THE PEOPLE AND THE N

"This book theoretically and empirically fills a void in populist studies. It explores systematically the relationships between territory, ethnicity, identity, and uneven development in European populist politics."
– **Carlos de la Torre**, *Professor of Sociology, University of Kentucky, USA. Editor of* The Routledge Handbook of Global Populism

"This volume is both welcome and distinctive. It is welcome in that it contributes to our knowledge on fundamental questions structuring political debates: questions of populism, nationalism, territory, and identity. It is distinctive in that its empirical basis is rich and wide, covering twelve Western and Central European cases."
– **Michaël Tatham**, *University of Bergen, Norway.*

"Based on a coherent and comprehensive analysis of relevant European political parties, the book is a timely analysis of the interactions between populist and ethno-territorial ideologies. It is a must-read for any student of contemporary political dynamics in Europe."
– **Régis Dandoy**, *Ghent University, Belgium*

The edited book brings together country experts on populism, ethno-territorial politics and party competition. It consists of eleven empirical chapters, covering eight Western European states (Austria, Belgium, France, Germany, Italy, Spain, Switzerland and the UK) as well as four Central European states (Croatia, Hungary, Serbia and Poland).

It is a collaboration by scholars from across Europe which contributes to the growing literature on populism by focusing on a relatively unexplored research agenda: the intersection of territoriality, ethno-politics and populism. Presenting an original perspective, contributing experts use case studies to highlight the territorial dimension of populism in different ways and identify that a deeper understanding of the interactions between populist actors and ethno-territorial ideologies is required.

This book will be of interest to academics, researchers and students of European politics, populism and ethno-territorial politics.

Reinhard Heinisch is Professor of Austrian Politics in Comparative European Perspective at the University of Salzburg, Austria.

Emanuele Massetti is Assistant Professor of Political Science at the University of Trento, Italy.

Oscar Mazzoleni is Professor in Political Science and Director of the Research Observatory for Regional Politics at the University of Lausanne, Switzerland.

Routledge Studies in Extremism and Democracy
Series Editors: Roger Eatwell, *University of Bath*, and **Matthew Goodwin**, *University of Kent*.
Founding Series Editors: Roger Eatwell, *University of Bath* and **Cas Mudde**, *University of Antwerp-UFSIA*.

This new series encompasses academic studies within the broad fields of 'extremism' and 'democracy'. These topics have traditionally been considered largely in isolation by academics. A key focus of the series, therefore, is the (inter-)*relation* between extremism and democracy. Works will seek to answer questions such as to what extent 'extremist' groups pose a major threat to democratic parties, or how democracy can respond to extremism without undermining its own democratic credentials.

The books encompass two strands:
Routledge Studies in Extremism and Democracy includes books with an introductory and broad focus which are aimed at students and teachers. These books will be available in hardback and paperback.

The People and the Nation
Populism and Ethno-Territorial Politics in Europe
Edited by Reinhard Heinisch, Emanuele Massetti and Oscar Mazzoleni

The Anti-Islamic Movement
Far Right and Liberal?
Lars Berntzen

Routledge Research in Extremism and Democracy offers a forum for innovative new research intended for a more specialist readership. These books will be in hardback only.

1. Uncivil Society?
Contentious Politics in Post-Communist Europe
Edited by Petr Kopecky and Cas Mudde

2. Political Parties and Terrorist Groups
Leonard Weinberg and Ami Pedahzur

3. Western Democracies and the New Extreme Right Challenge
Edited by Roger Eatwell and Cas Mudde

4. Confronting Right Wing Extremism and Terrorism in the USA
George Michael

5. Anti-Political Establishment Parties
A Comparative Analysis
Amir Abedi

For more information about this series, please visit:
www.routledge.com/politics/series/ED

THE PEOPLE AND THE NATION

Populism and Ethno-Territorial Politics in Europe

Edited by Reinhard Heinisch, Emanuele Massetti and Oscar Mazzoleni

LONDON AND NEW YORK

First published 2020
by Routledge
2 Park Square, Milton Park, Abingdon, Oxon OX14 4RN

and by Routledge
52 Vanderbilt Avenue, New York, NY 10017

Routledge is an imprint of the Taylor & Francis Group, an informa business

© 2020 selection and editorial matter, Reinhard Heinisch, Emanuele Massetti, and Oscar Mazzoleni; individual chapters, the contributors

The right of Reinhard Heinisch, Emanuele Massetti, and Oscar Mazzoleni to be identified as the authors of the editorial material, and of the authors for their individual chapters, has been asserted in accordance with sections 77 and 78 of the Copyright, Designs and Patents Act 1988.

All rights reserved. No part of this book may be reprinted or reproduced or utilised in any form or by any electronic, mechanical, or other means, now known or hereafter invented, including photocopying and recording, or in any information storage or retrieval system, without permission in writing from the publishers.

Trademark notice: Product or corporate names may be trademarks or registered trademarks, and are used only for identification and explanation without intent to infringe.

British Library Cataloguing-in-Publication Data
A catalogue record for this book is available from the British Library

Library of Congress Cataloging-in-Publication Data
Names: Heinisch, Reinhard, 1963- editor. | Massetti, Emanuele, editor. | Mazzoleni, Oscar, editor.
Title: The people and the nation : populism and ethno-territorial politics in Europe / edited by Reinhard Heinisch, Emanuele Massetti, and Oscar Mazzoleni.
Description: Abingdon, Oxon ; New York, NY : Routledge, 2020. | Series: Routledge studies in extremism and democracy | Includes bibliographical references and index. |
Identifiers: LCCN 2019025768 (print) | LCCN 2019025769 (ebook) | Subjects: LCSH: Populism–Europe. | Nationalism–Europe. | Ethnic identity–Political aspects–Europe. | Right-wing extremists–Europe. | Political parties–Europe. | Europe–Politics and government–21st century.
Classification: LCC JN40 .P46 2020 (print) | LCC JN40 (ebook) | DDC 320.56/62094–dc23
LC record available at https://lccn.loc.gov/2019025768
LC ebook record available at https://lccn.loc.gov/2019025769

ISBN: 978-1-138-57801-2 (hbk)
ISBN: 978-1-138-57802-9 (pbk)
ISBN: 978-1-351-26556-0 (ebk)

Typeset in Bembo
by Swales & Willis, Exeter, Devon, UK
Printed and bound by CPI Group (UK) Ltd, Croydon, CR0 4YY

CONTENTS

List of figures vii
List of tables viii
Preface ix
List of abbreviations xi
List of contributors xii

1 Introduction: European party-based populism and territory 1
   Reinhard Heinisch, Emanuele Massetti and Oscar Mazzoleni

2 Regionalist populism in Britain's "Celtic" peripheries: a longitudinal analysis of Plaid Cymru and the Scottish National Party 20
   Emanuele Massetti

3 Populism and ethno-territorial parties in Belgium 41
   Emilie van Haute

4 Claiming regionalism and nationalism at the same time: how the Italian and Swiss Leagues can engage in contradictory claims and get away with it 64
   Oscar Mazzoleni and Carlo Ruzza

5 The populist dimensions of Catalan secessionism: rhetoric, mobilization and institutional practices 88
   Astrid Barrio, Oscar Barberà and Juan Rodríguez-Teruel

vi Contents

6 Regional nativism in East Germany: the case of the AfD 110
  Hans-Georg Betz and Fabian Habersack

7 The Carinthian model: the role of sub-national claims in the
  Freedom Party's dominance in Austria's southernmost state 136
  Reinhard Heinisch

8 The territorialization of national-populist politics: a case study of
  the Front National in France 165
  Gilles Ivaldi and Jérôme Dutozia

9 Progressive regionalist populism vs. conservative nationalist populism in Poland: the case of the Silesian Autonomy Movement –
  RAŚ 189
  Magdalena Solska

10 Regionalist populism in Croatia: the case of the Croatian
   Democratic Alliance of Slavonia and Baranja – HDSSB 212
   Marko Kukec

11 Ethnic politics and competition between right-wing populist
   parties in Hungary 235
   Edina Szöcsik

12 A clash of myths: populism and ethno-nationalism in Serbia 256
   Bojan Vranić

13 Populism and ethno-territorial politics – conclusions: bridging
   legacies in understanding party mobilization 280
   Reinhard Heinisch, Emanuele Massetti and Oscar Mazzoleni

Index *291*

FIGURES

2.1	British parties' positions in 2014	30
5.1	Attitudes and opinions on politicians, parties, and government	92
5.2	'The will of the people' CDC poster for the 2012 regional election	96
6.1	Most important problems according to Eastern and Western German AfD voters (in percentage points)	122
6.2	Predicted effects of "lower class" (left) and "populist attitudes" (right) in interaction with "East"	126
A.1	Most important problems according to Eastern and Western German AfD voters (in percentage points); single statements and double mentions	128
7.1	Graph of FPÖ national and state elections results in comparison	143
8.1	FN share of vote by commune (% valid) in the 2015 regional elections (1st round)	169
10.1	Party results (per cent) at 2013 local elections (the red lines are the borders of the five Slavonian counties)	221
12.1	Parties' position on ethno-nationalism and the cultural dimension in 2017	261
12.2	Results of Serbian National Assembly elections for SPS, SRS and SNS from 1990 to present	263

TABLES

2.1	Plaid and the SNP's electoral results in general elections	26
2.2	Plaid and the SNP's electoral results in their respective regional elections	27
3.1	Hypotheses and case selection	44
3.2	Overview of the party leadership	46
3.3	Corpus of documents used in the analysis	50
3.4	Codebook populism	50
3.5	Codebook (sub-state) nationalism	52
3.6	Proportion of paragraph including populist and/or (sub-state) nationalist stances in party manifestos, 2010 and 2014	53
3.7	Occurrences of references to populism in manifestos and magazines, DéFI, N-VA, VB (2010–2014)	54
3.8	Occurrences of references to (sub-state) nationalism in manifestos and magazines, DéFI, N-VA, VB (2010–2014)	56
6.1	Binary logistic regression results	125
A.1	Reliability of measurements of populist attitudes (Cronbach's alpha)	128
A.2	Measurement and direction of effects	129
7.1	Elections to the National Parliament (Lower House, *Nationalrat*)	141
7.2	Results of the state elections in Carinthia 1999–2018 in %	144
8.1	FN national electoral results since 1984	166
8.2	Socio-economic, cultural and election indicators compared across PACA and HDF	176
9.1	The electoral results of the regional elections to the regional legislative assembly (Sejmik) in Silesian voivodeship in 2010 and 2014	199
12.1	Populism and ethno-nationalism in party programmes (SPS, SRS, SNS) in Serbia: 1990–2017	267

PREFACE

This book is the result of a scientific collaboration by scholars from across Europe. The starting point was an international workshop organized by the Research Observatory for Regional Politics at the University of Lausanne held from September 30 to October 1, 2016. This initial gathering, whose contributions focused on Western Europe, made it possible to produce a special issue of the journal *Comparative European Politics* (CEP) devoted to 'Populism and ethno-territorial politics in European multi-level systems' (volume 16, issue 6, 2018). A second international workshop, held at the Department of Political Science of the University of Salzburg on April 12–13, 2018, allowed for the development of a broader perspective, including important cases from Central and Eastern Europe. This book includes new contributions that complement and expand the CEP special issue, allowing for a wider geographical coverage of populism and ethno-territorial politics in contemporary Europe. The principal objective is to contribute to the growing of literature on populism by opening up a new and hitherto unexplored research agenda, which is the intersection of territoriality, ethno-politics, and populism, as well as the multi-level dimension of party-political contestation in connection with populist politics.

The editors aim to present an original perspective, supply a conceptual map for original research in this area, and make sense of the more or less systematic variation in ethno-territorial and populist politics that emerges from the individual case studies. Each case study highlights the territorial dimension of populism in various ways. First, it shows how statewide populist parties engage in territorial and sub-national strategies, either by adapting to region-specific grievances or by condemning and fighting against assertive regionalist claims. Secondly, it explores the way in which regionalist parties embrace populist stances with a view to strengthening their case (especially if it involves a push for independence) and/or to pursue electoral gains. Thirdly, it investigates the ambivalent multi-level strategies of some parties, be they regional, statewide, or in transition from one type of party organization to another. Finally, it places the relationship between populism and Euroscepticism in a wider territorial and multi-level analytical framework.

The analytical focus selected in this work connects two rich literatures: one on populism and the other on sub-state nationalism and regionalism, which had remained strangely separate from each other despite the many evident points of contact. In doing so, this book also addresses a gap in the scholarship on populism, in that this concept had seemed rather de-territorialized or devoid of a salient territorial dimension. Populism's focus on 'the people' apparently overshadows the question of the territory in which 'the people' live, as well as the relationship between people and territory. Yet, no matter how ambivalently the concept of 'the people' may be used, notions of territory (even in their generic form such as the 'heartland' or the 'periphery') often come with clear attributes and regional markers intended to resonate with distinct voter groups.

As simultaneous processes of political-territorial restructuring – devolution, secession attempts, European (dis-)integration and globalization – unfold, these provide a fertile ground for the emergence of new areas of contestation, which populist actors exploit by adopting ethno-territorial ideologies and, *vice versa*, regionalist and state-nationalist actors engage with, by increasingly adopting populist discourses. Scholars need to devote more attention to these interactions so as to provide a deeper understanding and more convincing explanations. The authors hope that this book will be a seminal text, prompting further exploration in this research agenda.

ABBREVIATIONS

Abbreviation	National party name	English party name
AfD	Alternative für Deutschland	Alternative for Germany
BZÖ	Bündnis Zukunft Österreich	Alliance Future Austria
CDC-PDCAT	Convergencia Democratica de Catalunya-Partit Demòcrata Català	Catalan European Democratic Party
CD&V	Christen-Democratisch en Vlaams	Christian Democratic and Flemish
CVP	Christlichdemokratische Volkspartei der Schweiz	Christian Democratic People's Party of Switzerland
DéFI	Démocrate fédéraliste indépendant	Democratic Front of Francophones
ERC	Esquerra Republicana de Catalunya	Republican Left of Catalonia
FDF	Front démocratique des francophones	Democratic Front of Francophones
FN	Front National	National Front (France)
FPÖ	Freiheitliche Partei Österreich	Austrian Freedom Party
HDSSB	Hrvatski demokratski savez Slavonije I Baranja Hrvatski	Croatian Alliance of Slavonia and Baranja
Jobbik	Jobbik Magyarországért Mozgalom	Movement for a Better Hungary
JxSi	Junts pel Si	Together for Yes
LN-Lega	Lega (Nord)	(Northern) League (Italy)
LT	Lega dei ticinesi	Ticino League
M5S	Movimento Cinque Stelle	Five Star Movement (Italy)
N-VA	Nieuw-Vlaamse Alliantie	New-Flemish Alliance
ÖVP	Österreichische Volkspartei	Austrian People's Party
Plaid	Plaid Cymru-The Party of Wales	Plaid Cymru-The Party of Wales
RN	Rassemblement National	National Rally
SNP	Scottish National Party	Scottish National Party
SNS	Srpska napredna stranka	Serbian Progressive Party
SPÖ	Sozialdemokratische Partei Österreichs	Social Democratic Party of Austria
SP	Sozialdemokratische Partei der Schweiz	Social Democratic Party of Switzerland
SPP	Ślůnsko Ludowo Partyjo	Silesian Regional Party of Poland
SPS	Socijalistička partija Srbije	Socialist Party of Serbia
SRS	Srpska radikalna stranka	Serbian Radical Party
SVP	Schweizerische Volkspartei	Swiss People's Party
VB	Vlaams Belang	Flemish Interest
VNP	Vlaams-Nationale Partji	Flemish National Party
VU	Volksunie	People's Union (Belgium)
VVP	Vlaamse Volkspartij	Flemish People's Party

CONTRIBUTORS

Oscar Barberà is associate professor at the Universitat de València (UV), Spain. His main areas of interest are party politics, decentralization, and political elites. His latest contributions on Spanish politics are published in *South European Society and Politics, Mediterranean Politics*, and *Comparative European Politics*.

Astrid Barrio is associate professor at the Universitat de València, Spain. Her research focuses on political parties and nationalism. She has published widely on Spanish politics and about Catalan nationalism.

Hans-Georg Betz is currently an adjunct professor of political science at the University of Zurich, Switzerland. Previously, he taught at York University in Toronto, the Paul Nitze School of Advanced International Studies (Johns Hopkins University) in Washington, DC, and Koc University in Istanbul. He is the author of several books, book chapters, and articles on the populist radical right, nativism, and Islamophobia. He is a senior fellow with the Centre for Analysis of the Radical Right (CARR) and regularly contributes short analytical essays to two major internet portals, opendemocracy.net, and fairobserver.com.

Jérôme Dutozia is a post-doctoral student in geography, currently at URMIS-University of Nice, France. His main research interests include spatial analysis, uncertainty and diagnostic, geomatics, geographic information systems (GIS) and risk analysis. Jérôme Dutozia is currently a research assistant to the SCoRE (Sub-national context and radical right support in Europe) international research program (2016–2019).

Fabian Habersack is a PhD fellow in the Department of Political Science, University of Salzburg, Austria. He obtained his MA degree in Political Science from the University of Salzburg, as well as the Université Sciences Po, Paris in 2017. His research and dissertation project focuses on populist radical right parties in regional and temporal context as well as political attitudes and voting behavior in a comparative perspective.

Reinhard Heinisch is Professor of Austrian Politics at the University of Salzburg, Austria where he also chairs the Department of Political Science. His main research interests are comparative populism, euroscepticism, and democracy. He is the author of numerous publications including *Understanding Populist Organization: The West European Radical Right* (Palgrave 2016, with O. Mazzoleni) and *Political Populism: A Handbook* (Nomos 2017, with O. Mazzoleni, C. Holz-Bacha). Other publication appeared in *Party Politics*, *West European Politics*, *Democratization*, *Comparative European Politics*, and others.

Gilles Ivaldi is a researcher in political science with the National Center for Scientific Research (CNRS) in France, currently at URMIS-University of Nice. His main fields of research include French politics, the comparative study of radical right parties, and the development of populist parties in Western Europe. He is the author of *The 2017 French Presidential Elections. A Political Reformation?*, Palgrave Macmillan, with Jocelyn Evans. His previous research has appeared in journals such as *Electoral Studies, the International Journal of Forecasting, French Politics or Political Research Quarterly*. Gilles Ivaldi is currently the French project leader of the SCoRE (Sub-national context and radical right support in Europe) international research program (2016–2019).

Marko Kukec is a post-doctoral researcher in the Institute for Political Science at the Helmut Schmidt University Hamburg. His research interests include political elites, legislative politics, and territorial politics, both in a comparative perspective and with a focus on Croatia.

Emanuele Massetti is Assistant Professor of Political Science in the School of International Studies and in the Department of Sociology and Social Research at the University of Trento, Italy. He is the co-editor of the JCMS Annual Review of the European Union. His research interests include political parties, ethno-territorial politics, federalism, the politics of European (dis)integration, and populism. His articles have appeared in several international journals, such as the *European Journal of Political Research, Party Politics*, and *West European Politics*.

Oscar Mazzoleni is Professor of Political science and the Director of the Research Observatory for Regional Research at the University of Lausanne, Switzerland. His research has been published in *Perspectives on European politics and Society, Government and Opposition, Party Politics, Swiss Political Science Review, Comparative European Politics*, amongst others. He is the co-editor of *Understanding Populist Party Organisation* (Palgrave 2016), *Regionalist Parties in Western Europe. Dimensions of Success* (Routledge 2017), and *Political Populism. A Handbook* (Nomos 2017).

Juan Rodríguez-Teruel is an associate professor at the University of València, Spain. His research fields are comparative politics and Spanish politics. His interests include political parties, party members, and executive elites. He was awarded with the 2007 Juan Linz Prize for his PhD dissertation on Spanish cabinet ministers.

Carlo Ruzza is Professor of Political Sociology at the University of Trento, Italy. His research interests focus upon populism, social movements, civil society groups, and right-wing parties. His books include *Europe and Civil Society* (Manchester UP 2007), *Reinventing the Italian Right: Populism, Post-Fascism and Territorial Identity* (Routledge 2009, with S. Fella) and *Europe's Prolonged Crisis* (Palgrave 2015, co-edited with H. Trenz and V. Guiraudon). He has also published in the *Journal of European Integration, Innovation, Theory and Society, Telos, West European Politics*, the *International Journal of Sociology, European Political Science*, the *Journal of Political Ideologies*, the *Journal of Civil Society*, the *Journal of Southern Europe and the Balkans*, and *Policy and Society*.

Magdalena Solska is a post-doctoral researcher and lecturer in political science at the University of Fribourg, Switzerland. Her research focuses on post-communist system transformation in Central and Eastern Europe, and, in particular, on the development of political parties and party systems and the political opposition in the post-communist democracies.

Edina Szöcsik is a post-doctoral researcher in the Department of Political Science at the University of Basel, Switzerland. In her research, she explores the dynamics of party competition and electoral participation in mature and young democracies. In particular, she is interested in the role of social identities in electoral politics. Her publications have appeared among others in the *European Journal of Political Research, Party Politics*, and *West European Politics*.

Emilie van Haute is Associate Professor and Head of the Department of Political Science at the Université libre de Bruxelles (ULB). She conducts her research at the Centre d'étude de la vie politique (Cevipol). Her main research interests include party membership, intra-party dynamics, participation, elections, and voting behavior. Her works have appeared in journals such as *Party Politics, Political Studies*, or *Electoral Studies*.

Bojan Vranić is an assistant professor at University of Belgrade – Faculty of Political Sciences. His fields of research are analytical political philosophy (conceptual structure of political theories) and political culture (preservation and changes of cultural patterns of political behavior). He has published papers in Serbian and German journals.

1
INTRODUCTION

European party-based populism and territory

Reinhard Heinisch, Emanuele Massetti, and Oscar Mazzoleni

Introduction

This edited book aims to investigate the relationship between party-populist mobilization and the territorial dimension in contemporary European politics. In recent decades, several successful Western European political parties have been labeled populist. Their discourses and strategies emphasize their role in defending the people's interests and identity, attacking the establishment, and claiming the power of the community (e.g. Betz 1994; March 2007; Mudde 2007; Albertazzi and McDonnell 2008; Stravakakis and Katsambekis 2014; Akkerman et al. 2016).

However, the territorial component has rarely been taken into account. Just as research on party politics has been largely shaped by what Jeffery and Wincott (2010) have dubbed "methodological nationalism", the literature on European party-based populism has also taken the nation-state as the natural context of analysis. In doing so, it avoided considering the relevance of a set of politically salient issues arising from the interaction of territory, ethnicity, identity, and uneven development. Thus, center-periphery dynamics have been given scant attention and have surfaced only incidentally in the literature, typically in cases in which the main populist protagonists were essentially regionalist parties and easily identifiable as such. The most prominent cases have been Vlaams Belang[1] in Belgium and the Lega Nord in Italy, both regionalist (or minority nationalist) parties (McDonnell 2006; Pauwels 2011; Biorcio 2017). However, as the latter case particularly suggests, these characteristics are not immutable, and regionalist parties can go national. By the same token, national parties can develop regional strengths or shift their base of support from one region to another, as this book will discuss. Nonetheless, in reference to right-wing populism, the scholarship has focused on societal changes toward greater multiculturalism, especially greater ethnic diversity (Van der Brug et al. 2000; Rydgren 2003, 2005, 2008;

Albertazzi and McDonnell 2008). This increase in ethnic diversity is seen as singularly responsible for the growing number of populist parties engaging in xenophobic, Islamophobic, and/or racist claims against immigrants.

By comparison, the link between populism and ethnic divisions within "native" populations has remained largely unexplored and untheorized in the European context. Beyond internal ethnic cleavages, there exist other regional divisions that allow populist actors to engage in identity politics, but that have yet to be fully explored by the scholarship. To the extent that populism, as defined below, is focused on an antagonism between "pure" people and corrupt elites, certain regions may constitute an alleged "heartland" containing the true representatives of the pure people. By contrast, other regions, particularly the metropolitan areas, may be seen as collective elites whose alien values and novel lifestyles present challenges to traditional society.

While regional disparities and differences between urban and rural are not new, the problem has become significantly more acute. In the US context, scholars have argued that, for much of the 20th century, regional differences in wages, unemployment, and the establishment of new businesses faded as the economy grew (Barro and Sala-i Martin 1991, 1992). The idea was that lagging regions would eventually close the gap with prosperous ones as business ideas diffused and cost differentials caused businesses to relocate to poorer areas. Indeed, until 1980, wage differentials were narrowing between places. Since then, the processes of globalization and modernization have not only produced external effects such as migration and greater economic interdependence, but have also substantially widened internal disparities (Hendrickson et al. 2018). Whereas certain regions may experience factory closures, capital drain, and the outmigration of young people and high-skilled workers; other areas, especially metropolitan regions and urban agglomerations – with their thriving services sectors, high-tech and advanced manufacturing industries, universities, and research facilities – have benefited. This has contributed to a growing disparity within many countries, which becomes an issue of not only economics and social concerns, but also one of identity and culture, which can readily be exploited by populist politicians.

Another crucial aspect of current European political systems, largely due to European integration, is the shift toward multilevel governance and the role of party competition in this context (e.g. Detterbeck 2012). However, while scholarship has widely investigated the relationship between populism and Euroscepticism (Taggart 1998; Krouwel 2007; Ruzza 2009; Harmsen 2010; Tournier-Sol 2015), few works have analyzed the regional level along with the national and EU levels (Mazzoleni 2005).

This book argues that territorial dimensions should be taken more seriously for understanding populist party mobilization. Territory is neither an "abstract concept" nor simply "a line on a map", but rather shapes social and political developments and institutions through the ways in which contextual factors influence political mobilization (see Hepburn and Detterbeck 2018: 2). For party-based populism, territorial dimensions are relevant in at least three principal and complementary respects:

1) First, territorial features need to be taken into consideration when analyzing populist mobilization by statewide political parties. Although such parties are organized on a national scale, their electoral support is rarely evenly distributed throughout the territory of the state. Therefore, territory plays a crucial role, and not only when these parties compete for local or regional elections. They are always confronted with regional and local peculiarities in national (or European) elections as well.
2) Second, regionalist or minority nationalist parties, which mobilize only in a specific region, may also develop populist claims and discourses. Although their ethno-territorial ideologies do not always mesh well with populist claims, especially when regionalist parties also present themselves as parties of current or aspired government, these themes – of a contest for a regional "heartland", or of native inhabitants supposedly discriminated against by the "center" or the nation-state – can be considered forms of populist mobilization.
3) Third, scholarship needs to be mindful of the chameleonic or shifting forms of territorial contention in European party politics, as the conventional dividing line between state-nationalist and regionalist parties is increasingly blurred. For instance, territorial issues come into play in a significant way when national-level populist parties adapt their own framing or agenda to constituencies for whom center-periphery cleavages are highly relevant. In turn, regionalist actors adjust themselves to multi-level opportunities and constraints and may take their regionally rooted parties national.

By exploring the complexity of the linkage between populism and territorial dimensions, this book addresses two main research questions that derive from the interplay between populism, state-nationalism, and regionalism: *Which role does the territorial dimension play in statewide populist party mobilization? How do regionalist and state-nationalist claims interact with populist discourses?* In order to answer to these questions, we need to rethink the ways in which the current literature conceptualizes party-populist mobilization in Europe. Thus, we will start by introducing a conceptual map of the relationship and linkages between populism, regionalism (or minority nationalism), majority state-nationalism, and Euroscepticism, so as to provide a common framework for analyzing different and shifting territorial scopes of populist mobilization in Europe.

In the first section, we discuss the traits of populism as a concept, then proceed to conceptualize and define specific ethno-territorial ideologies such as regionalism, majority nationalism, and Euroscepticism. This section also highlights potential linkages between each of these ideologies and populism. We then present several ideal-typical ideological combinations, examples of which will be discussed in the empirical chapters devoted to specific cases of party mobilization in different European political systems.

Between "thin" ideology and discourse

Many studies on populism have stressed the concept's contested nature (Berlin et al. 1968; Canovan 1981; Taguieff 1995; Taggart 2000). Leaving aside the ambiguous uses of the term in the mass media (Bale et al. 2011), two main factors seem to account for the conceptual slipperiness or disagreement present in the academic debate: first, the predominance of single-case studies or studies specific to a region – such as Latin America (Di Tella 1995; De la Torre 2010), North America (Kazin 1998; Berlet and Lyons 2000), Western Europe (Betz 1994; Taggart 1995; Rooduijn et al. 2014; Heinisch and Mazzoleni 2016; Akkerman et al. 2017), Central Eastern Europe (Mudde 2000; Minkenberg 2002; Vujacic 2003; Pirro 2014), etc. – often ignoring the contributions of other regional-comparative studies (De la Torre 2018); and second, a tendency to shift the discussion about the essence of the concept of populism to a debate over its appropriate conceptual categorization, whether populism should be considered an ideology (Mudde 2004; Stanley 2008), a discourse (Laclau 1977, 2005; Rooduijn and Pauwels 2011), a frame (Aslanidis 2016), or a strategy (Weyland 2001; Jansen 2011).

Within the community of populism scholars, it is possible to identify a certain convergence on how party-based populism is conceived (Panizza 2005; De la Torre 2014; Müller 2016; Mudde and Rovira Kalwasser 2017). Indeed, conceptual distinctions between populism as a strategy, discourse, or frame are often more superficial than substantive, given that proponents of "populism as a strategy" also include "populist rhetoric" (i.e., "discourse") as a defining element of said strategy (Jansen 2011: 83). As for the distinction between ideology and discourse, even the advocates of "populism as an ideology" typically narrow it by referring to populism as a "thin ideology" (Stanley 2008). As such, the distance between the two positions can be called into question even further by the fact that the "father" of the "thin ideology"[2] concept, Michael Freeden himself, has expressed doubt about populism even qualifying as an ideology at all, even a thin one (Freeden 2017). Instead, he appears to emphasize populism's borderline nature between (thin) ideology and discourse (Freeden 2017: 10).

If Freeden's contribution helps us reach an acceptable middle ground in the debate over the labeling of populism, a certain "center of gravity" on the key features of populism has emerged based on the definition proposed by Cas Mudde, which identifies the following components: a) a vision of society as divided into two groups, the "pure people" and the "corrupt elites"; b) the internal homogeneity of the two groups; c) the antagonistic relationship between the two groups; and d) always siding with the "pure people" as the only legitimate source of the "general will" (Mudde 2004: 543). Despite criticisms of this approach (see Aslanidis 2016), these defining criteria advanced by key proponents of "populism as an ideology" are largely compatible with most definitions proposed by advocates of "populism as a discourse" such as Laclau (2005) and Rooduijn and Pauwels (2011) as well as the advocates of "populism as a strategy" such as Jansen (2011).

Several scholars consider populism to be a more complex phenomenon than is captured by the Muddean definition (Finchelstein 2017; De la Torre and Anselmi 2018: 467). Other elements emphasized in the literature include a sense of crisis (Taggart 2000; Roodujin 2014). However, this can actually be defined as a contextual condition under which a populist discourse may be more viable or successful (Kriesi and Pappas 2015). Other recurring elements such as the stigmatization of "dangerous others" (Albertazzi and McDonnell 2008) may be better understood as "linkage nodes" to other (thick or thin) ideologies, such as in the connection between populism and the radical-right (Betz 1994; Rydgren 2005). Indeed, populism can be linked with very different ideological orientations: from radical-left to radical-right, from inclusionary to exclusionary, from socialist to neoliberal, from secular to religious, and from fanaticism for charismatic leadership to fanaticism for grassroots democracy (Otjes and Louwerse 2015; March 2017).

Populism's compatibility with completely different (and even opposing) ideological orientations is also due to its intrinsic ambivalence (Taggart 2000; Heinisch and Mazzoleni 2017). Populist politics is vaguely defined and its core terms might be seen as empty signifiers (Laclau 2005): "the people" or the "heartland" natives are depicted as a homogeneous and amorphous group generally without differences of interest and class; similarly, the group making up the (corrupt) "elites" is typically situational and may change from occasion to occasion to include the "political class", the "deep state", mainstream political parties, the media, bureaucrats, bankers, international business, experts, scientists, NGOs, European Union officials, and even specific individuals such as George Soros. Ambivalence may therefore be considered a key characteristic of populist mobilization, providing considerable flexibility and adaptability in party competition, especially in multi-layered arenas.

Ethno-territorial ideologies and their potential links with populism

From an ideational perspective, populism may intersect with ideological components of regionalism, majority (or state) nationalism, and Euroscepticism.

Regionalism

Regionalism can be defined as a thin ideology that politicizes the specificities of the population living in a certain sub-state region vis-à-vis the population of the state as a whole (Fitjar 2010). These specificities, which can be sociocultural (language, religion, prevailing ideological orientations, etc.) and/or socio-economic (type and degree of economic development, prevalent economic sectors, economic status of the region vis-à-vis the rest of state, etc.), are seen as the bases of a separate ethno-territorial identity that ought to be formally recognized and accommodated by the state. Indeed, regionalist parties are defined as self-contained political organizations that focus on the protection/enhancement of regional identities and interests, challenging the central state with their requests for some kind of territorial self-government (De Winter 1998; Massetti 2009; Alonso 2012; Mazzoleni and Mueller 2016).

The level of self-government advocated by regionalist parties can vary considerably. In this respect, Massetti and Schakel (2016) have identified a crucial distinction between those regionalist parties that pose a threat to the territorial integrity of the state ("secessionist") and those that do not ("autonomist"), highlighting how regionalist parties can change their positions over time. In addition, Dandoy (2010) has identified further differences within the "secessionist" category by distinguishing between "independentist", "irredentist", and "rattachist" parties.

Adopting different terminology, some scholars prefer to distinguish between "regionalist" and "stateless nationalist" (or "minority nationalist") parties (Elias 2008; Hepburn 2009). However, the distinction seems to lack a persuasive definition and, in the end, this distinction's limited additional explanatory value is attested by the fact that even its proponents believe that both regionalist and stateless nationalist parties belong to a common family of parties (Hepburn 2009). We therefore treat stateless (or minority) nationalism as an internal subcategory of regionalism – denoting those cases in which a claim to nationhood is made – bearing in mind that it does not necessarily coincide with the subcategory of secessionism. Like populism, regionalism can also be (and is) linked to all sorts of ideological orientations, from the radical-left to the radical-right (Massetti 2009; Massetti and Schakel 2015). The linkages with populism can thus be drawn within a broader ideological outlook.

As we touched on above, the most basic and most evident connection between regionalism and populism resides in the potential correspondence between the two foundational dichotomies. "People vs. elites" can be equated with "region (or minority nation) vs. state (or majority nation)" and vice versa. In the regionalist-populist synthesis, the "good people" are the people in the region while the elites are those politicians defending state interests at the expenses of the regional population. Regionalist populists typically focus on the putative incapacity or unwillingness of national elites in the distant capital to recognize, understand, or even consider the region's specific needs. As highlighted by Taggart (2000), the populist discourse often refers to a lost "heartland". Indeed, the politics of resentment and victimization, so typical of populism, might resonate well with ethno-regional minorities that perceive that the state elites have failed to recognize their region or treat it fairly. Given the structural antagonism between regionalist parties and the statewide parties' politicians who govern the state, we can expect to find this minimal level of populist discourse in virtually all regionalist parties. Similarly, we can expect a regional populist party, or a particularly autonomous regional branch of a statewide populist party, to back up their criticism of elites with a regionalist discourse. It is worth pointing out that both regionalist and populist parties can antagonize not only the state's political elites but, where a regional government is in place, also the regional political elites. Whether the regionalist-populist synthesis will target only the state elites or both the regional and state elites, will depend primarily on the role of the party in the regional and national party system (i.e., fringe party, relevant but not in office, relevant and in office, hegemonic and continuously in office) and on the age and/or history of the party (i.e., whether it is new or old and whether it has a history of cooperation or competition with statewide parties).

Besides this basic connection, populism and regionalism can combine within the frame of a broader ideological orientation. In these cases, the political actors forging the regionalist-populist synthesis may target not only (or not primarily) political elites, but also economic and/or intellectual elites. In addition, regionalist populists can target not only regional and state elites but also supranational and international ones (Mazzoleni 2005). In Laclau's terms (2005), they can challenge what they perceive as the dominant elite discourse from different ideological standpoints, such as challenging a dominant liberal/tolerant/pluralist discourse from a radical-right standpoint, or challenging a dominant neoliberal/economic conservative discourse from a radical-left standpoint, etc.

Special mention should be made of a distinct category of regionalist parties, unionist regionalist parties, which operate in ethnically divided regions and often find themselves fighting on two fronts. These parties are as much assertive advocates of a distinct regional identity and regional self-government as they are staunch supporters of state territorial integrity against other ethno-regionalist (potentially or openly secessionist) movements/parties that have claims on the same region (Massetti 2009: 504). In a way, like all regionalist parties, they are in a bargaining (and sometimes confrontational) relationship with the state for attaining a certain degree of self-government. At the same time, they fully side with the state against secessionist threats involving their region. It should be noted that highly autonomous regional branches of statewide parties can also engage in this type of two-front battle. Indeed, some of these parties can enter into close agreements with majority nationalist statewide parties, thus becoming their de-facto regional branches, for example the agreements between the Ulster Unionist Party (UUP) and the British Conservative Party in Northern Ireland and between Union of Navarrese People (UPN) and the Spanish People's Party in Navarra. If in such cases, parties make use of a populist discourse, the ambivalence of who "the people" really are can become even blurrier. When they act as regionalist parties, "the people" are likely to be the regional population (or a particular ethnic group). When they act as regional agents of majority (state) nationalism, "the people" will probably coincide with the majority (state) nation.

State (or majority) nationalism

Nationalism is widely considered a thin ideology that prioritizes national divisions over other political issues and promotes one's own nation over other nations (Freeden 1998). State-nationalism is the ideology that forms the foundation of the (putative) nation-state: the nation is presented as the prerequisite social entity and used to justify the state's *raison d'être*. In that respect, the nation-state becomes a political instrument of the nation. If the nation-state project is not internally contested, state-nationalism remains an implicit or dormant ideology. However, if the nation-state project is internally contested, different scenarios arise depending primarily on the level of democracy inherent in the political system and on the mobilization strategies and capacities of ethno-regionalist forces. Advanced liberal democracies tend to acknowledge the presence of ethno-regional identities as legitimate even if the latter represent a reminder that the nation-state project is not universally shared. This creates an uneasy relationship with those political forces who favor a strict pursuit/upholding of the nation-state project. Indeed, the same democratic freedoms that allow regionalists to raise identity claims before the state also allow state-nationalists to challenge and reject a pluralist revision of the nation-state project. Therefore, in these circumstances, state-nationalism remains a particularly potent force in the form of majority nationalism.[3]

The main concern of majority nationalists is the mobilization of ethno-territorial identities by regionalist parties/movements. In particular, majority nationalists tend to target ethno-territorial minorities that are perceived as a threat to national integrity, either because of their own strength or because they are protected/supported by a neighboring (kindred) state. In theory, majority nationalist parties can have different ideological orientations along the left-right continuum. However, in the context of Western liberal democracies, parties situated on the right of the political spectrum – particularly conservative and radical-right parties – tend to engage more with majority nationalism. Therefore, particularly in Western Europe, the populist-nationalist synthesis tends to manifest itself as a form of right-wing populism (Loch 2017).

The most obvious linkage between majority nationalism and populism may be found in the identification of the (majority) nation as "the good people", intended as a homogeneous group that does not permit internal (ethno-territorial) differentiation (Müller 2016): a person or group is either a member of the "nation/people" or they are not. Thus, while the main "enemies" of majority nationalists are regionalist (particularly secessionist) political forces, in their populist-nationalist synthesis, the targeted elites are the national parties and cultural elites, which are perceived as softer regarding regionalist claims. These elites (which might also include international or supranational elements) may be accused of offenses ranging from insufficient assertiveness/resolve in protecting the nation-state's unity and integrity to outright betrayal of the nation-state. It goes without saying that, beyond fighting against mobilized ethno-regional identities, majority nationalist parties also want to protect the national identity from the supposed threats posed by immigrant communities. In this case, their majority nationalism and exclusivist/xenophobic nativism results in the adoption of a radical-right ideology (Mudde 2007). The populist radical-right synthesis thus presents the "good people", understood as the majority/native nation (to the exclusion of ethno-territorial minorities and immigrant communities), against the "corrupt elites", understood as those (pluralist and multi-culturalist) political forces that do not protect (or work against) the homogeneity/purity of the nation.[4]

Euroscepticism

State-nationalism is not solely concerned with internal threats to the integrity of the nation-state. It can also aim outward and upward by identifying international and/or supranational actors that stand accused of conspiring against the interests of the nation-state and of depriving the nation/people of their sovereignty. In this case, the linkage with populism is rather immediate because the influence of external elites (usually with the alleged complicity of internal elites) is seen as diminishing the people's sovereignty. While overall "sovereignism" tends to target the main actors of globalization – especially transnational economic elites and international institutions such as the World Bank and the International Monetary Fund – sovereigntist political forces within Europe tend to direct their recriminations against European integration and its central protagonist, the European Union (EU). Euroscepticism can be seen, therefore, as a particular case of sovereignism and, in turn, a particular expression of state-nationalism.

Scholarship has identified different degrees and types of Euroscepticism. The Sussex school distinguishes between "soft" and "hard" Euroscepticism, whereby the former is defined as a qualified criticism of some EU policies (or integration in some policy areas) and the latter as an outright claim against EU membership (Taggart 1998; Szczerbiak and Taggart 2008). In contrast, Kopecky and Mudde (2002) differentiates between political forces that oppose the very idea of European integration (Euro-rejects) and those that, despite supporting the principle of European integration, openly criticize the ways in which the principle has been implemented in practice (Eurosceptic).

Like other ethno-territorial ideologies, Euroscepticism is compatible, in theory, with all types of leftist and rightist ideologies. In fact, empirical studies have found that Euroscepticism tends to combine with radical-left and radical-right ideologies (Hix 1999; Hooghe et al. 2002). In particular, hard and/or principled Euroscepticism tends to be found primarily among radical-right parties (Vasilopoulou 2011, 2018) whereas radical-left parties tend mostly to criticize the way the EU has been shaped (e.g., its allegedly neoliberal ethos).

Regionalist parties also pay close attention to European integration because the latter is seen as providing opportunities for territorial restructuring, with transfers of powers towards the regional level emerging as one of the most evident trends (Jeffery 2000; Keating 2004). Although most regionalist parties have generally been supportive of European integration (De Winter and Gomez-Reino 2002; Jolly 2015), Eurosceptic positions have become more common in the past two decades (Elias 2008). As for the relationship between Euroscepticism and other ideological orientations, regionalist parties tend to follow the same pattern as statewide parties: radical-right and radical-left regionalist parties tend to be more Eurosceptic than mainstream regionalist parties (Massetti 2009).

Since the process of European integration is a project devised by supranational elites, it is virtually self-evident why Euroscepticism can be easily expressed through a populist discourse: national sovereignty, which guarantees the democratic representation of the interests and identity of the people/nation, is seen as being sacrificed by supranational elites, who would rather go along with Brussels's centralizing tendencies than heed the will of the people (Taggart 1998; Harmsen 2010; Fabbrini 2017).

Given the additional (supranational) level of governance in the EU, European political parties – whether regional or statewide – have the opportunity to engage in "multi-level populism" (Mazzoleni 2005). This means that due to tactical or strategic considerations, some populist parties can shift the meaning of "good people" and "corrupt elites" depending on specific conditions such as the pattern of competition and the party's position within government (governing or opposition).

As this conceptual introduction has demonstrated, ethno-territorial ideologies have numerous potential links with populism. These concepts can go hand in hand, but the interaction is often complex and contingent on a variety of situational and contextual factors. Whether groups espousing ethno-territorial ideologies or their opponents will avail themselves of populist discourses and strategies frequently depends on the opportunities of a political moment or the pattern of political culture and party competition present in a given political system. The specific manifestations are best analyzed in the context of empirical cases, which will be introduced later in this volume. Before considering those cases, we need to review some important differences between European regions, discussing the peculiarities of Central Eastern Europe (as opposed to Western Europe).

The Central and Eastern European context

This book aims also to contribute to the discussion on populism by examining the central research questions in the context of both Western and Eastern European cases. This deserves a brief discussion of the relationship between nationalism and sovereignism in former Communist countries. There is an extensive literature suggesting that the widespread appeal of nationalism and nativism is strongly connected to that region's long history of multi-national empires, outside domination, and restricted national sovereignty. This caused competing historical narratives, unfulfilled national aspirations, and produced significant areas with religious or ethnic minority populations (Ishiyama and Breuning 1998; Henderson 2008; Minkenberg 2010, 2015; Hloušek and Kaniok 2014). Under communism, multiethnic discourses were either repressed or channeled through ideologically acceptable visions in which different peoples lived harmoniously together under socialism. Then, during the initial transition, when the political debate focused primarily on economic reform and market liberalization, sociocultural questions remained unresolved. Historical grievances and imagined or genuine national traumas therefore continue to serve as sociocultural sources of political contestation in the region (Minkenberg 2015: 27–42). Politically, this meant that calls for isolating the outgroup in an effort to bolster cohesion within the ingroup became a successful strategy for mobilizing popular support.

Moreover, the presence of external kinship-communities and ethnic diasporas served the exclusivist agenda of ethnocratic parties that either advocate irredentism or pledge to defend the national community against "dangerous others" in its midst.

Apart from national narratives and unresolved ethnic questions, the political systems of Central and Eastern Europe (CEE) have patterns of party competition that are distinct to those in Western Europe (Kitschelt 1992). These are largely the result of the transition legacy, delayed European integration, and the volatility and fragmentation of party systems across the region (Vachudova and Hooghe 2009). The regime legacies and the specifics of the post-Communist transition are useful for understanding the emergence of broad conflict dimensions that shape political contestation. Kitschelt et al. (1999) argue that the distinct Communist regime legacy resulted in a greater propensity of certain countries to develop political cleavages along the lines of transition winners and losers. In these, the political and economic reforms were often half-hearted and non-transparent, thus creating a new class of wealthy transition winners overnight. The ensuing resentment toward privileged elites, regions that seemingly unduly benefited from economic changes, or purportedly undeserving minorities became part of the political discourse (Minkenberg 2015: 29–47).

In certain countries, the nation-state project gains a sense of urgency from unresolved national traumas (Hungary) or existential threats to its national integrity (Poland). These elements make perceived supranational and sub-national challenges into important avenues for political mobilization. These sociocultural conflict dimensions become dominant or cause a realignment of the socioeconomic cleavages, such that parties of the right, not the left, espouse economic protectionism in the name of national sovereignty and welfare.

Delayed European integration has also been a crucial factor shaping the relationship among parties (Harmsen 2010). While joining the EU was initially supported by mainstream parties across the spectrum (Harmsen and Spiering 2004: 28; Riishøj 2007: 7), late accession meant that new member states had to accept terms of accession seen as unfavorable by the electorates. As a result, government parties were often held responsible for "selling out" the national interest, in response to which parties on the right and newly emerging protest parties championed nationalist causes and adopted increasingly Eurosceptical positions (Ishiyama and Bozóki 2002). In CEE, the two ideological sources of Euroscepticism – anti-market and anti-libertarian orientations – were frequently bundled together as a programmatic agenda for a single political party (Henderson 2008: 121–122; Neumayer 2008: 136). To the extent to which state-nationalist parties in CEE push the nation-state project and criticize the EU as an undesirable outside meddler, sub-national and regionalist interest may see Brussels as an ally against an overbearing national center. Hence, the EU represents a central issue in the antagonistic relationship between regionalist and state-nationalist parties. In particular, the EU is not only seen by both sides as affecting the opportunity structure with respect to greater autonomy or secession, but perceived by the nationalist right as an ideological antagonist whose liberal and pluralistic values threaten the nation-state project and unfairly aid and abet its enemies.

A third distinctive feature of CEE party systems is their greater degree of fluctuation compared to Western Europe (Bunce and Wolchik 2010). This "under-institutionalization" (Minkenberg 2015: 34) has resulted in frequent reconfigurations, making the parties "disconcertingly fluid" and contributing to "permeable borders between the radical right and the mainstream right" (ibid). As a result, the CEE party system became less structured than its Western European counterpart, especially in the first decade after the fall of Communist regimes (Sikk 2005). Fewer institutional constraints and greater fragmentation made it easier for ideological extremism to take hold. Yet, despite this fluidity, the ideological frames of party competition have remained surprisingly structured (Rovny 2014: 675). In the "crowded" world of populist and protest politics, populist actors needed to adopt a variety of positions to distinguish themselves in the political market place (Heinisch 2008). Pursuing national or sub-national narratives is clearly one such way of improving a party's competitive position vis-à-vis the targeted electorate.

Outline of the chapters

This book is concerned with the linkages between populism and various manifestations of ethno-territorial politics. As a result, we devote particular attention to recognizing which ideological/discursive elements in the empirical cases are distinctively populist, which ones come from ethno-territorial ideologies, and what the nodes of linkage are. This allows us to differentiate, for instance, between primarily (statewide) populist parties engaging with regionalist claims and primarily regionalist parties using a populist discourse. It will also allow us to explore how populist actors cope with the challenges arising from the ambivalence rooted in their often contradictory ideological patchwork, e.g., populism *and* regionalism *and* state-nationalism.

In order to comprehensively explore the complexity of the linkages between populism and the territorial dimensions, this edited volume consists of eleven empirical chapters focused on political parties across seven Western European political systems, four Eastern European political systems, and the Eastern part of Germany.

Six chapters analyze regionalist parties: in Western Europe, these include Emanuele Massetti's comparison between Plaid Cymru – The Party of Wales (Plaid) and the Scottish National Party (SNP) in the UK, Emilie Van Haute's comparison between DéFI and Vlaams Belang (VB) in Belgium, and Oscar Mazzoleni and Carlo Ruzza's comparison between the Lega dei Ticinesi (Ticino League) and Lega (Nord) (Northern League) in Switzerland and Italy, respectively. Additionally, Oscar Barberà, Astrid Barrio, and Juan Rodríguez-Teruell's chapter studies Catalan secessionist political actors, which consist of the Convergencia Democratica de Catalunya-Partit Demòcrata Català (Catalan European

Democratic Party/CDC-PDCAT) and Esquerra Republicana de Catalunya (Republican Left of Catalonia/ERC). In 2015, along with two secessionist movements, these parties formed the electoral coalition Junts pel Si (Together for Yes/JxSi). Magdalena Solska's analysis of the Silesian Autonomy Movement in Poland and Marko Kukec's chapter on Hrvatski demokratski savez Slavonije i Baranje (Croatian Alliance of Slavonia and Baranja Hrvatski) provide two examples of regionalist parties in Central and Eastern Europe.

Five chapters analyze territorial dimensions of statewide nationalist parties. Reinhard Heinisch's contribution focuses on the Freiheitliche Partei Österreichs (Austrian Freedom Party/FPÖ) in Austria, which despite its national orientation successfully pursued a marked sub-state agenda in one of Austria regions. Ivaldi and Dutozia's study of the Front National (FN), now Rassemblement National, in France highlights variation in the discourse and policy agenda that this state-nationalist party offers to different regional electorates. Hans-Georg Betz and Fabian Habersack present the case of the Alternative für Deutschland (Alternative for Germany/AfD) in the former East Germany, arguing that East Germans have begun to embrace this originally West German party to some extent out of resentment toward perceived West German domination. Edina Szoecisk's chapter on the Hungarian radical right-wing populist parties Fidesz and Jobbik highlights their competition over ethno-national politics, particularly regarding discrimination against internal minorities, especially the Roma community, and over "protecting" ethnic-Hungarian communities in bordering states. Bojan Vranic's study analyzes the constant presence of specific blends of populism and ethno-nationalism in the most important political parties in Serbia: the Socijalistička partija Srbije (the Socialist Party of Serbia), the Srpska radikalna stranka (Serbian Radical Party), and the Srpska napredna stranka (Serbian Progressive Party).

The selected cases permit us also to cover a large range of ideological orientation on the left-right axis. As for the parties' ideological position along this dimension, seven of them are placed to the right of the center, whereas four are positioned left of the center. The latter are all regionalist and mainstream left-wing parties (Plaid, SNP, ERC, RAS). In contrast, amongst rightist parties, only two are mainstream right (the regionalist DéFI and CDC-PDCAT), while eight are radical-right parties: two regionalists (VB, LT, Croatian Democratic Alliance of Slavonia and Baranja) and four statewide nationalists (FPÖ, FN, Jobbik, Fidesz, the Serbian socialist party), and finally two borderline cases, a statewide party with a strong regionalist stance (AfD in East Germany) and a regionalist party moving to become a nationalist one (Lega).

Regarding the parties' attitudes toward the EU, the radical-right parties are the only ones adopting a marked form of Euroscepticism (see chapters by van Haute; Mazzoleni and Ruzza; Heinisch and Marent; Dutozia and Ivaldi; Szoecsik; Vranic). Four of them, the statewide nationalist FN, FPÖ, Jobbik, Fidesz, and Serbian Radical Party criticize the EU, largely claiming that the interests of their respective nation-state are being infringed upon. Two of them, the regionalist VB and LT, attack the EU primarily for regional interests, and two others, the Italian League and the LT, voice their Euroscepticism while alternating between defending (and trying to reconcile) regional and national interests. Three parties express pro-European stances (the Silesian Autonomy Movement and the Serbian socialist and progressive parties). By presenting our readers with this assortment of cases, we hope to provide a comprehensive and interesting overview of the relationship between populism and territorial politics. In particular, readers interested in identifying patterns and trends will have the opportunity to use the material provided for engaging in multiple comparisons across European macro-regions (East/West), countries, sub-state regions, the territorial scope of parties (statewide/regionalist), and ideological positions.

Notes

1 This text refers to parties by their original names if these are commonly used in the literature. English translations of names are used in all other cases.
2 Freeden actually uses the expression "thin-centered ideology" to stress the limited coverage of the core component of some ideologies – such as feminism, environmentalism and nationalism – vis-à-vis the main ideologies – liberalism, socialism and conservatism (Freeden 1996, 1998).
3 It is worth noting that the ethno-demographic conditions of some countries (e.g. Belgium or Bosnia) make it extremely difficult to establish which group represents majority nationalism (Zuber and Szocsik 2018).
4 In countries where ethno-regional minorities are virtually absent (e.g. Germany or Denmark) or relatively scarcely mobilized (e.g. France or the Netherlands), populist radical-right parties are only concerned with immigrant communities.

References

Akkerman, T., de Lange, S. L., and Rooduijn, M. (eds.) (2016) *Radical Right-Wing Populist Parties in Western Europe: Into the Mainstream?* London: Routledge.

Albertazzi, D., and McDonnell, D. (eds.) (2008) *Twenty-First Century Populism.* New York: Palgrave Macmillan.

Alonso, S. (2012) *Challenging the State: Devolution and the Battle for Partisan Credibility.* Oxford: Oxford University Press.

Aslanidis, P. (2016) "Is Populism an Ideology? A Refutation and a New Perspective", *Political Studies*, 64(1), pp. 88–104.

Bale, T., van Kessel, S., and Taggart, P. (2011) "Thrown Around With Abandon? Popular Understandings of Populism as Conveyed by the Print Media: A UK Case Study", *Acta Politica*, 46(2), pp. 111–131.

Barro, R. J. and Sala-i Martin, X. (1991) "Convergence Across States and Regions", *Brookings Papers on Economic Activity*, 1, pp. 107–182.

Barro, R. J., and Sala-i Martin, X. (1992) "Convergence", *Journal of Political Economy*, 100(2), pp. 223–251.

Berlet, C., and Lyons, N. M. (2000) *Right-Wing Populism in America. Too Close for Comfort.* New York: The Guilford Press.

Berlin, I., Hofstadter, R., and MacRae, D. G. (1968) "To Define Populism", *Government and Opposition*, 3(1), pp. 137–179.

Betz, H.-G. (1994) *Radicalism and Right-Wing Populism in Western Europe*. New York: St. Martin's Press.

Biorcio, R. (2017) "The Northern League", In Mazzoleni, O. and Mueller, S. (eds.) *Regionalist Parties in Western Europe: Dimensions of Success*. London: Routledge, pp. 135–151.

Bunce, V. J., and Wolchik, S. L. (2010) "Defeating Dictators: Electoral Change and Stability in Competitive Authoritarian Regimes", *World Politics*, 62(1), pp. 43–86.

Canovan, M. (1981) *Populism*. New York and London: Harcourt Brace Jovanovich.

Dandoy, R. (2010) "Ethno-Regionalist Parties in Europe: A Typology", *Perspectives on Federalism*, 2(2), pp. 194–220.

De la Torre, C. (2010) *Populist Seduction in Latin America*. Athens: Ohio University Press.

De la Torre, C. (eds.) (2014) *The Promise and Perils of Populism: Global Perspectives*. Lexington: The University Press of Kentucky.

De la Torre, C. (eds.) (2018) *Routledge Handbook of Global Populism*. Abingdon: Routledge.

De la Torre, C. and Anselmi, M. (2018) "Epilogue. Areas for Future Research", In De la Torre, C. (ed.) *Routledge Handbook of Global Populism*. Abingdon: Routledge, pp. 467–474.

De Winter, L. (1998) "Conclusion: A Comparative Analysis of the Electoral, Office and Policy Success of Ethnoregionalist Parties", In De Winter, L. and H. Tursan (eds.) *Regionalist Parties in Western Europe*. London: Routledge, pp. 190–235.

De Winter, L., and Gomez-Reino, M. (2002) "European Integration and Ethnoregionalist Parties", *Party Politics*, 8(4), pp. 483–503.

Detterbeck, K. (2012) *Multilevel Party Politics in Western Europe*. New York: Palgrave Macmillan.

Di Tella, T. S. (1995) "Populism", In Lipset, S. M. (ed.) *The Encyclopedia of Democracy*, vol. 3. London: Routledge, pp. 985–989.

Elias, A. (2008) "From Euro-Enthusiasm to Euro-Scepticism? A Re-Evaluation of Minority Nationalist Party Attitudes towards European Integration", *Regional and Federal Studies*, 18(5), pp. 557–581.

Fabbrini, F. (2017) "The Euro-Crisis, EMU and the Perils of Centralisation", In Daniele L., Simone P., and Cisotta R. (eds.) *Democracy in the EMU in the Aftermath of the Crisis*. Cham: Springer, pp. 121–140.

Finchelstein, F. (2017) *From Fascism to Populism in History*. Oakland: The University of California Press.

Fitjar, R. D. (2010) *The Rise of Regionalism: Causes of Regional Mobilization in Western Europe*. Oxon: Routledge.

Freeden, M. (1996) *Ideologies and Political Theory: A Conceptual Approach*. Oxford: Oxford University Press.

Freeden, M. (1998) "Is nationalism a distinct ideology?", *Political studies*, 46(4), pp. 748–765.

Freeden M. (2017) "After the Brexit Referendum: Revisiting Populism as an Ideology", *Journal of Political Ideologies*, 22(1), pp. 1–11.

Harmsen, R. (2010) "Concluding Comment: On Understanding the Relationship between Populism and Euroscepticism", *Perspective on European Politics and Society*, 11(3), pp. 333–341.

Harmsen, R., and Spiering, M. (eds.) (2004) *Euroscepticism. Party Politics, National Identity and European Integration*. Amsterdam/New York: Rodopi B.V. Editions.

Heinisch, R. (2008) "Right-Wing Populism in Austria – A Case for Comparison?", *Problems of Post-Communism*, 53(3), pp. 20–34.

Heinisch, R., and Mazzoleni, O. (eds.) (2016) *Understanding Populist Party Organisation: The Radical Right in Western Europe*. London: Palgrave Macmillan.

Heinisch, R., and Mazzoleni, O. (2017) "Analysing and Explaining Populism: Bringing Frame, Actor and Context Back In", In Heinisch, R., Holtz-Bacha, C., and Mazzoleni, O. (eds.) *Political Populism. A Handbook*. Baden-Baden: Nomos, pp. 105–122.

Henderson, K. (2008) "Exceptionalism or Convergence? Euroscepticism and Party Systems in Central and Eastern Europe", In Szczerbiak, A. and Taggart P. (eds.) *Opposing Europe? The Comparative Party Politics of Euroscepticism Vol. 2: Comparative and Theoretical Perspectives*. Oxford/New York: Oxford University Press, pp. 103–126.

Hendrickson, C., Muro, M. and Galston, W. A. (2018). "Strategies for Left-Behind Places – Countering the Geography of Discontent", *Brookings Report*, November. www.brookings.edu/research/countering-the-geography-of-discontent-strategies-for-left-behind-places/.

Hepburn, E. (2009) "Introduction: Re-Conceptualizing Sub-State Mobilization", *Regional and Federal Studies*, 19(4–5), pp. 477–499.

Hepburn, E., and Detterbeck, K. (2018) "Introduction", In Hepburn, E., and Detterbeck, K. (eds.) *Handbook of Territorial Politics*. Cheltenham: Edward Elgar, pp. 1–14.

Hix, S. (1999) "Dimensions and Alignments in European Union Politics: Cognitive Constraints and Partisan Responses", *European Journal of Political Research*, 35(1), pp. 69–106.

Hloušek, V., and Kaniok, P. (2014) "Europe and the 2013 Czech Parliamentary Election, October 25- 26 2013", *EPERN Election Briefing*, no. 74.

Hooghe, L., Marks, G., and Wilson, C. (2002) "Does Left/Right Structure Party Positions on European Integration?", *Comparative Political Studies*, 35(8), pp. 965–989.

Ishiyama, J., and Bozóki A. (2002) "An Unfinished Story: Towards Explaining the Transformation of the Communist Successor Parties", In Bozóki, A., and Ishiyama, J. T. (eds.) *The Communist Successor Parties of Central and Eastern Europe*. Armonk, NY: M.E. Sharpe Inc., pp. 421–433.

Ishiyama, J., and Breuning, M. (1998) *Ethnopolitics in the New Europe*. Boulder, CO: Lynne Rienner Publishers.

Jansen, R. S. (2011) "Populist Mobilization: A New Theoretical Approach to Populism", *Social Theory*, 29(2), pp. 75–96.

Jeffery, C. (2000) "Subnational Mobilization and European Integration", *Journal of Common Market Studies*, 38(1), pp. 1–24.

Jeffery, C., and Wincott, D. (2010) "The Challenge of Territorial Politics: Beyond Methodological Nationalism", In Hay, C. (ed.) *New Directions in Political Science*. Basingstoke: Palgrave Macmillan, pp. 167–188.

Jolly, K. S. (2015) *The European Union and the Rise of Regionalist Parties*. Ann Harbor: University of Michigan Press.

Kazin, M. (1998) *The Populist Persuasion: An American History*. Ithacha, NY and London: Cornell University Press.

Keating, M. (2004) "European Integration and the Nationalities Question", *Politics and Society*, 32(3), pp. 367–388.

Kitschelt, H. (1992) "The Formation of Party Systems in East Central Europe", *Politics and Society*, 20(1), pp. 7–50.

Kitschelt, H., Mansfeldova Z., Markowski, R., and Tóka, G. (1999) *Post-Communist Party Systems: Competition, Representation, and Inter-Party Cooperation*. Cambridge: Cambridge University Press.

Kopecky, P., and Mudde, C. (2002) "The Two Sides of Euroscepticism. Party Positions on European Integration in East Central Europe", *European Union Politics*, 3(3), pp. 297–326.

Kriesi, H., and Pappas, S. T. (eds.) (2015) *European Populism in the Shadow of the Great Recession*. Colchester: ECPR Press.

Krouwel, A. (2007) "Varieties of Euroscepticism and Populist Mobilization: Transforming Attitudes from Mild Euroscepticism to Harsh Eurocynicism", *Acta Politica*, 42(2–3), pp. 252–270.

Laclau, E. (1977) *Politics and Ideology in Marxist Theory*. London: NLB.

Laclau, E. (2005) *On Populist Reason*. London: Verso.

Loch, D. (2017) "Conceptualising the Relationship between Populism and the Radical Right", In Heinisch, R., Holtz-Bacha, C., and Mazzoleni, O. (eds.) *Political Populism. A Handbook*. Baden-Baden: Nomos, pp. 73–86.

March, L. (2007) "From Vanguard of the Proletariat to Vox Populi: Left-Populism as a 'Shadow' of Contemporary Socialism", *SAIS Review*, 27(1), pp. 63–77.

March, L. (2017) "Left and Right Populism Compared: The British Case", *The British Journal of Politics and International Relations*, 19(2), pp. 282–303.

Massetti, E. (2009) "Explaining Regionalist Party Positioning in a Multi-Dimensional Ideological Space: A Framework for Analysis", *Regional and Federal Studies*, 19(4–5), pp. 501–531.

Massetti, E., and Schakel, A. (2015) "From Class to Region: How Regionalist Parties Link (and Subsume) Left-Right into Centre-Periphery Politics", *Party Politics*, 21(6), pp. 866–886.

Massetti, E., and Schakel, A. (2016) "Between Autonomy and Secession: Decentralization and Regionalist Party Ideological Radicalism", *Party Politics*, 22(1), pp. 59–79.

Mazzoleni, O. (2005) "Multi-Level Populism and Centre-Periphery Politics Cleavage in Switzerland: The Case of the Lega dei Ticinesi", In Caramani, D. and Meny, Y. (eds.) *Challenges to Consensual Politics: Democracy, identity and Populist Protest in the Alpine Region*. Brussels: Peter Lang, pp. 209–227.

Mazzoleni, O., and Mueller, S. (eds.) (2016) *Regionalist Parties in Western Europe: Dimensions of Success*. London: Routledge.

McDonnell, D. (2006) "A Weekend in Padania: Regionalist Populism and the Lega Nord", *Politics*, 26(2), pp. 126–132.

Minkenberg, M. (2002) "The Radical Right in Post-Socialist Central and Eastern Europe", *East European Politics and Societies*, 16(2), pp. 335–362.

Minkenberg, M. (2010) "Leninist Beneficiaries? Pre-1989 Legacies and the Radical Rights in Post-1989 Central and Eastern Europe", In Minkenberg, M. (ed.) *Historical Legacies and the Radical Right in Post-Cold War Central and Eastern Europe*. Stuttgart: Ibidem, pp. 11–28.

Minkenberg, M. (2015) "Profiles, Patterns, Process. Studying the East European Radical Right in its Political Environment", In Minkenberg, M. (ed.) *Transforming the Transformation? The East European Radical Right in the Political Process*. London: Routledge, pp. 27–56.

Mudde, C. (2000) "In the Name of the Peasantry, the Proletariat and the People: Populisms in Eastern Europe", *East European Politics and Societies*, 15(1), pp. 33–53.

Mudde, C. (2004) "The populist zeitgeist", *Government and opposition*, 39(4), pp. 541–563.

Mudde, C. (2007) *Populist Radical Right Parties in Europe*. Cambridge: Cambridge University Press.

Mudde, C., and Rovira Kalwasser, C. (2017) *Populism. A Very Short Introduction*. Oxford: Oxford University Press.

Müller, J.-W. (2016) *What's Populism*. Philadelphia: University of Pennsylvania Press.

Neumayer, L. (2008) "Euroscepticism as a Political Label: The Use of European Union Issues in Political Competition in the New Member States", *European Journal of Political Research*, 47(2), pp. 135–160.

Otjes, S., and Louwerse, T. (2015) "Populists in Parliament: Comparing Left-Wing and Right-Wing Populism in the Netherlands", *Political Studies*, 63(1), pp. 60–79.

Panizza, F. (2005) *Populism and the Mirror of Democracy*. London: Verso.

Pauwels, T. (2011) "Measuring Populism: A Quantitative Text Analysis of Party Literature in Belgium", *Journal of Elections, Public Opinion and Parties*, 21(1), pp. 97–119.

Pirro, A. L. (2014) "Populist radical right parties in Central and Eastern Europe: The different context and issues of the prophets of the patria", *Government and Opposition*, 49(4), pp. 600–629.

Pollak, M. (1962) *The Populist Response to Industrial America: Midwestern Populist Thought*. Cambridge: Harvard University Press.

Riishøj, S. (2007) "Europeanization and Euroscepticism: Experiences from Poland and the Czech Republic", *The Journal of Nationalism and Ethnicity*, 35(3), pp. 503–535.

Rooduijn, M. (2014) "The Nucleus of Populism: In Search of the Lowest Common Denominator", *Government and Opposition*, 49(4), pp. 573–599.

Rooduijn, M., de Lange, S. L. and van der Brug, W. (2014) "A Populist Zeitgeist? Programmatic Contagion by Populist Parties in Western Europe", *Party Politics*, 20(4), pp. 563–575.

Rooduijn, M., and Pauwels, T. (2011) "Measuring Populism: Comparing Two Methods of Content Analysis", *West European Politics*, 34(6), pp. 1272–1283.

Rovny, J. (2014) "Communism, Federalism, and Ethnic Minorities: Explaining Party Competition Patterns in Eastern Europe", *World Politics*, 66(4), pp. 669–708.

Ruzza, C. (2009) "Populism and Euroscepticism: Towards Uncivil Society?", *Policy and Society*, 28(1), pp. 87–98.

Rydgren, J. (2003) "Meso-Level Reasons for Racism and Xenophobia: Some Converging and Diverging Effects of Radical Right Populism in France and Sweden", *European Journal of Social Theory*, 6(1), pp. 45–68.

Rydgren, J. (2005) *Movements of Exclusion: Radical Right-Wing Populism in the Western World*. New York: Nova.

Rydgren, J. (2008) "Immigration Sceptics, Xenophobes or Racists? Radical Right-Wing Voting in Six West European Countries", *European Journal of Political Research*, 47(6), pp. 737–765.

Sikk, A. (2005) "How Unstable? Volatility and the Genuinely New Parties in Eastern Europe", *European Journal of Political Research*, 44(1), pp. 391–412.

Stanley, B. (2008) "The thin ideology of populism", *Journal of political ideologies*, 13(1), pp. 95–110.

Stravakakis, Y. and Katsambekis, G. (2014) "Left-Wing Populism in the European Periphery: The Case of SYRIZA", *Journal of Political Ideologies*, 19(2), pp. 119–142.

Szczerbiak, A. and Taggart, P. (eds.) (2008) *Opposing Europe? Comparative and Theoretical Perspectives*, vol. II. Oxford: Oxford University Press.

Taggart, P. (1995) "New Populist Parties in Western Europe", *West European Politics*, 18(1), pp. 34–51.

Taggart, P. (1998) "A Touchstone of Dissent: Euroscepticism in Contemporary Western European Party Systems", *European Journal of Political Research*, 33(3), pp. 363–388.

Taggart, P. (2000) *Populism*. Buckingham: Open University Press.

Taguieff, P.-A. (1995) "Political Science Confronts Populism: From a Conceptual Mirage to a Real Problem", *Telos*, 103, pp. 9–43.

Tournier-Sol, K. (2015) "Reworking the Eurosceptic and Conservative Traditions into a Populist Narrative: UKIP's Winning Formula?", *Journal of Common Market Studies*, 53(1), pp. 140–156.

Vachudova, M. and Hooghe, L. (2009) "Postcommunist Politics in a Magnetic Field: How Transition and EU Accession Structure Party Competition on European Integration", *Comparative European Politics*, 7(2), pp. 179–212.

van der Brug, W., Fennema, M., and Tillie, J. (2000) "Anti-Immigrant Parties in Europe: Ideological or Protest Vote?". *European Journal of Political Research*, 37(1), pp. 77–102.

Vasilopoulou, S. (2011) "European Integration and the Radical Right: Three Patterns of Opposition", *Government and Opposition*, 46(2), pp. 223–244.

Vasilopoulou, S. (2018) *Far Right Parties and Euroscepticism. Patterns of Opposition*. London: ECPR Press/Rowman & Littlefield.

Vujacic, V. (2003) "From Class to Nation", *East European Politics and Societies*, 17(3), pp. 359–392.

Weyland, K. (2001) "Clarifying a Contested Concept: Populism in the Study of Latin American Politics", *Comparative Politics*, 34(1), pp. 1–22.

Zuber, C., and Szocsik, E. (2018) "The Second Edition of the Expert Survey on Ethnonationalism in Party Competition – Testing for Validity and Reliability", *Regional & Federal Studies*, 29(1), pp. 91–113.

2

REGIONALIST POPULISM IN BRITAIN'S "CELTIC" PERIPHERIES

A longitudinal analysis of Plaid Cymru and the Scottish National Party

Emanuele Massetti

Introduction

Populism is not an exclusive feature of state-wide and/or majority nationalist parties. Regionalist (or minority nationalist) parties[1] can also develop a populist discourse either as a stable and defining characteristic or at specific times and under particular conditions. However, reflecting a marked tendency by the European scholarship on political parties to focus on right-wing (or radical-right) populism (e.g. Betz 1994; Betz and Immerfall 1998; Rydgren 2005; Mudde 2007), scholars have overwhelmingly identified cases of right-wing regionalist populism (Mazzoleni 2005; Albertazzi 2006; Jagers and Walgrave 2007; McDonnell and Vampa 2016). In contrast, with very few exceptions,[2] cases of neither-left-nor-right or left-wing regionalist populism have been largely overlooked. This chapter addresses this lacuna by presenting a longitudinal analysis of two regionalist (or minority nationalist) parties acting in the "Celtic" peripheries of Britain: Plaid Cymru – The Party of Wales (Plaid) and the Scottish National Party (SNP).

To be clear, this article does not claim that populism is a stable and core feature within Plaid and the SNP's ideology and discourse. Indeed, references to these two parties as being populist are extremely rare.[3] However, this chapter shows that these two parties have developed an extremely similar ideological trajectory which also featured the adoption of two different types of populist discourses in two different periods of their history: the long-formative phase which runs from the time of party formation in the late 1920s to the time in which these parties passed the threshold of representation in the 1960s (Elias 2011; Lynch 2011); and the most recent phase, characterized by the unfolding of the Great Recession and the return of the Conservative party in office at Westminster (since 2010). The longitudinal analysis allows to point out why and how the two "Celtic" parties have combined their regionalist ideology with populist discourses in different ways in the two periods. The empirical evidence shows that both parties adopted a neither-left-nor-right populist ideology in the 1920s–1960s period; while, in recent years, and particularly between the 2010 and the 2015 general elections, both have become typical examples of left-wing, anti-austerity populist parties, covering the role that in other Western European countries has been played by state-wide parties such as Syriza in Greece, Podemos in Spain, the Bloco de Esquerda in Portugal; La France Insoumise in France, Die Linke in Germany and, in a more ambiguous form, the Movimento Cinque Stelle in Italy (March and Mudde 2005; Stavrakakis and Katsambekis 2014; Lisi 2015; Kioupkiolis 2016; Ramiro and Gomez 2017; Segatti and Capuzzi 2016; Ivaldi et al. 2017).

Plaid Cymru and the SNP have tried, with very different levels of success, to play the same role in the UK, as representatives of primarily Welsh and Scottish interests. Incidentally, the implicit binary comparison allows to explain why the adoption of extremely similar strategies, ideologies and discourses by the two parties has led to remarkably different levels of electoral success, particularly in the recent years, with Plaid remaining a very peripheral force in British politics, while the SNP has become the third party in Westminster after the 2015 (and 2017) general election(s).

Neither-left-nor-right populism: social credit and *perchentyaeth* (1920s–1960s)

The 1926 Balfour Declaration, issued by the Imperial Conference of the British Empire, *de facto* sanctioned the independence of the then dominions of the Commonwealth: Australia, Canada, Free State of Ireland, Newfoundland (now part of Canada), New Zealand, and Union of South Africa. In this context of gradual but irreversible process of decolonization, nationalist instances in the "Celtic" peripheries of Britain intensified, giving birth to the parties that are analyzed in this article. Plaid Cymru was founded in 1925 from the merging of two newly-created organizations (Davies 1983: 61), while the SNP was born in 1928 – initially called the National Party of Scotland, it acquired its current name in 1934, after merging with the then two-year old Scottish Party (Hanham 1969: 154; Finlay 1994: 133).

The main initial challenge of both parties was their mere survival as unitary and independent political organizations. Indeed, many party members came from (or had ideological affinities with) the various British parties, thus bringing-in high ideological heterogeneity and low exclusive attachment to the new parties. As a consequence, both the Scottish and Welsh regionalist parties had to conceive themselves as "broad churches", kept together almost exclusively by the objective of achieving some territorial self-government for Scotland (in the case of the SNP)[4] and of protecting the Welsh language (in the case of Plaid Cymru).[5] In addition, class politics was already well covered by the two main

British parties, with the Conservatives representing the interests of the bourgeoisie and Labour being the political arm of the unionized working class (Jarvis 1996). In this context, the two minority nationalist parties recurred to populist discourses that allowed them to widen and qualify their nationalist message without, however, engaging too directly in (for them) divisive left-right politics. In particular, their minority nationalist ideology placed both parties in a position where they could easily exploit three interrelated populist themes: a) a recrimination for a lost "heartland" (Taggart 2000), in the forms of a "Free Scotland" and a "Free and Welsh Wales"; b) an *ante litteram* "small is beautiful" integral approach (Schumacher 1973), which justified the appreciation of small and peripheral nations, as well as the defense of small/diffused interests vis-à-vis big/organized interests;[6] and c) an antagonistic stance vis-à-vis the "power bloc" (Laclau 2005) or the detached elites (Mudde 2004), in this case identified in the British political, economic and cultural ruling classes.

This common nucleus of populist discourse was, however, bent and twisted differently by Plaid and the SNP due to some key differences across the two "Celtic" regions. First, Scottish and Welsh nationalism were based on partially different markers of national identity. While the Welsh language was perceived as the core source of Welsh national identity, the Scottish one was mainly based on its historical (an independent and united Scottish Kingdom) and present institutions, such as a separate legal system, Church (Kirk), educational system, etc. (Crick 1991). Secondly, there was substantial difference in the way and extent to which the two regions were integrated and embedded in the British economy. While Wales was a purely peripheral region divided between an agricultural North-(West) and an extractive South(-East), with the coal mining industry monopolized by English capital; Scotland, in spite of having her large agricultural and extractive sectors too, was still at the forefront of British heavy industry and had a more thriving autochthonous business community (Brand 1978). Thirdly, the electoral-political environment of the two regions was substantively different, with Wales being dominated by the Labour party (which had just replaced the Liberal party as the hegemon political actor in the region), while Scottish electoral politics (still heavily influenced by the intertwined issues of the Irish question and the confessional divide) was much more balanced and open to competition between the Conservative/Unionist coalition and the Labour party.[7] Finally, there was considerable difference in the personality, vocation and influence of party founders and/or early leaders across the two parties. The most influential founders/leaders of Plaid had a primarily spiritualist and humanist intellectual formation and approach.[8] In particular, the prolonged (1926–1939) and dedicated leadership of party founder Saunders Lewis had a tremendous and long-lasting impact on the ideological development of the party. In contrast, the founders and early leaders of the SNP stayed in charge for shorter periods and had less of a personal influence on the party. In addition, with the exception of poet and scholar of Latin/Greek literature Douglas Young (1942–1945), their formation was either professional/legalistic or technical/scientific.[9]

These factors produced some differences in the way the various elements of the nucleus of populist discourse were shaped, starting with the formulation of a lost "heartland". In the case of Scotland, the early leadership was extremely divided. On the one hand, people like Douglas Young wanted to revive the cultural bases of Scottish nationalism by proposing a romanticist view of national identity and an idealized version of Scottish history, which emphasized the victimization of Scotland as a country colonized by a foreign power. On the other hand, for people like Andrew Dewar Gibb the lost "heartland" was not an idealized independent Scotland of the middle-ages or the rebellious (Jacobite) Scotland of the early 18th century but, rather, the pick of the British Empire, in which Scotland featured as a "partner". Scottish "malaise", according to Gibb, did not originate from a loss of independence and inherently Scottish culture but, simply, from the need to re-balance the Anglo-Scottish partnership through constitutional reform. By the mid-1940s, both discourses had been largely replaced by a nostalgia for a radical Scotland which had fallen victim of a process of centralization and bureaucratization of the British state and its main socio-political institutions (SNP, Aims and Policy 1946: 3). In the case of Wales, the discourse of a lost "heartland" has been much more univocal and stronger, entailing a much deeper resentment against the "English colonizers". In the narrative of early Welsh nationalists, the loss of a Welsh civilization (Welsh Wales) was determined by the concurrent processes of Anglicization, capitalism, industrialization and urbanization (Davies 1983). This markedly anti-modernist sentiments appear to set early Welsh nationalist-populist discourse on a very similar tone as 19th century Russian populism (*Narodniki*) and Gandhi's Indian populism (Venturi 1960). In all three cases, intellectual (and urban) national elites put forward a nostalgia-dominated discourse in which they idealize and romanticize a faded/ing life style built around the rural community and its communal land – the *Gwele* (in Welsh populism), the *Obshichina* (in Russian populism) and the *Panchayat* (in early Indian populism) – in opposition to the most traumatic effects of modernization. In the narrative of early Welsh nationalists, in the turn of three centuries, the Welsh civilization, based on free men sharing a common culture heritage and the common use of the land, has been almost totally disrupted by annexation into England and by the exploitation of English greedy capitalists:

> From the cities of England, there flocked to Wales a horde of rootless capitalists to suck her lifeblood and leave her in a more miserable state than before... Modern Wales, as we know it, is the result of these centuries of exploitation... One industry alone flourishes in Wales today – that of draining the country of its best blood.
> *(Plaid Cymru, no date [between 1934 and 1939]: 3)*

The replacement of Welsh with English as the most spoken language in the industrialized and urbanized (and most populous) areas of Wales was seen as the most alarming effect of this deleterious process. Indeed, the early socio-economic plans of Plaid Cymru sounded more as a naïve attempt at restoring a lost civilization, and thereby reverting the decline of the Welsh language, than a realistic project for the future: "Agriculture should be the chief industry of Wales and the basis of its civilization … South Wales must be de-industrialised" (Lewis 1934: 4). Surely, a vision of a lost "heartland" similar to the one found in Scotland, i.e. as a harbour of radical culture and politics, was also well present in Wales, where the linkage between religious nonconformity, radicalism and nationalism has been stressed again and again in the nationalist narratives (Plaid Cymru, no date [between 1950 and 1964]: 10). However, this narrative remained subordinate to the anti-modernist one throughout the long leadership of Catholic-converted Sounders Lewis, gradually re-emerging during the leadership of Gwynfor Evans after World War Two.

Both discourses of a fading radical Scotland and a fading Welsh Wales tied up very well with what I called an *ante litteram* "small is beautiful" approach. Indeed, this type of discourse was not only used to praise the value of small independent nations – such as the Scandinavian states that have always been taken as examples by both Scottish and Welsh nationalists – but also to re-propose a decentralist and radical democratic discourse that allowed the parties to avoid taking a clear stance on the class-centered politics of the time. Concentration of political and economic power was presented by both parties as the real obstacle on the way of people's freedom. In this view, the SNP adopted a discourse very close to that of populist movements and parties in Western Canada (Hanham 1969: 175). In particular, the party adopted some key tenets of the Social Credit doctrine (Keating 1996: 182), stressing the importance of local, small town democracy, as well as the need to diffuse ownership as much as possible: "The economic safeguard of democracy lies in the diffusion of economic power" (SNP 1946: 6). Taking Western Canada as a benchmark of different types of peripheral populisms (Laycock 2005: 174–177), Plaid Cymru's socio-economic discourse had probably more in common with the left-leaning populism of the Cooperative Commonwealth Federation (CCF) than with that of the Social Credit parties. The strong emphasis on co-operation was brought into the party primarily by D. J. Davies who proposed, in his *The Economics of Welsh Self-Government* (1931), the adoption of a system based on co-operative socialism (Davies 1983: 88). However, this proposal was immediately edited by Lewis, who rejected with equal disdain both capitalism and socialism, framing D. J. Davies' project as "co-operative nationalism" (Massetti 2010: 59). Resorting to the Welsh concept of *perchentyaeth* (householdness), in Lewis' proposal the emphasis shifted from co-operation to the centrality of the economic wellbeing of the family. Eventually, the prevailing socio-economic discourse in early Welsh nationalism was very similar to that of the SNP: "to make the families of the nation as free, secure and independent as possible … It will be necessary to plan and legislate for a wide distribution of ownership, for ownership is the only guarantee of freedom" (Plaid Cymru, no date [between 1934 and 1939]: 10–11). The discourse of diffuse ownership was explicitly used to distance the parties from class politics and the capitalist vs. socialist ideological debate: "The concentration of economic power in the hands of either private or State monopolies is inimical both to the freedom of the individual and to the proper function of democratic government" (SNP 1946: 6), and

> Ownership should be so widely distributed as to make it impossible for the state (thus excluding Fascism, Communism, and many forms of Socialism) or individuals or groups of individuals (thus excluding Capitalism) to exercise economic tyranny over the families of the nation.
> *(Plaid Cymru, no date [between 1934 and 1939]: 11)*

The same discourse is also used to target the British elites, in the form of big business and trade unions, as well as their political (Conservative and Labour party) representatives.

These populist discourses and ideological stances have remained in place within both Plaid and the SNP well into the 1960s. An official document of the SNP, published in 1964, stated that the party aims "to reverse the harmful effects of the centralising forces which have been at work in government and industry and finance" (SNP 1964: 3); while a Plaid Cymru document published in 1969 reported the following quote from then party leader, Gwynfor Evans: "In politics, industry and social life, responsibility must be distributed as widely as possible if men are to achieve the quality of which life is capable" (Plaid Cymru 1969: 21).

Ideological in-fights, left-of-centrism and party mainstreamization (1970s–2000s)

By the mid-1970s, both parties were part of the anti-EEC front during the 1975 referendum on UK membership (Lynch 1996). In that occasion, they challenged the mainstream consensus for both strategic (i.e. gaining political visibility) and ideological (regionalist populist) reasons, joining forces with the left-wing (Tony Benn's Labour faction) and right-wing (Enoch Powell's Tory faction) populist actors of the time. However, the second part of that decade saw these parties concentrating their attention on devolution and on government policies. This was particularly the case for the SNP, which in 1977–1979 was the crucial supporter of the Labour minority government.

After the failures of the 1979 devolution referendums in both Scotland and Wales, coupled by the disappointing results at the general election later that year (see Table 2.1), the two minority nationalist parties went through a phase of soul (and strategy) searching (McAllister 2001; Lynch 2002). In the context of growing polarization within the British political system in the early 1980s, Plaid

Cymru and the SNP could not easily avoid left-right politics anymore. In both parties, factions that aimed at explicitly positioning the parties to the left of the political spectrum were born: the National Left within Plaid and the 79 Group within the SNP. Although, in the short run, the internal struggles had different endings in the two parties (the National Left won the battle within Plaid,[10] whereas the 79 Group was temporarily defeated by the traditionalists within the SNP),[11] the unfolding of the neo-liberal agenda carried out by the Thatcher governments in the 1980s did push both parties to explicitly position themselves to the left (Massetti 2010).

Internal tensions were gradually overcome during the 1990s also thanks to the emergence of a post-Thatcher consensus (Hay 1994), which allowed the regionalist parties to keep projecting a left-of-centre image without necessarily adopting a classic social-democratic economic approach. Indeed, during the 1990s and early 2000s, the two parties underwent a gradual process of "mainstreamization", which involved the completion of a U-turn on Europe (from anti-EEC in the 1970s to pro-EU in the early 1990s) and the *de facto* acceptance of a (Giddensian) "third way" approach to socio-economic policies (Lynch 2009). The left-of-centre image was mainly maintained by emphasizing new-leftist stances – pro-environment; against war and armament; pro-gender equality; against social discrimination; etc. – in what Peter Lynch described as a transformation "from Red to Green" (Lynch 1995). The process of normalization and mainstreamization, which was personified by Ieuan Wyn Jones[12] in Plaid Cymru and John Swinney[13] in the SNP, intensified in the early 2000s

TABLE 2.1 Plaid and the SNP's electoral results in general elections

Election year	SNP's votes (%) in Scotland	Plaid's votes (%) in Wales	SNP's number of seats in Scotland	Plaid's number of seats in Wales
1964	2.4	4.8	0/72	0/40
1966	5	4.3	0/72	0/40
1970	11.4	11.5	1/72	0/40
1974 (F)	21.9	10.7	7/72	2/40
1974 (O)	30.4	10.8	11/72	3/40
1979	17.3	8.1	2/72	2/40
1983	11.7	7.8	2/72	2/40
1987	14	7.3	3/72	3/40
1992	21.5	8.8	3/72	4/40
1997	22.1	9.9	6/72	4/40
2001	20.1	14.3	5/72	4/40
2005	17.7	12.6	6/59	2/40
2010	19.9	11.3	6/59	3/40
2015	50.0	12.1	56/59	3/40
2017	36.9	10.4	35/59	4/40

Source: Massetti (2018: 945)

when internal reforms aimed at limiting the influence of party activists were undertaken (Elias 2011; Lynch 2011). This process was primarily driven by the new opportunities that opened up with the approval of devolution (1997/1998) and the creation of elected regional governments in Scotland and Wales in 1999. The ambition to gain office at regional level, as well as the actual participation in regional executives, required the Scottish and Welsh regionalists to build up a reputation as competent and responsible parties of government (McAngus 2016). This reputation had to be obtained within the context of the consolidated consensus on "third way economics" which was in place in the late 1990s and throughout the 2000s (Milazzo et al. 2012). On the one hand, this strategy left the two parties more vulnerable on their left-flank in the 2003 regional elections, providing an advantage for Welsh Labour in Wales and for left-wing populist/nationalist competitors in Scotland, such as the Scottish Greens and the Scottish Socialist Party (Wyn Jones and Scully 2003; Massetti 2009b). On the other hand, both minority nationalist parties managed to get in (regional) office in 2007, though with a rather different electoral strength and via different governing formulas: the SNP became the biggest party in Scotland and formed a single-party minority government, while Plaid Cymru joined a Labour-led executive as a junior partner (see Table 2.2).[14]

The anti-austerity shield: left-wing populism after the great recession

With the start of the global financial crisis and the following Great Recession, new opportunities opened up for the two regionalist/leftist parties (especially for the SNP), particularly after the 2010 general election. They benefited from the results and the immediate consequences of that election in several ways. First, Labour's defeat – with (Scotsman) Gordon Brown's abandonment of active politics – and the Tories' return to office in Westminster represented a laceration between the UK political establishment and vast sectors of the two Celtic

TABLE 2.2 Plaid and the SNP's electoral results in their respective regional elections

Year	SNP vote (%)	Plaid vote (%)	SNP seats/total	Plaid seats/total	SNP in office	Plaid in office
1999	28.7	28.4	35/129	17/60	No	No
2003	23.7	21.2	27/129	12/60	No	No
2007	32.9	22.4	47/129	15/60	Yes – Single party minority	Yes – Coalition (junior partner)
2011	45.4	19.3	69/129	11/60	Yes – Single party majority	No
2016	46.5	20.5	63/129	12/60	Yes – Single party minority	No

regions' electorates. Second, the "suicidal" decision of the Liberal Democrats to enter a government coalition with the Conservatives, allowed the two minority nationalist parties to gather the fruits of the LibDems' subsequent electoral debacles, starting with the 2011 regional elections. Without the dramatic electoral losses of the LibDems the SNP would not have been able to gain a full majority in the Scottish parliament and, without that majority, it would have not been able to call (and pass regional legislation) for the independence referendum that was eventually held in September 2014. In turn, the possibility to hold a referendum on Scottish independence has given the SNP more than two years of unprecedented exposition in the media, not only in Scotland but also UK-wide and beyond (Keating 2017). Third, the new Con–LibDem government adopted a pro-austerity approach (Lee and Beech 2011), with important consequences on the capacity of the British welfare system (Grimshaw and Rubery 2012). This created an incentive for both Plaid and the SNP to strengthen their leftist (i.e. anti-austerity) and minority nationalist (i.e. more self-government to protect Scotland/Wales from London's austerity) discourses. Fourth, although the new UK Labour leader, Ed Miliband, deployed an anti-Blairite political discourse, by the time he led Labour into the 2015 general election, he had not been able to differentiate enough his party's macroeconomic approach from that of the governing Con–LibDem coalition. This gave the two regionalist parties the possibility to link their minority nationalist and leftist rhetoric with a populist discourse which targeted the whole British political elites, representing the latter as detached from the needs of the common citizens. This strategy was particularly easy for the SNP, which had been running a prolonged referendum campaign on Scottish independence (2012–2014), in which the Labour party had been part of a common unionist front together with the Conservatives and the LibDems.

The anti-austerity reputation of the two regionalist parties has been gradually built starting from the very electoral campaign of 2010. The SNP's manifesto explicitly asked Scottish voters to send as many minority nationalist MPs to Westminster as possible in order to protect Scotland from cuts to public spending: "The London parties all offer the same thing … At this election, more votes means more Nats, and more Nats means less cuts. Local services and recovery can and must be protected" (SNP 2010: 4–5). Plaid Cymru was even bolder in attacking the British political establishment and their common macroeconomic approach:

> Labour has slavishly followed Tory policies for 13 years and Cameron has modelled himself and his politics on Tony Blair… Neither Labour nor the Tories can be allowed to continue to wreak havoc on the Welsh economy and undermine our welfare state.
>
> *(Plaid Cymru 2010: 4)*

The same anti-austerity discourse was used by both parties in the 2011 regional elections:

> Wales continues to reel in the wake of Labour's financial and economic crises and the most savage cuts in public services since the 1930s inflicted on us by the Conservatives and Liberal Democrats... Drastic cuts to benefits will unfairly target the poorest in society, and will push them into a cycle of in-work and out-of-work poverty.
>
> *(Plaid Cymru 2011: 3)*

In addition, as mentioned above, the SNP had an opportunity to target the "London parties" during the long independence referendum campaign, as well as to present a social-democratic vision for an independent Scotland. In the document produced by the SNP Scottish Government in favor of independence, it can be clearly detected an attack against the rising (social and territorial) inequality that resulted from the policies of both Labour and Con–LibDem executives, as well as a series of counter-austerity measures that would be implemented in an independent Scotland, such as abolition of the measures of the Welfare Reform Act 2012 on housing benefits, minimum wage linked to inflation, re-nationalization of the Royal Mail, special measures to facilitate women's presence in the workforce (Scottish Government 2013). Given the positive reaction of many traditional Labour voters in Scotland to the pro-independence/leftist vision of the SNP, the regionalists kept emphasizing even more their anti-austerity populist discourse after the loss of the 2014 referendum pushed Scottish independence (temporarily) out of the agenda. As shown in Figure 2.1, by 2014, the two nationalist parties were occupying, together with the Greens, the left portion of the populist ground in British politics: a ground that was going to be ever more appealing to British voters (Flinders 2015). It is also worth noting that, being the right-wing populist UKIP virtually irrelevant in Scotland and having the SNP absorbed some of the themes of the Scottish left-wing populist parties, such as the Scottish Socialist Party (March and Mudde 2005), the Scottish nationalists acquired a sort of monopoly on anti-establishment politics in Scotland, particularly in the context of a general election.

In the absence of a UK-wide anti-austerity party, the two regionalist parties entered the 2015 general election campaign attacking immediately the "London parties" as indistinguishable defenders of austerity (McSmith 2015). This strategy clearly emerges once again from their manifestos: "All three Westminster parties are committed to slash and burn economics" (Plaid Cymru 2015: 3); "We propose a real alternative to the pain of austerity ... We will then use our influence to demand that Labour delivers the real change that people want and need – instead of just being a carbon copy of

30 Emanuele Massetti

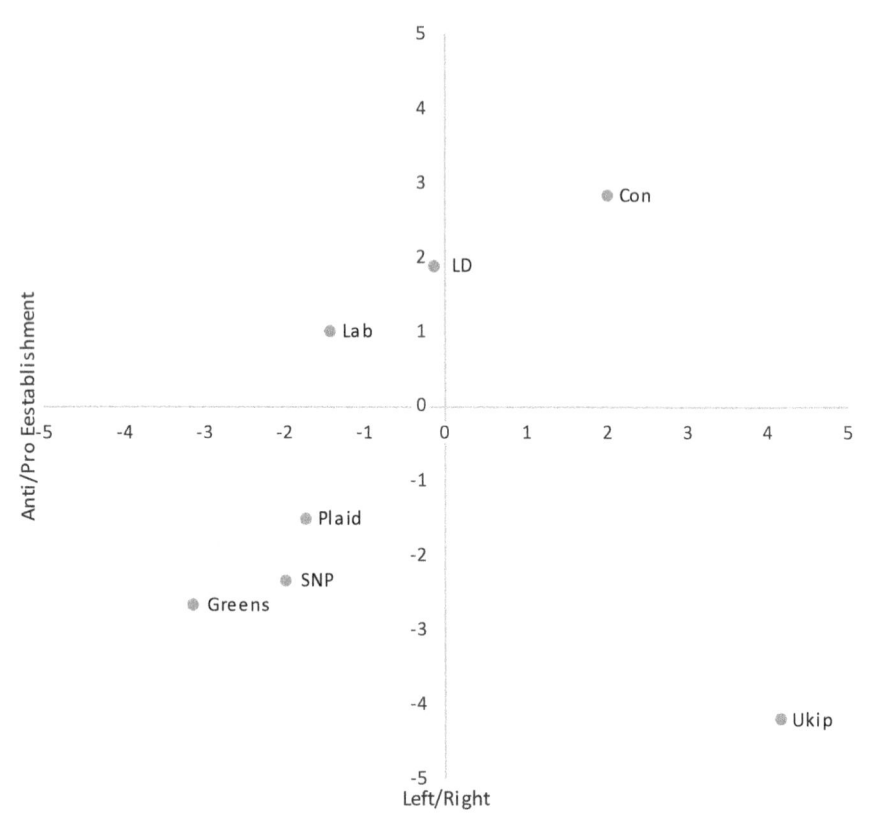

FIGURE 2.1 British parties' positions in 2014

Source: Author's elaboration on the bases of the 2014 Chapel Hill Expert Survey (CHES) data – Polk et al. (2017).

the Tories" (SNP 2015: 3). In the TV debates amongst party leaders during the campaign, the leaders of the SNP and Plaid Cymru were the ones who distinguished themselves for stigmatizing austerity policies more often and more openly than any other party leader. The results of the analysis conducted by Allen et al. (2017) shows that the time dedicated to austerity by the SNP's leader Nicola Sturgeon and Plaid's leader Leanne Wood was respectively 43% and 100% higher than the average of all leaders in the first TV debate, held on ITV on 2 April 2015 (Allen et al. 2017: 9). In the following debate, held on the BBC on 16 April 2015, they emphasized austerity respectively 33% and 50% more than the average of all leaders (Allen et al. 2017: 10). It is worth pointing out that austerity was the only issue, besides that of constitutional/territorial reforms, which clearly set the SNP and Plaid's leaders apart from the leaders of all the other parties that took part in the debates – i.e. Conservative, LibDems, Labour, UKIP and Greens in the ITV debate; Labour, UKIP and Greens in the BBC debate. It is probably superfluous to specify that Sturgeon and Woods' talking about austerity was, in fact, against austerity (BBC 2015).

In spite of adopting very similar discourses, the two nationalist parties diverged in terms of the space dedicated to their respective region's issues rather than to UK ones. In contrast to Plaid Cymru's focus on the constitutional question (i.e. more powers to the Welsh Assembly), the SNP presented a manifesto which was rather concerned with the generality of issues that Westminster has to deal with. The lack of concentration on constitutional matters was partially due to the fact that a referendum had just rejected the party long-term claim for independence. However, it was also due to the possibility of a hung Parliament, which would have given the SNP a potential role in the game of coalition government formation in London.[15] In this context, the party was pushed to show attention to general British issues, beyond (but surely not in contrast to) narrow Scottish interests – "The SNP will use our influence at Westminster to help deliver positive change for the benefit of ordinary people, not just in Scotland, but across the UK" (SNP 2015: 3). In this purpose, the party was also helped by the Tory strategy, which aimed to represent a possible Lab-SNP government as a "coalition of chaos", primarily by stigmatizing the SNP not only for its anti-Britishness but also for its rejection of strict fiscal discipline (*The Guardian* 2015). In this way, the SNP was legitimized not only in the eyes of Scottish leftist/nationalist voters but also in the eyes of some leftist voters south of the border, as it was represented by the Tories as the real "danger" for a possible turn in British economic policy. Occupying the anti-austerity niche in the British debate was the best way to reconcile the potentially contrasting needs of remaining the champion of Scottish interests and, at the same time, wining UK-wide sympathies and a role amongst anti-Tory forces. Indeed, during the 2015 election campaign, the SNP became a potential point of reference for voters deluded by Labour's timidity in challenging the status quo, not only in Scotland but throughout the UK. This explains why Nicola Sturgeon emerged as the most appreciated leader UK-wide after the first TV debate (YouGov's survey for the *The Guardian*, 3 April 2015). She kept adopting the same strategy during the second debate, where she offered Labour's leader Ed Miliband the support of the SNP for a possible anti-Tory government, while attacking him for his lack of courage in offering a clear alternative to the Tories' policies (BBC 2015). It was in this context and following this strategy that the SNP achieved, by far, its best electoral result ever in a general election (56 out of 59 seats won), virtually wiping out the three traditional British parties from Scotland. In contrast, in spite of adopting a very similar discourse and strategy, Plaid only managed to keep its 3 (out 40) seats, without substantive increases in vote share.

Left populism in Britain: an increasingly crowded political area (2015–2017)

The anti-austerity populist strategy of Plaid and the SNP continued after the 2015 general election, in spite of the Brexit referendum taking centre-stage in the political debate. In addition, the SNP could exploit the increased media attention due to the fact that it had become the third party in Westminster. In order to avoid any chance of getting identified as just another "London party", the SNP's group adopted different strategies that can be observed in many different populist parties (especially new ones) Europewide. For instance, the party resisted as much as possible symbolic forms of socialization and institutionalization within the Westminster's customs and traditions, such as the "Yah-Boo" and "bobbing up and down" during debates (Thompson 2018). In addition, they circulated pictures on social media that showed a virtually empty House of Commons in which the SNP group is the only one massively present in the room (Cowley 2015), thus implying that they are the only party respectful of tax-payers money and democratic institutions. At the same time, a marked over-representation of present MPs in parliamentary debates, especially in those that were particularly important for Scotland, such as the Scotland Bill, the Trident and "English-votes-for-English-laws" (Thompson 2018), gave the SNP the possibility of remaining very visible also in the UK media.

Yet, with the election of Jeremy Corbyn as leader of the Labour party in September 2015, and even more after his re-election a year later, anti-Austerity populism was not anymore an empty hunting ground for the two regionalist parties. As Corbyn's Labour closes in, advancing a more radical critique of the post-Thatcherite and post-Blairite consensus, some electoral damages for the two parties – especially for the SNP that had mostly benefited in the pre-Corbyn context – have started to materialize. To be sure, the Corbyn effect did not manifest itself in the 2016 regional elections, where the Labour party lost votes both in Wales and (heavily so) in Scotland. Arguably few months of unsettled leadership (with an overall negative media coverage) were not enough to have a positive impact. An SNP member of the Scottish Parliament who was previously a member of the Scottish Labour party proposed the following explanation:

> Labour has voted with the Conservatives for austerity policies many times in the last parliament, so that perception carries on. When Corbyn was elected as leader of the Labour party I was personally curious about possible consequences for Scottish politics too. But so far the effects of Corbyn's leadership have been virtually null in Scotland for three reasons: first, he has a reputation of being a leftist but also of being incompetent; secondly, the Labour party is very divided and people don't vote for divided parties; thirdly, in Scotland the party is not only divided but, amongst the Scottish leadership, it is more anti-Corbyn than pro-Corbyn, so people know that if they vote Labour in Scottish elections they actually vote for anti-Corbyn people.
>
> *(Ivan McKee MSP, interview conducted on 24 November 2016, Edinburgh)*

However, the campaign for the (snap) general election of June 2017 clearly marked the re-appearance of a more radical Labour party, potentially capable of re-attracting voters sensitive to left-populist appeals. The two nationalist parties kept using a strong anti-austerity rhetoric – "A vote for the SNP will strengthen Scotland's hand against further Tory cuts" (SNP 2017: 3); "Our economy, our communities and even our very identity as a nation is under threat from the cruel and reckless Tories" (Plaid Cymru 2017: 2) – but this time they could not accuse the Labour party of complicity or convergence with the Conservative government. Actually, it was the SNP's credentials as a genuine anti-austerity party that became a target. Indeed, Scottish Labour and the Scottish Greens started to criticize the Scottish executive for not using its new fiscal powers in order to increase taxes on the wealthy and fund more social services (Dugdale 2016); a criticism that was also used by Jeremy Corbyn himself (BBC 2017). The new polarization between the main British parties – interacting with the still divisive issue of Scottish independence and the increasingly salient and equally divisive issue of Brexit – determined a significant come-back of both the Conservatives and Labour in Scotland and Wales. Corbyn's Labour increased its vote share by nearly 3% points in Scotland (11.5% of its 2015 vote share) and more than 12 points in Wales (almost 33% of its 2015 vote). Plaid and the SNP lost respectively more than 14% and more than 26% of their 2015 vote share. To be sure, the SNP still remains, by far, the biggest party in Scotland. However, Labour much-better-than-expected UK-wide results have consolidated Corbyn's leadership and, with it, the party capacity to re-attract many voters that have switched from Labour to the SNP since 2010. In addition, the election of pro-Corbyn Richard Leonard as leader of Scottish Labour might increase Labour's electoral pressure on the SNP in future elections (*The Guardian* 2017). Competition on the leftist/populist quadrant of the British political space is, therefore, likely to increase further, with potential damages for the two "Celtic" regionalist parties. At the time of writing, however, they are still, particularly the SNP, relevant actors in British anti-austerity politics and, as long as there will be a Tory government in London, they are likely to remain so.

Discussion

The article sets out to investigate how different populist themes can be included into the ideological and discourse repertoire of minority nationalist parties. The inclusion of different sets of populist themes in different times appears to depend on the overall ideological profile of the parties, beyond the regionalist elements, which in turn is linked to strategic considerations based on the contextual socio-political conditions. The binary and longitudinal comparison between the SNP and Plaid Cymru shows a common, extremely similar, trajectory which has seen the two parties using a rather different populist discourse in two specific historical periods. From their birth in the 1920s/1930s to the 1960s both parties remained electorally irrelevant and refused to take a clear stance on the left-right ideological dimension. Their socio-economic proposals were very similar to those of some emerging third parties in 1930s–1960s Western Canada, which in turn re-proposed the ethos of the US Populist Party of the 1890s. While the centrality of agriculture, the agrarian society and spirit was more evident in Plaid Cymru than in the SNP, both parties deployed a discourse that pitted the small holders and small businessmen against the big organized interests of Trade Unions and Big Business. The former struggled and survived by their merits, providing society with a healthy combination of substantive equality and (diffused) private ownership; whereas the latter thrived with the protection of their respective political patrons, the Labour and Conservative parties. The attack on the British political elites, solidly grounded in their minority nationalist ideology, was thus integrated by a typical populist discourse which depicted the small middle classes against the political and economic elites. In addition, the minority nationalist and populist ideologies converged on specific Scottish and Welsh narratives of a lost "heartland".

Forty years later, in the aftermath of the Great Recession and under remarkably different socio-political conditions, we find the two parties operating a different synthesis of nationalist, populist and left-right ideological orientations. Indeed, since the 1970s the two parties have come out of electoral irrelevance, since the 1980s they have combined their regionalist stance with a leftist ideological orientation, since the late 1990s they have been able to compete in newly established regional institutions, and in 2007 they both got in office at regional level, although with important differences in the level of electoral support. Leaving aside their pro-independence (therefore anti-system) stance, at the start of the Great Recession in 2008 they had both become largely integrated in the British mainstream in terms political economic approach. However, the austerity measures adopted by the Con–LibDem coalition government in the 2010–2015 term, coupled by the rather timid opposition of the Labour party, has offered to both parties the chance to play the card of anti-austerity left-wing populism, which in other countries is primarily taken up by country-wide parties, such as Podemos, Syriza, La France Insoumise and, to some extent, the Movimento Cinque Stelle.

In spite of adopting the same strategy and discourse, the two parties have had very different results in the 2015 general election: with Plaid keeping the same number of MPs (three), the SNP rocketing from six to 56, and becoming the third party in Westminster. The binary comparison helps explaining the different outcome by pointing at a longer term electoral gap between the two parties, the different demographics of Scotland and Wales, the long campaign for Scottish referendum for independence (2012–2014) and the very different levels of media attention dedicate to the two parties. The SNP has been the party that, albeit maintaining the role of Scotland's independence advocate, has also covered the role of anti-austerity populism in British politics in the period 2010–2015. The ideal conjunction of minority nationalism and anti-austerity populism has been in place up to the election of Jeremy Corbyn as leader of the Labour party.

Until then, it was relatively easy for the two regionalist parties to represent the whole British elites ("London parties") as adopting a pro-austerity consensus against the interests of the common citizens. Since then, Corbyn's Labour appears to have regained the capacity to compete for the votes it lost in Scotland and Wales since 2010 (and before). The SNP has, however, established itself as the dominant party in Scotland, so competition on the left-side of the political spectrum amongst the two parties is likely to increase in the next years.

Notes

1 For a terminological/conceptual discussion of this party family, see Massetti (2009a, 2010). In this article the terms regionalist and minority nationalist are used interchangeably.
2 March and Mudde (2005) have pointed out the Scottish Socialist Party and the Eastern German PDS – which before the creation of Die Linke could also be considered as a regionalist party (Hough and Koss 2009) – as cases of left-wing populism.
3 To my knowledge, the only scholar that mentioned SNP's populism is Micheal Keating (1996: 182). While the only author that identified Plaid Cymru as a populist party is T. D. Combes (1977).
4 From 1928 to 1946 the SNP went through a series of internal struggles over the type/extent of self-government the party wanted to claim for Scotland (Massetti 2010: 100–102). In 1933 the moderate faction in favour of "Home Rule" took the upper hand, determining the expulsion of the most radical (republican and/or socialist) supporters of independence (Fry 1987: 216). In 1942, the tables were turned: the supporters of "Home Rule" left the party and some of those who had been expelled in 1933 re-joined. In 1946, the SNP set itself on a clear pro-independence stance (Hanham 1969: 213).
5 In the first five years of its life Plaid Cymru was exclusively concerned with the revitalization of the Welsh language and culture ("Welsh Wales"), while no mention was made to territorial self-government (Davies 1983: 82). From 1931, the party adopted ambiguously phrased stances on self-government – "dominion status"; "self-government", "full national status". Only in 2003 the party set itself on a clear pro-independence position (Massetti 2009a: 44–55). The preservation of the Welsh language has, anyway, remained the priority until the 1960s and one of the main concerns to this day.
6 The relationship between a "small is beautiful" approach (in both economics and politics) and populism has been explored in economic development studies – e.g. Kitching (1989) – and in political geography studies – e.g. Watts (2009).
7 In Wales, between the 1929 and the 1959 general elections the Labour party obtained between 70 and 80% of seats; in Scotland, in the same period, the Labour party came on top in four out of eight elections, thus trailing the Conservative/Unionist coalition in 50% of the elections.
8 The first leader, Lewis Valentine (1925–1926), was a Baptist pastor; the second, and by far most influential leader, Saunders Lewis (1926–1939), was a poet, dramatist and historian; while the third leader, John Edward Daniel (1939–1943), was theologian and philosopher.
9 The first two leaders of the SNP, Sir Alexander MacEwen (1934–1936) and Andrew Dewar Gibb (1936–1940), were respectively a solicitor and a barrister. The two leaders that set the SNP's aims and policies after WW2, Bruce Watson (1945–1947) and Robert McIntyre (1947–1956), were respectively a chemist and a physician.

10 In the following years, a traditionalist faction called the "Hydro Group" tried to push back the party towards a "neither right nor left" strategy. However, this group was largely unsuccessful and the leadership of Dafydd Elis Thomas (1984–1991) consolidated the leftist stance of Plaid Cymru (Massetti 2010).
11 Seven members of the 79Group, including future party leader Alex Salmond, were expelled from the party in 1982 (Levy 1990; Lynch 2002; Torrance 2009). The leftist faction started to regain ground from 1985, when they also launched the "Nationalist Left Review". By 1988, Alex Salmond had not only been re-accepted as party member but he had also been elected deputy leader. In 1990, he was elected leader of the SNP.
12 Ieuan Wyn Jones was the leader of Plaid Cymru from 2000 to 2012. He has been considered as a moderate pragmatist and broker between the traditionalist (mainly North-Western) and the leftist (mainly Southern) factions. He led Plaid into a coalition government with Welsh labour in the period 2007–2011, and was Deputy First Minister in that executive (Elias 2011).
13 John Swinney was the leader of the SNP from 2000 to 2004 and the inspirer of the internal party reforms (Lynch 2011: 247). He has been considered a moderate figure both in terms of left-right politics and self-government claims (Webb 2001). He was the Minister of Finance and Economy in the Scottish executive from 2007 to 2016.
14 Several factors can be held responsible for the fact that the SNP and Plaid had different electoral performances in their respective regional elections in spite of adopting very similar strategies. First, since the 1970s the SNP has had better electoral scores than Plaid, whose support has remained rather limited to the Welsh speaking areas of Wales. Secondly, Welsh Labour, which was led by a non-Blairite leader between 2000 and 2009, has been both more leftist and more (Welsh) nationalist than its Scottish counterpart (Clark and Bennie 2016). As a consequence, Plaid Cymru faced a stronger competition than the SNP in trying to establish itself as the nationalist/leftist party in the region.
15 As the below quotation shows, Plaid Cymru did try to increase its visibility by playing the card of a possible post-election anti-Tory coalition, also in virtue of its long relationship with the SNP:

> It is likely that there will be another hung parliament after the election. In that scenario, Plaid Cymru could hold the balance of power alongside our colleagues in the SNP. Should that happen, Plaid Cymru will seek a rebalancing of power and wealth in the UK. If the people of Wales return a strong team of Plaid Cymru MPs in May, then Wales will be best placed to secure an outcome to improve the prospects of our people and communities.
> *(Plaid Cymru 2015: 3)*

However, in contrast to the SNP, Plaid Cymru remained largely ignored in the UK-wide election debate.

References

Albertazzi, D. (2006) "The Lega dei Ticinesi: The Embodiment of Populism", *Politics*, 26 (2), pp. 133–139.
Allen, N., Bara, J., and Bartle, J. (2017) "Finding a Niche? Challenger Parties and Issue Emphasis in the 2015 Televised Leaders' Debates", *British Journal of Politics and International Relations*, Online first. doi:10.1177/1369148117715014.
BBC. (2015) "Election TV Debate: Leaders Clash over NHS, Cuts and Immigration". 3 April. www.bbc.co.uk/news/election-2015-32166354. Accessed 6 March 2017.
BBC News. (2017) 23 August 2017. www.bbc.co.uk/news/av/uk-scotland-41031109/jeremy-corbyn-calls-on-snp-to-use-powers-to-offset-austerity. Accessed 7 September 2017.

Betz, H.-G. (1994) *Radicalism and Right-Wing Populism in Western Europe.* New York: ST: Martin's Press.

Betz, H.-G. and Immerfall, S. (eds.) (1998) *The New Politics of the Right: Neo-Populist Parties and Movements in Established Democracies.* London: Macmillan.

Brand, J. (1978) *The National Movement in Scotland.* London: Routledge.

Combes, T. D. (1977) "The Party of Wales, Plaid Cymru: Populist Nationalism in Contemporary British Politics", PhD diss., University of Connecticut.

Cowley, P. (2015) "The Unusual Cohesion of SNP MPs". *Revolts*, 24 November. http://revolts.co.uk/?p=923. Accessed 6 March 2017.

Crick, B. (eds.) (1991) *National Identities: The Constitution of the United Kingdom.* Oxford: Blackwell.

Davies, D. H. (1983) *The Welsh Nationalist Party 1925–1945: A Call to Nationhood.* Cardiff: University of Wales Press.

Dugdale, K. (2016) "How a Small Tax Rise Exposed the SNP's Anti-Austerity Talk for Just That" *The New Statesmen*, 2 February. www.newstatesman.com/politics/economy/2016/02/how-small-tax-rise-exposed-snps-anti-austerity-talk-just. Accessed 6 April 2017.

Elias, A. (2011) "Plaid Cymru". In: Elias, A. and Tronconi, F. (eds.) *From Protest to Power: Autonomist Parties and the Challenges of Representation.* Vienna: Braumuller, pp. 261–282.

Finlay, R. J. (1994) *Independent and Free: Scottish Politics and the Origins of the Scottish National Party 1918-1945.* Edinburgh: John Donald.

Flinders, M. (2015) "The General Rejection? Political Disengagement, Disaffected Democrats and 'Doing Politics' Differently", *Parliamentary Affairs*, 68(1), pp. 241–254.

Fry, M. (1987) *Patronage and Principle: A Political History of Modern Scotland.* Aberdeen: Aberdeen University Press.

Grimshaw, D. and Rubery, J. (2012) "The End of the UK's Liberal Collectivist Social Model? The Implications of the Coalition Government's Policy under the Austerity Crisis", *Cambridge Journal of Economics*, 36(1), pp. 105–126.

Hanham, H. J. (1969) *Scottish Nationalism.* London: Faber and Faber.

Hay, C. (1994) "Labour's Thatcherite Revisionism: Playing the 'Politics of Catch-Up'", *Political Studies*, 42(4), pp. 700–707.

Hough, D. and Koss, M. (2009) "A Regional(ist) Party in Denial? The German PDS and its Arrival in Unified Germany", *Regional & Federal Studies*, 19(4–5), pp. 579–593.

Ivaldi, G., Zaslove, A., and Akkerman, A. (2017) "La France populiste?" *Note de recherche ENEF/Sciences Po-CEVIPOF*, 30, 1–10. https://halshs.archives-ouvertes.fr/halshs-01491961/document.

Jagers, J. and Walgrave, S. (2007) "Populism as Political Communication Style: An Empirical Study of Political Parties' Discourse in Belgium", *European Journal of Political Research*, 46(3), pp. 319–345.

Jarvis, D. (1996) "British Conservatism and Class Politics in the 1920s", *The English Historical Review*, 111(440), pp. 59–84.

Keating, M. (1996) *Nations Against the State: The New Politics of Nationalism in Quebec, Catalonia and Scotland.* Basingstoke: Palgrave.

Keating, M. (2017) *Debating Scotland.* Oxford: Oxford University Press.

Kioupkiolis, A. (2016) "Podemos: the Ambiguous Promises of Left-Wing Populism in Contemporary Spain", *Journal of Political Ideologies*, 21(2), pp. 99–120.

Kitching, G. N. (1989) *Development and Underdevelopment in Historical Perspective: Populism, Nationalism and Industrialization.* London: Routledge.

Laclau, E. (2005) *On Populist Reason.* London: Verso.

Laycock, D. (2005) "Populism and the New Right in English Canada". In: Panizza, F. (ed.) *Populism and the Mirror of Democracy*. London: Verso, pp. 174–201.

Lee, S. and Beech, M. (2011) *The Cameron-Clegg Government: Coalition Politics in an Age of Austerity*. Basingstoke: Palgrave.

Levy, R. (1990) *Scottish Nationalism at the Crossroads*. Edinburgh: Scottish Academic Press.

Lewis, S. (1934) *Ten Points of Policy, Deg Pwynt Polisi*. Canlyn Arthur: Gwasag Aberystwyth (republished in 1938).

Lisi, M. (2015) "U-Turn: The Portuguese Radical Left from Marginality to Government Support", *South European Society and Politics*, 21(4), pp. 541–560.

Lynch, P. (1995) "From Red to Green: The Political Strategy of Plaid Cymru in the 1980s and 1990s", *Regional and Federal Studies*, 5(2), pp. 197–210.

Lynch, P. (1996) *Minority Nationalism and European Integration*. Cardiff: University of Wales Press.

Lynch, P. (2002) *SNP: The History of the Scottish National Party*. Cardiff: Welsh Academic Press.

Lynch, P. (2009) "From Social Democracy back to No Ideology? The Scottish National Party and Ideological Change in a Multi-level Electoral Setting", *Regional and Federal Studies*, 19(4–5), pp. 619–637.

Lynch, P. (2011) "The Scottish National Party". In: Elias, A. and Tronconi, F. (eds.) *From Protest to Power: Autonomist Parties and the Challenges of Representation*. Vienna: Braumuller, pp. 233–260.

March, L., and C. Mudde (2005) "What's Left of the Radical Left? The European Radical Left after 1989: Decline and Mutation", *Comparative European Politics*, 3(1), pp. 23–49.

Massetti, E. (2009a) "Explaining Regionalist Party Positioning in a Multi-Dimensional Ideological Space: A Framework for Analysis", *Regional and Federal Studies*, 19(4–5), pp. 501–531.

Massetti, E. (2009b) "The Scottish and Welsh Party Systems Ten Years after Devolution: Format, Ideological Polarization and Structure of Competition". *SEI Working Paper*, 107.

Massetti, E. (2010) "Ideological and Strategic Adaptation in Regionalist Parties in Western Europe: A Comparative Study of the Northern League, Plaid Cymru, the Scottish National Party and the South Tyrolean People's Party", PhD diss., University of Sussex.

Massetti, E. (2018) "Left-wing regionalist populism in the 'Celtic' peripheries: Plaid Cymru and the Scottish National Party's anti-austerity challenge against the British elites", *Comparative European Politics*, 16(6), pp. 937–953.

Mazzoleni, O. (2005) "Multi-Level Populism and Centre-Periphery Cleavage in Switzerland: The Case of the Lega dei Ticinesi". In: Caramani, D. and Meny, Y. (eds.) *Challenges to Consensual Politics: Democracy, Identity, and Populist Protest in the Alpine Region*. Brussels: Peter Lang, pp. 209–228.

McAllister, L. (2001) *Plaid Cymru: The Emergence of a Political Party*. Cardiff: Seren.

McAngus C. (2016) "Party Elites and the Search for Credibility: Plaid Cymru and the SNP as New Parties of Government", *British Journal of Politics & International Relations*, 18(3), pp. 634–649.

McDonnell, D. and Vampa, D. (2016) "The Italian Lega Nord". In Heinisch, R. and Mazzoleni, O. (eds.) *Understanding Populist Party Organisation: The Radical Right in Western Europe*. Basingstoke: Palgrave, pp. 105–129.

McSmith, A. (2015) "SNP Leader Nicola Sturgeon Hits Out Against Austerity in Major New Election Pitch", *The Independent*, 2 February. www.independent.co.uk/news/uk/

politics/snp-leader-nicola-sturgeon-hits-out-against-austerity-in-major-new-election-pitch-10038677.html. Accessed 6 March 2017.
Milazzo, C., Adams, J. and Green, J. (2012) "Are Voters' Decision Rules Endogenous to Parties' Policy Strategy? A Model with Application to Elite Depolarization in Post-Thatcher Britain", *Journal of Politics*, 74(1), pp. 262–276.
Mitchell, J. and Bennie, L. (1996) "Thatcherism and the Scottish Question", *Journal of Elections, Public Opinion and Parties*, 5(1), pp. 90–104.
Mudde, C. (2004) "The Populist Zeitgeist", *Government and Opposition*, 39(4), pp. 542–563.
Mudde, C. (2007) *Populist Radical Right Parties in Europe*. Cambridge: Cambridge University Press.
Plaid Cymru. (1969) *This is Plaid Cymru*. Cardiff.
Plaid Cymru. (2010) *Think Different, Think Plaid*. Manifesto for the General Election. Cardiff.
Plaid Cymru. (2011) *For a Better Wales*. Manifesto for the Welsh Election.Cardiff.
Plaid Cymru. (2015) *Working for Wales*. Manifesto for General Election.Cardiff.
Plaid Cymru. (2017) *Defending Wales*. Manifesto for the General Election.Cardiff.
Plaid Cymru. (no date [1934–1939]) *The New Wales: Synopsis of the Policy of the Welsh Nationalist Party*. [translated from the Welsh pamphlet *Cymru Rydd: Braslun Polisi'r Blaid* by J. Gwilym Jones].
Plaid Cymru. (no date [between 1950–1964]) *The Welsh Political Tradition*. By Ioan Bowen Rees.
Polk, J. et al. (2017) "Explaining the Salience of Anti-Elitism and Reducing Political Corruption for Political Parties in Europe with the 2014 Chapel Hill Expert Survey Data", *Research and Politics*, Online first. doi: 10.1177/2053168016686915.
Ramiro, L. and R. Gomez (2017) "Radical-Left Populism during the Great Recession: Podemos and Its Competition with the Established Radical Left", *Political Studies*, 65(1), pp. 108–126.
Rydgren, J. (2005) *Movements of Exclusion: Radical Right-Wing Populism in the Western World*. New York: Nova.
Schumacher, E. F. (1973) *Small Is Beautiful: A Study of Economics as if People Mattered*. London: Blond & Briggs.
Scottish Government. (2013) "Scotland's Economy: The Case for Independence", May. www.scotland.gov.uk/Publications/2013/05/4084. Accessed 2 June 2014.
Segatti, P. and F. Capuzzi (2016) "Five Stars Movement, Syriza and Podemos: A Mediterranean Model?" In: Martinelli, A. (ed.) *Beyond Trump: Populism on the Rise*. Milan: ISPI, pp. 47–72.
SNP. (1946) *Aims and Policy of the Scottish National Party*. Glasgow.
SNP. (1964) *Aims and Fundamental Outlook of the Scottish National Party*. Stirling.
SNP. (2010) *Elect a Local Champion*. Manifesto for the General Election.
SNP. (2015) *Stronger for Scotland*. Manifesto for the General Election. Glasgow.
SNP. (2017) *Stronger for Scotland*. Manifesto for the General Election. Glasgow.
Stavrakakis, Y., and G. Katsambekis (2014) "Left-Wing Populism in the European Periphery: The Case of SYRIZA", *Journal of Political Ideologies*, 19(2), pp. 119–142.
Taggart, P. (2000) *Populism*. Philadelphia: Open University Press.
The Guardian. (2015) "Leaders' Debate: All You Need to Know about the 7-Way Clash" by Claire Phipps, 3 April. www.theguardian.com/politics/2015/apr/03/leaders-debate-all-you-need-to-know-about-the-seven-way-clash. Accessed 2 September 2015.

The Guardian. (2017) "Richard Leonard Wins Scottish Labour Leadership in Decisive Victory" by Severin Carrell, 18 November. www.theguardian.com/politics/2017/nov/18/richard-leonard-voted-scottish-labour-leader. Accessed 20 November 2017.

Thompson, L. (2018) "Understanding Third Parties at Westminster: The SNP in the 2015 Parliament", *Politics*, 38(4), pp. 443–457.

Torrance, D. (2009) "The Journey from the 79 Group to the Modern SNP". In: Hassan, G. (ed.) *The Modern SNP: From Protest to Power*. Edinburgh: Edinburgh University Press, pp. 162–176.

Venturi, F. (1960) *Roots of Revolution: A History of Populist and Socialist Movements in Nineteenth Century Russia*. London: Weidenfeld & Nicolson.

Watts, M. J. (2009) "Populism". In Gregory, D., Johnston, R. and Prat G. (eds.) *The Dictionary of Human Geography*. Chichester: Wiley-Blackwell, p. 556.

Webb, P. (2001) "Parties and Party Systems: Modernization, Regulation and Diversity", *Parliamentary Affairs*, 54(2), pp. 308–321.

Wyn Jones, R. and Scully, R. (2003) "Coming Home to Labour? The 2003 Welsh Assembly Election", *Regional and Federal Studies*, 13(3), pp. 125–132.

3

POPULISM AND ETHNO-TERRITORIAL PARTIES IN BELGIUM

Emilie van Haute

Introduction

In Belgium, three parties with ethno-territorial demands hold seats in the Belgian House of Representatives, a level of power towards which they hold a number of grievances (Democrat Federalist Independent/Démocrate Fédéraliste Indépendant – DéFI) or simply want to see disappear (Flemish Interest/ Vlaams Belang – VB; New Flemish Alliance/Nieuw-Vlaamse Alliantie – N-VA). This puts them in a paradoxical situation, especially when parliamentary representation leads to governmental participation.

Using Belgium as a case study, this chapter examines whether populism is intrinsically embedded or not in the discourse and ideology of ethno-territorial parties. We analyze how territorial demands formulated by these three parties overlap or not with a populist frame. We argue that the two are theoretically compatible, as they both oppose an "us" to a "them". In practice, we contend that the degree of overlap will depend on the parties' relation to power at the national and the sub-state levels. In doing so, the chapter attempts to bridge the literature on ethno-territorial parties and sub-state nationalism with the vast literature on populism. The two subfields largely ignore each other: the literature on populism is characterized by "methodological nationalism" (Jeffery and Schakel 2013) and mainly focuses on the national level (Mudde 2007; Rovira Kaltwasser et al. 2017), ignoring multi-level governance and territoriality; the literature on ethno-territorial parties and sub-state nationalism largely develops in parallel from populism scholars (Mazzoleni and Mueller 2016; Massetti and Schakel 2016).

The chapter first lays out how we combine the two literature to formulate our expectations. We then present our three cases, as well as the data mobilized in the chapter: party manifestos and membership magazines between 2010 and

2015. This material is analyzed in the subsequent section. We show that sub-state nationalism and populism do not always overlap and can be used by parties in parallel. We also show that the parties' relation to power matters, and that the overlap is higher when parties are sitting in power at the regional level and in the opposition at the national level. These findings stress the flexibility of the two ideologies and their adaptability to the parties' changing context.

Populism and sub-state nationalism: complementary or exclusive for political parties?

This chapter argues that sub-state nationalism and populism can partly overlap and be combined by political parties in their ideology and discourse. Along with major scholars in the discipline, this chapter regards nationalism as a political doctrine or ideology. Accordingly, it envisions nationalism as "a political principle that holds that the political and the national unit should be congruent" (Gellner 1983: 1), or as a doctrine developed by political elites to mobilize political support, as a "tool for a civic-territorial persuasion" (Hermet 1996: 85). In this conception, nationalism is a tool to construct a sense of identity. Breuilly (1994: 2) identifies three basic components of nationalism. Firstly, the nation has an explicit and exclusive character, which opposes a unique nation ("us") to an "other" against which the nation is built (see also Brubaker 1996; Wodak 2009). Secondly, the interests and principles of that nation take precedence over the rest. Finally, the nation must be independent and sovereign (Hobsbawm 1990). Conflict arises when the territory linked to a nation is incongruent with the state boundaries and can lead to sub-state nationalism. Sub-state nationalism therefore attacks the legitimacy of the state in which it operates and presents it as illegitimate and not "representative" of the nation (Conversi 2002).

Populism has also been given many definitions (Jagers and Walgrave 2007). First, it can refer to the mobilization of diverse social groups by a charismatic leader. Second, it can be defined as a thin-centered ideology that portrays "the people" as a virtuous and homogeneous group, lacking internal divisions, to "the elite". The corollary of portraying the people as one is the exclusion of "the others". These outsiders can be immigrants, ethnic communities, or "the elite". Populism negates horizontal divisions within the people. In doing so, it makes it easier to create vertical oppositions between the people and the elite, or inner circles of which "the others" are excluded. With vertical oppositions, the elite is also presented as homogeneous and ignorant of the interests of the people. Mudde (2004: 543) defines populism as an "ideology that considers society to be ultimately separated into two homogeneous and antagonistic groups, 'the pure people' versus 'the corrupt elite', and which argues that politics should be an expression of the *volonté générale* (general will) of the people". The populist ideology has been described as thin-centered, which means that it is not as complete as other ideologies such as socialism or liberalism. Consequently, it can be combined with other ideologies. This is what makes some scholars argue that "referring to the people can hardly be considered as a (new) ideology" (Jagers and Walgrave 2007: 322). These scholars argue that populism is a discourse, a communication style used by political actors to mobilize their basis. We argue that ideology and discourse are not necessarily incompatible.

Sub-state nationalism and populism translate into party politics and present similarities in that regard. In both cases, their core characteristics have been characterized as limited (Freeden 1998; Mudde 2004). The core oppositions remain the same ("the people" vs. "the elite"; "us" vs. "them" – which has led some to argue that they are indeed ideologies). However, parties use them in a loose manner and use inputs from other ideologies, which has led others contend that it is part of a discourse or communication style. In their discourse, parties and party actors can consciously or not adapt their content to mobilize their supporters. This adaptability has been shown in multiple studies on nationalism (see e.g. Danero Iglesias 2015). Both nationalism and populism can have an ad hoc content that fluctuates depending on the actors' strategic needs or the context in which they operate.

Furthermore, in both cases, their core characteristics can be combined with left- or right-wing positions on socio-economic issues. There are prominent left-wing (sub-state) nationalist parties, such as the Scottish National Party or Plaid Cymru in the UK, but also the Canadian Bloc Québécois. Though, most successful nationalist parties in Western Europe are radical right parties that focus primarily on (ethnic) nationalism, xenophobia, and authoritarianism. Among these, some have actually been categorized as sub-state nationalist parties (SSNPs) since they strive for an independent sub-state. It is the case for instance of the Northern League in Italy (Lega Nord – LN) and the VB in Dutch-speaking Belgium. SSNPs, also referred to as (ethno)-territorial or regionalist parties, are an important part of West-European politics and its center-periphery cleavage (Jeffery 2009: 693; Mazzoleni and Mueller 2016). SSNPs can have and have had a profound impression on the state structures and survival through their territorial demands and the mobilization of specific ethno-territorial groups. This impact is evident in an increasing number of Western countries in the past decades, with parties active in Flanders-Belgium (Sinardet 2012), Québec-Canada (Simeon and Conway 2001), Catalonia-Spain (Moreno 2001), and Scotland-UK (Mcewen and Petersohn 2015). These parties support self-government for a territorially located and ethnically different (language, religion, culture) people. In a much similar vein, populism too can be combined with left- or right-wing positions. For instance, most populists in Latin America are left-wing (e.g. Chavismo). In Europe too, populism can be found among radical left-wing parties such as the Greek communist party KKE or the French Lutte Ouvrière (Bonikowski and Gidron 2016), although most of the successful populist parties in Western Europe are located on the far right.

What is of interest for this chapter is that populism and nationalism can also be combined together. At the national level one often refers to "populist radical right parties" that combine radical right nationalism and populism (Mudde 2007). The combination has less been studied at the sub-state level. Yet when one looks at political legitimation of sub-state nationalism by SSNPs, the potential for combination becomes clear. To claim more self-rule, SSNPs can use either a nationalist frame and argue that the nation needs to be congruent with the state, an efficiency frame that contends that the sub-state entity is more efficient, or a democratic frame that supports that the sub-state entity is closer to the people (van Haute, Pauwels and Sinardet 2018). But a populist frame can also be used if the contours of "us" vs. "them" overlap: the "us" refer then at the same time to the people (for the populists) and to the nation (for the sub-state nationalists), and the "them" refers to the elite (for the populists) and the representatives of the other ethnic/language group (for the sub-state nationalists). Therefore, we argue that populism and sub-state nationalism are theoretically compatible, as they both oppose a "us" to a "them". We contend that the degree of overlap will depend on the parties' relation to power at the national and the sub-state levels.

When sitting in the opposition at either level, parties can mobilize populism with more ease as they can depict themselves as outsiders more convincingly. However, it does not mean that when in government, parties can no longer mobilize it (Albertazzi and McDonnell 2016). Similarly, parties can convey the sub-nationalist message with more ease when they sit in the opposition at either level as they do not have to face the practical complications of negotiating and implementing their sub-nationalist project. We therefore expect a high level of populism and sub-state nationalism when parties sit in the opposition at all levels, but only a partial overlap between the two as populism can be used indifferently towards various "others".

When parties sit in government at the sub-state level, we expect parties to mobilize a reduced level of populism as they become part of the sub-state ruling elite, but to maintain their sub-state nationalist demands. However, we expect the two to overlap more and populism to be used in a more targeted manner and more exclusively towards the national elite. Indeed, sub-state nationalists believe that their nation is unduly part of a state that is not consistent with their conception of the nation. Consequently, they should consider (part of) the state elite as illegitimate to govern the people of their nation. However, we expect this populism to be limited to that part of the political elite that governs at the state level. We expect that anti-elitism will not target the political elites at sub-state level.

TABLE 3.1 Hypotheses and case selection

Relation to power (national)	Relation to power (sub-state)	Populism	Sub-state nationalism	Case selection
Opposition	Opposition	+	+	DéFI 2010; VB 2010; VB 2014
Opposition	Government	–	+	N-VA 2010; DéFI 2014
Government	Government	–	–	N-VA 2014

When parties sit in power at the national level as well, we expect sub-state nationalists to mobilize a reduced level of populism and of sub-state nationalism. Indeed, in this configuration they face greater barriers to maintain their sub-state nationalism demands due to their commitment and loyalty to their governing partners. We explore these expectations, using sub-state nationalist or (ethno)-territorial parties in Belgium.

Case selection

Our analysis relies on the study of the policy positions of three sub-state nationalist or (ethno)-territorial parties in Belgium: the New Flemish Alliance (Nieuw-Vlaamse Alliantie – N-VA), the Flemish Interests (Vlaams Belang – VB), and Democrat Federalist Independant (Démocrate Fédéraliste Indépendant – DéFI). When it comes to SSNPs, Belgium is an interesting case study that provides a built-in comparative setting: these three SSNPs operate in two separate party systems (Deschouwer 2009). With the exception of the Radical Left Workers' Party (Parti du Travail de Belgique/Partij van de Arbeid van België – PTB-PVDA), there are no state-wide parties in Belgium. All parties restrict their activities to either the Dutch-speaking or the French-speaking electorate (with the exception of Brussels), that are concentrated territorially. To a certain extent, all parties in Belgium are sub-state or territorial parties, as they are elected by and represent the interest of part of the electorate. However, this chapter focuses on sub-state *nationalist* parties, that is, parties that clearly emerged on the center-periphery cleavage. The three above-mentioned parties fit that categorization.

The N-VA is the successor party of the (now disappeared) Flemish sub-state nationalist People's Union (Volksunie – VU) (Beyens et al. 2017). The VU was founded in 1954 and emerged from the center-periphery cleavage to defend the interests of Flanders and Flemish as a language and culture. The VU remained marginal politically and electorally for a while due to the high polarization on the philosophical cleavage after World War Two (van Haute and Pilet 2006). In 1954 and 1958, the VU scored around 3.5 per cent of the votes. In the 1960s, the center-periphery cleavage became again more salient as it intertwined with a shift of the economic balance of power from Wallonia, the former center of industrial revolution in Belgium, to Flanders. In the 1960s and the beginning of the 1970s, the party made considerable electoral progress, passing the ten per cent threshold in 1965 and the 15 per cent mark in 1968. In 1971, the VU obtained its best electoral result with almost 19 per cent of the votes, becoming the third party in Flanders. After its first governmental participation, the party was severely sanctioned at the 1978 elections, but it recovered in the 1981 elections. After that, the electoral decline was almost constant. In 1985, the VU lost more than 100,000 voters but remained the fourth party in Flanders. The 1987 elections confirmed this result. During the 1990s, the decline became even more pronounced. In 1991, the party lost again 130,000 voters and became the fifth party in Flanders. It reached a bottom in 1995 that brought the party back to its 1961 score. The 1999 elections ended up in a slight progress, but this was a last burst before the extinction of the party two years later. The VU ceased to exist as a party in 2001 because of irresoluble differences between a more moderate, progressive wing and a more radical, nationalist and conservative wing, which culminated during the negotiations on state reform in 2001 (van Haute and Pilet 2006). The more radical, sub-nationalist and conservative wing went on to form the N-VA and selected Geert Bourgeois as its first party leader (Table 3.2). The "new" party initially struggled at the polls, jeopardizing its survival. The N-VA therefore decided to form an electoral alliance with the Flemish Christian Democrats (Christen-Democratisch en Vlaams – CD&V). The alliance performed well but faced irreconcilable tensions on state reform issues when negotiating to form a federal government in 2007, leading up to the end of the cartel. However, the N-VA continued its electoral progress as an independent party and became the largest party in Flanders in 2014 under the leadership of Bart De Wever who took over from Geert Bourgeois in 2004.

From its creation in 2002, the first article of the N-VA statutes stipulates that the party strives towards an "independent republic of Flanders, member state of

TABLE 3.2 Overview of the party leadership

DéFI	VB	N-VA
1964–1967: Paul Brien	1979–1996: Karel Dillen	1954–1957*: Herman Wagemans
1967–1972: Albert Peeters	1996–2007: Frank Vanhecke	1957–1975*: Frans Van Der Elst
1972–1975: André Lagasse	2008–2012: Bruno Valkeniers	1975–1979*: Hugo Schiltz
1975–1977: Léon Defosset	2012–2014: Gerolf Annemans	1979–1986*: Vic Anciaux
1977–1982: Antoinette Spaak	2014–present: Tom Van Grieken	1986–1992*: Jaak Gabriels
1983–1984: Lucien Outers		1992–1997*: Bert Anciaux
1984–1985: Georges Clerfayt		1998–2000*: Patrick Vankrukelsven
1995–present: Olivier Maingain		2000–2001*: Geert Bourgeois
		2001–2004: Geert Bourgeois
		2004–present: Bart De Wever

Note: *VU
Source: author's own data.

a democratic European Union". It does not plead for immediate unilateral secession, but rather for a gradual process of disappearance of the Belgian state.

The Flemish Bloc (Vlaams Blok – VB) emerged in 1978 out of dissatisfaction with the VU. In the second half of the 1970s, part of the Flemish movement was increasingly unhappy about the VU and its positioning, considered as too moderate and left-leaning. This frustration peaked when the VU signed the so-called Egmont Pact, which envisioned a reform of the Belgian state that was seen as too favorable to the French-speakers, especially in the periphery of Brussels. One of the VU members, Lode Claes, quit the party and established the Flemish People's Party (Vlaamse Vokspartij – VVP). At the same time, Karel Dillen founded the Flemish-Nationalist Party (Vlaams-Nationale Partij – VNP). The two parties decided to participate in the federal elections of 1978 under the name Flemish Bloc (Vlaams Blok – VB). Dillen got elected and Lode Claes subsequently decided to leave politics. Dillen absorbed the nationalist wing of the VVP. In 1979 the VNP was dissolved and the VB was officially established (van Haute and Pauwels 2016). In its early years, the VB remained a small party dominated by Dillen (Table 3.2). Its programmatic focus was almost entirely directed against state reform while striving for Flemish independence. The party recruited mainly among Flemish nationalist movements such as Voorpost and Were Di. Despite the support from these organizations, the VB did not grow electorally. In 1981, Dillen was re-elected as MP but the vote share of the party declined from 2.1 to 1.8 per cent. In the second half of the 1980s, the VB started to broaden its ideology. It evolved towards a modern populist radical right party characterized by anti-immigrant rhetoric. Together with this ideological shift, the party started to change internally. Dillen integrated young members in the party (Gerolf Annemans, Filip Dewinter, and Frank Vanhecke). These changes provoked tensions that lead to the exit of dissatisfied VB members while strengthening the new course. The ideological and organizational changes started to pay off electorally at the end of the 1980s. The real breakthrough came when the party polled 10.3 per cent in the 1991 national elections. This "Black Sunday" alarmed all other Belgian parties, which agreed upon a *cordon sanitaire*, an agreement not to cooperate with the VB under any circumstances and on any political level.

However, the VB continued its electoral growth. In 1996, the leadership switched from Dillen to Vanhecke who was considered a figure of consensus between the Flemish nationalist and the anti-immigrant wings. At the national elections of 2003, the party obtained 18 per cent of the votes. One year later, the Court of Appeal of Ghent condemned several VB organizations for violating the anti-racism law. Yet the party polled its best result ever at the 2004 regional and European elections with 24 per cent of the votes and became the second largest party of Flanders (technically the first, since CD&V and N-VA arrived first but formed an electoral cartel of two distinct parties). After the appeal and the confirmation of the sanction by the Court in November 2004, the name Vlaams Blok was changed to Flemish Interest, Vlaams Belang. The party also moderated its external discourse to some extent, but the two are largely a continuation. Despite the party's electoral performances and parliamentary representation, it could not pass the governmental threshold because of the *cordon sanitaire*. In an attempt to further broaden the party's appeal, some young members such as Marie-Rose Morel and Jurgen Verstrepen were recruited. In 2008, Bruno Valkeniers replaced Vanhecke as party leader. Nevertheless, the growth of the VB had come to an end. In the 2006 local elections, the party faced its first symbolic defeats. At the national elections in 2007, the VB lost six percentage points and one seat. In 2009, the party lost one third of its votes (8.9 percentage points, 11 seats). A post-electoral survey showed that 15 per cent of the previous VB voters switched to the N-VA. Interestingly, a considerable part of switchers referred to the *cordon sanitaire* to motivate their switch to another party (Pauwels 2011). Since then, the electoral decline has continued. In 2012, Valkeniers stepped down and Annemans was elected as the new party leader but was not able to reverse the negative trend. In 2014, the party only scored 5.9 per cent of the votes in Flanders, flirting with the electoral threshold. Almost half of the VB voters in 2010 have opted for N-VA in 2014 (Deschouwer et al. 2015). Subsequently, Tom Van Grieken succeeded Annemans to become the youngest party leader ever in Belgium.

DéFI is the successor of the Front démocratique des francophones (Fédéralistes démocrates francophones since 2010 – FDF), a regionalist party based in Brussels. The FDF emerged as a reaction to the Flemish political demands. Their main goal was the defence of the French culture in and around Brussels, a largely French-speaking city in Flemish territory. In 1961, the Flemish marches on Brussels and the vote of the 1962–1963 laws on language use triggered a bigger movement among French-speakers. These laws translated several Flemish demands such as compulsory bilingualism in administrations or the inclusion of some municipalities of the Brussels periphery in the Flemish region. Such disposals were deep wounds for most French-speakers in the capital. In reaction, they created several associations to defend their rights. The movement was launched in the political arena and in universities. By the end of 1962, several university professors signed a "Manifesto for Brussels". The success of this action gave birth to a wider mobilization. In 1964, most of these movements united and gave birth to a political party, the Front démocratique des francophones (FDF) (Kesteloot and Collignon 1997). The party's project is initially a protectionist project, later embedded in a federalist project (van Haute and Pilet 2006).

The new party entered the political battlefield for the 1965 general elections. The first elections were a success for the FDF. The party submitted lists in the districts of Brussels and Nivelles where it respectively got 8.6 per cent and 4.6 per cent of votes. Between 1965 and 1971, the FDF rose quickly to win the position of first party in Brussels. From 1971 up to 1978, the party managed to secure scores around 30 per cent and to maintain its position of first party. At the turn of the 1980s, the party remained first but faced electoral losses (17.4 per cent in 1981). The electoral decline continued in the late 1980s, and in 1991 the FDF only received nine per cent of the votes.

In order to survive, the FDF signed in 1993 an agreement with the French-speaking Liberals (PRL) to form a federation. The alliance remained the first party in Brussels for the next ten years. Although allied in a cartel at elections, both parties remain independent organizations. Its electoral strength lies at the local level. By contrast with other Belgian new parties the FDF quickly built up strongholds in several municipalities, especially in the south and the east of Brussels. Yet, the most remarkable sign of this local strength is its performances at local elections. The FDF had four of the nineteen mayors of Brussels in 1970. At the 2000 local elections, it got five mayors and it took part to seven other executives. It is also characterized by the longevity of its party leader, Olivier Maingain. Comparably to what happened with the CD&V/N-VA alliance, the FDF/Liberals alliance faced tensions on state reform issues when negotiating to form a federal government in 2010–2011, leading up to the party taking back its independence in 2011. Since then, it has solidified its place in the Brussels region but struggles to expand, despite its program calling for a unified French-speaking community in Belgium between the Francophones in Brussels and Wallonia (Pilet and Dandoy 2014).

Data and methods

In order to test our expectations, we analyze the policy positions of these three parties between 2010 and 2015. This period was characterized by an important electoral cycle: the federal elections in 2010, and the federal, regional, and European elections in 2014. In doing so, we cover two legislatures, with variation in government/opposition status across the three parties synchronically, but also across the same party diachronically (Table 3.1). Indeed, the VB has been sitting in the opposition at the national and the sub-state levels during the two legislatures. Conversely, the N-VA has been sitting in government at the sub-state level during the entire period but went from opposition (2010–2014) to government (2014–2019) at the national level. DéFi went from opposition (2010–2014) to government (2014–2019) at the sub-state level and has been sitting in the opposition at the national level for the entire period.

We retrieve the policy positions of these three parties from election manifestos and membership magazines (Table 3.3).

The size of election manifestos greatly varies across parties, as does the number of issues per year for the membership magazine. Yet these two types of documents illustrate the positions of parties towards their two main publics: their (potential) voters – as the election manifestos are published and made publicly available ahead of elections to inform citizens about party positions –; and their members and supporters – as magazines are sent out to members and affiliates and are intra-party documents. This choice allows us to provide a balanced view of party positions and discourses and prevents us from focusing only on a public discourse that may be restrained to appeal to a larger electorate.

TABLE 3.3 Corpus of documents used in the analysis

DéFI	VB	N-VA
/ 2014 manifestos (456 pp) 2014–2015 magazines (3/y)	2010 manifesto (32 pp) 2014 manifesto (40 pp) 2014–2015 magazines (12/y)	2010 manifesto (70 pp) 2014 manifesto (96 pp) 2014–2015 magazines (10/y)

Note: in 2010, DéFI was running in alliance with the Liberals and did not produce a separate manifesto.

The corpus is analyzed via a content analysis using a codebook. We built the codebook with an abductive reasoning. We first elaborated a list of words that refer to populism and nationalism, based on existing research: we used Rooduijn and Pauwels (2011) to compile the codebook for populism, and Danero Iglesias (2013, 2015) to compile the codebook for sub-state nationalism. In a second phase, we went through the corpus and added or deleted some words from the codebook on this basis. Finally, the consolidated list of words was used to analyze the entire corpus. Tables 3.4 and 3.5 provide the final list of words included in the codebook as well as the list of suppressed words. We developed two distinct codebooks as one of our main ambitions is to examine to what extent populism and sub-state nationalism are used separately or overlap. For the coding of "us" vs. "them", at the core of the two ideologies, we have manually attributed the paragraph either to populism, sub-state nationalism, or both.

TABLE 3.4 Codebook populism

English	Dutch (VB – N-VA)	French (DéFI)
Anti-democratic	Antidemocratisch, anti-democratisch, ondemocratisch	Antidémocratique, anti-démocratique, non démocratique
Aristocra*	Aristocra*	Aristocra*
Autocra*	Autocra*, Totalitaire	Autocra*
Buddies	Vriend*	(petits) ami*
Capitalis*	Kapitali*	Capitalis*
Cartel*, Connection*	Connecti*, cartel*	Réseau*, cartel*, mainmise
Common sense	Gezond verstand	Bon sens
Coopted	*Coöpt*	Coopt*
Corrupt*	Corrupt*, zelfverdienend, postjescultuur	Corrompu, Corruption
Elit*	Elit*	Elit*
Enslave, slave*	Tot slaaf maken, voetvolk	Esclav*
Establishment	Establishment	Establishment, établissement

(Continued)

TABLE 3.4 (Cont.)

English	Dutch (VB – N-VA)	French (DéFI)
Eurocra★	Eurocrat★	Eurocrat★
Exploit★	Uitbuit★	Exploit★
Fed up with	Het beu zijn	En avoir marre
Greed	Hebzucht, graai	Cupid★
Guardianship	voogdij	tutelle
Imperialis★	Imperialis★	Impérialis★
Impose	Opleggen	Imposer
Loot	*Plunder★*	*Pill★*
Mainstream parties, Governing parties	Traditionele partijen, (alle) Vlaamse partijen, Regeringspartijen, Vlaamse politici, Vlaamse regering, Regerend	Partis traditionnels, Partis politiques, Partis du gouvernement, Partis au pouvoir, politisation
Monopoly	*Monopolie*	*Monopole*
Oligarch★	Oligarch★	Oligar★
Plutocra★	*Plutocrat★*	*Ploutocrat★*
Political class	Politieke klas★	Classe politique
Political games, Electoral games	Politieke spelletjes, Electorale spelletjes	(petits) Jeux politiques, électoraliste
Power hungry, Power cenacles, Power grip	Machtshonger, Machtcenakels, Machtsgreep, Machtsgeile, Machtmisbruik	Soif de pouvoir, Logique de pouvoir, Certitude du pouvoir, Le pouvoir pour le pouvoir
Propaganda	Propaganda	Propagande
Sold to	Uitverkoop	Vendu★
Technocrat★	Technocrat★, bureaucrat★	Technocrat★, bureaucra★
Unelected	*Onverkozen*	*Non-élu★*
Us (designating: the people)	Volk, bevolking	Peuple
Them (designating: elite, establishment, mainstream parties)	Zij, hen, hun	Eux

Note: In italics: words initially included in the corpus but that were not used in the analysis as they are not mobilized in the corpus.; ★ denotes that multiple endings of a word were taken into account (e.g.: bureaucra★ = bureaucrate, bureaucratie, bureaucratique, etc.).
Source: Adapted from van Haute, Pauwels and Sinardet (2018: 961–962)

We used a semi-automatic count system where we automatically identified all occurrences of each word from the codebook and then manually and qualitatively checked whether they were used in their expected meaning. In the case of the election manifestos, we counted the number of paragraphs that contained these words at least once, as well as the total number of paragraphs of each manifesto. This allowed to calculate the percentage of populist paragraphs, (sub-state) nationalist paragraphs, and paragraphs combining both or neither positions in each manifesto. Next to this semi-automatic content analysis, we also

TABLE 3.5 Codebook (sub-state) nationalism

English	Dutch (VB – N-VA)	French (DéFI)
Belgium	Belg★	Belg★
Belonging	Beho★	Apparten★
Borders (sub-state)	Grenzen, grens	Frontière
Community	Gemeenschapszin, gemeenschap	Communauté
Culture	Cultuur, cultureel, culturele	Culture★
Ethnic	Etnisch, etniciteit	Ethnique, ethnicité
Glory	Glorie	Gloire
Independence	Onafhankelijk★, soeverein, separatisme	Indépendant★
Language	Taal, taalgrens, taalgebied, taalwet, taalwetgeving, Nederlands	Langue, linguistique, Français
Legacy	Erfenis, erfgoed, heritage, geschiedenis	Héritage, Histoire
National spirit, nation, nationhood (sub-state)	Nationale geest/(nationale) identiteit, natiegevoel, nationalistisch, nationaliteit, natie, vlaams-nationalisme	Identité nationale, esprit national, nationaliste
People (sub-state)	Volk, bevolking	Peuple
Pride	Trots, eer, liefde	Fierté, honneur, amour
Region	Vlaanderen, Vlaamse Gemeenschap, Vlaams, Vlaming (exc. VB), Vlaamse overheid, Vlaamse regering, Vlaamse partijen	Wallon★, Bruxell★, Communauté française, Périphéri★
Self-government	Zelfbestuur, zelfbewust, zelfbeschikking, eigen bestuur, eigen handen	Auto-gouvernement, auto-détermination, disposer d'eux-mêmes
State reform	Staatshervorming, staatsvorming, staatswording	Réforme de l'état
Territory (sub-state)	Grondgebied, gebied	Territoire
Tradition	Traditi★	Tradition
State, Citizen (country)	Staat, burger, deelstaat, lidstaat, land	Etat belge, état fédéral, citoyen★
State, Citizen (sub-state)	Staat, burger, deelstaat, lidstaat, land	Etat, citoyen★
Them (other country)	Vreemdelingen, migranten, allochtonen, asielzoekers, illegalen, deze mensen, zij, hen, hun	Etrangers, migrants, allochtones, demandeurs d'asile, illégaux, ces gens, eux, ils
Them (other sub-state)	Franstaligen, Wallonië, walen, waalse partijen, verfrans★, zij, hen, hun	Flamand★, Flandre, eux, ils
Us (country)	Wij, we, ons, onze	Nous, notre, nos
Us (sub-state)	Wij, we, ons, onze	Nous, notre, nos

Note:★denotes that multiple endings of a word were taken into account (e.g.: bureaucra★ = bureaucrate, bureaucratie, bureaucratique, etc.).
Source: Adapted from van Haute, Pauwels and Sinardet (2018: 963–964)

performed a more qualitative analysis and mobilize excerpts from the corpus to exemplify populist and sub-state nationalist stances, but also to illustrate how these two ideologies are sometimes combined.

Analysis

The VB is the party that mobilizes populism and (sub-state) nationalism the most in its party documents, be it separately or in combination. In 2010, populist positions represented 4 per cent of the manifesto's paragraphs (VB 2010). This proportion increased to 9 per cent in 2014 (Table 3.6). Interestingly, sub-state nationalism is more dominant (23 per cent in 2010 and 33 per cent in 2014). The two ideological dimensions are frequently combined, especially in 2010 where they constituted 16 per cent of the paragraphs. This proportion diminished in 2014 to 6 per cent. Overall thus, about half of the 2010 and 2014 election manifestos were coded as populist, sub-state nationalist, or both. Only the distribution between these categories varies. Populism and sub-state nationalism are also dominant throughout the party magazines.

Populism is used to criticize the "mainstream parties", "the elite", "the establishment" (Table 3.7). This criticism is targeted towards all political elite, be it European, national, but also from Flanders, and extends to academics and journalists. In the party magazine, one finds negative references to the politically correct elite (VB 2014a: 16), the academic, intellectual elite (VB 2015f: 24), the political and media elite (VB 2015i: 17), and the technocratic and bureaucratic elite (VB 2015i: 18). This populist critique defines the "other" as everyone but the "pure" (Flemish) people ("us"). This critique is combined with radical right positions, as foreign-born citizens are *de facto* excluded from this definition of the Flemish people: "We Flemings derive for a large part our identity from our heritage" (VB 2014l: 31).

TABLE 3.6 Proportion of paragraph including populist and/or (sub-state) nationalist stances in party manifestos, 2010 and 2014

	VB 2010 N	VB 2010 %	VB 2014l N	VB 2014l %	N-VA 2010 N	N-VA 2010 %	N-VA 2014k N	N-VA 2014k %	DeFI 2013 N	DeFI 2013 %
Populism	4	3.7	11	9.3	1	0.3	5	0.5	5	2.5
Sub-state nationalism	25	22.9	39	33.1	80	24.1	102	10.7	50	24.9
Both	17	15.6	7	5.9	10	3.0	42	4.4	3	1.5
Neither	63	57.8	61	51.7	241	72.6	803	84.3	143	71.1
TOTAL	109	100.0	118	100.0	332	100.0	952	100.0	201	100.0

Note: Given the redundancy of many paragraphs in the various DéFi manifestos for the 2014 elections, the calculation of the proportion of paragraphs was not performed.
Source: Adapted from van Haute, Pauwels and Sinardet (2018: 966)

TABLE 3.7 Occurrences of references to populism in manifestos and magazines, DéFI, N-VA, VB (2010–2014)

English	VB 2010	VB 2014 a–l; VB 2015 a–k	VB Mag 2010	N-VA 2010	N-VA 2014 a–k; N-VA 2015 a–j	N-VA Mag	DéFI 2013	DéFI 2014 a–e; DéFI 2015	DéFI Mag
Anti-democratic	0	1	6	0	0	0	0	0	0
Autocra★	0	2	3	0	0	0	0	0	0
Buddies	0	0	11	0	0	3	0	0	0
Capitalis★	0	0	3	0	0	0	0	0	0
Cartel★, Connection★	0	1	0	0	0	0	0	1	1
Common sense	0	2	13	0	0	2	0	2	1
Corrupt★	1	0	2	0	0	0	0	16	0
Elit★	1	0	43	0	0	3	0	1	0
Enslave, slave★	0	0	16	0	0	0	0	0	0
Establishment	2	0	18	0	0	1	0	0	0
Eurocra★	0	2	11	0	0	0	0	1	0
Exploit★	0	0	1	0	0	0	0	0	0
Fed up with	0	0	4	3	0	1	0	0	0
Greed	0	0	7	1	0	1	0	0	0
Guardianship	1	2	3	0	0	0	0	0	0
Imperialis★	0	2	3	0	0	0	0	0	0
Impose	0	1	0	0	0	0	1	0	0
Mainstream parties, Governing parties	3	7	119	2	4	39	5	11	6
Oligarch★	0	0	0	0	0	0	0	1	0
Political class	1	1	13	0	0	1	0	0	1
Political games, Electoral games	1	2	3	1	0	5	1	0	0
Power hungry, Power cenacles, Power grip	2	3	31	0	0	3	2	0	1
Propaganda	0	0	10	0	0	1	0	0	0
Sold to	1	0	0	0	0	0	0	0	0
Technocrat★	0	1	6	0	0	0	0	4	0
Us (designating: the people)	1	6	71	1	10	2	1	2	1
Them (designating: elite, establishment, mainstream parties)	5	4	32	3	1	12	2	0	0
Total occurrences	19	37	429	11	15	74	12	39	11

Note: ★denotes that multiple endings of a word were taken into account (e.g.: bureaucra★ = bureaucrate, bureaucratie, bureaucratique, etc.).
Source: Adapted from van Haute, Pauwels and Sinardet (2018: 968–969)

Sub-state nationalist stances are also mobilized, with reference to the Flemish culture, language, and sense of nationhood (Table 3.8). The party clearly positions itself in favor of Flemish independence and self-government. The first section of the 2010 manifesto is titled *Project Flemish State* (VB 2010: 4–6). The 2014 manifesto advocates "state formation, rather than state reform" (VB 2014d: 10). In the same vein, all references to the federal state are always negative (for instance, by referring to the size of the national debt); the same holds for all references to Europe, described as the "EU-super State", or the "totalitarian EU integration" (VB 2015h: 10). When referring to Flanders, references are more neutral or positive. Interestingly, the manifestos refer to Belgium as "that country" where nothing works, and to Flanders as "our country". In this view, the "us" clearly refers to Flanders and Flemish citizens sharing a common heritage ("our identity", "our culture"). The "others" are foreign-born citizens, but also citizens from the other sub-states in Belgium, and the Belgian state more generally. This is where populism and sub-state nationalism combine. The populist critique of the elite and the establishment often refers to the European or the national political elite (VB 2010: 3, 19, 2014h: 9) or the elite from the other sub-state, the francophone elite, depicted as the heavyweights or the imperialists (VB 2010: 5–6, 2014l: 5).

Overall thus, the VB portrays the "we" as the Flemish people, and the "them" as everyone else, including the Flemish political elite (populism), the French-speakers (sub-state nationalism), the Belgian and the francophone elite (populism and sub-state nationalism), but also the foreign-born citizens (radical right), leading to only a partial overlap between sub-state nationalism and populism.

Contrary to the VB, the N-VA rarely uses populism on its own in its party manifestos: less than 1 per cent of the paragraphs are coded as populist. Populism is somewhat more present in its party magazines that criticize the traditional parties or the mainstream parties in power, the Christian Democratic State, the Socialist model (N-VA 2014i), or "friends" politics from authorities (N-VA 2015g: 20). Conversely, sub-state nationalism is N-VA's dominant ideology (Table 3.6). However, the references to its sub-state nationalist project differ from the VB. The VB refers to Flanders as a State, while the N-VA refers to it as a sub-state. There is a clear double treatment: the N-VA avoids references to independence in its election manifestos, but does refer to it in its magazines. Furthermore, while the VB refers to a Flemish *nation* opposed to French-speakers, the N-VA refers to a Flemish *community*, and to Wallonia as a distinct sub-state region, thereby using a vocabulary linked to federalism and insisting on a dual conception of federalism in Belgium, ignoring the other entities such as Brussels and the German-speaking community. Much as the VB, the N-VA depicts the federal state as a failed state (N-VA 2014c: 65), as old and static, and characterized by a fading glory (N-VA 2014c: 5, 73–75). In contrast, they present Flanders as dynamic, entrepreneurial and modern (N-VA 2015d: 17): "Flanders is more advanced than the federal level" (N-VA 2014k: 75), "Belgium is hopelessly hopping behind" (N-VA 2014k: 22).

TABLE 3.8 Occurrences of references to (sub-state) nationalism in manifestos and magazines, DéFI, N-VA, VB (2010–2014)

English	VB 2010	VB 2014 a–l; VB 2015 a–k	VB Mag	N-VA 2010	N-VA 2014a–k; N-VA 2015a–j	N-VA Mag	DéFI 2013	DéFI 2014 a–e; DéFI 2015	DéFI Mag
Belgium	77	52	704	57	63	306	23	329	14
Belonging	1	0	0	2	0	0	3	0	0
Borders (sub-state)	3	1	227	9	5	13	8	2	0
Community	2	2	13	14	23	65	1		1
Culture	12	15	189	2	42	50	12	27	7
Ethnic	3	0	21	0	0	0	0	0	0
Glory	0	0	0	0	0	2	0	0	0
Independence	20	18	318	0	1	9	1	1	0
Language	8	10	391	9	35	208	49	269	3
Legacy	1	1	41	0	24	16	0	0	0
National spirit, nation, nationhood (sub-state)	13	3	281	14	3	27	17	5	5
People (sub-state)	1	6	71	1	10	2	1	2	1
Pride	0	0	13	0	0	7	4	1	0
Region	209	189	2,208	146	323	1,752	243	1,906	306
Self-government	5	6	43	3	4	11	1	0	1
State reform	16	10	71	7	27	50	10	30	2
Territory (sub-state)	5	0	2	4	8	0	6	24	0
Tradition	0	1	5	0	5	0	0	4	0
State, citizen (country)	14	14	1	40	27	143	8	40	7
State, Citizen (sub-state)	11	14	10	6	34	11	14	33	1
Them (other country)	41	19	584	40	41	107	0	16	0
Them (other sub-state)	57	38	263	59	35	182	60	152	15
Us (country)	1	2	2	20	36	12	0	48	0
Us (sub-state)	3	44	36	11	60	12	1	119	3
Total occurrences	503	445	5,494	444	806	2,985	462	3,008	369

Source: Adapted from van Haute, Pauwels and Sinardet (2018: 970–971)

In the "us" vs. "them" categorization, the N-VA has evolved over time. When referring to Flemish parties at the national level in 2010, the party combines populist and sub-state nationalist stances: "the governing parties CD&V and OpenVLD gave all the keys of the migration policy in the hands of the PS and the cdH" (N-VA 2010: 53). Later on, the party mostly includes all Flemish parties as part of "us" (sub-state nationalism) rather than as part of "them" (populism).

Populist positions are related to the idea of Belgium as a failed state: the current situation is depicted as "not logical" (N-VA 2014k: 73) and the need for reform as "common sense" (N-VA 2014k: 73). Populism and sub-state nationalism are also combined to oppose a positive image of the hardworking Flemish citizens against the negative image of the lazy and corrupted Walloons:

> The Flemings are also tired of it. They are tired of finding that the tax authorities in Flanders are acting more severely than elsewhere, that the policeman is firing more in Flanders than in Wallonia, that the social rules in Flanders are adhered to more strictly than in the rest of the country.
> *(N-VA 2014k: 5).*

Interestingly, populist sub-state nationalist positions are also used to criticize the federal level as a whole, but only until the end of 2014 (date of accession of the N-VA in the federal government). The N-VA criticizes the "oversized" federal state whereas Flanders is equated to be lean and efficient: "Politicians must give the good example and first sweep at their own door. In Flanders, this happens and it is done with fewer government jobs. At the federal level, people do the opposite" (N-VA 2010: 36). In the same vein, the federal level is depicted as plagued with corruption, clientelism and patronage whereas Flanders is equated with good governance:

> under the Di Rupo government (…) all the little positions to be distributed were recorded in a "cadastre" and then for months they were pushed, pulled, blocked, negotiated and tinkered to nicely distribute all these little positions among parties of the majority.
> *(N-VA 2014k: 78).*

Overall, the party uses an ambiguous definition of the contours of the sub-state nation. Its uses the "we" to refer both to Belgium (often to criticize the current state of affairs) and to Flanders (to refer to how "we" are doing better). It uses the "them" to equally refer to (citizens from) other countries or other sub-states in Belgium. Contrary to the VB, the party rarely uses a "we" to exclude the Flemish elites (pure populism) or foreign-born citizens (radical right).

In its founding manifesto, DéFI (2013) clearly rejects of "all forms of conservatism (…), environmental or populist protectionism, and of nationalism"

(DéFI 2013: 5). However, their party documents are not exempt of some forms of both populism and sub-state nationalism.

Populist stances are used to reject "growing corruption" and to portray itself as the champion of transparency and good governance. The party criticizes "mainstream parties" for their lack of political courage and their catch-all, vote-seeking behavior: "Too often, in order to avoid long-term decisions, even more if they are electorally risky, traditional parties refuse to engage in necessary reforms" (DéFI 2014d: 4); "stop the inertia of traditional parties that promise a lot, election after election, but do not achieve anything" (DéFi 2015: 4).

All references to sub-state nationalism or independence are negative. They are mainly used in association with Flanders: The party criticizes the aspirations of Flanders to become an independent state (DéFI 2013: 32, 39). It only refers to the Wallonia-Brussels Federation as a state as a possible outcome or reaction to Flemish independence (DéFI 2013: 37). Similarly, all references to nationalism in the DéFI magazines are negative. Its sub-state nationalist stances refer to French as a language and a culture, and to the linguistic border. Its sub-state nationalism is conceived as a reaction to its Flemish political opponents, and the "us" refers to the Francophones (French-speaking elite and citizens altogether), and the "them" as Flanders. While the party defends French as a language and a Francophone culture, their "us" is also inclusive. The party favors multiculturalism and diversity, in opposition to a "them" (Flanders) that would be exclusive. However, the party also sometimes uses the "we" to refer to Belgium, as does the N-VA.

Populism and sub-state nationalism are rarely combined in DéFI's documents. When it is the case, it is when targeting the federal level as a whole, thereby including the French-speaking parties who are considered as "traitors" of the francophone interests and unskilled negotiators in the state reform process:

> The sixth reform of the state, poorly prepared and therefore poorly negotiated by the French-speaking parties involved, is fully in line with the dynamics desired by the more autonomous parties in the North of the country. (...) The disarray is total and, once again, these French-speaking parties are entering the process backwards. They run without knowing where they are going.
>
> *(DéFI 2013: 32).*

Our analysis shows that each of the three parties has a specific relation to populism and sub-state nationalism. It matches their particular status in the Belgian multi-level system. The VB sits in the opposition at all levels during the entire period, and this translates into stronger sub-state nationalist and populist positions in their party documents. These positions were even more pronounced in 2014, maybe due to electoral difficulties that lead to a radicalization strategy (van Haute and Pauwels 2016). Populism and sub-state nationalism tend to overlap more than in the case of the other two parties.

The N-VA sits in government at the sub-state level during the entire period. As expected, it goes hand in hand with lower levels of populist stances. The party mainly adopts sub-state nationalist positions, but these were mitigated after its accession to the national government in 2014. The N-VA almost exclusively uses populism when in combination with sub-state nationalism. This was made more difficult after the accession to the national government at the end of 2014, and it shows in the later party magazines. Lastly, DéFI adopts "enlightened" populist stances that criticize the "cartel" of corrupted mainstream parties, even after its accession to power in the Brussels regional government. It adopts a similar level of sub-state nationalist positions as the N-VA when the party was sitting in the opposition at the national level. However, the party rarely mobilizes populist stances in combination with its sub-state nationalist positions.

Conclusion

This chapter assessed the populist and/or sub-nationalist stances of three SSNPs in Belgium (VB, N-VA, DéFI) between 2010 and 2015, based on an analysis of their party documents (election manifestos and membership magazines). Overall, the analysis confirms that parties do present themselves differently to various publics and adopt stronger stances in their membership magazines than in their election manifestos. We showed how much these parties rely on these two thin ideologies and highlighted that the three parties differ in that regard. Sub-state nationalism and populism do not always overlap and can be used by parties in parallel. The VB displays the highest proportion of party documents relying on these ideologies separately. Conversely, the N-VA and DéFI primarily mobilize sub-nationalism over populism.

The analysis also shows how these two ideologies are combined. The VB is also the party that combines populism and sub-state nationalism the most. If the N-VA seldomly uses populism on its own, it does use it primarily in combination with sub-state nationalism. Conversely, DéFI mostly mobilizes populism as stand-alone and rarely in combination with sub-state nationalism. We argue that these specific uses of populist and sub-state nationalist positions are partly due to the parties' relationship to power (government vs. opposition) at the sub-state and national levels. Our longitudinal analysis shows that parties such as the N-VA and to a lesser extent DéFI have adapted their combination of populism and sub-state nationalism after their change of status in 2014. These findings stress the flexibility of the two thin ideologies and their adaptability to the parties' changing context. Parties' relation to power matters, and the overlap is higher when parties are sitting in power at the regional level and in the opposition at the national level. These findings stress the flexibility of the two ideologies and their adaptability to the parties' changing context. Overall, this study uniquely relates populism to the (ethno)-territorial dimension of Belgian politics and contributes to a better understanding of the contextual factors that shape the relation between the two ideologies.

References

Albertazzi, D. and McDonnell, D. (2016) *Populists in Power*. London: Routledge.
Beyens, S., Deschouwer, K., van Haute, E. and Verthé, T. (2017) "Born Again, or Born Anew. Assessing the Newness of the Belgian Political Party New Flemish Alliance (N-VA)", *Party Politics*, 23(4), pp. 389–399.
Bonikowski, B. and Gidron, N. (2016) "Populist Claims-Making in the Fifth European Parliament, 1999–2004". Paper presented at the *Annual Meeting of the American Sociological Association*.
Breuilly, J. (1994) *Nationalism and the State*. Chicago: University of Chicago Press.
Brubaker, R. (1996) *Nationalism Reframed: Nationhood and the National Question in the New Europe*. Cambridge: Cambridge University Press.
Conversi, D. (2002) "Conceptualizing Nationalism. An Introduction to Walker Connor's Work". In: Conversi, D. (ed.) *Ethnonationalism in the Contemporary World. Walker Connor and the Study of Nationalism, Routledge Advances in International Relations and Global Politics*. London: Routledge, pp. 1–23.
Danero Iglesias, J. (2013) "Constructing National History in Political Discourse: Contradiction (Moldova, 2001–2009)", *Nationalist Papers*, 41(5), pp. 780–800.
Danero Iglesias, J. (2015) "An Ad Hoc Nation. An Analysis of Moldovan Election Campaign Clips", *East European Politics and Societies*, 29(4), pp. 850–870.
DéFI (2013) *Manifeste. La force gagnante des libéraux sociaux pour donner de l'ambition à la Wallonie et à Bruxelles*, https://defi.eu/wp-content/uploads/2016/09/manifeste_des__fdf_28-04-2013.pdf. Accessed 1 January 2018.
DéFI (2014a) *Programme elections européennes 2014*, https://defi.eu/wp-content/uploads/2016/02/Programme-européenne-2014-FDF.pdf. Accessed 1 January 2018.
DéFI (2014b) *Programme fédéral 2014*, https://defi.eu/wp-content/uploads/2016/02/Programme-fédéral-2014-FDF.pdf. Accessed 1 January 2018.
DéFI (2014c) *Programme Région Bruxelloise et Fédération Wallonie-Bruxelles*, https://defi.eu/wp-content/uploads/2016/02/Programme-régionale-Bruxelles-2014-FDF.pdf. Accessed 1 January 2018.
DéFI (2014d) *Programme Région Wallonne et Fédération Wallonie-Bruxelles*, https://defi.eu/wp-content/uploads/2016/02/Programme-régionale-Wallonie-2014-FDF.pdf. Accessed 1 January 2018.
DéFi (2014e) *Dimension. Le bimestriel des Fédéralistes démocrates francophones*. December.
DéFi (2015) *Dimension. Le bimestriel des Fédéralistes démocrates francophones*, 4, https://defi.eu/dimension-n-4/. Accessed 1 January 2018.
Deschouwer, K. (2009) "Coalition Formation and Congruence Between the Federal and the Regional Level", *Regional and Federal Studies*, 19(1), pp. 13–35.
Deschouwer, K., Delwit, P., Hooghe, M., Rihouw, B. and Walgrave, S. (2015) *Décrypter l'électeur/De kiezer ontcijferd*. Leuven: Lannoo Campus.
Freeden, M. (1998) "Is Nationalism a Distinct Ideology?" *Political Studies*, 46(4), pp. 748–765.
Gellner, E. (1983) *Nations and Nationalism*. Oxford: Blackwell.
Hermet, G. (1996) *Histoire des nations et du nationalisme en Europe*. Paris: Seuil.
Hobsbawm, E. J. (1990) *Nations and Nationalism since 1780. Programme, Myth, Reality*. Cambridge: Cambridge University Press.
Jagers, J. and Walgrave, S. (2007) "Populism as Political Communication Style: An Empirical Study of Political Parties' Discourse in Belgium", *European Journal of Political Research*, 46(3), pp. 319–345.
Jeffery, C. (2009) "New Research Agendas on Regional Party Competition", *Regional and Federal Studies*, 19(4), pp. 639–650.

Jeffery, C. and Schakel, A. (2013) "Are Regional Elections Really 'Second Order' Elections?" *Regional Studies*, 47(3), pp. 323–341.
Kesteloot, C. and Collignon, A. (1997) "Le FDF: l'échec d'une expérience pluraliste". In: Delwit, P. and De Waele, J.-M. (eds.) *Les partis politiques en Belgique*. Brussels: Edition de l'Université de Bruxelles, pp. 169–180.
Massetti, E. and Schakel, A. (2016) "Decentralisation Reforms and Regionalist Parties' Strength: Accommodation, Empowerment or Both?" *Political Studies*. Online first. doi:10.1177/0032321716644612
Mazzoleni, O. and Mueller, S. (eds.) (2016) *Regionalist Parties in Western Europe. Dimensions of Success*. London: Routledge.
Mcewen, N. and Petersohn, B. (2015) "Between Autonomy and Interdependence: The Challenges of Shared Rule after the Scottish Referendum", *The Political Quarterly*, 86 (2), pp. 192–200.
Moreno, L. (2001) "Ethno-Territorial Concurrence in Multinational Societies: The Spanish Comunidades Autonomas". In: Gagnon, A. G. and Tully, J. (eds.) *Multinational Democracies*. Cambridge: Cambridge University Press, pp. 201–221.
Mudde, C. (2004) "The Populist Zeitgeist", *Government and Opposition*, 39(4), pp. 542–563.
Mudde, C. (2007) *Populist Radical Right Parties in Europe*. Cambridge: Cambridge University Press.
N-VA (2010) *Verkiezingsprogramme 13 juni 2010. Nu durven veranderen. Een sterk sociaal en economisch perspectief voor Vlaanderen en Wallonië*.
N-VA (2014a) "Nieuw-Vlaams Magazine", 1, www.n-va.be/sites/default/files/generated/files/magazine/n-vmnr1_2014.pdf. Accessed 1 January 2018.
N-VA (2014b) "Nieuw-Vlaams Magazine", 2, www.n-va.be/sites/default/files/generated/files/magazine/n-vmnr2_2014.pdf. Accessed 1 January 2018.
N-VA (2014c) "Nieuw-Vlaams Magazine", 3, www.n-va.be/sites/default/files/generated/files/magazine/n-vmnr3_2014.pdf. Accessed 1 January 2018.
N-VA (2014d) "Nieuw-Vlaams Magazine", 4, www.n-va.be/sites/default/files/generated/files/magazine/n-vmnr4_2014.pdf. Accessed 1 January 2018.
N-VA (2014e) "Nieuw-Vlaams Magazine", 5, www.n-va.be/sites/default/files/generated/files/magazine/n-vmnr5_2014.pdf. Accessed 1 January 2018.
N-VA (2014f) "Nieuw-Vlaams Magazine", 6, www.n-va.be/sites/default/files/generated/files/magazine/n-vmnr6_2014.pdf. Accessed 1 January 2018.
N-VA (2014g) "Nieuw-Vlaams Magazine", 7, www.n-va.be/sites/default/files/generated/files/magazine/n-vmnr7_2014.pdf. Accessed 1 January 2018.
N-VA (2014h) "Nieuw-Vlaams Magazine", 8, www.n-va.be/sites/default/files/generated/files/magazine/n-vmnr8_2014lres_6.pdf. Accessed 1 January 2018.
N-VA (2014i) "Nieuw-Vlaams Magazine", 9, www.n-va.be/sites/default/files/generated/files/magazine/n-vmnr9_2014lres_.pdf. Accessed 1 January 2018.
N-VA (2014j) "Nieuw-Vlaams Magazine", 10, www.n-va.be/sites/default/files/generated/files/magazine/n-vmnr10_2014lres_7.pdf. Accessed 1 January 2018.
N-VA (2014k) *Verkiezingsprogramma Vlaamse, federale en Europese verkiezingen 25 mei 2014. Verandering Voor Vooruitgang*.
N-VA (2015a) "Nieuw-Vlaams Magazine", 1, www.n-va.be/sites/default/files/generated/files/magazine/n-vmnr01_2015.pdf. Accessed 1 January 2018.
N-VA (2015b) "Nieuw-Vlaams Magazine", 2, www.n-va.be/sites/default/files/generated/files/magazine/n-vmnr2_2015lres_6.pdf. Accessed 1 January 2018.
N-VA (2015c) "Nieuw-Vlaams Magazine", 3, www.n-va.be/sites/default/files/generated/files/magazine/n-vmnr3_2015.pdf. Accessed 1 January 2018.

N-VA (2015d) "Nieuw-Vlaams Magazine", 4, www.n-va.be/sites/default/files/generated/files/magazine/n-vmnr4_2015.pdf. Accessed 1 January 2018.
N-VA (2015e) "Nieuw-Vlaams Magazine", 5, www.n-va.be/sites/default/files/generated/files/magazine/n-vmnr5_2015.pdf. Accessed 1 January 2018.
N-VA (2015f) "Nieuw-Vlaams Magazine", 6, www.n-va.be/sites/default/files/generated/files/magazine/n-vmnr6_2015lres_def.pdf. Accessed 1 January 2018.
N-VA (2015g) "Nieuw-Vlaams Magazine", 7, www.n-va.be/sites/default/files/generated/files/magazine/n-vmnr7_2015lres_6.pdf. Accessed 1 January 2018.
N-VA (2015h) "Nieuw-Vlaams Magazine", 8, www.n-va.be/sites/default/files/generated/files/magazine/n-vmnr8_2015_defdefires.pdf. Accessed 1 January 2018.
N-VA (2015i) "Nieuw-Vlaams Magazine", 9, www.n-va.be/sites/default/files/generated/files/magazine/n-vmnr09_2015.pdf. Accessed 1 January 2018.
N-VA (2015j) "Nieuw-Vlaams Magazine", 10, www.n-va.be/sites/default/files/generated/files/magazine/n-vmnr10_2015_def_lr2.pdf. Accessed 1 January 2018.
Pauwels, T. (2011) "Explaining the Strange Decline of the Populist Radical Right Vlaams Belang in Belgium. The Impact of Permanent Opposition", *Acta Politica*, 46(1), pp. 60–82.
Pilet, J.-B. and Dandoy, R. (2014) "L'évolution programmatique du FDF, d'un parti mono-enjeu à un parti régionaliste à vocation généraliste". In: Dujardin, V. and Delcorps, V. (eds.) *FDF. 50 ans d'engagement politique*. Brussels: Racine, pp. 395–423.
Rooduijn, M. and Pauwels, T. (2011) "Measuring Populism: Comparing Two Methods of Content Analysis", *West European Politics*, 34(6), pp. 1272–1283.
Rovira Kaltwasser, C., Taggart, P. A., Ochoa Espejo, P. and Ostiguy, P. (eds.) (2017) *The Oxford Handbook on Populism*. Oxford: Oxford University Press.
Simeon, R. and Conway, D.-P. (2001) "Federalism and the Management of Conflict in Multinational Societies". In: Gagnon, A. G. and Tully, J. (eds.) *Multinational Democracies*. Cambridge: Cambridge University Press, pp. 338–365.
Sinardet, D. (2012) "Is There a Belgian Public Sphere? What the Case of a Federal Multilingual Country Can Contribute to the Debate on Transnational Public Spheres. And Vice Versa". In: Seymour, M. and Gagnon, A.-G. (eds.) *Multinational Federalism: Problems and Prospects*. New-York: Palgrave MacMillan, pp. 172–204.
van Haute, E. and Pilet, J.-B. (2006) "Regionalist Parties in Belgium (VU, RW, FDF): Victims of Their Own Success?" *Regional and Federal Studies*, 16(3), pp. 297–313.
van Haute, E. and Pauwels, T. (2016) "The Vlaams Belang: Party Organization and Party Dynamics". In: Heinisch, R. and Mazzoleni, O. (eds.) *Understanding Populist Party Organisation*. London: Palgrave, pp. 49–78.
van Haute, E., Pauwels, T. and Sinardet, D. (2018) "Sub-State Nationalism and Populism: The Cases of the Vlaams Belang, New Flemish Alliance and DéFI in Belgium", *Comparative European Politics*, 16(6), pp. 954–975.
VB (2010) *Programma Federale verkiezingen 2010. Vlamingen eerst*.
VB (2014a) *Vlaams Belang. Echt onafhankelijk. Ledenblad van de Vlaams-Nationale partij*, 1, www.vlaamsbelang.org/vbmagazine/vbm-2014-01/. Accessed 1 January 2018.
VB (2014b) *Vlaams Belang. Echt onafhankelijk. Ledenblad van de Vlaams-Nationale partij*, 2, www.vlaamsbelang.org/vbmagazine/vbm-2014-02/. Accessed 1 January 2018.
VB (2014c) *Vlaams Belang. Echt onafhankelijk. Ledenblad van de Vlaams-Nationale partij*, 3, www.vlaamsbelang.org/vbmagazine/vbm-2014-03/. Accessed 1 January 2018.
VB (2014d) *Vlaams Belang. Echt onafhankelijk. Ledenblad van de Vlaams-Nationale partij*, 4, www.vlaamsbelang.org/vbmagazine/vbm-2014-04/. Accessed 1 January 2018.
VB (2014e) *Vlaams Belang. Echt onafhankelijk. Ledenblad van de Vlaams-Nationale partij*, 5, www.vlaamsbelang.org/vbmagazine/vbm-2014-05/. Accessed 1 January 2018.

VB (2014f) *Vlaams Belang. Echt onafhankelijk. Ledenblad van de Vlaams-Nationale partij*, 6, www.vlaamsbelang.org/vbmagazine/vbm-2014-06/. Accessed 1 January 2018.
VB (2014g) *Vlaams Belang. Echt onafhankelijk. Ledenblad van de Vlaams-Nationale partij*, 7–8, www.vlaamsbelang.org/vbmagazine/vbm-2014-07-08/. Accessed 1 January 2018.
VB (2014h) *Vlaams Belang. Echt onafhankelijk. Ledenblad van de Vlaams-Nationale partij*, 9, www.vlaamsbelang.org/vbmagazine/vbm-2014-09/. Accessed 1 January 2018.
VB (2014i) *Vlaams Belang. Echt onafhankelijk. Ledenblad van de Vlaams-Nationale partij*, 10, www.vlaamsbelang.org/vbmagazine/vbm-2014-10/. Accessed 1 January 2018.
VB (2014j) *Vlaams Belang. Echt onafhankelijk. Ledenblad van de Vlaams-Nationale partij*, 11, www.vlaamsbelang.org/vbmagazine/vbm-2014-11/. Accessed 1 January 2018.
VB (2014k) *Vlaams Belang. Echt onafhankelijk. Ledenblad van de Vlaams-Nationale partij*, 12, www.vlaamsbelang.org/vbmagazine/vbm-2014-12/. Accessed 1 January 2018.
VB (2014l) *Verkiezingsprogramma. Uw stok achter de deur.*
VB (2015a) *Vlaams Belang. Echt onafhankelijk. Ledenblad van de Vlaams-Nationale partij*, 1, www.vlaamsbelang.org/vbmagazine/vbm-2015-01/. Accessed 1 January 2018.
VB (2015b) *Vlaams Belang. Echt onafhankelijk. Ledenblad van de Vlaams-Nationale partij*, 2, www.vlaamsbelang.org/vbmagazine/vbm-2015-02/. Accessed 1 January 2018.
VB (2015c) *Vlaams Belang. Echt onafhankelijk. Ledenblad van de Vlaams-Nationale partij*, 3, www.vlaamsbelang.org/vbmagazine/vbm-2015-03/. Accessed 1 January 2018.
VB (2015d) *Vlaams Belang. Echt onafhankelijk. Ledenblad van de Vlaams-Nationale partij*, 4, www.vlaamsbelang.org/vbmagazine/vbm-2015-04/. Accessed 1 January 2018.
VB (2015e) *Vlaams Belang. Echt onafhankelijk. Ledenblad van de Vlaams-Nationale partij*, 5, www.vlaamsbelang.org/vbmagazine/vbm-2015-05/. Accessed 1 January 2018.
VB (2015f) *Vlaams Belang. Echt onafhankelijk. Ledenblad van de Vlaams-Nationale partij*, 6, www.vlaamsbelang.org/vbmagazine/vbm-2015-06/. Accessed 1 January 2018.
VB (2015g) *Vlaams Belang. Echt onafhankelijk. Ledenblad van de Vlaams-Nationale partij*, 7–8, www.vlaamsbelang.org/vbmagazine/vbm-2015-07-08/. Accessed 1 January 2018.
VB (2015h) *Vlaams Belang. Echt onafhankelijk. Ledenblad van de Vlaams-Nationale partij*, 9, www.vlaamsbelang.org/vbmagazine/vbm-2015-09/. Accessed 1 January 2018.
VB (2015i) *Vlaams Belang. Echt onafhankelijk. Ledenblad van de Vlaams-Nationale partij*, 10, www.vlaamsbelang.org/vbmagazine/vbm-2015-10/. Accessed 1 January 2018.
VB (2015j) *Vlaams Belang. Echt onafhankelijk. Ledenblad van de Vlaams-Nationale partij*, 11, www.vlaamsbelang.org/vbmagazine/vbm-2015-11/. Accessed 1 January 2018.
VB (2015k) *Vlaams Belang. Echt onafhankelijk. Ledenblad van de Vlaams-Nationale partij*, 12, www.vlaamsbelang.org/vbmagazine/vbm-2015-12/. Accessed 1 January 2018.
Wodak, R. (2009) *The Discursive Construction of National Identity*. Edinburgh: Edinburgh University Press.

4

CLAIMING REGIONALISM AND NATIONALISM AT THE SAME TIME

How the Italian and Swiss Leagues can engage in contradictory claims and get away with it[1]

Oscar Mazzoleni and Carlo Ruzza

Classifications of political parties typically distinguish sub-national regionalist parties from statewide nationalist ones. There is a general acceptance of the thesis that contemporary Western European regionalist parties develop strategies that aim to defend territorial interests in opposition to statewide authority. It would seem unlikely, therefore, to be able to identify a combination of regionalist claims and 'statewide' nationalism coexisting within the strategy of a single party. Thus, a party strategy combining a regionalist *and* a nationalist frame seem inherently contradictory, or unlikely to succeed. This also reflects the scholarship specialization, which distinguishes the literature on (statewide) right-wing parties from studies on regionalist parties and movements. This chapter contends, however, that a dual frame, namely a co-occurrence between regionalist and nationalist claims, might emerge and develop over time.

A dual frame might occur once supranational power – particularly in the form of the EU – is targeted as a more dangerous threat to regional interests than any perceived threat at the statewide level. This contribution addresses the question of how Eurosceptic parties rooted in regionalism develop and sustain themselves with a populist discourse that also incorporates national statewide claims. To illustrate how such a dual frame occurs – that is, a simultaneous emphasis on a regionalist *and* a nationalist ethos – we will focus on two Eurosceptic regionalist and populist parties, namely the Italian Northern League (NL), which was recently renamed with the abbreviated name of Lega (League), and the Swiss Lega dei Ticinesi (LT). This contribution is organized as follows: first, we will discuss the current literature and propose our framework for analysis; second, we will present and justify the selection of our two empirical cases; third, we will focus on each party's development over time and space; and finally, we will show how our research suggests the need to consider more carefully the links between regionalism, statewide nationalism, and supra-nationalism in the current context of Eurosceptic parties.

The anti-European opposition

The relationship between 'minority' nationalism and 'majority' nationalism has been explored by a rich literature that has often stressed the incompatibilities and tensions between the two constructs (e.g. Keating and McGarry 2001). Tensions occur because 'nationalism' as a legitimating ideology is interpreted in radically different ways according to the two perspectives. Statewide nationalism is intent on promoting a parallel process of state-building and nation-building, under which internal ethnic, linguistic, and sub-national minorities should integrate or assimilate (e.g. Gellner 1983; Breuilly 1993). This perspective is typically opposed by minority nationalism or regionalism, which redefine the concept of nation or region at a different – and smaller – territorial level and do not accept the idea of acquiescing to overarching nation-state-building imperatives (Gagnon and Keating 2012). At the same time, when focusing on political mobilization strategies, and on the discourse of political actors, the literature appears less univocal. This is because nationalism, regionalism, and ethnicism are 'chameleonic' terms (Connor 1994) and consequently, several scholars tend to make interchangeable use of 'regionalism' and 'nationalism', as if they were synonymous, or assume that they are somewhat overlapping. Such ambivalent usage occurs especially in studies of separatist movements, which are sometimes labelled as 'nationalist' rather than 'regionalist', or which are presented as 'regional nationalist' (e.g. Hueglin 1986; Christiansen 1998).

However, the possibility of combining a regionalist claim and a statewide nationalist claim within the same party's strategic narrative appears difficult to sustain, especially within a single political party. In other words, political parties that characterize themselves as regionalist parties would stand in contradiction to statewide nationalism, which traditionally belongs to other party families and – within the context of current Western European countries – to the right-wing parties in particular.

Nevertheless, one might argue that a co-occurrence of these two distinct types of nationalism can arise, especially once a common threat and target are seen to emerge, providing both an internal and external bridging of regionalism and statewide nationalism. One such case is the perception of the EU as a threat to both regional and statewide interests, as the EU is represented as a common challenge for national and regional sovereignty. In Western Europe, from a perspective of statewide nationalism, an increasing number of movements and parties have in recent decades been mobilizing against European integration (e.g. Ignazi 2006; Mudde 2007), although Euroscepticism is not specific to right-wing parties (Szczerbiak and Taggart 2008; Topaloff 2012). For instance, in Austria, Switzerland, and France, some of the most successful formations, especially those that are labelled extreme or right-wing populist parties, have portrayed the EU as posing a threat to national identity and national sovereignty including the Freiheitliche Partei Österreichs, the Schweizerische Volkspartei, and the Rassemblement National (formerly Front National). By contrast, the literature has often emphasized that so far as the 'family' of regionalist parties is concerned, EU integration has been embraced in several countries, especially under the notion of a 'Europe of the regions' (De Winter and Gomez-Reino Cachafeiro 2002). However, some scholars have recently pointed to increasing levels of Euroscepticism in the family of regionalist parties (Keating and Hooghe 2006: 272; Elias 2008; Gomez-Reino Cachafeiro 2014).

This change can be explained with reference to the trajectory of European integration in recent years. In the 1970s and 1980s, there was a transfer of power from nation states to regional authorities – often newly formed and encouraged by EU-funding dynamics (Harvie 1994; Keating 2013). In such a context, regionalist movements and parties came to see the EU as an empowering construction and often embraced it wholeheartedly. However, successive decades showed that such a process remained of limited relevance. The functions of regional bodies such as the Committee of the Regions remained confined to an advisory role, and a more intergovernmental conception of the EU came to prevail. The limited relevance of the myth of the 'Europe of the regions' was particularly evident during the 2007 financial crisis and its aftermaths, whose responses occurred predominantly at the intergovernmental level. In this context, regionalist parties' support for European integration began to waver, causing a narrowing of differences, if not a convergence, with the Euroscepticism of nationalist formations. Nowadays, when we examine the make-up of the Europe of Freedom and Democracy group of MPs in the European Parliament, we note that it includes both statewide nationalists, like members of UKIP and the Danish Folkspartei, and parties with a regionalist roots agenda, namely Lega (Nord) and Vlaams Belang.

Although it can hardly be said that regionalist parties constitute an anti-EU family of their own, scholars' interest has increasingly focused on the nature of their anti-EU sentiments. These are typically rooted in a perceived EU centralism and 'dirigisme', and in the consequences of the austerity measures that have been imposed by the EU, especially in the period since 2008/2009, and in migration policies, in which migrants are conceived as contenders for the resources of the welfare state and competitors on the regional job market (Verney 2012; Caiani and Conti 2014; Jolly 2015, Chapter 4). As some scholars have pointed out, the EU policies that facilitate regional autonomy have diminished, and there were fewer opportunities for regional autonomy in the 2000s (Keating and Hooghe 2006; Elias 2008). The opposition also involves EU governance (intergovernmental powers against supranational rules) and emerges as a populist claim (Harmsen 2010: 335). Moreover, a recent comparative analysis shows the salience of the right-left cleavage among several regionalist parties, as the right-wing and left-wing regionalist parties tend to be more anti-EU than centrist parties (Gomez-Reino Cachafeiro 2014).

However, it remains unclear under what conditions Eurosceptic regionalist parties might express support for statewide nationalism. We argue that since the EU is often framed as a rival construct by regionalists, some of them in a period of rising Eurosceptic orientations might see the defence of national interest as an acceptable if undesirable option. In other words, it is the best way to address some of the policy issues with which they are particularly concerned. For instance, statewide involvement appears the best way of strengthening national borders and thereby limiting immigration. Our question thus concerns the conditions under which regionalist Euroscepticism comes to be combined with 'statewide' nationalism.

Case selection and hypotheses

In our attempt to grasp the possibility of a nationwide nationalist frame within a regionalist party, we adopt an actor-centred approach where parties and their representatives are not cohesive organizations and they behave in a complex environment (Hellmann 2011). We focus on two political parties, namely the Lega (formerly Lega Nord) in Italy, and the Lega dei Ticinesi in Switzerland, which run in political systems that are substantially different in terms of state structure, which is federal in the case of Switzerland and one in which regional reform has only been (weakly) implemented relatively recently, and one in the case of Italy that has been superimposed on a historically centralistic structure. The two systems also differ substantially with respect to the fact that only one of them is set within a member state of the EU. Nonetheless, these two parties have combined two ideologies that appear contradictory to many observers. We thus adopt a 'most different systems design' for comparative research (Przeworski and Teune 1970; Anckar 2008). In other words, having identified similarly coexisting nationalist and regionalist frames in the two parties, we examine the conditions that are likely to have produced them within the two different political systems.[2]

Among facilitating conditions, a crucial role is played by the so-called configuration of political opportunities (Kitschelt 1986; Meyer and Minkoff 2004). Within the broad literature on political opportunities, we refer to opportunities particular to a specific sector (Giugni 2009). Political opportunities may relate to various structural factors. There is also, however, a class of opportunities that derive from embracing a particular political discourse, or an ideology such as the ideology of the extreme right. We will refer to them as 'discursive opportunities' (Koopmans and Olzak 2004). More generally, the concept of 'discursive opportunities' relates to the research tradition that studies the role of ideational constructs in political contexts (Schmidt 2008). This tradition shows how ideas emerge in response to specific social and political challenges and illustrates how political actors utilize emerging ideas to pursue a variety of organizational goals, including party competition.

We then focus on the opportunities that characterize the radical right (Arzheimer and Carter 2006) and investigate the opportunities that are likely to promote the co-occurrence of regionalist and nationalist frames. Our analysis emphasizes four aspects, concerning both intra-party and inter-party features: (1)

the relevance of the type of regionalism at stake (whether it is more or less 'moderate'); (2) the degree of competition and cooperation with radical right-wing parties; (3) the complexity of multi-level competition; and (4) the 'chameleonic' and often contradictory logic of populist discourse (Taggart 2000). For each of these aspects, we formulate a specific hypothesis.

Firstly, given that minority nationalist movements are typically positioned ideologically on an axis that ranges between advocating separatism and a greater degree of regional independence – that is, 'autonomism' – our first hypothesis concerns the likelihood of incorporating nation-state nationalism in relation to parties' self-positioning on such an axis. As regionalist parties provide strong ideological variation (Massetti 2009), our first hypothesis contends that 'separatism' creates less of a bond with statewide nationalism than 'autonomism' or 'integrationism' (Keating 2003), that is, with moderate forms of regionalism. This moderation towards statewide power also implies the potential to easily integrate other cleavages. In fact, one might expect a relatively strong link with the left-wing cleavage, in particular through open competition with nationwide radical right-wing parties. In this sense, our second hypothesis posits that the stronger the rival relationship with radical right-wing parties is – in terms of competition and/or cooperation – the higher the possibility for regionalist parties to integrate a nationwide claim.

Moreover, following our rationale that the dual frame is expressed through a mix of goals, tactics, and expectations that can vary in space and time, our third hypothesis contends that the presence of a dual frame in regionalist parties is partially a by-product of an adaptive strategy. Each party strategy necessarily depends on internal dynamics, such as the evolution of the dominant coalition and the emergence of new leaders. As parties are not unitary organizations, claiming and changes are not necessarily shared by members as a whole. The (public) self-representation of the party does not always fit with the members' political culture and behaviour, and the legitimacy of individuals within the party might be a very crucial issue in the way that it relates to parties' discursive strategy. Moreover, party strategy can be an adjusting response to challenges related to the uncertainty of electoral achievements in a multi-layered system. Party competition occurs in different (legislative and executive) arenas and on different (sub-national, national, and supranational) levels. These are characterized by a varying set of structures of opportunity and constraint (Detterbeck 2012), favouring distinctive tactics and strategies in linking with different alliances and constituencies (e.g. Bottel et al. 2016).

While all successful European regionalist parties tend to adjust their discourse to different arenas and levels, in the case of *populist* regionalist parties, this malleability is enhanced. According to the literature, populist parties share a claim to represent the unified category of 'the people', while representing this entity in different ways, as a community, a region, or a nation. The 'enemies' of populist parties also vary and include the likes of 'political elites', 'bureaucrats', and 'immigrants'. (Rovira Kaltwasser et al. 2018; de la Torre 2019). Taking advantage of their own particular environment, regionalist parties may provide a 'multi-level populism' in order to target different constituencies of the notionally unified, but in fact differentiated 'people' (situated locally, regionally and nationally), and to fight against the elites related to each arena at local, regional and national levels (Mazzoleni 2005: 210). Moreover, populists tend, more than non-populists, to share a fluid style underlying a chameleonic logic (Taggart 2000; Heinisch and Mazzoleni 2017). Although this does not necessarily avoid intra-party tensions, in particular between a more moderate and government-oriented wing and the protest wing, one can nevertheless expect – and this is our fourth hypothesis – that populist regionalist parties can sustain and succeed in managing 'minority' and 'majority' nationalism with varying degrees of tension and ambiguity.

Bridging regionalism and nationalism in party mobilization

In an attempt to test our four hypotheses, we compare two parties with a strong regionalist background that have experienced a long period of success since the 1990s and which allow a dual frame: Italy's Lega and the Swiss Lega dei Ticinesi (LT). Founded in the 1970s, the Italian League provides the example of a regionalist party emerging in a centralist state that has recently experienced a shift from a regionalist and anti-statewide discourse to a combined Eurosceptic regionalist and nationalist discourse and a statewide electoral strategy. These features contrast with those of the LT, which was created in 1991 and which expresses a persistent Euroscepticism along with an 'integrationist' approach to regionalism within strong federal institutions. The LT also retains its regional constituency over time, notwithstanding its direct competition with right-wing parties nationwide. Despite these diversities, the question arises as to how these different types of regionalism, as well as the patterns of party competition and multi-level populism, contribute to sustaining a dual-frame strategy. Our analysis is based on several sources, including electoral results, party manifestos, in-depth interviews with activists, and cadres' speeches.

The League and the enduring tension within the dual frame

As has already been pointed out, the coexistence of party loyalties striding the divide between the nation and the region can mask an underlying internal ambivalence and an ongoing struggle between regionalism and statewide nationalism. This is the case with the (Northern) League, which has been one of the principal actors in Italian politics in recent decades (Ruzza and Fella 2009; Curcio and Perini 2014; Passarelli and Tuorto 2018). In the early years of its existence, the League took a positive stance towards Europe and the process of European integration. For its members in the eighties and nineties, EU-level politics appeared relatively more efficient than the discredited and corrupt Italian system, and more congruent with the neo-liberal pro-market vision that the

League espoused at that time. Also, and crucially, the European system of governance appeared to compete with those of the member states, and in several ways, a pro-EU stance seemed to undermine the centralist Italian system that the League despised. However, since the early 2000s, the League's position on European integration has increasingly shifted towards a radically Eurosceptic view. As an example of radical anti-EU sentiments, one could consider excerpts from a speech Matteo Salvini made at the European Parliament on 5 July 2017: 'I will now speak to those who are following us from outside of this building, not to those who govern this European Union, because they are accomplices, fake, hypocritical, incompetent or naïve'. (Salvini 2017, our translation).

The recent evolution of the League confirms our hypothesis on the political opportunities that contribute to triggering the emergence of a dual-frame strategy. First, in contrast with the legacy of secessionist claims, the regionalist claim by the League has tended to become increasingly moderate in recent years. The League has, over time, quickly and skilfully adapted to changing political contexts, often shifting positions on the basis of its role vis-à-vis its incorporation (or the lack of it) in central government coalitions, the mix of institutional actors that have supported it at subnational levels of government, and the nature of the prevalent political and media discourse in the country. In particular, on the key issue of whether the party should pursue a secessionist or a regionalist agenda, the preference for a federalist agenda has dominated the party during its stints in government, as was the case during the period of a Berlusconi government in 1994, during a second period in government in 2001–2006, and during a third period in 2008–2011. Conversely, the secessionist agenda has typically emerged during phases of radicalization after leaving government – such as was seen in the period of 1994–1999 (Ruzza 2004). However, these evolutions underwent a turning point that took place soon after Salvini became the leader of the party in December 2013.

The secessionist agenda remained a key theme in the concerns of the activist base and in the official statutes of the League, confirmed in June 2015, which still cite the 'independence of Padania' as the party's principal goal,[3] although this seems in perfect contrast with the new party agenda as laid out by the leader, Salvini. The strategic goal of independence for Padania was explicitly ruled out by Salvini, whose main efforts have been designed to persuade the party that his proposed turn to the right would bring new and important opportunities for growth (Madron 2015; Albertazzi et al. 2018). In effect, the national elections of March 2018 proved him right as the League achieved 17.64% of the vote in the Senate and 17.4% in the lower chamber, thereby becoming the largest party in the centre-right coalition. This trend continued in the European elections of 2019 as the League achieved 34.3% of the vote. As has been said, the League's turn to the right is not a new development, but the extent of the ideological shift spurred by Salvini was unprecedented until his leadership and this shift strongly influenced the national election results, which constituted a watershed in Italian politics. His move to the right, and even, according to his critics, to the extreme right, became increasingly controversial over time but allowed a distancing of the party from the previously widely shared perception of an anti-Southern ethos. This transformation was strengthened by renaming the party as simply Lega or 'League', thus dropping the reference to the North, which was prominent in the old name of 'Lega Nord'.[4]

These ideological changes and the ambivalent existence of the party organization (between two names and two statutes) have resulted in an increase of the Lega's vote in the South, although its electoral roots largely remain in the North and to some extent in the centre of the country (Passarelli and Tuorto 2018: 58 ff.). Meanwhile, another larger transformation occurred in the South, which voted massively for the largest populist actor in the Italian political scene: the Five Star Movement (5SM). Therefore, a radically transformed political system emerged from the 2018 national elections and the subsequent new government – one in which two large populist parties are now the central actors on the political scene, whereby the country is radically split between the League, which is now strongly dominant in the North of the country, and the 5SM, which is overwhelmingly dominant in the South (Biorcio and Natale 2018).

The success of the new nationalist League was confirmed and in many cities amplified in the local elections of June 2018 (Testa 2018). Even more importantly, the League consolidated and expanded its successes in the South, although the old autonomist focus remained viable in the Northern regions. This coexistence was evident, for instance, in the July 2018 speeches of the League's regional governors – all from the North of the country – who participated in one of the League's traditional ritual events, the 'Pontida Festival', which is held annually and attracts a vast audience of activists. They often praised the newly arrived Southern representations at the festival, but emphasized that the key focus on regional autonomy had not been abandoned and remained a central focus of the League's activities.

Conversely, Southern governors, such as the Sicilian centre-right governor Nello Musumeci, stressed the importance of keeping the North and the South of the country united, for several reasons, but notably to confront the fact that 'as Italians are divided between North and South the godfathers of Europe laugh at us' (from live radio reports; see also Staff Reporter 2018c). On the same occasion, after several interventions on this topic, Salvini concluded that 'it is not the League that has changed, it is the world that has changed. In order to win we must unite' (Salvini 2018). Thus, Salvini acknowledged the tensions between the regionalist and statewide nationalist views, but strongly reasserted his new approach of combining the two and justified it as a historical necessity. Of course, this debate is important not just because of the new pro-Southern ethos, but because it is a proxy for the League's paradigm change in political discourse.

Nonetheless, despite the League's changing political discourse, a substantial conflict persists on how to allocate resources between the North and the South of the country, and the League still often expresses its traditional Northern preferences. For instance, an extensive debate on the vexed question of the fiscal autonomy of Northern regions re-emerged at the beginning of 2019. The 'governors' of the rich regions of Lombardy and Veneto challenged Salvini to use his now influential role in government to revamp the League's traditional demands for regional fiscal autonomy (see, for example, Valentini 2019). They even suggested that without real progression on this topic, the League should reconsider its alliance with the Five Star Movement and its permanence in government. The Five Star Movement, which represents a mainly Southern constituency, is ambivalent and often opposed to such a reform. It is torn between the desire to retain good relations with its government ally and pressure from civil society in the South of the country where, for instance, a petition entitled 'No to the Secession of the Rich' has been organized on the online platform *change.org*. In this context, Salvini has, for the time being, sided with its Northern component and has assured it of his support for regional fiscal autonomy. This is clearly a complex issue, which will not be rapidly settled, but on which the tension between the two frames remains unresolved.

Thus, the dual-frame stance of the League is far from being a single-minded defence of statewide sovereignism. It is a more nuanced position in which contrasts remain between regionalism and nationalism, but in which a new enemy is identified, distinguishing the power of the central institutions and the rights of nations. As Salvini has pointed out:

> I remain persuasively autonomist and federalist. And independentist, because peoples have the right to choose, in Quebec, Brittany, Salento, Scotland, and Crimea. Unlike twenty years ago, the Europe of today is now massacring, killing and levelling everything and everyone. This is an emergency that did not exist back then. Now my problem is Brussels. [...] The problem now is national ...
>
> *(Franzi and Madron 2015: 79–80, our translation; see also Rapisarda 2015: 44)*

The current leader of the League pursues a dual strategy to give credibility to his stance of combining regionalism and nationalism, without appearing inconsistent and disloyal to his past. In this vein, in keeping with the strategy to build a nationwide party in Italy, Matteo Salvini attended rallies in Naples, a city that stands in Italian imagery as a symbol for southern Italian poverty, crime, and social problems. His visits, with the list 'Noi con Salvini' in 2015 were meant to attract new followers to his new party with a nationalist platform. However, the internal impact of this reframing is complex, as his forays in the South attract 'reframing' attempts within Northern constituencies, traditionally responding to the regionalist anti-'nationwide' claims. Having abandoned secessionist claims, they typically now argue that enhanced Northern independence is still a viable goal, which is, however, to be generalized to all the regions. The tension within the dual frame is then typically left to the mediating and interpreting role of the League's cadres and leaders. Tensions with ex-leader Bossi, who is particularly critical of the right-wing turn, have in recent years flared up on frequent occasions, but he is now completely marginalized within the party. His role is confined to representing a connection to a glorious past – he is seen as the noble founding father of the party – but his following is now very limited, and he is generally excluded from all relevant arenas.

All attempts to combine the two frames are now left to the present leadership. Salvini frequently argues that the federalist agenda that characterized the regionalist phase of the League is now a viable strategy for the entire country. The previous regionalist-centred ideology emphasized a set of supposedly distinctive virtues of the Northern part of the country, such as a stronger work ethic and a glorious historical past. These specificities were celebrated with distinctive collective rituals and symbols that had a manifest nation-building intent. Salvini has recently reframed the League's ideological package and asserts that every Italian location has a right and even a duty to celebrate its distinctive features and traditions. To that effect he has created new rituals that celebrate all the localities he visits. They include sporting T-shirts with the name of each locality printed in big characters, which he wears at political rallies in front of its now broader audiences.

Thus, the League can now argue that each region will be strengthened thanks to the new nationwide ideology, and all will benefit from a more regionalized state structure. In this way, the regionalist ethos still survives but can be married to a nationalist ideology. This said, in terms of saliency, the new leadership is clear that the fight with 'Europe' is where the energy of the League should now be focused. This allows the party to enjoy several advantages that on the one hand displace old tensions with the South by identifying and pursuing an alternative enemy, and on the other hand, allow the benefits of membership in a growing party family – that of the Eurosceptic populist right. Over time, we are gradually witnessing the institutionalization in the party's ideology of the dual frame, which is still vigorously asserted but in a context in which unashamed regionalist are now excluded. For instance, at the aforementioned Pontida Festival of 2018, the 'old guard' and their key spokespersons – the former leader Umberto Bossi and his ally, Roberto Maroni, the former governor of the Lombardy region – were, for the first time, pointedly not included among the speakers, as their differences with the leader are well known (see Staff Reporter 2018a, 2018b).

Inter-partisan relations play a crucial role in these changes. While the League's strategy towards the radical right-wing parties has changed over time, in recent years, the League has increasingly been competing across the country around the same issues and constituencies of the radical right and the centre right. Thus, together with Euroscepticism, statewide nationalism is a key component of the right-wing radicalization of the League. This is quite clear to see in its agenda, for instance, through alliances with the extreme right designed to enable them to respond to the 'threat of migration' with similar policy proposals, but also through similar ideological stances taken with statewide nationalists. This discursive change is accompanied by a recurring concern about immigration, a preoccupation with the defence of European borders, and a preference for intergovernmental approaches and the preservation of the veto powers of member states to 'protect democracy and the rights of the European people' (Caiani 2014: 189). Thus, although the League is the junior partner in this government, its impact on a range of the League's characteristic signature policies has been extremely noticeable. This has particularly been the case for migration policies, which have radically changed with the League in power, leading to a virtual stalling of NGO-led consolidated humanitarian missions to rescue migrants attempting to cross the Mediterranean.

When trying to explain the League's anti-EU turn, researchers (e.g. Chari 2004) have pointed out the need to improve the coalitional power of the League vis-à-vis other Eurosceptic centre-right parties in Italy. For the League, a strong alliance with Forza Italia and Alleanza Nazionale was of paramount importance at a time when potentially EU-endorsed secessionism appeared increasingly unfeasible. Lately, the most important turning point is represented by the unexpected success in the 2014 European elections, when the League's parliamentarian Mario Borghezio won a seat with the support of voters from the centre of Italy and the alliance with Rome's extreme-right formation Casa Pound (Rapisarda 2015: 45–46). In the meantime, however, the competition with the radical right continues, sometimes to the benefit of the League, and at other times in a way that enables extreme-right formations to take substantial proportions of the League's vote. This was the case in the local election in Bozen of 5 June 2016, when the extreme-right formation Casa Pound attracted significant support from the League's electorate (Maggi 2016). However, in recent years the move to the right has not been motivated by a desire to facilitate and unite the centre-right coalition, as Chari (2004) had argued, but to erode the support of Berlusconi's centre-right Forza Italia – a formation by now led by an ageing and discredited leader. This strategy has paid off, particularly in the North of the country, where the League acquired votes from several parties but notably from Forza Italia, as some electoral analyses suggest (Vignati 2018).

As we have stated, one distinctive aspect of populist discourse enables it to deal easily with heterogeneous enemies and virtuous communities located in a multi-layered environment (Mazzoleni 2005). In other words, a key aspect of the populist claim is its relatively unstructured nature and the often charismatic following of parties that embody them. These two aspects contribute to providing a degree of distinctive flexibility in their policies and political proposals. To a greater extent than other parties, they are able to speak in different ways to different audiences. This also means that they can more easily seize emerging discursive opportunities and re-fashion their ideological core according to emerging opportunities for forming alliances. So far as the League is concerned, this aspect clearly emerges in the speeches delivered at the Pontida Festival in 2018. In that context, the image is of a Europe made of 'peoples' with strong identities who 'love each other', as opposed to a Europe made up of the bureaucrats and financiers who dominate the EU. People who work with their hands – or as

Salvini argued in his speech, 'those with corns on their hands' – are opposed to people who ruin uncountable lives on a whim (Salvini 2017). Strong communities are praised, while cosmopolitans are despised. In this context, Salvini looks forward to the forthcoming European election of 2019, when he believes a strong partnership of like-minded parties will emerge and win. In this context, Euroscepticism becomes an appealing choice to solidify EU-wide alliances with like-minded parties and to possibly benefit from a range of rewards, ranging from those accrued by forming large and cohesive parties in the European Parliament to those deriving from collective and concerted activism in the public sphere. From this point of view, a set of well-publicised events have shown what has been termed as a 'populist international' being formed and solidified by meetings and supportive statements. For instance, Marine Le Pen was one of the first politicians to congratulate Salvini for the 2018 electoral gains (Staff Reporter 2018d).

A chameleon-like inconsistency and substantial discursive variations in different arenas facilitate the difficult task of managing the aforementioned ongoing tensions resulting from the dual-frame strategy of the League. If 'the people of reference' is no longer reserved for the ranks of Northern Italians and local communities, but increasingly includes all Italians, thereby marking a transition to a 'majoritarian' nationalist frame (Caiani and Conti 2014: 189), the anti-establishment criticism targets the EU, but also sub-national and national authorities, including the government of Rome, which represent a continuity in the League's regionalist frame. As previously mentioned, specific references to 'Northern people' are not abandoned, as anti-Southern sentiments continue to be voiced, for example, at League events such as the annual Pontida meetings. Moreover, in Lombardy and Veneto – two of the largest and richer Italian regions administered by League governors – regionalist issues remain prominent, as was shown in a recently launched referendum on fiscal autonomy, which was also espoused by Salvini. A chameleonic populist discourse thus plays a crucial role in managing inconsistencies in the definition of the people of reference – national or regional. To sum up, as expected, the variety of political discourses and ambivalent ideological positions enabled by a multi-layered discursive environment contribute to the capacity to sustain a dual frame.

The LT: the dual frame as a legacy

Without doubt, the Lega dei Ticinesi (LT) has been a regionalist party since its foundation in 1991 in the southern part of Switzerland. Its ideological background has traditionally emphasized the centre-periphery cleavage, targeting the national centre as being unable to respect the expectations of Ticino, the Italian-speaking canton in southern Switzerland, in terms of economic prosperity and identity (Albertazzi 2006). With its first electoral platform, the LT denounced a lack of financial support from the central national authorities, discriminatory wages for federal public servants located in Ticino, and limited transportation access to the rest of

Switzerland because of the natural obstacle of the Alpine Chain (Rusconi 1994: 159–160). Despite some changes in certain policies, its ideological supply has largely persisted over time (Mazzoleni 2016).

Moreover, the LT has been a Eurosceptic party since its first steps in the 1990s. Founded when European integration was becoming a crucial issue in the Swiss political agenda and the federal government was pushing toward European integration, the LT was one of the few Swiss formations to mobilize against the referendum targeting Switzerland's entry into the European economic space (EES) in 1992. At that time, within the Swiss People's party, which was to become in the 2000s the main Swiss national-populist and Eurosceptic formation, only a minority faction was against the EES (Mazzoleni 2018). By contrast, in the LT's agenda, the Eurosceptic orientation was already strongly dominant within the party. Against European integration, the party denounced the 'betrayed' promises of the Swiss national elites, especially in the face of the risk of losing national and popular sovereignty. At that time, the pursuit of European integration was rejected by this party more because it was perceived to be a threat to national independence, sovereignty, and direct democracy than a direct threat to regional interests (Maspoli 1992). Later on, especially since the 2000s, which were marked by increasing levels of European integration, the LT has reshaped its anti-EU frame. This is characterized by an ideological stance in which the EU is increasingly seen as constituting a threat to the regional prosperity and job market of Ticino – a canton which is the territorial base of this party and is located on the border of Northern Italy. While the LT has been able to develop a strong and influential regionalist frame within the cantonal party system – across traditional party cleavages – it has, since the mid-2000s, taken advantage of the expanding political opportunities related to the application of Swiss-EU bilateral agreements and the ongoing Italian socio-economic crisis, which has pushed an increasing number of people toward seeking a job in Southern Switzerland (Mazzoleni 2016, 2017). Thus, in the LT agenda, border issues with Italy have become more and more relevant. They include the denunciation of the flow of cross-border workers and Swiss–Italian fiscal treaties, as well as the claim for regional protectionism in the face of increasing economic competition over the cantonal market (Mazzoleni and Mueller 2017). Within the LT's agenda, therefore, national sovereignty and federal autonomy are not opposites, but complementary stances.

Thus, the LT confirms our hypotheses of conditions favouring the dual-frame strategy. First, in contrast to the autonomism and previously separatist claim of the League, the regionalism of the LT is persistently based on an 'integrative' stance, aiming for stronger federalism within the current statewide system (Keating 2003). The LT defends the widely accepted characterization of Switzerland as a federal and multinational state, which can protect its minorities in matters of cultural recognition, the welfare state, and economic well-being. However, according to the LT, the Ticino is currently going through a decline in its prosperity because of the undermining role of the federal state, which prioritizes supranational agreements and migrants instead of its internal minorities. Consequently, a stronger national federal state is seen as a condition for the defence of Ticino's interests. Bridging Euroscepticism and nationwide claim, the LT has been able to persist in framing the centre-periphery cleavage against the national elites, as conditions for the regional autonomy and prosperity that it asks to be restored. Thus, despite the criticism of federal authorities, the LT's representatives emphasize their view of Switzerland as a 'free and safe country' and proudly celebrate Swiss National Day each year on 1 August. This is shown, for instance, in a speech by one of the LT's members of the cantonal government:

> today more than ever, on the Christmas Day of our homeland, we must be protagonists in the political choices that concern us, we must fight for the Ticino we want; we cannot and must not passively accept what is imposed on us from outside, but above all, we must reaffirm our will to be masters in our own home … we want to live 'free and Swiss'! Let us remember it every day. For our sake. For the good of Ticino and Switzerland.
> *(Gobbi 2016, our translation; see also, 2017)*

Second, since its foundation, the LT's strategy has been closely shaped by a mix of cooperation and competition with the populist 'nationwide' right-wing parties, both at the regional and national level. In 1992, the LT took part in the referendum against the EES alongside the party of Swiss Democrats, which is a right-wing party settled in the Swiss-German cantons. At that time, the LT also made a parliamentary agreement with the Swiss Democrats and then, after the latter's decline, with the SVP. As the latter is more liberal in economic issues, the LT's representatives in the federal parliament have sometimes voted against their group by supporting legislative reforms endorsed by left-wing parties intended to defend the regional labour market and regulate the effects of the free circulation of persons. However, open conflict with the national SVP has rarely arisen. As the LT recently pointed out, the party 'shared 80% of its positions with the SVP in federal issues' (LT 2015), although alliances at cantonal level cannot be taken for granted. The LT also competes with the SVP's cantonal branch for the same electorate, not only in terms of attitudes and values but also in terms of socio-demographic features, including voters with low levels of education and unskilled workers (Mazzoleni et al. 2017: 23–24). However, far from being placed under lasting tensions, either at the national level or at cantonal level – where the SVP cantonal branch remains less successful than that of the LT – a collaboration persists on issues related to Swiss sovereignty and independence from any supranational power. The durable relationship with the 'nationwide' radical right, also shared with the SVP of the canton of Ticino, reflects the persisting relevance of anti-immigrant issues throughout the claim for strengthening national borders against foreign criminals and for restrictive laws against immigrants and asylum-seekers. This also implies recurrent electoral agreements, such as is the case for the 2019 cantonal and national elections.

Third, the intra-party dynamics also tend to contribute to the durable, albeit ambivalent strategy. Until 2013, the LT was headed by its founder, Giuliano Bignasca, a businessman whose statements mainly embodied the regionalist claim against the Swiss political centre (i.e. Bern) and who openly disliked the German-speaking part of Switzerland, as he clearly stated in an interview in 1992 (De Lauretis and Giussani 1992: 153). However, in the early years, Bignasca shared the leadership with a former journalist, Flavio Maspoli, who was proud to speak Swiss-German. After Maspoli's death, other representatives of the LT, in particular, the MPs Lorenzo Quadri and Norman Gobbi – who had been a member of the cantonal government since 2011 and a candidate for the federal government in 2015 – took on prominent roles in dealing with the German-speaking population of Switzerland. They were also instrumental in strongly mobilizing the nationwide sense of belonging to Switzerland, while Giuliano Bignasca's son, Bobo, a member of the cantonal parliament, tends to focus more on the regional issues. Despite some ambivalence, the lasting electoral success of the LT has contributed to limiting intra-party tensions. Since 2011, the LT has been a dominant party within the cantonal government, having already been part of the cantonal government in 1995, with between one member and five represented. Moreover, in the cantonal elections of 2015, the League became the second-strongest party in the parliament of Ticino, with about 28% of voter support, and gained two MPs in the lower chamber of the federal parliament, where the LT has been continuously represented since 1991.

Fourth, within the LT's agenda, the combination of regionalism and nationalism also benefits from the multi-level populist stance of the party targeting different elites and communities, including local ones (Mazzoleni 2005). While the LT criticizes the federal establishment in the name of the citizens of the canton of Ticino as a whole, it also defends the interests of particular municipalities, like Lugano – the largest city in Ticino and the base for the LT's biggest electoral constituency – against the canton of Ticino's establishment. Its recurrent attacks against the federal government, blamed for betraying national sovereignty *and* regional interests in the face of Brussels, make it possible to legitimize its reference to the cantonal community *and* the national community. In this vein, each federal referendum – of which there are several every year – represents a crucial opportunity for its multi-level populism, as the LT often mobilizes strongly on the cantonal level against cantonal and federal policy-making. Its multi-level discourse and mobilization also take benefit from the LT's achievements at the national level. The most powerful 'nationwide' success for the LT occurred on 9 February 2014 in the popular initiative 'against massive immigration' launched by the SVP, the results of which will strongly influence relations between Switzerland and the EU in the years ahead. Strongly committed to this initiative, the LT and the cantonal branch of the SVP (whose Ticino branch remains much smaller than that of the LT) have contributed to the national success, as an average of 50.5% support the constitutional change at national level, whilst voting support in Ticino was at 68.2%, which is the highest score among all the Swiss cantons. In 2016, the LT also supported the cantonal initiative 'Ours First', which was launched and won by the SVP's cantonal branch and its bid to prioritize residents for employment and access to the labour market. Once again, the application of these initiatives allows an example of multi-level populist discourse, as a statement from Lorenzo Quadri (2017) shows: 'it becomes increasingly urgent to concretize the initiative in Ticino, "Ours First", since Bern does not miss a chance to sabotage every little hint of indigenous preference and to crawl in front of the rulers of the EU'.

Discussion

As we have seen, the Italian and Swiss Leagues exhibit several differences, as the combination of the two frames with other features of these two parties clearly illustrates. There is a significant dissimilarity in the internal and external environment of these parties. The Italian League experienced several changes and oscillations, which in the last decade transformed it into a Eurosceptic regionalist party, prompted it to abandon its previous emphasis on separatisms, and led it to develop a strong statewide nationalism and a right-wing radicalization. This dual frame reflects, above all, the changing nature of the party competition over time and the party's recent move towards a statewide electoral strategy. With its consolidated and enduring radical-right positioning, a competitive relationship was also present in the past, especially under the Berlusconi governments, but in recent years, the League has developed a stronger competition with the right over issues as well as constituencies, becoming one of the more influential Italian parties at the national level. The recent accentuation of its radical-right transformation has occurred not without internal tensions and a strong shift towards nationalist stances. Nonetheless, the malleability of the populist discourse and the multi-layered environment in which the party operates help to retain a perception of the unity of the party and to avoid splits. This means that, in contrast with what is generally assumed, the move toward adopting the nationwide turn is far from being a linear progression, as the party and its leaders persist in their efforts to bridge Euroscepticism and nationalism with regionalism, with the aim of preserving the traditional Northern constituencies.

Aiming to explain the League's strong turn to the right in comparison with the LT, one needs to also focus on the broader ideational and economic contexts that sharply differentiate Switzerland and Italy. There are of course several readings with respect to which differences are more crucial in engendering populist voting, but they tend to emphasize the theme of the 'losers of globalization' or cultural changes towards securitarian values, or a combination of both (Inglehart and Norris 2016). Italy was particularly strongly hit by the financial crisis of 2007 and its aftermaths, as well as by the 'migration crises' of recent years. Its geographical position and a weak state unable to control its borders exposed it to uncontrolled migratory flows. Its under-performing economy also points to the causal impact of distinctive economic dynamics on the diffusion of populist sentiments (Gross 2016). Thus, in economic and ideational terms, the Italian turn to the right was facilitated by cultural and economic factors that provided an emerging opportunity for the Lega, but much less so for the LT.

By contrast, as an originally and enduringly Eurosceptic regionalist party, the LT constitutes a somewhat rare example among regionalist parties in the Western European family, not only on the grounds of its successful anti-EU strategy, but also because its fundamental ideological make-up is based on a combination of regionalist and nationalist claims avoiding any strong tensions among them. The LT articulates its ideological roots – an integrative regionalism – and the strong autonomy already granted to the Swiss cantons, with the duration and stability of its electoral success over time – factors that confirm the foundational strategy simultaneously based on regional claim and nationwide nationalism. In addition, since the foundation of the LT, typical right-wing signature issues have also been part of the LT's legacy, especially the concern with immigration. In its regional constituency, where it exclusively runs for electoral gains, the party competes with the same electorate as the radical right-wing SVP. However, within the LT, distinctive representatives express the two components of the dual frame, and intra-party tensions appear less relevant than is the case in the Italian League.

However, despite the differences between the two Leagues, a common discourse emerges in which statewide nationalism is the means by which the parties oppose the EU and, at the same time, defend the regional interests of their respective constituencies. The current incarnation of the League and the LT belong to the family of Eurosceptic regionalist parties and exhibit a common targeting of the EU as the prevalent threat. In both cases, EU bureaucracy and free-market globalization are at stake, and in both cases, Euroscepticism articulates the fears that a neo-liberal, globalizing EU and the related circulation of labour tend to spark in these constituencies. This enables them to take a rather favourable appraisal of the 'nationwide' frame, for instance on economic issues, with a claim for protectionism, but with sceptical attitudes towards statewide central powers. At the same time, they tend to imply a rather limited demand for autonomist policies. Their version of regionalism is different from the radical and often uncompromising version that has emerged in other European countries, such as Spain or the UK. In this sense, our first hypothesis, which contends moderate forms of regionalism fit better with a dual frame, appears confirmed. Moreover, for both cases, the expanding family of populist radical-right parties and the complex relations with them also offer significant political opportunities for the dual frame. The salience of statewide nationalism in the League and the LT, combined with Euroscepticism, is also clearly a product of anti-immigrant and border-security stances, as well as populist standpoints that make it possible to adapt the discourse to the diversity of arenas and constituencies in which the parties operate. Moreover, for both selected parties, the dual frame might also provide an adaptive resource that highlights the relevance of a set of evolving political opportunities and related strategic changes, but also engendering ongoing and sometimes unresolved tensions between two different conceptions of nationalism, reflecting multi-level settings and constituencies in which the parties compete and form allegiances. Finally, the considerable flexibility of populist stances boosts an aspect also frequently noted in other populist parties, that is their chameleonic ideological nature and a political variability in their multi-level actions (Heinisch and Mazzoleni 2017), which also permits to comprehend the capacity of both parties to articulate the dual frame.

Conclusion

In sum, there is widespread acceptance of the opinion that regionalist parties in Western Europe develop strategies that aim to defend territorial interests against statewide authority, as the latter naturally tends to be the main polemic target of regionalist parties. However, this opinion is not always confirmed by empirical evidence. Based on the above analysis, we can argue that the co-occurrence of the facilitating conditions enables some parties to sustain over time a dual-frame discourse of coexisting and seemingly contradictory claims. We contend that the durable adoption of such a dual frame arises once regionalist parties do not share a secessionist perspective and perceive statewide nationalism as being less of a threat to regional interests than EU-promoted policies and politics. Moreover, the regional party also has to be strong enough to cope with populist radical-right parties. The appeal of this different and in some ways opposed party family is context-dependent and will become more relevant in those political contexts that feature the distinctive traits associated with the success of the radical right. It is then argued that such a dual frame is likely to consolidate when political opportunities emerge that reward a concomitant nationalist and regionalist strategy. This dual frame is likely to take place in contexts in which anti-system parties have acquired a strong foothold in institutional settings and benefit from relations with the currently successful family of radical-right populist parties, or when emerging political opportunities materialize at an international level. Moreover, the populist stance also has to do with the capacity to combine the regionalist and nationwide discourse. The inherent flexibility of populist stances – an aspect also frequently noted in other populist parties, with their chameleonic ideological nature and a political variability in their multi-level actions (Heinisch and Mazzoleni 2017) – boosts the capacity of both parties to develop their dual frame. This also allows us to return to the initial question about the coexistence of different types of ethnos. Of course, redefining fundamental ideological stances, such as the community of reference and therefore the contrast between ethnos, poses the question about the ability of parties rooted in regionalism to address different and sometimes opposed constituencies. In assessing this ability, much explanatory power is rooted in the typical flexibility of populist claims, but also of nationalism as an equally ambivalent ideology. Of course, the relation between populism and nationalism is complex (e.g. De Cleen 2017). However, populism and nationalism, regionalism, and ethnicism might all be seen as 'chameleonic'. This suggests the relevance of a future research agenda bridging Euroscepticism, regionalism, populism, and nationalism (Heinisch et al. 2018). From this perspective, populism and nationalism are ideologies still undergoing a process of definition, with low formalization and high adaptability as tools for a durable and successful party strategy.

The adoption of the dual frame also allows these parties to connect to the emerging ideational set that has diffused populist formations throughout the Western world. In so doing they can then retain political relevance for their original ideations set. They are thereby effecting a de-facto strategic frame bridging, whereby they provide legitimacy to a weaker political frame by borrowing it from an emergent frame (Benford and Snow 2000; Brown 2017). In addition, at least for the League, espousing the dual frame allows this party to engage in strategies of cooperation and triangulation at EU-level with like-minded parties. This is particularly important in the run up to the 2019 Parliamentary elections, for which Salvini advanced his candidacy for the Commission Presidency – a symbolic move that is meant to signify his desire to become the leader of the radical-right populists in the European Parliament (Baume 2018; Wax 2018). The EU-level then fosters processes of ideational convergence, which are paralleled within leftist forces and focus on their respective signature policies, such as migration policy (Monforte 2014).

Thus, for both parties, the dual frame provides an adaptive resource that highlights the relevance of a set of evolving political opportunities and related strategic shifts, but also engenders ongoing and sometimes unresolved tensions between two different conceptions of nationalism, reflecting multi-level settings and constituencies in which the parties compete and form allegiances. At the same time, the expanding family of populist radical-right parties and the complexity of relations with them also offer significant political opportunities. The salience of statewide nationalism in the League and the LT, combined with Euroscepticism, is also clearly a product of anti-immigrant and border-security stances, as well as populist standpoints that make it possible to adopt the discourse to the diversity of arenas and constituencies in which the parties operate.

At the same time, this chapter raises the question of a potentially new party family claiming for Euroscepticism and its limits. It appears that such an extension of members of a nascent party family is limited not only by the limited audience of strong Eurosceptic sentiments, which is shaped by the future vicissitudes of the project of European construction. It is also limited by the fact that the political opportunities documented in this chapter conflict with strong ideological positions, which, in the case of many European minority nationalist parties, are rooted in century-old political histories.

Parties might then well attempt to exploit emerging political opportunities, such as those offered by a right-wing turn in a period of widespread anti-immigrant sentiments. However, they cannot easily redefine the priorities that have been cemented by a shared history and strong common identities, such as is the case, for instance, with Catalan, Basque, or Scottish parties. It is hard to believe, therefore, that an expansion of this potentially nascent party family is likely to occur in the short and medium period, although we do not exclude this possibility in the long term.

Notes

1 A previous and substantially different version of this book chapter was published in the journal *Comparative European Politics* (Volume 16, Issue 6, November 2018).
2 There are other potential cases that combine state-wide nationalism and minority nationalism (or regionalism), such as the Vlaams Belang, which is however rather different from our two cases. Unlike the Italian League and the Swiss League, the trajectory of Vlaams Belang has been shaped by a powerful and sustained cordon sanitaire, depriving it of the ideological and policy impact that our two cases have achieved thanks to their recurrent incorporation in government coalitions (Pauwels 2011).
3 Article 1 of the 2015 Statutes of the Northern League states: 'Lega Nord per l'Indipendenza della Padania (hereinafter referred to as "Lega Nord", "Lega Nord-Padania" or "Movimento") is a confederal political movement constituted in the form of an unrecognised association whose aim is to achieve the independence of Padania through democratic methods and its international recognition as an independent and sovereign Federal Republic'.
4 In November 2017, the statutes of the 'League for Salvini Premier' were officially registered (see *Gazzetta Ufficiale della Repubblica Italiana*, no. 292, 14.12.2017), although the former statutes of the League Nord still remain valid. Article 1 of the new statutes do not mention Padania: 'Lega per Salvini Premier is a confederal political movement constituted in the form of a non-recognised association which has the following aims: the peaceful transformation of the Italian State into a modern federal state through democratic and electoral methods. Lega per Salvini Premier promotes and supports freedom and the sovereignty of peoples at European level'.

References

Albertazzi, D., Giovannini, A. and Seddone, A. (2018) "No Regionalism Please, We are 'Leghisti!' the Transformation of the Italian Lega Nord under the Leadership of Matteo Salvini". *Journal of Regional and Federal Studies* 28(5): 645–671.

Albertazzi, D. 2006. The Lega dei Ticinesi: The Embodiment of Populism. *Politics* 26(2): 133–139.

Anckar, C. (2008) "On the Applicability of the Most Similar Systems Design and the Most Different Systems Design in Comparative Research". *International Journal of Social Research Methodology* 11(5): 389–401.

Arzheimer, K. and Carter, E. (2006) "Political Opportunity Structures and Right-Wing Extremist Party Success". *European Journal of Political Research* 45(3): 419–443.

Baume, M. D. L. and Borrelli, S. S. (2018) "Welcome to Europe's 'Club' for Populists". *Politico*, 10 September, www.politico.eu/article/euroskeptics-steven-bannon-mischael-modrikamenwelcome-to-europes-first-populist-club/.

Benford, R. and Snow, D. (2000) "Framing Processes and Social Movements: An Overview and Assessment". *Annual Review of Sociology* 26: 611–639.

Biorcio, R. and Natale, P. (2018) *Il Movimento 5 stelle: dalla protesta al governo*. Milano: Mimesis.

Bottel, M., Mazzoleni, O. and Pallaver, G. (2016) "Are Government Regionalist Parties Mainstream Parties? A Comparison between the Südtiroler Volkspartei, the Union Valdôtaine, and the Lega dei Ticinesi". *Contemporary Italian Politics* 8(2): 160–179.

Breuilly, J. (1993) *Nationalism and the State*. Manchester: Manchester University Press.

Brown, A. (2017) "The Dynamics of Frame-Bridging: Exploring the Nuclear Discourse in Scotland". *Scottish Affairs* 26(2): 194–211.

Caiani, M. and Conti, N. (2014) "In the Name of the People: The Euroscepticism of the Italian Radical Right". *Perspectives on European Politics and Society* 15(2): 183–197.

Chari, S. R., Suvi, I. and Kritzinger, S. (2004) "Examining and Explaining the Northern League 'U-Turn' from Europe". *Government and Opposition* 39(3): 423–450.

Christiansen, T. (1998) "Plaid Cymru: Dilemmas and Ambiguities of Welsh Regional Nationalism". In: De Winter, L. and Türsan, H. (eds.) *Regionalist Parties in Western Europe*. London: Routledge, pp. 125–142.

Connor, W. (1994) *Ethnonationalism. The Quest of Understanding*. Princeton: Princeton University Press.

Curcio, A. and Perini, L. (eds.) (2014) *Attraverso la Lega*. Bologna: Il Mulino.

De Cleen, B. (2017) "Populism and Nationalism". In: Rovira Kaltwasser, C., Taggart, A. P., Ochoa Espejo, P. and Ostiguy, P. (eds.) (2018) *The Oxford Handbook of Populism*. Oxford: Oxford University Press, pp. 342–362.

de la Torre, C. (ed.) (2019) *Routledge Handbook of Global Populism*. London and New York: Routledge.

De Lauretis, M. and Giussani, B. (1992) *La Lega dei Ticinesi: Indagine sul fenomeno che ha sconvolto il Ticino politico*. Locarno: Armando Dadò.

De Winter, L. and Gomez-Reino Cachafeiro, M. (2002) "European Integration and Ethnoregionalist Parties". *Party Politics* 8(4): 483–503.

Detterbeck, K. (2012) *Multilevel Party Politics in Western Europe*. New York: Palgrave MacMillan.

Elias, A. (2008) "From Euro-Enthusiasm to Euro-Scepticism? A Re-evaluation of Minority Nationalist Party Attitudes towards European Integration". *Regional and Federal Studies* 18(5): 557–581.

Franzi, A. and Madron, A. (2015) *Matteo Salvini, Il militante*. Firenze: Goware.

Gagnon, A.-G. and Keating, M. (eds.) (2012) *Political Autonomy and Divided Societies*. Basingstoke: Palgrave.

Gellner, E. (1983) *Nation and Nationalism*. London: Blackwell.

Giugni, M. (2009) "Political Opportunities: From Tilly to Tilly". *Swiss Political Science Review* 15(2): 361–367.

Gobbi, N. (2016) "Liberi e svizzeri, ricordiamocelo ogni giorno!". http://vais.ch/liberi-e-svizzeri-ricordiamocelo-ogni-giorno. Accessed 20 March 2018.

Gobbi, N. (2017) "La Svizzera è un paese libero …". 9 June, www.lega-dei-ticinesi.ch. Accessed 27 July 2017.

Gomez-Reino Cachafeiro, M. (2014) "European Integration and an Alternative Party Family: Regionalist Parties and the European Question". In: Gould, C. A. and Messina, M. A. (eds.) *Europe's Contending Identities. Supranationalism, Ethnoregionalism, Religion and New Nationalism*. Cambridge: Cambridge University Press, pp. 118–140.

Gross, D. (2016) "Is Globalization Really Fueling Populism?". Project Syndicate, 6 May, www.project-syndicate.org/

Harmsen, R. (2010) "Concluding Comment: On Understanding the Relationship between Populism and Euroscepticism". *Perspectives on European Politics and Society* 11(3): 333–341.

Harvie, C. (1994) *The Rise of Regional Europe*. London: Routledge.

Heinisch, R., Massetti, E. and Mazzoleni, O. (2018) "Populism and Ethno-Territorial Politics in European Multilevel Systems". *Comparative European Politics* 16(4): 923–936.

Heinisch, R. and Mazzoleni, O. (2017) "Analysing and Explaining Populism: Bringing Frame, Actor and Context Back". In: Reinhard, H., Holz-Bacha, C. and Mazzoleni, O. (eds.) *Political Populism. A Handbook*. Baden-Baden: Nomos, pp. 105–122.

Hellmann, O. (2011) *Political Parties and Electoral Strategy. The Development of Party Organization in East Asia*. London and New York: Palgrave MacMillan.

Hueglin, T. (1986) "Regionalism in Western Europe: Conceptual Problems of a New Political Perspective". *Comparative Politics* 18(4): 439–458.

Ignazi, P. (2006) *Extreme Right Parties in Western Europe*. Oxford: Oxford University Press.

Inglehart, R. F. and Norris, P. (2016) *Trump, Brexit, and the Rise of Populism: Economic Have-Nots and Cultural Backlash*. Kennedy School of Government, Harvard University, Faculty Research Working Paper Series.

Jolly, K. S. (2015) *The European Union and the Rise of Regionalist Parties*. Ann Harbor: University of Michigan Press.

Keating, M. (2003) "The Invention of Regions: Political Restructuring and Territorial Government in Western Europe". In: Brenner, N., Jessop, B., Jones, M. and MacLeod, G. (eds.) *State/Space: A Reader*. Oxford: Wiley-Blackwell, pp. 257–277.

Keating, M. (2013) *Rescaling the European State: The Making of Territory and the Rise of the Meso*. Oxford: Oxford University Press.

Keating, M. and Hooghe, L. (2006) "Bypassing the Nation-State: Regions and EU Process". In: Richardson, J. J. (ed.) *European Union: Power and Policy-Making*. London: Routledge, pp. 239–256.

Keating, M. and McGarry, J. (2001) *Minority Nationalism and the Changing International Order*. Oxford: Oxford University Press.

Kitschelt, H. (1986) "Political Opportunity Structures and Political Protest". *British Journal of Political Science* 16: 57–85.

Koopmans, R. and Olzak, S. (2004) "Discursive Opportunities and the Evolution of Right-Wing Violence in Germany". *American Journal of Sociology* 110: 198–230.

LT. (2015) "L'alleanza con l'UDC alle nazionali si può fare, a patto che …". 3 June, www.lega-dei-ticinesi.ch. Accessed 27 July 2017.

Madron, A. (2015) "Lega Nord, la base chiede ancora la secessione a Salvini: 'ok il consenso, ma non dimenticare il tuo popolo'". *Il Fatto Quotidiano*, 22 November.

Maggi, A. (2016) "Elezioni, Salvini perde voti a favore di Casapound e alza i toni". *Affari Italiani: Quotidiano Digitale*, www.affaritaliani.it/politica/lega-salvini-casapound-elezioni-421199.html?refresh_ce/ Accessed 20 April 2017.

Maspoli, F. (1992) "Chi vuole l'Europa?". *Il Mattino della Domenica*, 24 May.

Massetti, E. (2009) "Explaining Regionalist Party Positioning in a Multi-Dimensional Ideological Space: A Framework for Analysis". *Regional and Federal Studies* 19(4–5): 501–531.

Mazzoleni, O. (2005) "Multilevel Populism and Centre-Periphery Cleavage in Switzerland. The Case of the Lega dei Ticinesi". In: Mény, Y. and Caramani, D. (eds.) *Challenges to Consensual Politics: Democracy, Identity, and Populist Protest in the Alpine Region*. Bruxelles: PIE-Peter Lang, pp. 209–227.

Mazzoleni, O. (2016) "A Regionalist League in Southern Switzerland". In: Mazzoleni, O. and Mueller, S. (eds.) *Regionalist Parties in Western Europe. Dimensions of Success*. Abingdon and New York: Routledge, pp. 152–168.

Mazzoleni, O. (2017) *Les défis du régionalisme politique en Suisse. Le Tessin et ses relations avec Berne*. Geneva: Slatkine.

Mazzoleni, O. (2018) "Political Achievements, Party System Changes and Government Participation: The Case of the 'new' Swiss People's Party". In: Zaslove, A. and Wolinetz, S. (eds.) *Absorbing the Blow: Populist Parties and Their Impact on Parties and Party Systems*. Colchester: ECPR Press, pp. 83–102.

Mazzoleni, O. and Mueller, S. (2017) "Cross-Border Integration through Contestation? Political Parties and Media in the Swiss–Italian Borderland". *Journal of Borderlands Studies* 32(2): 173–192.

Mazzoleni, O., Rossini, C., Pilotti, A. and Debons, V. (2017) *Partecipazione, partiti, personalizzazioni e temi*. Lausanne: Les Cahiers de l'IEPHI.

Meyer, D. and Minkoff, D. (2004) "Conceptualizing Political Opportunity". *Social Forces* 82(4): 1457–1492.

Monforte, P. (2014) "The Cognitive Dimension of Social Movements' Europeanization Processes. The Case of the Protests against 'Fortress Europe'". *Perspectives on European Politics and Society* 15(1): 120–137.

Mudde, C. (2007) *Populist Radical Right Parties in Europe*. Cambridge: Cambridge University Press.

Passarelli, G. and Tuorto, D. (2018) *La Lega di Salvini. Estrema destra di governo*. Bologna: Il Mulino.

Pauwels, T. (2011) "Explaining the Strange Decline of the Populist Radical Right Vlaams Belang in Belgium: The Impact of Permanent Opposition". *Acta Politica* 46 (1): 60–82.

Przeworski, A. and Teune, H. (1970) *The Logic of Comparative Social Inquiry*. New York: John Wiley.

Quadri, L. (2017) "Amministrazione federale: njet alla preferenza indigena!". *Il Mattino della Domenica*, 5 March.

Rapisarda, A. (2015) *All'armi siam leghisti. Come e perché Matteo Salvini ha conquistato la Destra*. Roma: Aliberti Wingsbert House.

Rovira Kaltwasser, C., Taggart, A. P., Ochoa Espejo, P. and Ostiguy, P. (eds.) (2018) *The Oxford Handbook of Populism*. Oxford: Oxford University Press.

Rusconi, G. (1994) "Gegen die Tessiner 'Partitokratie'". In: Altermatt, U., Furrer, M., Gutknecht, B., Rusconi, G., Skenderovic, D. (eds.) *Rechte und Linke Fundamentaloppisition. Studien zur Schweizer Politik. 1965–1990*. Frankfurt am: Helbing & Lichtenhahn, pp. 154–173.

Ruzza, C. (2004) "The Northern League: Winning Arguments, Losing Influence". *Current Politics and Economics of Europe* 13(4): 309–34.

Ruzza, C. and Fella, S. (2009) *Re-Inventing the Italian Right: Territorial Politics, Populism and 'post-fascism'*. London: Routledge.

Salvini, M. (2017) "Salvini, Governo si fa prendere in giro dall'UE". 5 July, www.prpchannel.com/blog/salvini-governo-si-prendere-giro-dallue. Accessed 20 January 2017.

Salvini, M. (2018) "Matteo Salvini a Pontida. Il discorso integrale dal palco del raduno leghista". Bergamonews, 1 July.

Schmidt, V. A. (2008) "Discursive Institutionalism: The Explanatory Power of Ideas and Discourse". *Annual Review of Political Science* 11(1): 303–326.

Staff-Reporter. (2018a) "La Lega non ha dimenticato il federalismo". *Il Foglio*, 27 February.

Staff-Reporter. (2018b) "Scontro nella Lega, Maroni contro Salvini: trattato con metodi stalinisti". *Il Sole 24 Ore*, 11 January.

Staff-Reporter. (2018c) "Musumeci a Pontida alla festa della Lega: 'Senza Sud il Nord non va da nessuna parte': Il presidente della Regione Siciliana dal palco ha parlato di Mezzogiorno ma anche della perfetta intesa politica con il partito di Salvini". *La Sicilia*, 1 July.

Staff-Reporter. (2018d) "Le Pen fa i complimenti all'invidiato Salvini. E ricorda la caduta di Renzi, il Macron italiano". *Huffington Post*, 11 March.

Szczerbiak, A. and Taggart, P. (2008) *Opposing Europe: The Comparative Party Politics of Euroscepticism*. Vol. 2. Oxford: Oxford University Press.

Taggart, P. (2000) *Populism*. Buckingham: Open University Press.

Testa, T. (2018) "Ballottaggi, cadono le roccaforti rosse: Massa, Pisa e Siena al centrodestra, Imola ai 5 Stelle. Vola la Lega. M5S conquista Avellino". *La Repubblica*, 24 June.

Topaloff, L. K. (2012) *Political Parties and Euroscepticism*. Basingstoke: Palgrave.

Valentini, V. (2019) "L'autonomia delle regioni del nord in agonia", *Il Foglio*, 4 May.

Verney, S. (2012) *Euroscepticism in Southern Europe. A Diachronic Perspective*. New York: Routledge.

Vignati, R. (2018) *Elezioni Politiche 2018: le prime analisi sui flussi di voto. Il Pd cede voti al M5s e a Leu Nel Centro-nord, la Lega attrae voti pentastellati Al Sud, un M5s 'pigliatutti'*. Bologna, Istituto Carlo Cattaneo, www.cattaneo.org. accessed 25 January 2019.

Wax, E. (2018) "Matteo Salvini Mulls Bid for Commission Presidency". *Politico*, 18 October, www.politico.eu/article/matteo-salvini-commission-presidency-european-elections-2019-mulls-bid/

5

THE POPULIST DIMENSIONS OF CATALAN SECESSIONISM

Rhetoric, mobilization and institutional practices

Astrid Barrio, Oscar Barberà and Juan Rodríguez-Teruel

Introduction

The sudden increase of secessionist values and mobilization in Catalonia and their political consequences is indeed one the most shocking phenomenon of contemporary Spanish politics. This change has been expressed by transformations in both the supply (political parties, interest groups) and the demand (public opinion) sides of the Catalan political system. Since the mid-2000s, support for secessionism grew steadily, but the big turning point was in 2012 when this reached around 40 per cent of the population. This shift has unfolded in parallel to the emergence of new groups and to important changes in the political positions of several regionalist parties. The emergence of secessionism has redefined Catalan party politics producing polarization, several party splits, unseen political coordination strategies and, overall, a substantial transformation of the party system.

This chapter will provide evidence on how the adoption of secessionism by the main Catalan regionalist parties can be linked to a "populist drift" in their discourses that have also affected their mobilization strategies and institutional practices. Taking into account the major approaches to understand populism (Mudde 2004; Kriesi and Pappas 2015), we will illustrate in which ways this "populist drift" might be connected with some of the distinctive features of the populist discourse and its main varieties (Ivaldi, Lanzone and Woods 2017). Second, the chapter will explore how these grievances and new political discourses have been translated into mobilization practices (Burg 2015). Secessionist Catalan parties and interest groups have promoted a wide range of initiatives in order to keep the social mobilization going. And finally, we will analyze how this new populist discourse has also been translated into new institutional practices by both the regional executive and legislative powers. As it will be pointed out, some of these new initiatives have clashed with key liberal democratic principles and widened Spain's constitutional crisis.

In order to properly explore these phenomena, in the first section, a theoretical framework is developed. The second section provides a short overview of the Catalan case. The third part analyzes the linkages between Catalan secessionism and the populist discourse, which leads, in the fourth and fifth sections, to a proper examination of its quite successful mobilization efforts and new institutional practices. A short conclusion wraps up the article's main ideas.

Connecting populism with regionalism and exploring its political consequences

The study of populism has extensively analyzed how this phenomenon has spread in the last twenty years. Indeed, different approaches have allowed researchers to capture the specificities of several populist waves in Europe, the United States, and Latin America (e.g., Taggart 1995; van Kessel 2015). In Europe, populism has generally been associated with the radical right (e.g., Mudde 2007, 2016; Heinisch and Mazzoleni 2016) and linked to a clear nativist dimension (Betz 2017). Alternatively, some scholars have observed that new regionalist parties, such as the Lega Nord (LN) in Italy, have combined regional claims with populism, presenting a sort of "regionalist populism" (McDonnell 2006) and emphasizing economic grievances more than nativism. More recently, some new challenger parties with populist features have emerged in the Southern European countries as a consequence of the economic crisis (Bosco and Verney 2012; della Porta et al. 2017).

Following Mudde's definition, this article understands populism as

> an ideology that considers society to be ultimately separated into two homogeneous and antagonistic groups, 'the pure people' versus 'the corrupt elite', and which argues that politics should be an expression of the *volonté générale* (general will) of the people.
>
> *(Mudde 2004: 543)*

This approach points out four relevant features of the populist phenomenon: the existence of two homogeneous groups, the people and the elite; their political antagonism; the shared belief that sovereignty relies on the people; and a Manichean perspective that puts into opposition a positive idea of the people and a stigmatized view of the elites (Stanley 2008; Kriesi and Pappas 2015). In addition, several authors have recently stressed the relevance of populism's illiberal conception of democracy (Zakaria 1997), which mainly refers to the literal adherence to the government by the people and, hence, the repudiation of liberal checks and balances; the hostility towards intermediation and representative politics, while it claims for plebiscitary forms of democracy and direct links between the people and its leaders; and a monolithic view of the *volonté générale* that is hardly compatible with pluralism (Pappas 2014; Kriesi and Pappas 2015).

The literature has highlighted a strong relationship between nationalism and populism, particularly for the radical right (e.g. McGann and Kitschelt 1995; Mondon 2015; Heinisch, Massetti and Mazzoleni 2018). In this vein, nationalism, regionalism, and populism have been branded as thin ideologies that are easy to combine (e.g., Stanley 2008). Following the concepts mentioned above, there are at least two particular ways in which regionalism and populism might be mixed. The first one concerns the transformation of people-centrism into "the right to decide", placing an emphasis on people within a region as the true holders of sovereignty, who can express their will through plebiscitary forms of democracy. The second one adapts its anti-elitism to a multilevel dimension in order to oppose the regionalist demands imposed by the corrupt and/or Machiavellian manners of the state elites, hence opening up a debate on the legitimacy of the state institutions. The expression of this particular combination of ideologies might be purely rhetorical or, as in the Catalan case, it can also be carefully translated into political action through mobilization strategies.

There is, however, a lively debate on the links between regionalist parties and populism, as noted by Gómez-Reino (2002). Some academics point out the populist features of some regionalist movements like the Lega Nord (Biorcio 1991; Woods 1995). Mazzoleni (2003) has shown how regionalist parties may accommodate their populist rhetoric to a multilevel political environment, as illustrated by the Lega dei Ticinesi. Similarly, several studies on populism have generally used the Vlaams Blok as a case study (de Vos 2005). On the other hand, Diani (1992: 83) highlighted key differences between the two phenomena: populism has an anti-elitist appeal, while regionalism usually relies on local elites; charismatic leadership might be a facilitator for the rise of populism (Mudde and Rovira Kaltwasser 2013), but this is not necessarily the case for regionalism; and, finally, while populism is usually focused on external threats (e.g., foreigners), regionalism mostly embraces diversity. That is why the linkages among regionalism, populism, and nativism remain controversial; while some parties such as the Vlaams Blok might fit well into all these categories, others are mainly focused on the mobilization of political and economic issues and might barely qualify as populist (e.g., De Winter, Gómez-Reino and Lynch 2006).

On the other hand, Moffit and Tormey have recently suggested that populism might also be expressed through political styles defined as repertoires of performance that are used to create political relations (Moffitt and Tormey 2014: 7). When populists get in power, their political decisions seek the maintaining of power through the capture of political institutions to avoid being voted out (Taggart and Kaltwasser 2016; Chesterley and Roberti 2018). Thus, a populist move by regionalist parties is also expected to produce specific actions and styles in their collective action and their institutional behaviour, particularly when they are in government power. Hence, we are going to focus on the main grievances and features of the new secessionist discourse, how they have influenced the collective performances of populist supporters and affected their behaviours in the institutions.

The transformation of mainstream Catalan politics: from regionalism to secessionism

Catalonia is a Spanish region with high levels of self-government and a particular party system structured around the socio-economic and centre-periphery divides. Since the return of democracy (1977), moderation in the left-right divide and dual forms of identification either with Catalonia or Spain have been predominant (Botella 1998). Mainstream contemporary Catalan regionalism has been a wide phenomenon adopted by most of the Catalan parties and traditionally close to a civic-territorial ideal type of nation. The main aim of the movement has been the quest for more devolved powers and economic autonomy. In this sense, the preferred means of achieving these objectives have mostly been through negotiation (although not without conflicts) and pragmatism either within the Catalan parties or between the Catalan and the Spanish governments (Guibernau 2004). That said, even the most subjective forms of regional identification have added a cultural side linked with the use of the Catalan language. Class or birthplace differences (e.g., migrants from the rest of Spain) have traditionally been recognised but downplayed or subjected to assimilation efforts (Conversi 2000). Ethnic exclusivism or even violent forms of Catalan regionalism have been historically marginal. Correspondingly, the preference for outright secession has also been insignificant in Catalonia up until the 2010s (see Figure 5.1).

Since the late 1990s, most of these moderate features have changed: the centre-periphery divide gained relevance and competition amongst the Catalan parties increased (Barberà, Barrio and Rodríguez-Teruel 2011); the 2008 economic crisis and subsequent austerity policies altered key citizens' opinions and attitudes promoting a deep change in support for independence (see Figure 5.1), and a new rise in the outbidding competition (Barrio and Rodríguez-Teruel 2017); and some political scandals deepened the population's already low evaluation of political parties. As a result, new secessionist groups and political parties have emerged, and Catalan politics has been deeply transformed (Barrio, Barberà and Rodríguez-Teruel 2018)

The rest of this section is devoted to analyzing the main groups and political parties involved in the transformation of Catalan regionalism into a new secessionist movement. In this respect, Omnium Cultural and the newly created Assemblea Nacional Catalana (National Catalan Assembly, ANC) have been two of its most prominent players. Omnium Cultural is a group set up in 1961 as a platform to promote the Catalan language and culture during the Francoist regime. The group relevance substantially decreased since the 1980s because most of its aims were developed by the Catalan regional government. However, since the late 2000s Omnium started to actively denounce Catalonia's economic grievances and, later on, to promote secessionist ideas. Since 2012, Omnium has received the support of the ANC, a new group formed with secessionist members of several regionalist parties. As the chapter will show later on, both groups have been instrumental in the secessionist movement's adoption of a new discourse and repertoire of protest, and in the success of its massive mobilization efforts.

92 Astrid Barrio et al.

FIGURE 5.1 Attitudes and opinions on politicians, parties, and government

Another key actor in the mainstream adoption of the Catalan secessionism was Convergència Democràtica de Catalunya (Democratic Convergence of Catalonia, CDC). CDC was a moderate regionalist party that, in the late 1970s, formed a long-lasting alliance with Unió Democràtica de Catalunya (Democratic Union of Catalonia, UDC) a small Christian Democratic party. The alliance was called Convergència i Unió (Convergence and Union, CiU) and, through

CDC's party leader Jordi Pujol, was in charge of the regional government between 1980 and 2003. Although CiU accessed the regional government, by 2010 the alliance's hard stance on austerity policies, the emergence of some corruption scandals and the swift change in the pro-independentist public opinion mood led to radical changes in both the alliance and the party. Along with other parties, by the 2010s CDC promoted the emergence of Catalan economic grievances with the campaign "Spain steals from us". By 2012, CDC decided to actively join, with UDC's reluctance, the ANC's first secessionist efforts.

After the 2012 snap elections, CiU formed a new minority government with the parliamentary support of Esquerra Republicana de Catalunya (Catalonia's Republican Left, ERC). ERC was a left regionalist party founded in 1931 that was in charge of the regional government during the 1930s. The party hardly recovered after the Francoist regime and didn't come back to power till the 2000s in coalition with the Catalan socialists. Many ERC supporters got disappointed by the content of the Statute Reform promoted by the regional government, which led to several party splits. Many of the splitting ERC party elites joined smaller groups promoting secessionism, which forced the party to embrace stronger stances on this issue after its defeat in the 2010 Catalan elections. By the end of 2012, ERC and CiU had contested the regional elections with pro-secessionist platforms, that is why both parties agreed to call for an independence referendum in November 2014.

Shortly after the 2014 referendum simulation (see below), UDC held an internal consultation in order to decide whether to continue supporting the secessionist movement. The faction opposing independence won by a slim margin, which led to UDC exiting the regional government, a deep party split, and the end of the CiU alliance. UDC decided to contest the approaching 2015 regional elections, but it was not able to secure representation which led to the death of the party. On the other hand, UDC's secessionist faction promoted a new party called Demòcrates de Catalunya (Catalonia's Democrats, DC). The DC joined the secessionist alliance Junts pel Sí (Together for the Yes, JxSí) with CDC and ERC for the 2015 regional snap elections and secured two seats. In that election, JxSí got the explicit support of the main secessionist groups and won a plurality of the seats.

However, all secessionist parties received less than 50 per cent of the votes in what was seen as a plebiscitary election on independence. In addition, JxSí needed additional parliamentary support in order to form a government. That support came from the Candidatura d'Unitat Popular (Popular Unity Candidature, CUP), a newly formed far left and secessionist party that made its breakthrough in the 2012 regional elections. In exchange for the CUP's support, JxSí had to replace its leadership from Artur Mas to the newly elected regional prime minister, Carles Puigdemont. The end of Mas leadership also led to CDC rebranding itself into the newly Partit Demòcrata Europeu Català (Catalan European Democratic Party, PDeCAT). Puigdemont committed himself to a new independence referendum by October 2017. The referendum was preceded by a huge expectation, the approval of some highly controversial laws and by several efforts of the Spanish government to stop it. That forced Puigdemont's government to co-organize it with several secessionist groups and to transform it into a new referendum simulation.

After the 1 October 2017 referendum simulation and the 27 October Declaration of Independence, the relations between the Spanish and the Catalan governments became truly strained. In the end, the Spanish government dismissed the Catalan one, sued its members and called for a snap regional election on 21 December 2017. Puigdemont and other regional ministers fled to Brussels while others were arrested and jailed. The elections indeed took place in an exceptional climate of polarization. That said, no joint candidatures were agreed upon for either side. ERC formed an alliance with DC and some former socialist members. Puigdemont formed a list of so-called Junts per Catalunya (Together for Catalonia, JxCAT) composed of many independents, namely being the ANC leader and several members of the PDeCAT. The call reached unprecedented mobilization on both sides. The winner was Ciudadanos (Citizens), an openly anti-secessionist party. However, the secessionist side (JxCAT, ERC and the CUP) achieved a majority of seats. Since Puigdemont was banned from forming a government, after some months, JxCAT and ERC were able to secure the support of the CUP and to select a new regional prime minister, Joaquim Torra.

Populist features of the secessionist discourse

This section will analyze how Catalan secessionist parties and pressure groups have used some key rhetorical arguments that were closely connected with the main dimensions and varieties of the populist discourse. Our analysis will be based on several documents released since 2012 (party platforms, electoral campaign material, working papers) and press sources reporting on their political initiatives (interviews, in-depth press reports, etc.)

The classical populist opposition between the people and the elite (e.g., Mény and Surel 2000) has been adapted to pit the good and naïve Catalan people against the oppressive and corrupt Spanish State. This general argument is presented under different guises. In a broad sense, the external adversary of the Catalan people is usually defined as the Spanish political class, identified with a widely Machiavellian and corrupt political system in the hands of a small bureaucratic and economic elite, and supported by the Spanish media (including the main journals and TV networks). Occasionally, those Catalan politicians (usually linked to state-wide political parties) and influential interest groups in Catalonia who are opposed to the secessionist movement (particularly the Catalan business elite) are also presented as an internal adversary.[1] That might suggest the use of some kind of "multi-level populist" arguments (Mazzoleni 2003). In any of these alternative versions, the Catalan people always become the subject suffering oppression from the corrupt elites,[2] and the Catalan government appears to be powerless to stop them. Following this argument, the claim for a new state would be the natural reaction of the Catalan people against the Spanish establishment. The reasons underlying the opposition between the Catalan people and the Spanish state and its elites are often expressed with arguments of moral superiority, aiming to make the secessionist claim a moral cause for everyone.[3]

Another paradigmatic example of these arguments is illustrated by the longterm debate over fiscal grievances summarized under the slogan "Espanya ens roba" ("Spain steals from us"), which became the battle cry of the independence campaign with the 2008 economic downturn and, more particularly, with the failed negotiations in the early 2010s over a new fiscal deal for Catalonia (Dowling 2014: 229). As stated above, comparative grievances are not new in Catalonia or Spain. However, these ideas were, for a long time, a common feature of minor left-wing secessionist parties, and their inclusion by the regional mainstream ERC or centre-right parties such as CDC constituted a main change in their rhetoric. Since the 2010s, statements like "the subsidized Spain is living from the productive Catalonia" or "Spain steals from us" have been some of the mottos employed by ERC and CiU in their electoral messages.[4] A relevant added feature of these campaigns has to do with the bad manners and mocking political style (Moffitt and Tormey 2014) in which they were presented.

Another of the central pleas of the Catalan secessionist movement is the call to follow the people's will. Although other minor parties previously made a claim for a referendum, ERC was the first regional mainstream party to include the plebiscite as a central demand at the 2010 Catalan elections. After a massive demonstration in September 2012, CDC also took up this request. The emphasis on the "right to decide" or the "will of the people" was obvious in CDC's electoral motto at the 2012 Catalan elections (see Figure 5.2). Since then, the secessionist movement has defended the idea that only a referendum and plebiscitary elections would allow for such political expression of the people's will, to the detriment of political representation and other kinds of consociational arrangements. The plebiscite has become the moral principle under the idea that "democracy is principally counting votes". That is why both Catalan referendum simulations, on 9 November 2014 and 1 October 2017, were maintained despite being declared null and unconstitutional by the Constitutional Court some weeks before (see next section). A similar situation happened with polemical moves such as the alleged declaration of independence on 27 October 2017.

Furthermore, an appeal is made to the people as the ultimate source of legitimacy (e.g. Canovan 2005: 80; Kriesi and Pappas: 2015). This raises an opposition between legitimacy and legality, which has been exploited to confront the legal arguments permanently presented by the Spanish institutions. As the Spanish government has rejected the negotiation of terms and conditions for a legal referendum on secession beyond the current constitutional framework, the Catalan secessionist movement has continued to insist on the lack of legitimacy of those public institutions. Hence, the legal resistance of the Spanish institutions to accept unilateral secession may be defeated by the moral legitimacy that the

FIGURE 5.2 "The will of the people" CDC poster for the 2012 regional election

international community would give to the Catalan cause. Recently, the opposition between legitimacy and legality has achieved new and increasing importance as some relevant Catalan representatives have been found guilty of disobeying the Constitutional Court (CC) after sidestepping its orders regarding the referendum simulation held in November 2014 and October 2017 (see next section). In this context, secessionist political leaders have repeatedly insisted on their will to disobey any legal requirement that would contradict the popular mandate.[5] As the ERC's spokesman in the national low chamber stated, "If we are imprisoned, we will be released by the Catalan people" (Del Riego 2016). In the same vein, the ERC party leader and regional deputy (Nació Digital 2014) prime minister, Oriol Junqueras, has argued that "voting is a right that prevails over any law" That was the same argument that led to the controversial results of the so-called 2017 Catalan referendum and the even more polemical declaration of independence. After the 2017 elections and the problems to select a viable would-be candidate to the regional premiership, the president of the Catalan Parliament stated, after Puigdemont's arrest by the German police, that "Puigdemont is president by the free, sovereign and democratic decision of the Catalan voters expressed through the Parliament. No judge, government or public official has the legitimacy to dismiss, nor prosecute the president of all Catalans" (El Punt Avui 2018) These statements seem to imply an illiberal version of democracy where the rule of law and the separation of powers are presented as a trade-off with democracy, and where a monolithic conception of the people's will could eventually harm minority rights (Kriesi 2014).

The predominance of the popular will unsurprisingly entails and accepts praise for the unity of the people. This idea of a nation expressing a unified voice and seeking a common goal is shared by regionalism and populism. At its extremes, however, this might lead to dismissal, if not denial, of the division of interests and pluralism within society. It might also involve a rejection of the legitimacy of either the external or internal opponents because they are not merely political actors with different priorities or views on the Catalan issue, but adversaries to the people's will (Mudde 2004). Hence, in this Manichean confrontation of ideologies, secession is the only fair outcome of the process, and any other option or compromise would harm the people's interest. This helps to explain the strong polarization of Catalan politics during the last years, as any non-supporter of the secessionist movement has actually been considered an anti-secessionist actor.[6] In this vein, political parties have occasionally been suspicious of dividing the unity of the people and, hence, becoming an obstacle for secession.[7] Independent, nonpartisan politicians or activists from secessionist interest groups such as the ANC or Omnium Cultural have eventually been seen as more reliable agents than party members. Similarly, from time to time these groups have acted as brokers (Heaney 2010) and have been instrumental in promoting initiatives to bring parties, interest groups, and institutions together, and in restoring the unity and cohesion of the movement (see next section).

The judicialization of the process has led to the implied political prosecution of all the Catalan people. The President of the Catalan Parliament recently stated: "the thirst for vengeance of the Spanish State is never-ending (...). Through these actions the State is not only persecuting people, it is also kidnapping the will of the Catalan people expressed through the ballots". According to this argument, secession is portrayed as a just cause linked to democracy and human rights. And any dissent might automatically be portrayed as non-democratic.

Likewise, the aim of keeping national unity has downgraded other traditional political divisions in the party competition, particularly the left-right cleavage. Although, once again, these are shared ideas between regionalism and populism, they resemble Laclau's arguments that populism tends to downplay the left-right divide and turn it into a new logic dominated by the fight for hegemony (Laclau 2005). In this sense, Catalan regionalist parties and interest groups have long considered the left-right divide as a threat to the unity of the movement and its mobilization potential, particularly in times of crisis. In order to overcome the social debate, two main arguments have been presented. On the one hand, secession has strong social content, as independence will provide sufficient economical tools to solve most of Catalan's social and economic problems. This was the explicit argument behind the 2014 campaign "Ara és l'hora" ("Now is the time"), with several mottos such as "We want ice cream for dessert everyday" and "A country where it only rains on school days", among others, meaning that there will be no limits on the people's will after Independence Day. On the other hand, people must focus on the national question, not on social issues, as the latter will favour the status quo and will erode Catalan national aspirations. That is why several calls for dismissing the left-right divide have been made during this time. As a Catalan government spokesman stated, "the left-right debate makes us Spaniards and subordinate" to Spain (Bassas 2014). In the same vein, regional prime minister Artur Mas has often argued, as he did on 16 June 2015, that "independence is neither left-wing nor right-wing, it is for everybody".[8] The CUP's (a left-wing party) support of Carles Puigdemont (member of a liberal party such as CDC) is also an evidence of the secondary relevance of the left-right divide.

Populism and political mobilization

This section will highlight the links between the main grievances, the core arguments behind the discourse of the Catalan secessionist parties and groups (unity of the Catalan people, the right to decide, etc.), and their mobilization efforts. The repertoire ranges from the classical modes of performance (electoral mobilization, mass demonstrations) to new societal forms such as referenda simulations.

Massive demonstrations

From the 1980s until the 2000s, demonstrations in favour of independence were testimonial. However, for the secessionist movement, massive demonstrations have been a key instrument to reinforce the messages of unity and further spread those of defiance towards a Spanish state that supposedly denies or ignores the democratic right to decide. In this sense, they have become an icon and a practical representation of the whole people of Catalonia, in contrast to the Spanish political elites. This is why they also have given much relevance to the figures of participants, to mirror the idea of "millions" of citizens marching for the aim.[9]

A big turning point in the process of secessionist mobilization was the 2010 rally after the Constitutional Court (CC) ruling annulling several articles of the reformed Catalan Statute of Autonomy of 2006 and (as pointed out below), which ruling was widely interpreted as a strong political grievance. The polarization and media attention over this issue in both Catalonia and Spain, the disputed legitimacy of the CC members, and the watering down of key aspects of the reform (e.g. Catalonia's definition as a nation) led to a massive demonstration of hundreds of thousands of people organized by Omnium Cultural and supported by all Catalan parties except the PP and Ciudadanos. The slogan "We are a nation, we decide", however, was still ambiguous on the issue of independence. Shortly after the 2010 rally, the political debate quickly shifted towards the economic crisis, and Catalan parties focused on preparations for the upcoming 2010 Catalan regional elections.

The ANC inception in 2012 made a huge impact on the secessionist movement. The ANC was instrumental in reframing the economic crisis as a new step in the centre-periphery conflict, and it called, with the support of other groups such as OC, for a big demonstration on 11 September 2012 with the unambiguously pro-independence slogan "Catalonia, new European State". Both groups then organized all types of meetings at the local level and through social media to support the demonstration. The event received a significant amount of media attention mostly because some regionalist parties unsuccessfully tried to downgrade or change its main aim. At the end, the rally was supported by some but not all regionalist parties, which caused disagreements within the moderate ones such as the Socialists. The peaceful demonstration held in Barcelona gathered hundreds of thousands of individuals. One year later, by September 2013, the ANC and other secessionist groups emulated the human chain organized in 1989 in the Baltic states. In an extraordinary display of strength, the groups successfully organized a 400 km human chain from tip to tip of Catalonia and gathered hundreds of thousands of people in favour of secession. The event captured major international and regional media attention (Crameri 2015).

Since 2014, the demonstrations slightly changed their orientation and became more in line with the aims of the main secessionist parties. They were called in order to mobilise support for the referendum simulations promoted by the Catalan government (2014 and 2017) or for the regional elections (2015). Despite a slight decrease of people attending the secessionist demonstrations, they still represented symbols of unity and determination. In addition, following the October 2017 referendum, the separatist movement held two partially successful general strikes, one supported by the regional government, and the other organized by a minor secessionist union without the support of the main labour organizations. Since the 2017 referendum, the mobilization has been focused on the liberation of all the leading figures arrested. The main grievances are now based on Spain's violations of Human Rights, the country's lack of democratic quality and its ineffective division of powers.

Referendum simulations

The mass mobilization repertoire of the Catalan secessionist movement has also introduced new performances, the main novelty being the introduction of referendum simulations, an initiative that was firstly at the local level between 2009 and 2011 (Vilaregut 2012; Muñoz and Guinjoan 2013).[10] At the regional level, the two more relevant simulations were held on 9 November 2014 and 1 October 2017, which are notably known through media and political news as 9-N and 1-O, respectively.

The 9 November 2014 consultation was attended by 2,344,828 people (under 40 per cent of the population), 1,897,271 of whom voted yes to Catalonian independence. This nonbinding vote had a low turnout but was deemed a success by the regional media. 1 October 2017 the participation rate was 43 per cent (2,266,498) of the population, with 2,044,038 voting yes (92 per cent). Moreover, the organization of this referendum also relied on a wide and new repertoire of protest: volunteers occupied a vast number of schools where the voting was to take place, and people safeguarded and secured ballot boxes and other electoral material (ballots), etc. However, the most widely disseminated actions constituted passive resistance of many activists and voters trying to block the police operations; with the resulting police charges, several people were wounded.

Like massive demonstrations, referendum simulations highlight the expression of the people's voice but also take the argument a step forward: as expressions of civil disobedience they force the Spanish institutions to intervene, hence stressing the already stated clash between the (legitimate) general will of the Catalan people against the "corrupt", "violent", "repressive" Spanish (illegitimate) law. This has been made even more obvious when some Catalan representatives have been sentenced by the courts for leading and organizing such events.

Electoral mobilization

Catalan political parties and secessionist groups have also tried to transform electoral competition into a broader campaign for independence. Hence, they have presented recent elections in a plebiscitarian mode in order to facilitate the expression of the people about their future as a nation against the oppression of the Spanish institutions. Their efforts have not always been successful. At the level of national, European, and local elections, this plebiscitarian mode was weakened by other political dynamics. That was also the case with the 2010 regional elections, when the economic crisis became one of the most predominant issues despite the efforts of other minor secessionist parties.

The 2012 regional campaign was the first occasion that revolved around secessionist issues, as two of the main regionalist parties – CiU and ERC – suggested proposals for self-determination. However, the 2012 campaign was also centred on CiU's implementation of harsh austerity policies to overcome the economic crisis. The 2015 and 2017 regional votes were more successful attempts to transform a regular election into a sort of plebiscite on independence. The 2015 campaign was preceded by the aim of forging a single candidature with all secessionist parties and key interest groups such as the ANC and Omnium Cultural. Although that proved not to be possible, an electoral agreement was built between CDC, ERC, and other secessionist parties and interest groups under the name Junts pel Sí (Together for the Yes, JxSí). That candidature did succeed in framing the election as an exceptional event with just two sides (Medina, Barrio and Rodríguez-Teruel 2016). However, these efforts were distorted by the presence of other regionalist parties such as the Socialists and Catalunya Sí Que Es Pot (Catalonia Yes We Can) defending self-determination, but not independence. The 2017 campaign presented very similar dynamics but was affected by the exceptional consequences of the events that occurred in the previous weeks (referendum simulation, Declaration of Independence, arrest of leading secessionist figures) and also featured a division between the two major secessionist parties, ERC and the PDeCAT alliance, the so called Junts per Catalunya (Together for Catalonia, JxCAT). Both the 2015 and 2017 elections registered the highest turnout rate since the 1980s, but the results were somehow controversial: the secessionist parties did not achieve 50 per cent of the votes although they kept a narrow (absolute) majority in seats, a constant in the Catalan parliament since 1984.

Populism and institutional behaviour

Like the previous section, this one will point out the links between the main arguments of the Catalan secessionist parties and groups, and their institutional behaviour, the latter being defined as the main practices and actions taken by these political actors in order to achieve the goals stated through their rhetoric.

Local level

One of the first attempts to build and show institutional consensus on secession at the local level was the forging of the Association of Towns for the Independence (AMI) by 2011. This interest group brought together 787 out of 947 Catalan local councils and other supra-municipal institutions. So far, however, some of the most relevant cities, such as Barcelona, have not been represented. The AMI has recently promoted the so-called "Assembly of Elected Representatives", aimed to work as an alternative Catalan legislature in case the regional MPs were to be barred from office by the Constitutional Court in the final steps of secession. So far, the "Assembly of Elected Representatives" has never met.

Parliamentary and governmental actions

As stated above, since 2012, several secessionist initiatives have been launched at the regional level aiming to show that both the legislative and the executive powers were taking steps towards secession. In addition, Catalan secessionist leaders have tended to behave with a populist political style characterized by acting decisively and urgently, favouring short-term and swift decisions that responded to the "historical moments" or "critical junctures" that Catalan people were facing (Moffitt and Tormey 2014: 391–392). Their institutional actions have also aimed to stress the connections with the grassroots secessionist movement and, more broadly, with the people, through collective decisions mirroring unity and internal cohesiveness. "National agreements" and "declarations" have usually been the tools to express these actions and goals.

One of the first initiatives of the newly formed Catalan government was the 2013 creation of the Advisory Council for the National Transition (ACNT), a new agency conceived to draft proposals and reports in order to organize the 2014 Independence Referendum and take the following steps towards independence. The ACNT drafted 19 reports written by several renewed social scientists, lawyers and economists that were included in the so-called *White Book for the Catalan National Transition*. This *White Book* analyzed different scenarios and suggested different institutional paths toward Independence, and also was instrumental in framing the political debates of the following years.

Another institutional initiative was the National Pact for the Right to Decide (NPRD), a political forum promoted by the regional government in order to merge together political parties, local councils, civil society groups and to legitimize the 2014 Independence Referendum. This initiative was joined, among others, by: several parties such as CDC, UDC, ICV, EUiA and the CUP; several business-firm organizations and Chambers of Commerce[11]; Trade unions such as CCOO, UGT, USOC, Unió de Pagesos; several local level associations such as the previously stated Association of Towns for the Independence or the Catalan Association of Towns; some provincial governments and individual councils; or some civil society groups such as the Third Sector Board, the Federation Catalan Pupils' Parents, Omnium Cultural, the ANC; and cultural institutions such as the Institute for Catalan Studies. Collecting a wide range of institutional and civil society support was instrumental in highlighting the idea that the "right to decide" and the 2014 Independence Referendum had massive support and consensus. By 2016, the National Pact for the Right to Decide transformed itself into the National Pact for the Referendum in order to do the same with the new 2017 Independence Referendum.

Beyond these advisory initiatives, the Catalan government – with the support of the regional parliament – have also taken more serious steps towards the disobedience of the Spanish institutions and, more particularly, to the Constitutional Court rulings. All these steps have, of course, been immediately banned by the Constitutional Court itself. As stated before (see previous sections), all these initiatives have been justified with the argument that the will of the people and, more generally, democracy is above the Spanish law.

One of the more relevant disobedience actions was the organization of the 2014 referendum simulation. The event was held after the Spanish parliament formally denied any possibility of the Catalan region to hold any kind of (binding or nonbinding) referendum on Independence. The Catalan Parliament then decided to pass a law on referendums and public consultations that was partially suspended by Spain's Constitutional Court. The Catalan government then shifted to organizing a nonbinding referendum simulation that upset ERC and the ANC. In order to avoid its suspension, the consultation was formally called by the government but organized with the assistance of 40,000 volunteers. The Catalan government denied any real participation in the process, but this was a highly contested issue. That is why this nonbinding consultation was also suspended by the Constitutional Court. In a controversial move, the Catalan government decided then to disobey the CC ruling and proceed with the consultation. In the wake of the consultation, all parties and secessionist groups actively campaigned to mobilise the population to attend the referendum simulation. The active opposition of the Spanish government and the resultant media attention favoured the mobilization.[12] By early 2017, the former regional prime minister and other regional ministers were barred from office for two years and fined with a burdensome fee for their disobedience to the Constitutional Court ruling.[13]

By 2016, the Declaration of Sovereignty made by the Catalan Parliament was also a new step toward the open defiance of the Constitutional Court. One of the main points of that Declaration was indeed the future disobedience to the

Constitutional Court's rulings. That law was not only ruled out, but also got the Board of the Catalan Parliament to trial for disobedience. The sentence has not been issued yet.

The referendum on 1 October 2017 followed a similar process, although there were also some relevant differences. The main one was its formal nature, as the coalition government (formed by CDC and ERC) decided to conduct the process in a legalistic manner, aiming to produce a binding vote. By September 2017, the Catalan parliament passed the Referendum Bill and the Juridical Transition Bill, from the Spanish Law to the Catalan Law. Although both laws were approved without the presence of any opposition party and were later on ruled unconstitutional by the CC, they were framed as evidence of secessionist unity and determination against the Spanish state. They were also presented as responses to the "democratic mandate" given by the people in the regional elections. Despite the Constitutional Court having also declared this referendum unconstitutional, the vote was finally held although, in some voting precincts, it was amid police repression due to several protests from supporters. The judicial consequences of the 2017 referendum will probably be very harsh but are yet to be seen.

Internationalization

Since 2012, one of the main aims of the Catalan government has been to disseminate information and frame the international perception of the Catalan problem in order to win new supports within the international arena. In order to better promote this objective, in 2013 a new agency was built, the DIPLOCAT (short for Catalan Diplomacy). The main aim of the Diplocat was to promote international relations despite this being an exclusive prerogative of the central government. The night of the 9-N (9 November 2014), the DIPLOCAT organized an unofficial press conference inviting several international media outlets and causing great annoyance with the Spanish government. After the 2015 elections, the DIPLOCAT agency was transformed into a proper department of the Catalan government led by a senior member of the regional cabinet. This department led several road-shows with an approximate cost of around 30 million euros. The day of the official referendum 1-O (1 October 2017), the Catalan government once again organized an unofficial press conference with national and international media.

The international mobilization efforts have been emphasized since the referendum simulation. The Catalan government successfully framed the police intervention of the 1-O as a violent repression of the Spanish State against the Catalan people. Puigdemont's move to Brussels, the heart of the EU, was conceived as a way to attract international media attention to the Catalan conflict. Puigdemont also organized several lectures in different EU countries to intentionally foster international attention. It was actually after one of these lectures in Finland that the former regional prime minister was arrested in Germany. For the same reason, several other senior members of the Catalan government and leading figures of the Catalan secessionist movement have also fled to Scotland and Switzerland.

Despite all these efforts, the EU countries have all insisted that this is an internal affair. And after the Declaration of Independence of 27 October 2017, none of them recognised Catalonia as a sovereign State. So far, most of the international support of the Catalan secessionist movement is limited to unofficial statements from politicians of several parties, most of them populist ones.

Conclusions

This chapter aimed to illustrate a case where mainstream regionalist parties and groups, in a context of increasing political and economic dissatisfaction, can adopt populist strategies, particularly when this fosters the perception of both old and new grievances. We elucidated this argument with the case of the Catalan secessionist movement, focusing on the "populist drift" and the changes in the political discourse of the main regionalist parties and groups, and then linking that to their repertoire of collective actions and institutional behaviours.

Our first main point stressed the evolution from a traditional, pragmatic, regionalist discourse towards a new populist rhetoric characterized by several important traits: the opposition of the Catalan people to the Spanish state and its political class; a constant appeal to the will of the Catalan people; an emphasis on direct and plebiscitary forms of democracy; and the predominance of popular legitimacy against legality (leading eventually to civil disobedience). Our second main point highlighted how the secessionist movement has adapted mobilization strategies to reflect the new populist rhetoric and to display the firm determination of the Catalan people to exercise their "right to decide". Hence, the populist message has been reflected in several massive demonstrations, referendum simulations, the attempt to transform elections into plebiscitary votes, and the adoption of a populist style at the institutional level. Finally, our third point has also tried to point out the steps taken by the Catalan secessionist parties through the regional executive and legislative powers to express their defiance and disobedience to the rule of law and, more particularly, to the Constitutional Court rulings. This approach has shown an illiberal perspective on democracy, to the detriment of both liberal checks and balances and the representative mechanisms linking voters and institutions.

However, as in other cases of populist parties, the Catalan secessionist movement displays other features that do not easily fit within the populist framework. Hence, the public discourse of the main Catalan secessionist parties and organizations can hardly be identified with anti-immigration issues or explicit nativist claims – to mention just two issues often associated with populism as manifested in other countries and regions. Unsurprisingly, the definition of the "Catalan people" is often vague and blurred, as any attempt to set boundaries to define political or ethnical boundaries has become highly controversial and counter-productive for this secessionist movement. Although the opposition between Catalonia and Spain has occasionally led some partisans to dismiss those Catalan voters who do not support independence (especially those born in the rest of Spain), considering them simply as non-Catalan, "invaders", or outsiders,[14] such statements have usually been disapproved by the party leaders. The main threat to the Catalan people is essentially posed by the Spanish establishment and its elites, not by other levels of governance (as, for instance, the EU) or by people from other countries. However, "euroscepticism" started to emerge after the lack of support for the October 2017 declaration of independence that was displayed by EU institutions and European governments.[15]

Moreover, the leadership in the Catalan secessionist movement can hardly be represented solely by a charismatic leading figure, despite the attempts by some party leaders to perform as the main representatives of the whole movement. These attempts have usually been contained by the tendency toward collective leadership emerging from both the political parties and key interest groups such as the ANC. Nevertheless, the evolution of the process during 2017 contributed to reinforce the personalization around Puigdemont, especially after his escape to Brussels and the making of the personal candidature for the regional election in December 2017.

Similarly, the potential illiberal threat is not present in the real day-to-day life of the Catalan regional institutions. Still, some parliamentary or executive decisions aiming to promote a binding referendum of independence have aimed to break with the constitutional framework. Although they can hardly be qualified as anti-democratic, they pose legitimate doubts about their liberal nature. Indeed, the legislation passed in September 2017 calling for the referendum and organizing a new institutional framework, afterwards included some controversial aspects considered contradictory to liberal values.[16]

In the end, this shift of Catalan politics poses questions as to what extent this rhetoric – based as it is on grievances, the will of the people, and opposition to the Spanish state and its elites – is an inherent feature of populism or is a new (and more radical) form of nationalism or regionalism. Does all regionalism contain a hidden populist dimension ready to emerge, or does it sometimes simply comprise phenomena that converge under quite specific circumstances? The Catalan case seems to be closer to the second answer, but there is definitely a need for more research to be carried out in this area.

Notes

1 In the last speech of the 2017 regional campaign, Marta Rovira, ERC's secretary general, asked for the vote against those who put Oriol Junqueras in jail, namely "the Catalan establishment, the elite, the oligopolis, and the Spanish government".
2 In his speech two weeks before the 2014 referendum simulation, Artur Mas identified Mariano Rajoy (Spain's prime minister) as the "real opponent and powerful" enemy of the Catalan people. This idea has been rephrased several times. Mas has also presented CDC as the true party "fighting against the powerful".

3 It is a commonplace to compare the allegedly higher amount of corruption in the rest of Spain to its lower levels in Catalonia. Carme Forcadell, leader of the ANC, stated that "it is true we have corrupted politicians in Catalonia – something which is employed [by our adversaries] to erode our self-esteem – but there are many more in Spain, so do not pay attention to those that are employing the issue against us" (Sallés 2013).
4 Although Catalonia is a developed region, most of these arguments indeed resemble the ones from internal colonialism theories (Hetcher 1975).
5 Declaration of the Initiation of the Process of Independence of Catalonia, approved by the Catalan parliament on 9 November 2015.
6 Junqueras stated, "the enemies of freedom and democracy are those who fight to prevent Catalonia to hold a vote to decide its future" (Regió 7 2013)
7 After being forced to resign as prime minister, Mas warned about the role of political parties, as they were likely to get involved in internal fights and competition, becoming an obstacle for the secession. (Diari de Girona 2016)
8 www.president.cat/pres_gov/AppJava/president/notespremsa/285087/president-mas-independencia-desquerres-dretes.html, Accessed 2 January 2019
9 In fact, figures about participants have always been very controversial, as different sources have given highly fluctuating estimates. For instance, at the 2012 demonstration, the organisers reported 2 million attendees and the regional police estimated 1.5 million, while the national police and some nonpartisan sources reduced the amount to 600,000 or even lower.
10 The first initiative was held in Premià de Mar in 2009 and then was replicated in several other Catalan towns and cities until 2011. The nonbinding vote on independence was supported first by the local representatives and then organized by an interest group called Platform for the Right . This initiative was not accepted in all Catalan towns, and the participation rates were also highly asymmetrically distributed. It is estimated that around 800,000 people participated in all of them. The last and more important of these was the one held in Barcelona a few weeks before the 2011 local elections. Although 240,000 people supported independence, the overall participation rate was very low (around 18 per cent).
11 All 13 Catalan commerce Chambers and business-firm organizations such as CECOT, FEPIME, AMEC, PIMEC, FemCAT and the Federaton of business-firms from Girona displayed their support to this initiative through the so-called Manifest del Far (The Lighthouse Manifesto) signed 8 May 2014.
12 The results provided by the regional government may be consulted at www.participa2014.cat. The level of turnout is an estimate by the media, as the government never provided results of the turnout.
13 After the trial, Mas stated that "In the Spanish state, the law is not the same for everybody" (The Guardian 2017).
14 As stated by Carme Forcadell, the ANC's main leader, in 2014, "Our adversary is the Spanish state. Let's be clear about something: the Spanish parties in Catalonia, such as Citizens and the Popular Party – that should not be called PP of Catalonia but PP in Catalonia – are our adversaries, the rest is the Catalan people". Some years later, when Forcadell had become the parliament's speaker, he regretted these words.
15 After the declaration of independence, support for the EU among pro-independence supporters declined slightly. Former regional prime minister Carles Puigdemont recently proposed the possibility of a vote about the EU in Catalonia, although the other parties and regionalist leaders did not back the proposal.
16 Among other controversial aspects, the transition law reinforced the prime minister's powers to appoint judges and implemented a unilateral breakup with the Spanish public administration and institutions.

References

Barberà, O., Barrio, A. and Rodríguez-Teruel, J. (2011) "Political Developments and Party Changes in Catalonia", In van Haute, E. (ed.) *Party Membership in Europe: Exploration into the Anthills of Party Politics*. Brussels: Editions de l'Université de Bruxelles, pp. 109–128.

Barrio, A., Barberà, O. and Rodríguez-Teruel, J. (2018) "Spain steals from us! The 'populist drift of Catalan regionalism", *Comparative European Politics*, 16(6), pp. 993–1011.

Barrio, A. and Rodríguez-Teruel, J. (2017) "Reducing the Gap between Leaders and Voters? Elite Polarization, Outbidding Competition, and the Rise of Secessionism in Catalonia", *Ethnic and Racial Studies*, 40(10), pp. 1776–1794.

Bassas, A. (2014) "Francesc Homs: "Alguns ho volen tot alhora i volent-ho tot no s' aconsegueix res", *Ara*, 11 October www.ara.ad/premium/tema_del_dia/Francesc-Homs-alhora-volent-ho-saconsegueix_0_1264673554.html. Accessed 2 January 2019.

Betz, H.-G. (2017) "Nativism Across Time and Space", *Swiss Political Science Review*, 23(4), pp. 335–353.

Biorcio, R. (1991) "The Rebirth of Populism in France and Italy", *Telos: Critical Theory of the Contemporary*, 90, pp. 43–56.

Bosco, A. and Verney, S. (2012) "Electoral Epidemic: The Political Cost of Economic Crisis in Southern Europe, 2010–11", *South European Society and Politics*, 17(2), pp. 129–154.

Botella, J. (1998) "El comportament electoral català", In Giner, S. (ed.) *La Societat Catalana*. Barcelona: Institut d'Estadítica de Catalunya, pp. 1111–1119.

Burg, S. L. (2015) "Identity, Grievances, and Popular Mobilization for Independence in Catalonia", *Nationalism and Ethnic Politics*, 21(3), pp. 289–312.

Canovan, M. (2005) *The People*. Cambridge: Cambridge University Press.

Chesterley, N. and Roberti, P. (2018) "Populism and Institutional Capture", *European Journal of Political Economy*, 53, pp. 1–12.

Conversi, D. (2000) *The Basques, the Catalans, and Spain: Alternative Routes to Nationalist Mobilisation*. Reno: University of Nevada Press.

Crameri, K. (2015) "Political Power and Civil Counterpower: The Complex Dynamics of the Catalan Independence Movement", *Nationalism and Ethnic Politics*, 21(1), pp. 37–41.

de Vos, P. (2005) "Righ-wing Populism and the Radical Centre: Explaining the Electoral Growth of the Vlaams Blok in Belgium", In Howarth, D. and Torfing, J. (eds.) *Discourse Theory in European Politics. Identity, Policy and Governance*. Basingstoke and New York: Palgave Macmillan, pp. 190–210.

De Winter, L., Gómez-Reino, M. and Lynch, P. (2006) *Autonomist Parties in Europe: Identity Politics and the Revival of the Territorial Cleavage*. Barcelona: Institut de Ciències Polítiques i Socials.

Del Riego, C. (2016) "Tardà a Rajoy: "Si nos meten en la cárcel, los catalanes nos liberarán", *La Vanguardia*, 31 August. www.lavanguardia.com/politica/20160831/4115172888/tarda-rajoy-debate-investidura.html. Accessed 2 January 2019

Della Porta, D., Fernández, J., Kouki, H. and Mosca, L. (2017) *Movement Parties Against Austerity*. Cambridge: Polity.

Diani, M. (1992) "Lo sviluppo dei movimenti etnico-nazionali in Occidente, 1960–1990", In Rusconi, G. (ed.) *Nazione Etnia Cittadinanza in Italia e in Europa*. Brescia: Editrice La Scuola, pp. 175–185.

Diari de Girona. (2016) "Mas diu que el procés es complica perquè els partits posen pedres al camí," 30 March. www.diaridegirona.cat/catalunya/2016/03/30/mas-diu-que-proces-complica/774976.html, Accessed 2 January 2019.

Dowling, A. (2014) "Accounting for the Turn towards Secession in Catalonia", *International Journal of Iberian Studies*, 27(2–3), pp. 219–234.
El Nacional. (2014) "Junqueras: Votar és un dret que preval per sobre de qualsevol llei", 14 September. www.naciodigital.cat/noticia/74423/junqueras/votar/dret/preval/sobre/qualsevol/llei. Accessed 2 January 2019.
El Punt Avui. (2018) "Es l'hora de la política", 26 March. www.elpuntavui.cat/politica/article/17-politica/1364229-es-l-hora-de-la-politica.html. Accessed 2 January 2019.
Gómez-Reino, M. (2002) *Ethnicity and Nationalism in Italian Politics, Inventing the Padania: Lega Nord and the Northern Question*. Farnham: Ashgate.
Guibernau, M. (2004) *Catalan Nationalism: Francoism, Transition and Democracy*. London: Routledge.
Heaney, M. T. (2010) "Linking Political Parties and Interest Groups", In Maisel, S. and Berry, J. (eds.) *Oxford Handbook of American Political Parties and Interest Groups*. Oxford: Oxford University Press, pp. 568–587.
Heinisch, R. Massetti, E and Mazzoleni, O. (2018) "Populism and ethno-territorial politics in European multi-level systems", *Comparative European Politics*, 16(6), pp. 923–936. doi:10.1057/s41295-018-0142-1.
Heinisch, R. and Mazzoleni, O. (2016) *Understanding Populist Party Organisation: The Radical Right in Western Europe*. London: Palgrave Macmillan.
Hetcher, M. (1975) *Internal Colonialism: The Celtic Fringe in British National Development (1536–1966)*. London and Berkeley: Routledge & University of California Press.
Ivaldi, G., Lanzone, M. E. and Woods, D. (2017) "Varieties of Populism across a Left-Right Spectrum: The Case of the Front National, the Northern League, Podemos and Five Star Movement", *Swiss Political Science Review*, 23(4), pp. 354–376.
Kriesi, H. (2014) "The Populist Challenge", *West European Politics*, 37(2), pp. 361–378.
Kriesi, H. and Pappas, T. S. (2015) *European Populism in the Shadow of the Great Recession*. Colchester: ECPR Press.
Laclau, E. (2005) *La razón populista*. Buenos Aires: Fondo de Cultura Económica.
Mazzoleni, O. (2003) "Multi-Level Populism and Centre-Periphery Cleavage in Switzerland The Case of the Lega dei Ticinesi", In Caramani, D. and Mény, Y. (eds.) *Challenges to Consensual Politics. Democracy, Identity, and Populist Protest in the Alpine Region*. Brussels: Peter Lang, pp. 209–227.
McDonnell, D. (2006) "A Weekend in Padania: Regionalist Populism and the Lega Nord", *Politics*, 26(2), pp. 126–132.
McGann, A. J. and Kitschelt, H. (1995) *The Radical Right in Western Europe: A Comparative Analysis*. Ann Arbor: University of Michigan Press.
Medina, I., Barrio, A. and Rodríguez-Teruel, J. (2016) "Assessing the Identity Politics Hypothesis: Political Parties and Interest Groups Linkages in the Case of Junts pel Sí". Paper presented at the *ECPR General Conference*, Prague, 7–9 September.
Mény, Y. and Surel, Y. (2000) *Par le peuple, pour le peuple*. Paris: Fayard.
Moffitt, B. and Tormey, S. (2014) "Rethinking Populism: Politics, Mediatisation and Political Style", *Political Studies*, 62(2), pp. 381–397.
Mondon, A. (2015) ""Populism, the 'People' and the Illusion of Democracy – The Front National and UKIP in a Comparative Context", *French Politics*, 13(2), pp. 141–156.
Mudde, C. (2004) "The Populist Zeitgeist", *Government and Opposition*, 39(4), pp. 542–563.
Mudde, C. (2007) *Populist Radical Right Parties in Europe*. Cambridge: Cambridge University Press.
Mudde, C. (2016) "Europe's Populist Surge: A Long Time in the Making", *Foreign Affairs*, (November–December), pp. 25–30.

Mudde, C. and Rovira Kaltwasser, C. (2013) "Exclusionary vs. Inclusionary Populism: Comparing Contemporary Europe and Latin America", *Government and Opposition*, 48 (2), pp. 147–174.

Muñoz, J. and Guinjoan, M. (2013) "Accounting for Internal Variation in Nationalist Mobilization: Unofficial Referendums for Independence in Catalonia (2009–11)", *Nations and Nationalism*, 19(1), pp. 44–67.

Pappas, T. S. (2014) *Populism and Crisis Politics in Greece*. Basingstoke: Palgrave Macmillan.

Regió 7 (2013) "Junqueras: "És un Diada que demostrarà al món la nostra voluntat de continuar sent"", 11 setptembre, www.regio7.cat/arreu-catalunya-espanya-mon/2013/09/11/junqueras-diada-demostrara-mon-nostra/243777.html, Accessed 2 January 2019.

Sallés, Q. (2013) 'No som espanyols» o l'Evangeli segons Forcadell', *El Nacional*, 16 March. www.naciodigital.cat/noticia/52836/no/som/espanyols/evangeli/segons/forcadell. Accessed 2 January 2018.

Stanley, B. (2008) "The Thin Ideology of Populism", *Journal of Political Ideologies*, 13(1), pp. 95–110.

Taggart, P. (1995) "New Populist Parties in Western Europe", *West European Politics*, 18(1), pp. 34–51.

Taggart, P. and Kaltwasser, C. R. (2016) "Dealing with Populists in Government: Some Comparative Conclusions", *Democratization*, 23(2), pp. 345–365.

The Guardian (2017) "Catalan ex-president Artur Mas barred from holding public office", *The Guardian*, 13 March. www.theguardian.com/world/2017/mar/13/catalan-ex-president-artur-mas-barred-from-holding-public-office. Accessed 2 January 2018

van Kessel, S. (2015) *Populist Parties in Europe. Agents of Discontent?* Basingstoke and New York: Palgrave Macmillan.

Vilaregut, R. (2012) *Memòria i emergència en l'independentisme català. El cas de la Plataforma pel Dret de Decidir*. Barcelona: Universitat Autònoma de Barcelona, Departament de Ciència Política i Dret Públic.

Woods, D. (1995) "The Crisis of Center-Periphery Integration in Italy and the Rise of Regional Populism: The Lombard", *Comparative Politics*, 27(2), pp. 187–203.

Zakaria, F. (1997) "The Rise of Illiberal Democracy", *Foreign Affairs*, 76(6), pp. 22–43.

6
REGIONAL NATIVISM IN EAST GERMANY

The case of the AfD

Hans-Georg Betz and Fabian Habersack

Introduction

Until recently, Germany was somewhat of a political outlier among advanced liberal democracies. Unlike its neighbors, Germany proved relatively resilient to the sirens of radical right-wing populism. The success of the Alternative for Germany (AfD) in the federal election of 2017 marks a decisive break with this past. With more than 12 per cent of the vote it became the third largest party in the newly elected Bundestag. The results sent shock waves through Germany's political establishment and across the entire country. With the AfD, a party entered the Bundestag, which in the run-up to the election had introduced a new confrontational and aggressive tone into the political discussion, designed to irritate and polarize. Leading party members used provocation to push the boundaries of acceptable speech and break established taboos (Steffen 2017). They justified their strategy arguing that they were only lending voice to ordinary people and providing a platform for their views. A number of its candidates, however, made no secret of their extremist views; nor did they try to hide their ties to right-wing extremist groups, both domestically and abroad, nor their amicable contacts with like-minded parties abroad, most prominently the Austrian Freedom Party (FPÖ), the Swiss People's Party (SVP), and the Dutch Party for Freedom (PVV).

The AfD is not a regionalist party. It started out as a largely Western German single-issue party of bourgeois protest against eurozone bailouts in Southern Europe (Arzheimer 2015; Schmitt-Beck 2017). Led by prominent academics, the AfD promoted the orderly dissolution of the monetary union and a return to national currencies. Riding a wave of growing popular Euroscepticism, it failed only by a hair to enter parliament in the 2013 federal election (Grimm 2015). With 7 per cent of the vote in the European elections of 2014, it won seven seats in the European Parliament. Notable gains in subsequent regional elections confirmed the party's appeal to a relatively small but growing segment of the German electorate.

Political success tends to invite rivalries, internal strife, power struggles, and programmatic trench warfare. This was also the case with the AfD following the European elections. The internal confrontation pitted economic liberals, focussing on economic issues, against "national conservatives" intent on putting the emphasis on identitarian positions. The factional infighting ended with the breakaway of the liberal wing of the party; its core members founded a new party, which was a political nonstarter (Franzmann 2016). Against that, the national-conservative AfD quickly rose in the polls, boosted by the "refugee crisis" of late 2015, early 2016, which provoked widespread anxieties and resentment across the country.

The AfD's appeal was particularly pronounced in the Eastern part of the country. One of the most significant results of the 2017 election was the electoral disparity between the territory of the former FRG and that of the former GDR. In the former, the AfD received roughly 11 per cent of the vote; in the latter, it garnered more than double (22.5 per cent). In the West, it came out third, in the East, second (in one state, Saxony, even first). The party won three direct mandates, all in the East. In the analysis that follows we will attempt to provide a plausible explanation for the AfD's disproportionate success in the East. The argument consists of three parts. First, we establish that the AfD is a typical radical right-wing populist party, which promotes an emphatically nativist discourse. The second part lays out the particular features that distinguish the Eastern part of Germany from the rest of the country. Finally, we explore to what degree understanding Eastern Germany's regional idiosyncrasies might help to explain the AfD's disproportionate appeal there.

Radical right-wing populism made in Germany: the AfD after 2015

German political analysts in academia and the media generally agree that the AfD represents Germany's version of radical right-wing populism. A close analysis of the party's discourse since 2015 largely supports this contention.

Radical right-wing populism

Contemporary radical right-wing populism is a composite of two ideational elements: populism and nativism. Populism is defined as a political doctrine that holds that society is divided into two antagonistic groups – the vast majority of ordinary people and a relatively small elite that acts in its own interest. Populism claims for itself to restore voice to the people and thus assure that politics once again becomes a true reflection and expression of the popular will.

Nativism holds that the "descendants of the original inhabitants" of a country should be accorded priority, if not exclusivity, with respect to rights and resources –

i.e., that 'the own people' should always come first. Government should show "reasonable partiality towards compatriots" by protecting and promoting the welfare and wellbeing of the native-born (Kuper 2003: 390; Miller 2005: 79).

Nativism's appeal lies in the fact that it responds to the search for comprehensive protection of those who perceive the world as an inherently insecure and dangerous place. Populism's appeal lies in the fact that it pretends to explain why comprehensive protection is not forthcoming. Radical right-wing populist supporters tend to heap blame primarily on left-wing/liberal elites. They accuse them of systematically giving preference to non-natives, either in the name of political correctness or for self-serving reasons, when, in reality, preference should be accorded to the native population. What links populism and nativism furthermore is a common appeal to affect and emotions – particularly resentment born of a profound sense of injustice (in the case of populism) and anxiety born of a deep sense of cultural disorientation (in the case of nativism).

The AfD as a populist party

The AfD's growing appeal after 2015 was largely owed to the new leaders' ability to frame their discourse in a way that resonated with widespread and enduring undercurrents in German public opinion. The result was a radical right-wing populist discourse, tailored to the idiosyncrasies and sensibilities of the German public (Arzheimer 2015; Lewandowsky 2015).

In Germany today, the AfD is generally characterized as a right-wing populist party comparable to the French National Rally (RN), the PVV, and the Danish People's Party (DF). What distinguishes these parties is a rhetoric that charges that contemporary democracies are democracies in word only. In reality, political power has been "confiscated" by a self-serving political class or caste – a new oligarchy, unresponsive to, if not dismissive of the real-life concerns of ordinary people. While in theory, democracy is supposed to express the political will of the people, in real life, politics has largely escaped popular control. Against that, right-wing populist parties promote themselves as disinterested and dedicated advocates of ordinary people and the only genuine defenders of "true democracy" (Betz 2017a: 174–176).

With the programmatic reorientation following the split of 2015, the AfD radicalized its populist rhetoric while adopting core elements of a nativist discourse. Its narrative was centered upon a frontal assault on the established political parties, collectively dismissed as "Altparteien" ("old parties"), and the political elite, denigrated as a "Politik-Kaste" ("political caste"). Thus, in one of its main political manifestos, the party conjured up the paranoia of conspiracy:

> Behind the scenes a small and powerful elite within the political parties is secretly in charge, and is responsible for the misguided development of past decades. It is this political class of career politicians whose foremost interest is to retain their own power base, status, and material wellbeing.
>
> *(AfD 2016a: 7)*

Against that, the AfD claims that it stands for a "genuine democratization of politics", a process intent on allowing ordinary people not only to participate in the decision-making process and have greater influence on it but also to exercise an effective control of government. In order to achieve that, the AfD calls for the introduction of an expanded array of instruments of direct democracy at all levels of government, modelled after the Swiss system.

The AfD's nativist turn and the rhetoric against "Islamization"

The AfD's failure to enter parliament in 2014 demonstrated that populist rhetoric was clearly not sufficient to motivate a substantial part of the electorate to vote for the new party. If the party wanted to broaden its electoral appeal, it had to seize upon an issue that not only fired people's passions but was also unlikely to disappear from the political agenda anytime soon.

Following the defection of its liberal wing, the AfD's discourse dramatically shifted away from its earlier emphasis on economic issues toward cultural issues. Within a relatively short time, the party adopted a panoply of nativist tropes and positions, largely imported from abroad. Most prominently among them an emphasis on collective identity based on the notion that the national community rests on a distinctive, historically evolved culture and value system that is paramount to preserve, defend and, if necessary, restore (Betz 2017b).

On the contemporary populist radical right, identitarian positions are intricately linked with the question of the place of Islam in Western societies. In Western Europe, the radical right has established itself as the most intransigent anti-Islamic voice, determined to contain and roll back the 'Islamization' of our culture and way of life. This anti-Islamic discourse has a strong populist appeal, directed against the cultural and political establishment elite charged with being complicit in undermining and weakening the liberal foundations of Western culture.

Given Germany's relatively visible, and well-organized Muslim community the question of Islam's place in society is a particularly sensitive issue. It became a subject of public debate following statements by various prominent politicians that "Islam belongs to Germany" (Süddeutsche Zeitung 2018). The claim was quickly adopted by large parts of the political and cultural establishment, yet largely rejected by the German population. In 2015, more than 70 per cent of respondents voiced opposition, only 23 per cent agreed (Schmidt 2015). The gap between elite and popular opinion gave the AfD the opportunity to fill the issue space and promote itself as the voice of the silent majority, making the notion that Islam was not part of Germany central to its mobilization campaign. Adopting the radical right's anti-Islamization rhetoric, the AfD argued that Germany was subject to a "creeping" process of Islamization intent on subverting the country's secular constitutional order in order to "establish an Islamic political and social regime" (Henkel 2017: 107). A leading AfD politician charged Germany's center-left parties with actively promoting the expansion of Islam because they "hated everything German" and desired to see it get "destroyed" (Cramer 2016).

In response, AfD officials demanded that Islam "be outlawed in Germany", charging that Sharia law was irreconcilable with the German constitution (AfD 2017). Leading party politicians also promoted the "theory" of the "great replacement" according to which native-born Europeans were on their way to be replaced by non-natives in a secular process of population exchange, which would invariably lead to the extinction of European culture and identity.

Like other radical right-wing populist parties, the AfD frames German identity primarily in "civilizationalist" terms (Brubaker 2017b): On this reading, German identity is grounded in "the traditions of the Christian Occident" as well as Western "ideas of freedom, human dignity, equality, a secular conception of the state, democracy and enlightenment". Islam does not belong to Germany since it neither shaped German history nor the country's self-understanding (AfD 2016b: 31). In fact, it "is incompatible with Germany's liberal democratic order" and can therefore never be part of the country's identity (*Epoch Times* 2017).

Contextual factors

The radicalization of the AfD's right-wing populist discourse was one of the major factors behind the party's dramatic upsurge of electoral support on the regional and federal level. By laying claim on sensitive and controversial questions such as national identity, multiculturalism, and the place of Islam in German society, the AfD hit the nerve of an increasingly jittery zeitgeist, particularly with respect to the question of Islam. This jibes well with the recent "cultural turn" in the study of radical right-wing populism (Brubaker 2017b; Jones, Cox and Lienesch 2017; Rensmann 2017).

Cultural anxiety: the impact of Islam

An article from 2006 published in the *Frankfurter Allgemeine Zeitung* set the tone: A majority of Germans, the title suggested, saw in Islam a "foreign, menacing world" (Noelle and Petersen 2006). The article summarized recent findings on public attitudes toward Islam, which revealed the depth of German anxiety and apprehension. More than 80 per cent of respondents equated Islam with fanaticism; more than 70 per cent with intolerance; more than 60 per cent saw it as "backward" and "undemocratic"; more than 90 per cent associated it with discrimination against women. A majority of respondents saw in the rise of Islamic fundamentalism the beginning of a "clash of cultures", which could only but increase in intensity. The extent of German apprehensiveness can also be seen in the fact that in 2016, 40 per cent of respondents thought that German society was being "subverted" by Islam (FES 2016).

Islam's negative image in Germany was cultivated by a slew of media reports and publications. It culminated in Thilo Sarrazin's polemic *Deutschland schafft sich ab* (2010), which quickly topped the bestseller lists (Geyer 2010). The central thesis was that if Germany failed to regulate the influx of migrants from Muslim countries, the country's culture and "Volkscharakter" (national character) would invariably be altered in a highly undesirable direction (Sarrazin 2010: 330). Sarrazin's anti-Islamic theses were largely rejected by the entire political establishment while partly falling on more sympathetic ears among the supporters of established parties, and notably among voters of the Christian Democratic Union of Germany/ Christian Union in Bavaria (CDU/CSU), the Free Democratic Party (FDP), and the AfD. In late 2010, only 40 per cent of interviewed Social Democratic Party (SPD) voters disagreed with the author; about a third expressed their agreement (Reinbold 2010). At the same time, nearly 50 per cent of the public agreed with Sarrazin's notion that Germans were in danger of becoming "strangers in their own country" (HaGalil 2010).

Given the depth of anti-Islamic sentiments in Germany, the AfD's electoral gains were hardly surprising. These sentiments were particularly pronounced in the Eastern part of the country, not only in comparison to the Western part, but also in comparison to other countries in Western Europe (Pickel and Yendell 2016: 290). The most prominent illustration of Eastern German anti-Muslim affect was, of course, the Pegida (Patriotic Europeans Against the Islamisation of the Occident) movement, which, starting in late 2014 in Dresden, managed to mobilize thousands of demonstrators against "the Islamization of the West".

At first glance, the extent and intensity of hostility toward Islam in Germany might be expected to go a long way to explain the success of the AfD, particularly in the Eastern part of the country. There is little evidence, however, to support this assumption. Take, for instance, the distribution of the Muslim population in Germany. According to an official study from 2008, the vast majority of Muslims resided in the West; a mere 2 per cent in the East, thus "practically not present" (Haug, Müssig and Stichs 2009: 106). Xenophobic sentiments tend to increase in response to the visible "other". Yet, greater contact with "the other" also tends to attenuate fears, reservations, and prejudices with regard to the "other" (Pettigrew and Tropp 2008). This might explain the high level of Islamophobia in the East, yet not necessarily the disproportionate support for the AfD there. The results of a comprehensive study of Pegida participants support this contention. It found that only a tiny minority of participants were motivated by anti-Islamic sentiments (Vorländer, Herold and Schäller 2015: 58). Islam, albeit central to the AfD's discourse, hardly accounted for the party's substantial gains in the East, gainsaying the explanatory power of a cultural framework to account for the AfD's success there.

Economic anxiety: globalization, modernization and positional deprivation

Gidron and Hall have recently argued that "an effective analysis" of the right-wing populist phenomenon "must rest on understanding how economic and cultural developments interact to generate support for populism" (2017: 57). In the past, economic arguments largely centered upon the "losers of modernization" thesis; more recently, however, the emphasis has shifted to notions of "positional deprivation" and "relative economic decline" (Gest, Reny and

Mayer 2017; Gidron and Hall 2017; Kopetsch 2017; Rooduijn and Burgoon 2017; Burgoon 2018).

From an economic perspective, the modernization loser thesis is closely linked to globalization. The intensification of trade flows associated with globalization creates winners and losers. Competitive pressures from newly emerging economies have led to the elimination of routine manual and basic service jobs in advanced industrial countries. Workers disposing of relatively low levels of human capital are threatened with obsolescence and structural unemployment. Largely abandoned by the traditional left, they represent a reservoir of disenchanted (lower-class) voters for the populist right.

Positional deprivation largely stems from socio-economic inequality, measured in terms of changes in individual or group socio-economic status compared to others. It reflects perceived relative socio-economic decline, as reflected in the notion of the "declining middle". It is reasonable to expect that individuals experiencing socio-economic status decline develop resentment stemming from feelings of economic unfairness, particularly if they attribute their situation to elite indifference to their plight (Burgoon 2018).

Although appealing, neither analytical approach provides an empirically grounded explanation for the disproportionate success of the AfD in Eastern Germany. Empirical studies suggest that Germany has been far less impacted by trade with low-wage countries than other advanced capitalist countries. Actually, in Germany trade slowed down the decline in the manufacturing sector "because rising exports to the new markets stabilized industry jobs" (Dauth, Findeisen and Suedekum 2017: 341). There has been some globalization-induced impact on a few select locations; but the regional impact has not been more pronounced in the East than in the West (Südekum, Dauth and Findeisen 2017). This is partly owed to Eastern Germany's distinctive manufacturing infrastructure largely dominated by small and medium-sized companies presumably less exposed to international competition (Arnold et al. 2015). Additional evidence comes from individual-level data. They suggest that the vast majority of AfD supporters are hardly typical *Modernisierungsverlierer* (losers of modernization). On the contrary, "people of a middle- or upper-class status" tend to have "a stronger intention to vote for the AfD" than lower status groups (Lengfeld 2017a: 210; see also Bergmann, Diermeier and Niehues 2017).

Positional deprivation theory does not much better to explain the disproportionate support the AfD receives in the East. It has been shown that between 2004 and 2014, the fear of social decline fell significantly in all social groups throughout Germany. In fact, in 2014, it reached the low point of 1991. This development was particularly marked in the Eastern part of the country, where fear of social decline decreased to a much larger degree (albeit from a far higher initial level) than in the West (Lengfeld 2017b: 3; see also Lengfeld and Ordemann 2016). Studies of income polarization tell a similar story. Focusing on urban agglomerations in the period after 2006, Jan Goebel and Martin Gorni have shown that in the Eastern part of the country, income polarization decreased somewhat whereas in the West, it continued to grow. In fact, in the East, "the percentages in the low-income group have dropped significantly and those in the middle-income group are increasing slightly" (Goebel and Gornig 2015: 18). Positional deprivation theory clearly falls short of explaining the AfD's disproportionate appeal in the East.

In the remainder of this essay we propose an alternative explanation and put it to the empirical test. It takes as point of departure a third approach, which has recently gained growing prominence in the literature on the populist right – the role of emotions (Rico, Guinjoan and Anduiza 2017; Salmela and von Scheve 2017). The argument is that the AfD's success in Eastern Germany is to a large extent an expression of a panoply of pent-up emotions provoked and engendered by the collective psychological shocks, traumas, and injuries sustained in the years following unification, which have apparently never fully healed.

The affective roots of populist mobilization in Eastern Germany

The sociologist Robert Jansen defines populism as a political project that mobilizes ordinary people into contentious political action while "articulating an anti-elite, nationalist rhetoric that valorizes ordinary people" (2011: 82). Jansen's formulation makes an important point with regard to an essential facet of populism: the fact that populism accords recognition to ordinary people, their anxieties, and concerns. It does this by satisfying the need for psychological compensation via rhetoric that appeals to emotions.

Contemporary politics is increasingly driven by a range of emotions; and the appeal to emotions increasingly conditions the success of populist politics. Germany is no exception, as the repetitious reference by the media to the *Wutbürger* (transl: irate citizen) demonstrates. "Word of the year" in 2010, it has been used as a *passe-partout* phrase to explain the growing support for radical right-wing populism, from Pegida to the AfD (Nachtwey 2015; Jensen 2017: 10; Vorländer, Herold and Schäller 2017).

Anger and rage are, however, hardly the only emotions motivating support for the populist right. In fact, what prompts the success of the AfD in the east is to a significant extent a combination of positive and negative sentiments and emotions, most notably anger, resentment, embitterment, and nostalgia. What all of these emotions, save nostalgia, have in common is that they represent reactions to perceived moral injuries, insults, and injustices (Haidt 2003; Fassin 2013). Embitterment, for instance, is an emotive response to "persistent feelings of being let down, insulted or being a loser", a "feeling and perception of injustice together with the urge to fight back but the inability to identify the proper goal", a sentiment of "being revengeful but helpless" (Linden 2003: 197). Available evidence suggests that in the decades following unification, these sentiments have come to be widely shared by a considerable portion of the Eastern population and now define to a significant extent Eastern German identity (Kubiak 2018). Politically, they have engendered a profound sense of political disenchantment and alienation, which provides fertile ground for populist mobilization.

Opinion polls speak a clear language. In 2016, roughly two thirds of West Germans declared themselves to be satisfied with democracy. By contrast, in the East, only about half of the population did so (Belock and Faus 2017). Explanations for the divergence are easily found: Easterners are considerably more likely than Westerners to consider themselves politically powerless. In 2009 more than four out of ten Eastern respondents thought they had no influence on the truly important political decisions, all of which were made by Westerners (Köcher 2009: 52). There was a strong sense that what they thought and desired politically did not really count for much.

This sense of powerlessness is also reflected in the fact that until today, a significant number of Eastern Germans perceive themselves to be second-class citizens. In 2009, four out of ten respondents said they felt that way (Köcher 2009: 53). Recent regional-level studies indicate that these sentiments have hardly diminished. Thus in 2017, 44 per cent of Saxons agreed with the statement; more than two thirds said they felt that the achievements of Eastern Germany were not sufficiently recognized (*Leipziger Volkszeitung* 2017). One year earlier, more than half of respondents in Thuringia said they felt that they were treated like second-class citizens (Best, Niehoff, Salheiser and Vogel 2016: 74). These happened to be the two Länder where the AfD did exceptionally well in the 2017 federal election.

The result is a paradoxical situation: while the vast majority of Eastern Germans generally indicate a high level of satisfaction with their personal circumstances, a significant number are resentful for not being appreciated by the West. This has resulted in a kind of permanent regional psychological trauma, for which Eastern analysts have coined the notion of *Ostdeprivation* (transl: East deprivation) (*Frankfurter Allgemeine Zeitung* 2017). *Ostdeprivation*, in turn, has engendered political disaffection, fueled by suspicion of having been "written off" by the political establishment. With Pegida and the AfD, these sentiments ultimately found a political outlet in the form of right-wing populism. The case of Pegida is particularly instructive: when asked why they took part in Pegida demonstrations, more than 50 per cent of participants explained their support for the movement with "dissatisfaction with politics" rather than concerns about the alleged advance of Islam in the West (Vorländer, Herold and Schäller 2015: 58).

The refugee crisis of 2016 only exacerbated Eastern resentments while provoking nativist resentments grounded in hearsay that refugees received more social benefits than did Germans. Particularly elderly Eastern Germans, who had worked all their lives, felt unfairly treated. As an Eastern German resident resentfully stated to a journalist: "We cannot even afford a piece of new clothing while they get everything" (Schmidt 2017). These resentments, in turn, added to political disaffection, engendered by charges that politicians accorded preference to the newcomers instead of making sure that the "own people" would come first. One regional government even saw the need to issue fact sheets explaining, for instance, why refugees disposed of smartphones (Sander 2015).

The resentments engendered by the arrival of hundreds of thousands of refugees within a relatively short time provoked strong nativist sentiments. These, in turn, provided ample fuel for the AfD's nativist mobilization particularly because it fed into an emotion, which has received growing attention from students of the populist right – nostalgia (Gest, Reny and Mayer 2017; Kenny 2017). Eastern German nostalgia is hardly a new phenomenon. Nostalgic sentiments appeared first during the late 1990s, provoked by growing Eastern German anger and resentment over the pejorative tone of much of the reporting in Western German media about the former GDR and about Eastern Germans. The perception of denigration by Westerners, in turn, contributed to the emergence of a distinct sense of togetherness and regional identity, grounded in the shared experience of historically-grounded "otherness" (Kubiak 2018). The result was what observers characterized as *Ostalgie* – a rose-colored view of life before unification, reflecting as much a genuine yearning for certain positive aspects of the "good old days" (such as community and social security) as it was an act of anti-Western defiance. Thus, in the late 1990s half of the Eastern German population rejected the official negative depiction of the GDR as distorting reality; a quarter considered the way the GDR was treated as "hurtful" (Rudolph 2016: 91).

In the years following unification, the Eastern German emotional state reflected in this *Ostalgie* was politically served by the Party of Democratic Socialism (PDS), the legal successor to the Socialist Unity Party (SED). Nominally a left-wing party, the PDS represented a part of the Eastern German population that significantly deviated from the party's official positions. This was particularly pronounced with regard to immigration. In 2000, almost 60 per cent of PDS supporters agreed with the statement that there were too many foreigners living in Germany, compared to 44 per cent among SPD voters and 8 per cent among Green voters (RP Online 2000; *Spiegel Online* 2000).

The PDS, as the only party of East German origin in the German party system until 2007 (when the party merged into "The Left"), found it relatively easy to politicize East-West discrepancies and to position itself as the prominent voice of East German nostalgia and anti-establishment sentiments, both nationally and on the state level (Jun 2017: 98). Despite considerable discrepancies between PDS voters' attitudes and party positions, the PDS successfully mobilized protest votes and deep-rooted discontent with the political and economic conditions East Germans confronted after reunification. This ended with the foundation of "The Left" which positioned itself as an all-German party that sought to win elections in both parts of the country (Mielke and Eith 2017: 17). This gradually opened up space for new parties to embrace anti-systemic and anti-establishment messages as well as the PDS's former symbolic and clientelistic representation of East Germany. Presently, the AfD appears to have seized the opportunity to fill this void. In 2017, 85 per cent of AfD voters stated that they considered the AfD "the only party with which one can express one's protest" (Infratest dimap 2017). AfD voters appear to be the only electorate to base their vote on "disappointment with the other parties" (61 per cent) rather than the "belief in one's own party" (31 per cent) (Infratest dimap 2017). Against this backdrop, support for the anti-establishment program of the AfD can also be interpreted as an expression of a distinctly Eastern German nostalgia, reflecting a strong desire to keep it that way and not end up like the West. Surveys reveal a significantly higher level of agreement in the East (46 per cent) than in the West (35 per cent) with the statement that Germany should return to its traditional values and ensure that "our Christian-Western culture [will] not get lost" (Belock and Faus 2017: 10).

If the AfD's anti-elite rhetoric has resonated with East German voters, it has also allowed the party to establish itself as a welcome "alternative" for those voters who once felt close to the PDS but always held nativist and xenophobic attitudes. It is the combination of protest and right-wing radical discourse which has guaranteed the AfD's success at the polls. Not surprisingly, the radical right and more extremist faction of the AfD is situated in the East. Under the GDR regime, foreigners largely lived in social isolation from Germans – yet, especially the 1960s and 1970s saw some level of right-wing activism and politically motivated violence directed at foreigners and "guest workers" brought into the GDR from "friendly" socialist countries such as Vietnam, Mozambique, and Cuba. Given the GDR's perennial labor shortage, job competition was not a problem. Rather, East Germans' hostility towards these guest workers was "essentially a form of socio-economic chauvinism" rooted in the country's "shortage economy" (Dennis 2007: 351; see also: Poutrus, Behrends and Kuck 2000).Even though a considerable number of foreign workers left the country after unification (especially in the 1990s), hostility and criticism directed against foreigners remained relatively high. At present, anti-foreigner aggression continues to influence politics as the AfD's dramatic gains in 2017 in Saxony and particularly the region around Dresden, where xenophobia has been particularly pronounced (Hornuf and Rieger 2017), have demonstrated.

This suggests that the AfD's appeal lies in its nativist claim for protection against the threat of international and global processes, combined with the populist blaming of "the West" and "the elites" held responsible for failing to protect "the people" and "the East" from them. The combination of the textual factors, party system developments and affective roots of voter mobilization in East Germany outlined above support the contention that the AfD serves primarily as a vehicle of protest, particularly for Eastern German voters, providing them with a voice for their frustrations and disenchantment. This projection takes place first and foremost on two dimensions: first, citizens frustrated with the "Westernized" political system or parliamentarism itself are disproportionately prone to vote AfD (*populist dimension*). Second, frustration over economic conditions and relative deprivation also increases the likelihood of East Germans – more so than is the case for West Germans – to vote AfD (*socio-economic dimension*).

AfD voters in East and West Germany: do regional sentiments matter?

In a final section, we put these theories to the empirical test. Do voters in the East feel excluded from the political system and treated as second-class citizens? Are there structural differences between AfD supporters in the West and those in the East – and do they explain the party's regional support? To answer these questions we draw on data from the German Longitudinal Election Study (GLES) – comprising a pre- and post- election wave for the 2017 election (Roßteutscher et al. 2018).

To date, no study has examined the role of regional interaction effects in the context of voter support for the AfD. Hambauer and Mays (2018) come closest with their study of who votes AfD. The authors look at GLES voter data from 2015 and 2016 and even introduce an East/West dummy to their model, yet their results are sobering: for one, voters in the East do not even seem to be significantly more prone to voting AfD than voters in the West after controlling for several other variables (Hambauer and Mays 2018: 150). For another, regional *interaction* effects (e.g. regionally stronger sentiments of discrimination and exclusion from political decisions) are not even tested, due to the small sample sizes (Hambauer and Mays 2018: 140). In 2017, almost three times as many people voted AfD, first and foremost in the Eastern *Bundesländer*. We take this surge in voter support in the East (yet also in the West) as motivation to model and shed more light on differences in motives and voter characteristics between the two regions.

In a first step, we cast a glance at two open questions (variable names (vn) vn22s and vn23s; Roßteutscher et al. 2018) asking respondents what would be the first and second most important problem Germany is facing at the time. We coded and categorized the 454 responses from Eastern and Western AfD voters that we found into statements revolving around negative opinions towards refugees and immigrants (1) statements dealing with social issues, sentiments of social injustice, and concerns with basic resources and infrastructure (2), again statements expressing disenchantment with the political system and elites as well as frustration over political decisions being made "over the people's heads" (3), as well as finally into those statements dealing with regional matters and East/West differences (4). Do descriptive differences among AfD voters from East and West Germany exist?

As shown in Figure 6.1, they do indeed. Both the refugee crisis and social issues feature prominently in AfD voters' statements: across regions, the two issues account for around 80 per cent of all statements made. There are however some noteworthy differences. As becomes immediately discernable, Western AfD voters do not think in terms of regional disparities while 5 per cent of Eastern German AfD voters do express concern. As an example, one Eastern German AfD voter noted that "as East German citizen, I feel patronized by West Germans. For West Germans, we only count as lowest-class people".[1] Another statement combines concerns over regional disparities with socio-economic matters: "Wages and salaries and pensions should be adjusted to West German levels!".[2] Second, an equally high share of West Germans mentioned concerns that did not fall within any of these four categories. Most often mentioned by respondents that fall within these 5 per cent were issues pertaining to the EU, criticism directed against the Euro as common currency, or bailout measures (alongside other statements). This focus on the EU and its common currency by Westerners lends credence to the claim that the AfD's transition from a Eurosceptic single-issue party to a right-wing populist entity in parliament (Arzheimer 2015; Schmitt-Beck 2017) also manifests itself in two different kinds of voters: "early supporters" drawn to the AfD mainly for its Eurosceptic past and "late supporters" for its radical right and populist present (Schmitt-Beck 2017: 129). By contrast, all statement made by East German voters were clearly tackling one of the four above mentioned categories. Lastly, almost twice as many Eastern German AfD supporters (around 17–18 per cent) were critical of the political system, expressed anger with the political "elites" and blamed "out-of-touch" politicians for a number of negative developments and social disparities.

In addition to these findings, Figure A.1 (appendix) also reveals that most statements combined two categories, for instance complaining about the "refugee situation" only to go into more detail about socio-economic matters, pensions, wages, and sentiments of social injustice in the second half. In fact, this combination of categories 1 and 2 appeared most often in the data (about 45 to 50 per cent of all statements, single and double, taken together). These combined statements are indicative of a strong interaction of different motives: anti-immigration attitudes, concerns over social injustice, and a widening income gap and disenchantment with the political system can hardly be seen separate from each other.

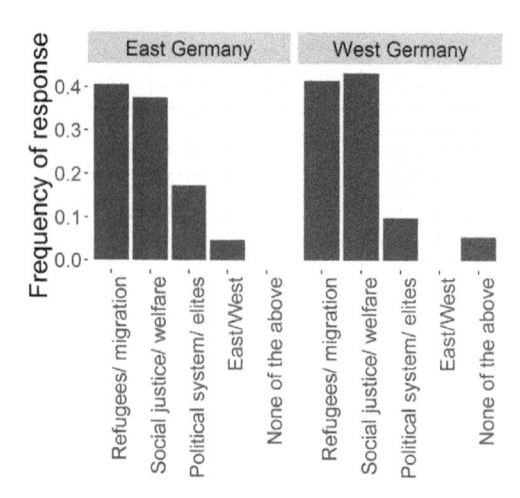

FIGURE 6.1 Most important problems according to Eastern and Western German AfD voters (in percentage points)

Note: N = 454; based on GLES data/ZA6802 (Roßteutscher et al. 2018)

Taken together, these *descriptive* results point towards striking differences in AfD voters' opinions – and possibly also behind their motives to support the AfD. For Western Germans, among other things, the EU, regulation, and particularly the common currency appear to be problematic issues. On the other side, out-of-touch politicians, corruption within the political system, and lack of representation of people's interests and needs are prominent points of critique among Eastern German AfD supporters. The refugee crisis, migration, and social justice appear more or less equally important to the West and East. Most obvious, however, is the fact that a substantial share of East Germans claims that, compared to "Westerners", people living in the East are systematically discriminated against, excluded from political decisions, and economically worse off than the rest. This matches perfectly with previous findings that show how East Germans feel discriminated against and portrayed as second-class citizens (Best et al. 2016; see also Hensel 2018).

East and West German voters are clearly divided, view different things as problematic and would, perhaps, put different issues on the agenda when it comes to political decisions. Yet, do these differences translate also into distinct motives and decide over the path that leads to voting for the AfD?

In a second step, we illuminate the causal mechanism of support for the AfD and examine whether citizens in the East and West take indeed different routes to their voting decisions. The underlying question is: can differences in motives and in voter characteristics explain the disproportionate success of the AfD in East Germany? Methodologically, we would assume that if "region" turns out to be a significant factor driving vote choice, this does not necessarily mean that voters differ in their respective motives to vote AfD. Rather, it would suggest that regional contexts and/or the party's image and key messages make a difference. By contrast, if we were to find that the place of residence voters identify with *mediates* the effect of specific motives and voter attributes on support for the AfD in a meaningful way, this would allow us to infer that regionally different voting patterns and AfD vote shares can be traced back to distinct mechanisms and demand-side factors.

Our variable selection leans on earlier studies of AfD support (e.g. Hambauer and Mays 2018). Compared to Hambauer and Mays's (2018) study however, we go further into detail regarding populist attitudes, interest in politics, the regional dimension of economic developments as well as the mediating effect of region.

As expected, Eastern respondents turn out to be more supportive of the AfD. Overall, both electoral support for, and a favorable opinion about the AfD among survey respondents increased from 2013 to 2018. Nonetheless, the share of self-reported AfD voters slightly lags behind the official election results of 2017 by around 4 percentage points (for the results of the *Bundestagswahl* 2017, see Bundeswahlleiter 2017). In order to correct for the oversampling of non-AfD voters, the regression results are weighted by the 2017 election outcome.

Our analysis contains a binary variable that controls for different levels of support for the AfD in the East and West of Germany ("East"). We expect this variable to moderate third variables that are directly or indirectly linked to sentiments of discrimination and exclusion from the political discourse. Variables capturing these sentiments can either operate on a *socio-economic dimension* thus addressing social disparities and "relative [here: regional] economic deprivation" (Gest, Reny and Mayer 2017; Gidron and Hall 2017; Kopetsch 2017; Rooduijn and Burgoon 2017; Burgoon 2018) or operate on a second, *populist dimension* measuring frustration with political elites that seemingly do not care about Eastern interests.

In order to take both of these dimensions into account and ascertain as to what extent they interact with region ("East"), we introduce "Populist attitudes" and two economic variables ("Lower class" and "Economy negative") to our model. The first consists of five out of six survey questions intended to tap populism.[3] Testing for the overall reliability of this index reveals that including the sixth survey question would have reduced Cronbach's alpha from.78 to.75 (see Table A.1, appendix). More importantly, however, the sixth survey item does not conform well with the definition of populism: as expected, many respondents endorse the statement that politicians should represent the people in parliament ("vn66c"), yet the item does not directly tap into populist attitudes.

"Lower class" and "Economy negative" tap into sentiments of economic deprivation and poor standards of living often related to support for the populist radical right (Dippel, Gold and Heblich 2015; Betz 2017a). Importantly, the first variable asks respondents to identify which social class they feel they belong to and takes on 1 if they indicated "Lower class" and otherwise takes on 0, while the latter asks whether respondents think that Germany's current economic situation is bad.

Aside from these factors that can be linked to region, our model controls for several other factors previous studies have found to be relevant or at least included in their empirical models of AfD support (e.g. Hambauer and Mays 2018). These survey questions tap into anti-immigrant sentiments that have especially been associated with more recent AfD supporters (Schmitt-Beck 2017: 129), but which also tap into discontent arising from globalization/denationalization processes that leave parts of national populations feeling powerless (Dippel, Gold and Heblich 2015; Betz 2017a). Additionally, we control for respondents' ideological orientation, their interest in politics, and a number of demographic characteristics. Table 6.1 summarizes our main model regression results on a binary AfD support dependent variable.

The results largely confirm the assumption that region can mediate the effect of political and socio-economic attitudes on the support for the populist right. The overall fit is higher than compared to Hambauer and Mays (2018) which may be explained by several different factors: a larger overall sample size, larger share of AfD voters and weighting according to official election results enabling us to compare AfD and non-AfD voters in East and West Germany and lastly by our model specification itself which takes important additional factors into account.

TABLE 6.1 Binary logistic regression results

	Model 1: Electoral support for the AfD(Odds Ratios)
Fear globalization	1.74★★★
Immigration (weighted)	3.64★★★
Left-right self-placement	1.66★★★
Interest in politics	0.25★★★
Populist attitudes	7.10★★★
Populist attitudes × East	1.48★★★
Lower class	5.44★★
Lower class × East	1.17★
Economy negative	4.49★★★
Economy negative × East	0.59
East	2.87★★★
Age	0.97★★★
Male	1.48★★★
Education (middle)	1.05★★
Education (high)	0.64★★★
Intercept	3.72★★★
Cox & Snell R^2	0.62
Nagelkerke R^2	0.67

Note: ★★★ $p<0.001$, ★★ $p<0.01$, ★ $p<0.5$; dependent variable weighted by AfD results in the general election in 2017; N=2990.[1] A detailed overview of the survey questions we used can be found in the appendix (Table A2)

Beginning with populist attitudes, higher scores are strongly associated ($p<0.001$) with the likelihood of voting AfD. Importantly, this is also the case for the interaction of region and populist attitudes: a sense of powerlessness, the feeling that traditional parties appear to regard Easterners as second-class citizens, and frustration with a party system that has been gradually moving away from its electorate in the East – all of this draws Eastern voters towards the AfD. Alienated from the traditional party system as well as Die Linke, citizens regard the AfD as a last resort of protest against a system seen as corrupt and dysfunctional (see also Hagen 2017; Machowecz 2018). For West German voters, by contrast, this does not appear to be a very prominent motive behind support for the AfD.

Sentiments of relative economic deprivation and personal identification with the "lower class" are generally linked to AfD support, but – just like populist attitudes – also interact with region (see also Figure 6.2 which displays the predicted probabilities for both interaction terms). These results match perfectly with what a number of Eastern German AfD voters state (see p.121): "Wages and salaries and pensions should be adjusted to West German levels!". However, whereas respondents' own wellbeing and own class identification clearly interact with region, the assessment of the current economic situation of

Germany ("Economy negative") does not. On their own, economic concerns do play a role. Yet, these concerns impact on voting decisions in East and West Germany equally so that no regional interaction effects can be discerned. The story these findings tell is that while voters in East Germany are not disproportionally concerned with the state of the economy Germany is facing, personal levels of wellbeing and regional deprivation are often problematized. On the contrary, AfD voters might even argue that while Germany as a whole (or: West Germany) is doing well economically, one feels left out and *relatively* disadvantaged.

Figure 6.2 summarizes these two effects: on the left side, the positive effect of lower class self-identification on being sympathetic to the AfD in East Germany can clearly be discerned. On the right, the figure shows that populist attitudes are more directly linked to AfD support in East Germany (dark grey) compared to West Germany (light grey).

In sum, the empirical results largely confirm both of our theoretical claims. Populist attitudes do not only drive citizens to vote AfD but are also, as expected, mediated by region (1). And even though a negative assessment of general economic conditions does not interact with region, identification as "lower class" does, suggesting that (perceived) relative economic deprivation among Easterners also increases the likelihood of voting AfD (2). These two results are best reflected in statements among East German AfD supporters such as this: "As East German citizen, I feel patronized by West Germans. For West

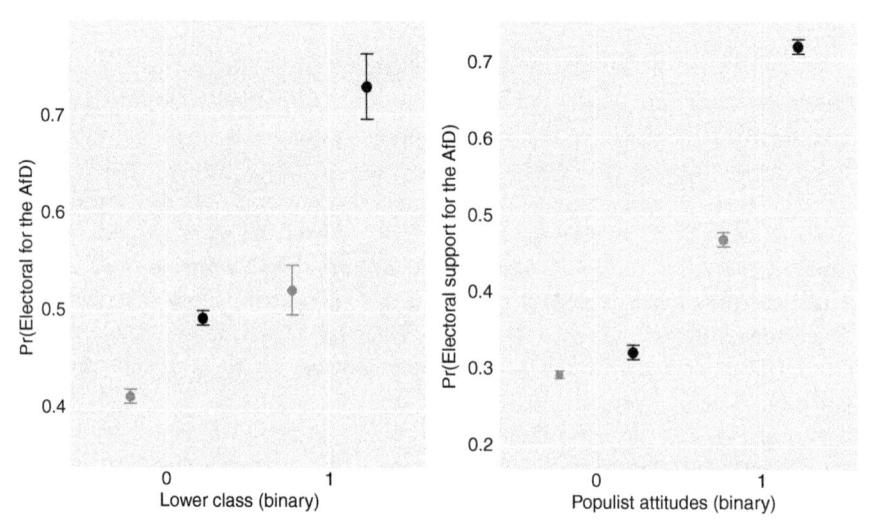

FIGURE 6.2 Predicted effects of "lower class" (left) and "populist attitudes" (right) in interaction with "East"

Note: East Germany (dark grey); West Germany (light grey); 95 per cent CIs; based on model 1

Germans, we only count as lowest-class people". Though levels of anti-immigration sentiments among Easterners and the affinity of segments of the Eastern German electorate with radical right discourse are both pronounced, this study demonstrates that it is worthwhile to shed more light on the exact mechanisms linking specific sentiments to radical right populist support.

Conclusion

The evidence presented in this chapter suggests that it is reasonable to interpret the disproportionate success of the AfD in the Eastern part of Germany as an expression of regionalist nativism largely motivated by the misgivings and resentment that continue to haunt Eastern Germany some 25 years after unification. It is hardly a coincidence that the AfD has replaced Die Linke – a party that resulted from the merger of the (Eastern German) PDS and (Western German) SPD defectors – as a regional catch-all party of protest representing the East (Hagen 2017; Machowecz 2018). Its success in the East is largely owed to the "emotional injuries" a large number of Eastern Germans have sustained in the decades following unification, but which were downplayed or ignored for too long. It is only now, in the aftermath of the 2017 federal election that these issues have become the topic of public debate (FES 2018).

These tensions are immediately discernable from our voter data analysis as well: for one, anti-elitist sentiments bring elite vs. ordinary people discourses to the fore and give them an additional territorial dimension. The traditional party system has, according to East Germans, moved away from their concerns and interests – thus making way for a new *Ostpartei* (party of East Germany) to fill the void (see also: Machowecz 2018). East Germans feel relatively deprived both in a social sense ("second-class citizens") and in an economic sense when it comes to East German pensions and parameters indicating that the East is still lagging behind West German standards, more than 25 years after unification – both culminating in a higher likelihood of voting AfD.

Against the backdrop of these findings, a further avenue for research would be to shift focus to the supply-side. Our analysis assumes that differences among voters and between regions can explain differences in AfD vote shares. And we found evidence that corroborates this claim: the regional strength of the AfD can be directly linked to regional idiosyncrasies and East German frustration with national elites as well as economic developments. Yet, this does not mean that the AfD had no role in these events. Did the AfD campaign on different slogans tailored to its audience and set different policy priorities in the East and in the West? Is it the AfD that learned to understand East Germany while others have lost this connection?

Appendix

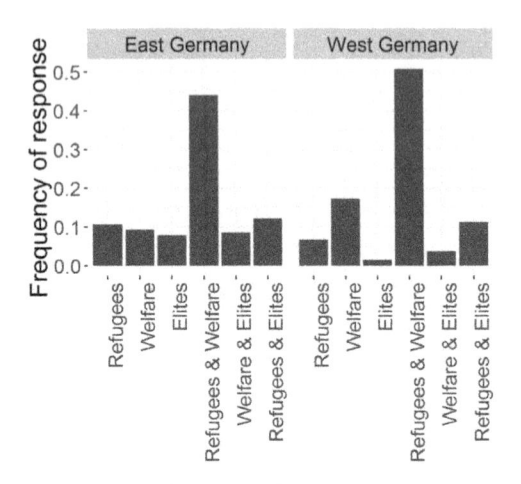

FIGURE A.1 Most important problems according to Eastern and Western German AfD voters (in percentage points); single statements and double mentions
Note: N = 454; based on GLES data/ZA6802 (Roßteutscher et al. 2018).

TABLE A.1 Reliability of measurements of populist attitudes (Cronbach's alpha)

	Raw alpha	Reliability if an item is dropped Std. alpha	SE
Item 1: "vn66a"	.70	.70	.007
Item 2: "vn66b"	.71	.71	.007
Item 3: "vn66c"	.78	.78	.006
Item 4: "vn66d"	.74	.74	.006
Item 5: "vn66e"	.73	.73	.006
Item 6: "vn66f"	.71	.71	.007

Note: Overall reliability of 6 items: alpha=.75

TABLE A.2 Measurement and direction of effects

Location in dataset	Name in regression model	Survey question (own translation)	Scale	Predicted direction
n11ba	Support for AfD	In the general election, you could cast two votes. The first vote for a candidate from your constituency, the second one for a party list. Here is a sample ballot similar to the one you received in the general election. What did you tick on your ballot?	Dummy (1 = AfD)	
n55d	Fear globalization	How scared are you about globalization?	Dummy (1 = scared)	+
vn60	Immigration	What is your opinion on access for foreigners into the country?	(-5) should be facilitated; (+5) should be restricted; weighted by vn63; Dummy: 3Q = cut-off	+
vn 63	[Immigration salience]	How important is the issue of access for foreigners to you?	(1) not at all important; (2) very important	
vn54	Left-right self-placement	In politics people often talk of "left" and "right". Where would you place yourself on a scale from 1 to 11?	(1) left; (11) right	+
vn3	Interest in politics	How much are you interested in politics?	(1) not at all interested; (5) very interested	+
vn66a-b; d-f	Populist attitudes	(a) What is called "compromise" in politics really just means betrayal of principles. (b) The people should take important political decisions, not politicians. (d) The political differences between elites and the people are larger than differences among the people. (e) Another citizen would represent my interests better than a career politician. (f) Politicians talk too much and do too little.	Dummy (1 = agree)	+

(Continued)

TABLE A.2 (Cont.)

Location in dataset	Name in regression model	Survey question (own translation)	Scale	Predicted direction
	Populist attitudes × East			+
vn167	Lower class	Which of the following classes you feel you belong to?	(1 = lower class)	+
	Populist attitudes × East			+
vn26	Economy negative	How do you evaluate the general economic situation of Germany at the moment?	(1 = very bad)	+
	Economy negative × East			(+)
ostwest2	East	[Interviewer: coded "East Germany" if place of residence is in one of the East German *Bundesländer* or East Berlin; otherwise coded "West Germany"]	Dummy (1 = East Germany)	+
vn2c	Age	In what year were you born?	Metric scale	+
vn1	Male	[Interviewer: coded male or female]	Dummy (1 = male)	+
vn136	Education	What is your highest level of educational attainment? [recoded]	(1) low [elementary school or lower]; (2) middle; (3) high [college degree or higher]	−

Source: Roßteutscher et al. (2018). *Note:* hypothesized effects not found to be sig. are in brackets.

Notes

1 Own translation; the original statement reads: "Als ostdeutscher Einwohner fühle ich mich durch die Westdeutschen bevormundet und entmündigt. Für die Westdeutschen zählen wir doch bloß als Menschen letzter Klasse". Source: GLES / ZA6802 (Roßteutscher et al. 2018).
2 Own translation; the original statement reads: "Lohn und Gehalt und Rente angleichen an Westniveau!". Source: GLES / ZA6802 (Roßteutscher et al. 2018).
3 For the complete list of questions that went into this index, see Table A2, appendix.

References

AfD. (2016a) *Manifesto for Germany: The Political Programme of the Alternative for Germany.* www.afd.de/grundsatzprogramm. Accessed 11 December 2018.

AfD. (2016b) *Wahlprogramm zur Landtagswahl am 13. März 2016.* Magdeburg: AfD Landesverband Sachsen-Anhalt. https://afd-lsa.de/fraktion/wahlprogramm. Accessed 11 December 2018.

AfD. (2017) "'Der Islam müsste in Deutschland verboten sein' – André Poggenburg – 5. Bürgerdialog des Landtages von Sachsen-Anhalt". *AfD Fraktion im Landtag Sachsen-Anhalt*, www.afdfraktion-lsa.de/der-islam-muesste-in-deutschland-verboten-sein-andre-poggen burg-5-buergerdialog-des-landtages-von-sachsen-anhalt. Accessed 11 December 2018.

Arnold, M., Eickelpasch, A., Fritsch, M., Mattes, A. and Schiersch, A. (2015) "Die ostdeutsche Wirtschaft ist zu kleinteilig strukturiert". *DIW Wochenbericht*, pp. 764–772.

Arzheimer, K. (2015). "The AfD: Finally a Successful Right-Wing Populist Eurosceptic Party for Germany?". *West European Politics*, 38(3), pp. 535–556.

Belock, F. and Faus, R. (2017) *Kartografie der politischen Landschaft in Deutschland: Die wichtigsten Ergebnisse für Ostdeutschland.* Berlin: Forum Berlin/Friedrich Ebert Stiftung.

Bergmann, K., Diermeier, M. and Niehues, J. (2017) "Die AfD: Eine Partei der sich ausgeliefert fühlenden Durchschnittsverdiener?". *Zeitschrift für Parlamentsfragen*, 48(1), pp. 57–75.

Best, H., Niehoff, S., Salheiser, A. and Vogel, L. (2016). "Thüringen nach der 'Flüchtlingskrise': Ergebnisse des Thüringen-Monitors 2016". *Kompetenzzentrum Rechtsextremismus: Friedrich-Schiller-Universität Jena.* www.thueringen.de/mam/th1/tsk/thuringenmonitor_2016_mit_anhang.pdf. Accessed 11 December 2018.

Betz, H.-G. (2017a) "Nativism and the Success of Populist Mobilization". *Revista Internacional de pensamiento politico*, 12, pp. 169–188.

Betz, H.-G. (2017b). "Nativism Across Time and Space". *Swiss Political Science Review*, 23 (4), pp. 335–353.

Brubaker, R. (2017b). "Between Nationalism and Civilizationalism: The European Populist Moment in Comparative Perspective". *Ethnic and Racial Studies*, 40(8), pp. 1191–1226.

Bundeswahlleiter. (2017). "Bundestagswahl 2017: Endgültige Ergebnisse". Homepage, https://bundeswahlleiter.de/bundestagswahlen/2017/ergebnisse.html. Accessed 11 December 2018.

Burgoon, B. (2018) "Positional Deprivation and the Economic Roots of Radical Right and Radical Left Voting". Paper presented at *EZH*, Zurich, March 8.

Cramer, E.-M. (2016) "Interview mit dem Chef der AfD Bayern über Muslime, Moscheen, die 'Blaue Allianz' mit der FPÖ". Bayern Depesche, 20 April. www.bayerndepesche.de/politik/petr-bystron-afd-„der-islam-muss-sich-an-die-normen-und-werteder-aufgeklärten-moderne-anpassen".html. Accessed 11 December 2018.

Dauth, W., Findeisen, S. and Suedekum, J. (2017). "Trade and Manufacturing Jobs in Germany". *American Economic Review: Papers and Proceedings*, 107(5), pp. 337–342.

Dennis, M. (2007). "Working under Hammer and Sickle: Vietnamese Workers in the German Democratic Republic, 1980–89". *German Politics*, 16(3), pp. 339–357.

Dippel, C., Gold, R. and Heblich, S. (2015) "Globalization and Its (Dis-)Content: Trade Shocks and Voting Behaviour". *National Bureau of Economic Research working paper*, 21812.

Epoch Times. (2017). "AfD-Pressekonferenz: Islam ist nicht mit 'freiheitlichen, demokratischen Grundordnung Deutschlands vereinbar'". 19 September. www.epochtimes.de/politik/deutschland/afd-pressekonferenz-islam-ist-nicht-mit-freiheitlichen-demokra

tischen-grundordnung-deutschlands-vereinbar-a2219620.html. Accessed 11 December 2018.
Fassin, D. (2013). "On Resentment and Ressentiment. The Politics and Ethics of Moral Emotions". *Current Anthropology*, 54(3), pp. 249–267.
FES. (2018) "Wie viel Westen steckt im Osten? Westdeutsche Eliten und ostdeutsche Befindlichkeiten". 22 March. www.fes.de/landesbuero-sachsen/artikelseite-landesbuero-sachsen/wie-viel-westen-steckt-im-osten-westdeutsche-eliten-und-ost deutsche-befindlichkeiten. Accessed 11 December 2018.
FES – Friedrich Ebert Stiftung. (2016) "Studie zeigt Stabilität rechtsextremer und - populistischer Einstellungen". 21 November. www.fes.de/e/studie-zeigt-stabilitaet-rechtsextremer-und-populistischer-einstellungen. Accessed 11 December 2018.
Frankfurter Allgemeine Zeitung. (2017). "Mehrheit der Thüringer fühlt sich ungerecht behandelt". 1 November. www.faz.net/aktuell/politik/inland/thueringen-monitor-mehrheit-fuehlt-sich-ungerecht-behandelt-15272597.html.
Franzmann, S. T. (2016) "Von AfD zu ALFA: Die Entwicklung zur Spaltung". *Mitteilungen des Instituts für Deutsches und Internationales Parteienrecht und Parteienforschung*, 22, pp. 23–37.
Gest, J., Reny, T. and Mayer, J. (2017). "Roots of the Radical Right: Nostalgic Deprivation in the United States and Britain". *Comparative Political Studies*, 51(13), pp. 1694–1719.
Geyer, C. (2010) "So wird Deutschland dumm". *Frankfurter Allgemeine Zeitung*, 26 August. www.faz.net/aktuell/feuilleton/sarrazin/das-buch/sarrazins-thesen-so-wird-deutschland-dumm-11029081.html. Accessed 11 December 2018.
Gidron, N. and Hall, P. A. (2017). "The Politics of Social Status: Economic and Cultural Roots of the Populist Right". *British Journal of Sociology*, 68(S1), pp. 57–84.
Grimm, R. (2015). "The Rise of the German Eurosceptic Party Alternative für Deutschland, between Ordoliberal Critique and Popular Anxiety". *International Political Science Review*, 36(3), pp. 264–278.
HaGalil. (2010) "Sarrazin: Umfragen". 2 September. www.hagalil.com/2010/09/sarrazin-8. Accessed 11 December 2018.
Hagen, K. (2017) "Das Ende der Ost-Partei". *Der Spiegel*, 29 September. www.spiegel.de/politik/deutschland/die-linke-nach-der-bundestagswahl-2017-das-ende-der-ost-partei-a-1170037.html. Accessed 11 December 2018.
Haidt, J. (2003) "The Moral Emotions". In: Davidson, R. J., Scherer, K. R. and Goldsmith, H. H. (eds.) *Handbook of Affective Sciences*. Oxford: Oxford University Press, pp. 852–870.
Hambauer, V. and Mays, A. (2018). "Wer wählt die AfD? Ein Vergleich der Sozialstruktur, politischen Einstellungen und Einstellungen zu Flüchtlingen zwischen AfD-WählerInnen und der WählerInnen der anderen Parteien". *Zeitschrift für Vergleichende Politikwissenschaft*, 12(1), pp. 133–154.
Haug, S., Müssig, S. and Stichs, A. (2009) *Muslimisches Leben in Deutschland. Forschungsbericht 6*. Berlin: Bundesamt für Migration und Flüchtlinge.
Henkel, M. (2017) *Der Islam: Fakten und Argumente*, 3 ed. Erfurt: Fraktion der Alternative für Deutschland (AfD) im Thüringer Landtag.
Hensel, J. (2018) "Ostdeutschland – Willkommen im Club". *Die Zeit*, 20 May. www.zeit.de/politik/deutschland/2018-05/ostdeutschland-erfahrungen-migration-naika-forou tan. Accessed 11 December 2018.
Hornuf, L. and Rieger, M. O. (2017) "Can Television Reduce Xenophobia? The Case of East Germany". *IAAEU Discussion Paper Series in Economics*, 2.

Infratest dimap. (2017) "Bundestagswahl 2017 Deutschland: Umfragen zur AfD". https://wahl.tagesschau.de/wahlen/2017-09-24-BT-DE/umfrage-afd.shtml. Accessed 11 December 2018.

Jansen, R. S. (2011). "Populist Mobilization: A New Theoretical Approach to Populism". *Sociological Theory*, 29(2), pp. 75–96.

Jensen, U. (2017) *Zornpolitik*. Berlin: Suhrkamp Verlag.

Jones, R. P., Cox, D. and Lienesch, R. (2017) "Beyond Economics: Fears of Cultural Displacement Pushed the White Working Class to Trump". *PRRI/The Atlantic Report*, www.prri.org/research/white-working-class-attitudes-economy-trade-immigration-election-donald-trump. Accessed 11 December 2018.

Jun, U. (2017) "Repräsentation durch Parteien. Die Entwicklung des deutschen Parteiensystems und Parteienwettbewerbs nach 1945". In: Koschmieder, C. (ed.) *Parteien, Parteiensysteme und politische Orientierungen. Aktuelle Beiträge der Parteienforschung*. Wiesbaden: VS Verlag für Sozialwissenschaften, pp. 87–112.

Kenny, M. (2017). "Back to the Populist Future? Understanding Nostalgia in Contemporary Ideological Discourse". *Journal of Political Ideologies*, 22(3), pp. 256–273.

Köcher, R. (eds.) (2009) *Allensbacher Jahrbuch der Demoskopie. Vol. 12 (2003–2009)*. Berlin: Walter de Gruyter.

Kopetsch, C. (2017). "Rechtspopulismus, Etablierte und Außenseiter. Emotionale Dynamiken sozialer Deklassierung". *Leviathan*, 45(32), pp. 208–232.

Kubiak, D. (2018). "Der Fall 'Ostdeutschland': 'Einheitsfiktion' als Herausforderung für die Integration am Fallbeispiel der Ost-West-Differenz". *Zeitschrift für Vergleichende Politikwissenschaft*, 12(1), pp. 25–42.

Kuper, A. (2003). "The Return of the Native". *Current Anthropology*, 44(3), pp. 389–402.

Leipziger Volkszeitung. (2017). "Zufriedene Sachsen hegen weiter viele Ressentiments". 28 November. www.lvz.de/Region/Mitteldeutschland/Zufriedene-Sachsen-hegen-weiter-viele-Ressentiments. Accessed 11 December 2018.

Lengfeld, H. (2017a). "Die 'Alternative für Deutschland': eine Partei für Modernisierungsverlierer?". *Kölner Zeitschrift für Soziologie und Sozialpsychologie*, 69(2), pp. 209–232.

Lengfeld, H. (2017b). "Abstiegsangst in Deutschland auf historischem Tiefstand". *Arbeitsbericht des Instituts für Soziologie, Universität Leipzig*, (73), 21 August 2017, pp. 1–18.

Lengfeld, H. and Ordemann, J. (2016) "Die Angst der Mittelschicht vor dem sozialen Abstieg revisited. Eine Längsschnittananlyse 1984–2014". *SOEP papers on Multidisciplinary Panel Data Research*, no. 862, pp. 1–30.

Lewandowsky, M. (2015). "Eine rechtspopulistische Protestpartei? Die AfD in der öffentlichen and politikwissenschaftlichen Debatte". *Zeitschrift für Politikwissenschaft*, 25(1), pp. 119–134.

Linden, M. (2003). "Postraumatic Embitterment Disorder". *Psychotherapy and Psychosomatics*, 72(4), pp. 195–202.

Machowecz, M. (2018) "Ist die Linke schuld am Aufstieg der AfD?". *Die Zeit*, 6 May. www.zeit.de/2018/19/ostdeutschland-linke-afd-aufstieg.

Mielke, G. and Eith, U. (2017) "Auf dem (Rück-)Weg zur Demokratiewissenschaft? Anmerkungen zur Parteien- und Wahlforschung". In: Koschmieder, C. (ed.) *Parteien, Parteiensysteme und politische Orientierungen. Aktuelle Beiträge der Parteienforschung*. Wiesbaden: VS Verlag für Sozialwissenschaften, pp. 11–26.

Miller, D. (2005). "Reasonable Partiality Towards Compatriots". *Ethical Theory and Moral Practice*, 8(1–2), pp. 63–81.

Nachtwey, O. (2015). "Rechte Wutbürger: Pegida oder das autoritäre Syndrom". *Blätter für deutsche und internationale Politik*, 60(3), pp. 81–89.

Noelle, E. and Petersen, T. (2006) "Eine fremde, bedrohliche Welt". *Frankfurter Allgemeine Zeitung*, 17 May. www.faz.net/aktuell/politik/inland/allensbach-analyse-eine-fremde-bedrohliche-welt-1328270.html. Accessed 11 December 2018.

Pettigrew, T. F. and Tropp, L. R. (2008). "How Does Intergroup Contact Reduce Prejudice? Meta-Analytic Tests of Three Mediators". *European Journal of Social Psychology*, 38 (6), pp. 922–934.

Pickel, G. and Yendell, A. (2016). "Islam als Bedrohung? Beschreibung and Erklärung von Instellungen zum Islam im Ländervergleich". *Zeitschrift für Vergleichende Politikwissenschaft*, 10(3–4), pp. 273–309.

Poutrus, P., Behrends, J., and Kuck, D. (2000). "Historische Ursachen der Fremdenfeindlichkeit in den neuen Bundesländern". *Aus Politik und Zeitgeschehen*, 26(May), pp. 15–21.

Reinbold, F. (2010) "42 Prozent der Deutschen lehnen Sarrazins Thesen ab". *Der Spiegel*, 14 September. www.spiegel.de/politik/deutschland/umfrage-42-prozent-der-deutschen-lehnen-sarrazins-thesen-ab-a-717267.html. Accessed 11 December 2018.

Rensmann, L. (2017). "The Noisy Counter-Revolution: Understanding the Cultural Conditions and Dynamics of Populist Politics in Europe in the Digital Age". *Politics and Governance*, 5(4), pp. 123–135.

Rico, G., Guinjoan, M. and Anduiza, E. (2017). "The Emotional Underpinnings of Populism: How Anger and Fear Affect Populist Attitudes". *Swiss Political Science Review*, 23 (4), pp. 444–461.

Rooduijn, M. and Burgoon, B. (2017). "The Paradox of Well-Being: Do Unfavorable Socio-Economic and Socio-Cultural Contexts Deepen or Dampen Radical Left and Radical Right Voting among the Less Well-Off?". *Comparative Political Studies*, 51(13), pp. 1720–1753.

Roßteutscher, S., Schmitt-Beck, R., Schoen, H., Weßels, B., Wolf, C., Bieber, I., Stövsand, L.-C., Dietz, M., Scherer, P., Wagner, A., Melcher, R. and Giebler, H. (2018) "Pre- and Post-Election Cross Section Cumulation/GLES 2017". GESIS Data Archive, Cologne. ZA6802 Data file Version 1.1.0. doi:10.4232/1.13139.

RP Online. (2000) "Forsa-Umfrage ergab: Mehrheit für Einwanderungsgesetz mit Asylrechtsbeschränkung". 5 July. https://rp-online.de/politik/mehrheit-fuer-einwanderungsgesetz-mit-asylrechtsbeschraenkung_aid-8264165. Accessed 11 December 2018.

Rudolph, N. (2016) "Ostdeutsche Besonderheiten 25 Jahre nach dem Beitritt zur Bundesrepublik". In: Thieme, T. (ed.) *25 Jahre deutsche Einheit*. Chemnitz: Universitätsverlag Chemnitz, pp. 85–99.

Salmela, M. and von Scheve, C. (2017). "Emotional Roots of Right-Wing Political Populism". *Social Science Information*, 56(4), pp. 567–595.

Sander, B. (2015) "Bekommen Flüchtlinge mehr Geld als Hartz IV-Empfänger?". *Schweriner Volkszeitung*, 9 December. www.svz.de/regionales/mecklenburg-vorpommern/politik/bekommen-fluechtlinge-mehr-geld-als-hartz-iv-empfaenger-id12164336.html. Accessed 11 December 2018.

Sarrazin, T. (2010) *Deutschland schafft sich ab: Wie wir unser Land aufs Spiel setzen*. Munchen: DVA.

Schmidt, C. (2017) "Mehr als Hartz IV? Was Flüchtlinge vom Staat bekommen". *Märkische Allgemeine*, 13 February. www.maz-online.de/Lokales/Havelland/Mehr-als-Hartz-IV-Was-Fluechtlinge-vom-Staat-bekommen. Accessed 11 December 2018.

Schmidt, M. (2015) "Der Islam gehört für Viele immer noch nicht zu Deutschland". *YouGov*, 24 September. https://yougov.de/news/2015/09/24/der-islam-gehort-fur-viele-immer-noch-nicht-zu-deu. Accessed 11 December 2018.

Schmitt-Beck, R. (2017). "The 'Alternative für Deutschland in the Electorate': Between Single-Issue and Right-Wing Populist Party". *German Politics*, 26(1), pp. 124–148.

Spiegel Online. (2000) "Geschäftsführer Bartsch: Rassismus auch bei PDS-Wählern". 6 December. www.spiegel.de/politik/deutschland/geschaeftsfuehrer-bartsch-rassismus-auch-bei-pds-waehlern-a-106462.html. Accessed 11 December 2018.

Steffen, T. (2017) "Alternative für Deutschland: Der ganz normale Rassismus". *Die Zeit*, 31 August. www.zeit.de/politik/deutschland/2017-08/afd-alexander-gauland-volksverhetzung-aydan-oezoguz. Accessed 11 December 2018.

Süddeutsche Zeitung. (2018) "Merkel widerspricht Seehofer: 'Islam gehört zu Deutschland'". 16 March. https://www.sueddeutsche.de/news/politik/migration-merkel-widerspricht-seehofer-islam-gehoert-zu-deutschland-dpa.urn-newsml-dpa-com-20090101-180316-99-512690.

Südekum, J., Dauth, W. and Findeisen, S. (2017). "Verlierer(-regionen) der Globalisierung in Deutschland: Wer? Warum? Was tun?". *Wirtschaftsdienst*, 97(1), pp. 24–31.

Vorländer, H., Herold, M. and Schäller, S. (2015) "Wer geht zu PEGIDA und warum? Eine empirische Untersuchung von PEGIDA-Demonstranten in Dresden". *Schriften zur Verfassungs- und Demokratieforschung*, 1(1), Dresden: ZVD, pp. 1–80.

Vorländer, H., Herold, M. and Schäller, S. (2017). "Entfremdung, Empörung, Ethnozentrismus. Was PEGIDA über den sich formierenden Rechtspopulismus verrät". *Leviathan*, 45(32), pp. 138–159.

7

THE CARINTHIAN MODEL

The role of sub-national claims in the Freedom Party's dominance in Austria's southernmost state

Reinhard Heinisch

Introduction

The Austrian Freedom Party (FPÖ) is best known for national campaigns based on a right-wing populist agenda, by advocating nativism, ethnic identity, Euroscepticism, and a selective mix of market liberal and protectionist policy position. In the past, the FPÖ had been closely associated also with German-nationalist, anti-Semitic, and anti-Slavic claims, from which the party has now officially distanced itself. In fact, liberalism and (German) nationalism were – before the party's conversion into a populist radical right party (PRRP) – the FPÖ's core ideologies. All of this identifies the FPÖ as a national political party with a national agenda implying that sub-national claims should not matter or would in fact detract from its national message.

Yet, when the Freedom Party was headed by Jörg Haider – the party leader who transformed it into a populist party at the national level –, he was closely associated with the Austrian state (province) of Carinthia, which also served as the FPÖ's stronghold. In fact, the Carinthian party organization, called since 1986 FPK or Freedom Party in Carinthia, at the time dominated the FPÖ. In that state, Haider not only achieved substantial electoral majorities but it is from Carinthia that he and his party could exert political influence at the national level. However, this constitutes something of a puzzle. How can a political actor and party excel both at the national and sub-national level? This is even more remarkable, given that Carinthia is only a small and economically somewhat backward province among nine states that make up the Federal Republic of Austria. In other countries where regional party organizations dominate the national party, such as Zurich in the Swiss People's Party, Antwerp in the case of the Belgian Vlaams Belang, and even Lombardy in the case of the Lega Nord, these are generally the politically most relevant and prosperous parts of their respective countries. Carinthia is in many ways the opposite and has been struggling to keep up with the modernization and economic growth underway in the richer parts of Austria.

As will be shown in this chapter, the Carinthian case is special in that the messages by the FPÖ at the regional level were not merely extensions of the national-level but rather distinct. It is also not the case that the FPÖ's national policy positions are simply an especially close fit for the Carinthian context. Nor can it be argued that the Carinthian electorate is configured such that it has a special socio-demographic affinity for the Freedom Party. Even the claim that Haider resonated especially with Carinthians because he, as one of their own, rose to international prominence is not convincing because he was originally not even from that state but had moved there as a young party functionary. This leads to two related research questions this chapter seeks to answer: First, what were the special political characteristics of Carinthia that Haider and his party could exploit to construct a series of claims that were effective at the sub-national level[1]? Second, what was the effect of having a PRRP as the dominant party in government for more than a decade? Specifically, do we see a regional populist model of governing?

Theoretical discussion

Theories explaining the success of populist parties have focused on two sets of factors: opportunity structures in terms of demand-side explanations (Arzheimer and Carter 2006) and winning formulas in terms of the supply side (Kitschelt 2007). When applying explanations to the regional level, we have to look for factors that pertain more directly to certain sub-national territories versus others. These include existing *ethnic and socio-cultural cleavages* as well as historical legacies that shape some regions more than others. Certain regional peculiarities may also lend themselves to center-periphery mobilization (Alonso 2012) and lead to a separate identity formation vis-à-vis the nation state. This in turn, may provide a fulcrum for populist mobilization because it allows political actors to portray the state's population as the "good/pure people" (Mudde 2007) aggrieved or threatened by (national elite) outsiders. Populists can then campaign on a platform against national elites, the media, and other outside "meddlers" who are claimed to be ignorant of the region's true history and culture.

Other literature on the causes of populism has centered on political systems suffering from *crises of legitimacy* due to political corruption, influence peddling, and a lack of responsiveness to voter demands (Van Kessel 2011). This explanation also follows the arguments about former mass parties having turned into cartel parties which, through the penetration of state institutions, can extract resources to such an extent that they become isolated from voters and their own activist base (Katz and Mair 1995). There are of course important supply-side explanations having to do with the attractiveness of the candidate, the winning formula of the messages propagated, and the strategic deftness of party-political competitors (Van der Brug, Fennema and Tillie 2005).

Based upon the preceding discussion, I formulate the following empirical expectations: (1) Sub-state territorial claims-making is more likely to occur in states in which political trends are likely to be most different from national and other state-level trends (general opportunity structure). (2) In terms of opportunity structures, the FPÖ is more likely to be successful if it is able to exploit ethnic and socio-cultural cleavage conditions and/or if the legitimacy of the established local political power structure is severely compromised (specific opportunity structure). (3) In terms of supply-side factors, the FPÖ is more likely to be regionally successful if it can provide a political offer that uniquely resonates with the voters in the region (winning formula).

When measuring regional RRPP success, this work focuses on two criteria: electoral results based on votes achieved in relation to other provinces and the extent of government participation. Whereas the first criteria is straightforward, the latter is more complicated. As accepting the burden of government always proves difficult because this step may compromise the credibility of RRPPs with its voters (McDonnell and Newell 2011), it poses organizational and logistical challenges such parties cannot easily meet (Bolleyer 2008: 35–38). In terms of regional Austrian politics, there is a second problem when applying this criterion. Thus, we should note here that in some Austrian regions, government positions are allocated proportionally to all parties, depending on their share of the votes. This peculiar feature of parties being automatically represented in government is dubbed *Proporz* referring to influence based on proportionality. Under this arrangement, an undesirable party may be formally in government but its portfolios are heavily curtailed as it is relegated to politically unimportant responsibilities.[2]

In order to examine the claims made by the FPÖ, this work draws on the analysis of manifestos, campaign materials by the regional party organizations, and statements by regional party leaders as well as media reports and interviews to determine whether they pertained to a sub-national agenda and notions of territoriality.

The FPÖ: its regional organization and geographic divisions

The Freiheitliche Partei Österreichs (Freedom Party of Austria) was established by predominantly German-nationalist activists on 7 April 1956. Organizationally, it was both the successor to a short-lived predecessor, dubbed Federation of Independents (Verband der Unabhängigen/VdU),[3] and heir to a long and well-entrenched ideological orientation in Austrian history dating back to the German-nationalist stirrings in post-Napoleonic imperial Austria. In fact, the FPÖ views itself as the inheritor of the national-liberal legacy enshrined in the bourgeois-democratic (anti-imperial) Revolution of 1848. Its very name "Freedom" Party recalls this tradition directed against a centralized (formerly imperial) state closely connected with the Catholic Church (Riedlsperger 1978).

Whereas Social Democrats, Conservatives, and Communists enjoyed the active support or at least the passive toleration by the Allies, which occupied Austria from 1945 to 1955, former Nazi-party members were formally banned from political participation until 1949. Later they found a natural political home in the FPÖ. Many of its leaders served prison sentences for being implicated in Nazi war crimes such as the founder of the FPÖ, Anton Reinthaller,[4] himself. Although the Third Camp was rather fragmented, it received crucial support from the large number of former Nazi-party members, who resented the job restrictions and political prohibitions they were confronting in the immediate postwar years (Höbelt 1999). Another important group for the party were the ethnic Germans expelled from Eastern Europe, who had found a new home in Austria but had no particular ties to Austria's other parties (Riedlsperger 1978). Politically, the new party was locked into an ideological corner. Moreover, Christian Democratic Austrian People's Party (ÖVP) and the Social Democratic Party (SPÖ) formed successive coalition governments, using their hegemonic position in Austrian politics to build a clientelistic following while cutting the FPÖ off from the channels of power.

In the 1960s a new leadership tried to overcome the FPÖ's ghetto position by recruiting members of a new generation, especially from academic circles and more liberal elites so as to reduce the influence of the wartime cohorts. Modernizing the party also required a more consistent and intellectually sound programmatic basis designed to consolidate the position of the FPÖ as a small nationalist-libertarian party. The FPÖ's change in direction toward greater political liberalism and opening itself toward cooperating with the Social Democrats met with tremendous internal resistance. Especially anti-leftist circles and the radical nationalist right wing in the party rejected the new course. Eventually, the leadership faced a challenge by Neo-Nazi extremists several of whom subsequently left the party and founded the right-wing extremist National Democratic Party (NDP) (Luther 1995: 438). The German-nationalist far-right was particularly strong in the Carinthian party organization. Its leading figure was Otto Scrinzi who in 1968 became deputy leader of the national FPÖ party executive against the expressed wishes of the national party leadership. A former high-ranking member in Hitler's SA, Scrinzi was a tireless promoter of radical German-nationalist and far-right causes (e.g. a general amnesty for Nazi war criminals). He was also a father figure of sorts to the young Haider whose seat in the Austrian parliament the latter inherited in 1979 (Höbelt 2003).

The deep ideological divisions between the nationalist and liberals as well as anti-clerical and more conservative pro-Catholic tendencies, not to mention those willing to work with the Social Democrats followed partially the regional and geographic divisions within the FPÖ. This meant that the regional party chapters in Upper Austria and Carinthia emerged as the most nationalist whereas for example the Salzburg and Vienna chapters were more liberal. The bottom-up federal organizational structure of the Freedom Party implied that the national leadership had relatively little power in affecting developments at the regional level. At the same time, the regional-level power structure ensured the recruitment of like-mined party activists, thereby strengthening the specific ideological profile of the regional chapter.

Within this structure of vertical integration, the state branches also dubbed the "state party" are the organizational backbone of the FPÖ as it provides the party with a remarkable organizational reach. Its bottom-up organization makes national top-down decision-making generally difficult. This is because at every level, lower ranking units may send delegates to the next higher level and thus enjoy representation all the way of to the Federal Party Congress. The nine state party organizations are also important because they possess the organizational wherewithal to function, if necessary, as autonomous and cohesive units. This is because they mirror the national party's organizational structure and can autonomously elect their leaders. They also determine the composition of the state party's decision-making bodies and are the principal sources of party revenue. In fact, the provincial party branches are the general gateway to FPÖ membership because new recruits typically affiliate with the FPÖ by joining up at a local chapter (Heinisch 2016). Thus, the state party can in most instances determine on its own the terms of membership, set a membership fee independently of the Federal Party, and has wide-ranging discretion in selecting local and regional candidate slates. It is noteworthy that more than half of party revenue are derived through the state party organizations. This provides regional party organs with significant leverage not only vis-à-vis the center but also each other (Sickinger 2009: 145). It also explains both the limited outside control FPÖ regional chapters have to fear and its relative influence at the national level.

In order to survive politically, the national FPÖ leadership was often forced to make concessions to the internal opposition,[5] manage party fragmentation,[6] and run the organization by relying on alliances with various regional chapters. In 1980 the party was evenly divided between liberals and right-wing nationalists when the liberal Norbert Steger was elected as national party leader by a slim 55.3 per cent majority. He subsequently accepted a coalition offer by the Social Democrats in 1983 in hopes of positioning his party more like an Austrian version of German Free Democrats. The heterogeneity of the FPÖ was an even greater problem in government because the party received much greater public scrutiny. The organizational looseness and lax party discipline translated into a public perception of discord and incompetence aggravated by the FPÖ's general inexperience in government. Following sharply declining poll numbers for Freedom Party nationally, Haider – then the young and charismatic head of the FPÖ's Carinthian branch – emerged as the unofficial leader against the more liberal national party elite. When sensing an opportunity to challenge the leadership of Norbert Steger in 1986, Haider and his supporters convened a party congress in which they mobilized the grassroots to depose Steger. This event was a watershed for the Freedom Party as Haider would not only transform the FPÖ into a radical right-wing populist formation but also lead the Carinthinan organization to play the preeminent role in the national party.

From 1986 to 1999, the FPÖ increased its electoral share from 5 to 26.9 per cent (Table 7.1) and the party's share of seats in parliament grew from 5 to 52. By the end of the 1990s, the Freedom Party had also greatly expanded its power at the regional and local level, emerging as the second largest party in five of Austria's nine provinces (including the capital of Vienna). However, in Carinthia it emerged as the dominant party and had a lock on the governorship for over a decade (Dachs 2008: 97–99). How was this possible?

If we summarize the discussion thus far, we would conclude that already prior to the FPÖ's conversion to a RRPP, it had developed a distinct far-right German-nationalist and nativist profile in Carinthia. This allowed the party to appeal credibly to segments of the Carinthian electorate that shared similar views and was willing to defect from their traditional party-political loyalties. The growing strength of the FPÖ at the regional and national level could be leveraged against each other and establish the party as a credible political force.

Examining regional and national trends

In order to determine whether sub-national territorial claims-making is more pronounced in a region that exhibits a political pattern distinct from the rest of

TABLE 7.1 Elections to the National Parliament (Lower House, *Nationalrat*)

Year of election[2]	Greens	Social Democrats (SPÖ)	People's Party (ÖVP)	Freedom Party (FPÖ)	Alliance (BZÖ)	Team Stronach	Liberals NEOS	Liste Pilz
1983		47.7	43.2	5.0				
1986	4.8	43.1	41.3	9.7				
1990	4.8	42.8	32.1	16.1				
1994	7.3	34.9	27.7	22.5			6.0	
1995	4.8	38.1	28.3	21.9			5.5	
1999	7.4	33.2	26.9	26.9				
2002	9.5	36.5	42.3	10.0^3				
2006	11.1	35.3	34.3	11.0	4.1			
2008	10.4	29.3	26.0	17.5	10.7			
2013	12.4	26.8	24.0	20.5	–	5.7	5.0	
2017	3.68	26.8	31.4	25.9	–	–	5.3	4.4

1 The parties are ordered along the left-right dimension. Grey cells indicate the parties forming the government after the respective elections.
2 Legislative and government periods do not always correspond exactly. General elections often take place at the end of the calendar year, that is why most new governments only take office at the beginning of the following year (this was, e.g., the case in 1987, 1996, 2000, 2003, and 2007).
3 The second ÖVP-FPÖ cabinet lasted only until April 2005, when the BZÖ formally replaced the FPÖ as the ÖVP's coalition partner, without new elections being called.

Source: Federal Ministry of the Interior.

the country, we need to examine FPÖ's success at the regional level over time. This can be done by plotting the trend lines in terms of vote shares for each of the nine states and the national level from the mid-1980s to the present. We clearly notice in Figure 7.1 that the fortunes of the Freedom Party both at the national and the regional levels have varied considerably. Following the party's breakthrough election in 1986, it continued to increase its electoral gains in every subsequent national election (except for 1995) until peaking in 1999, when it even surpassed the People's Party. The two parties then formed a national coalition government from 2000 through 2005. Proving unfit for national government (Heinisch 2003), the FPÖ subsequently collapsed in the polls, losing nearly two of every three voters. In 2005 its internal crisis resulted in a split of the party when the moderate office-seeking wing led by Jörg Haider broke away to form a new party called Alliance Future Austria (BZÖ). At the time, the rump FPÖ left the coalition and reverted to a more radical populist vote-seeking strategy under its new leader Heinz-Christian Strache. A visual inspection of Figure 7.1 clearly indicates that the trend lines in nearly all states shadow the FPÖ's development at the national level, albeit departing from different starting points and modulated by the regional election cycle. In all states except for one, we notice the troughs and peaks in the rate of success all roughly coincide. The amount of variation observed is clearly attributable to a variety of factors pertaining to the individual races. Nonetheless, the overall uniformity in these trend lines is rather striking and points to a close correlation between the national and regional level, which is not surprising for a nationwide populist party.

However, Figure 7.1 also points to one glaring exception in which the trend lines follow a different path, which is the state of Carinthia. Not only is the starting point there significantly higher than at the national level or in any other state, but the curve indicating success at the polls reached its plateau before it does elsewhere and remains high throughout the mid-2000s while it drops in all other states. At its peak, the Carinthian Freedom Party was nearly twice as successful as the party was in rest of the country. Even more astonishing is that the party maintained this rate of success despite switching affiliations at the national level and undergoing a leadership change. In 2005 the Freedom Party in Carinthia (FPK) broke with the national party to join Haider's newly founded BZÖ only to return to the FPÖ's fold in 2013. Yet, during all this time, the Carinthian branch remained politically and organizationally de facto the same – I will treat the Freedom Party in Carinthia (FPK), which incidentally kept its name, despite its affiliation with its BZÖ, as a continuous entity.

Likewise, the Carinthian FP entered a precipitous decline in 2013 (see Figure 7.1) when the FPÖ was rebounding elsewhere in the country. Thus, the national and Carinthian trend lines are quite different, which suggests the presence of factors that matter locally but are absent nationally and elsewhere in the country. By contrast, two other cases of recent government participation by the Freedom Party, the states of Burgenland and Upper Austria, exhibit no

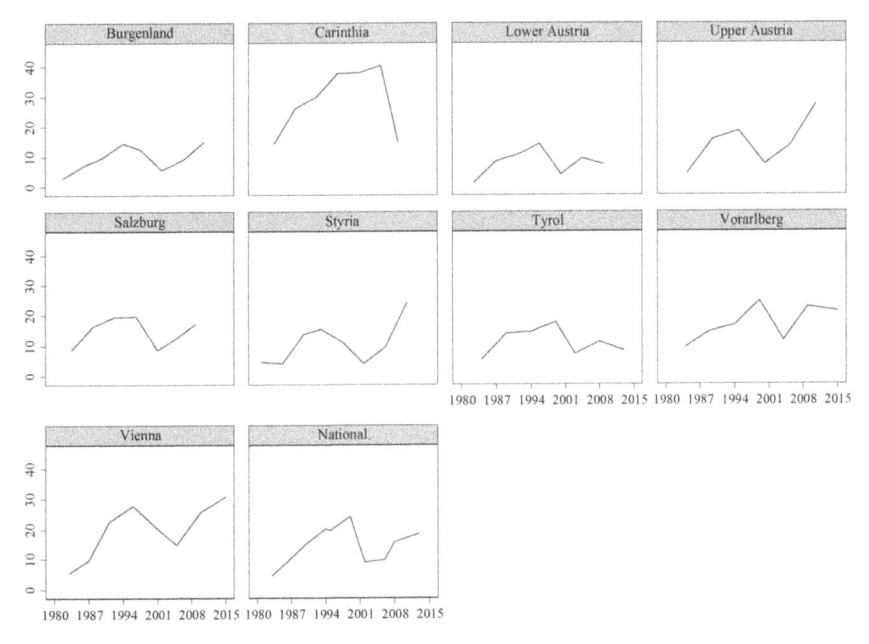

FIGURE 7.1 Graph of FPÖ national and state elections results in comparison
Source (Heinisch and Marent 2018: 1020)

particularly deviant or unusual pattern except that the most recent trend line is pointing upward as one would expect for a party entering public office.

What can account for these different trends given that for much of the time period under investigation, Jörg Haider was the leader of both the national and provincial party? From our discussion, thus far we can sketch out the following theoretical assumption: A combination of factors unique to the Carinthian context allowed the FPÖ to develop a particular strength in Carinthia early on and from where Haider was then able launched his national career. The subsequent analysis will explore the Carinthian case in detail and examine to what extent sub-national territorial claims were employed by the Freedom Party.

The Freedom Party's success in Carinthian state politics

Carinthia is a largely alpine state, representing less than 10 per cent of the national population. Its main industries have included agriculture, forestry, manufacturing, mining, and tourism. In recent decades, its economic and demographic development increasingly lagged behind the rest of the country. In 1999 the Freedom Party trounced the long dominant Social Democrats in state elections, wining over 42 per cent and gaining the biggest advantage in votes and seats (see Table 7.2). It was the first time in Austria's Second Republic that a third party achieved such a success, claiming even the governorship.

TABLE 7.2 Results of the state elections in Carinthia 1999–2018 in %

	Greens	SPÖ	ÖVP	FPÖ/FPK*	BZÖ/FPK*	TS/TK
1999	–	32.9	20.7	42.1	–	–
2004	6.7	38.4	11.6	42.4	–	–
2009	5.2	28.7	16.8	3.8	44.9	–
2013	12.1	37.1	14.4	16.9	6.4	11.1
2018	3.1	47.9	15.4	22.9	0.3	5.6

Source: Ministry of the Interior. Grey cells indicate principal governing party, (*) note that the FPK (Freedom Party in Carinthia) shifted affiliations at the national level from FPÖ to BZÖ and back to FPÖ but remained for all practical purposed organizationally and ideologically the same in Carinthia. TS/TK denotes the party Team Stronach/Team Carinthia.

Already in 1984, under Haider's new leadership, the FPK had gained 4.25 per cent achieving about 16 per cent of the vote in state elections. In 1989 the party gained another 13 per cent, obtaining a total of 29 per cent and moving past passed the ÖVP (20.9 per cent) to become the second largest party in the state – the first time the FPÖ or any third party had done so anywhere in Austria. The SPÖ had lost a total of 8 per cent in two successive elections and thus also their absolute majority. This defeat cost the Social Democrats the governorship which initially went to Haider and then, after he was forced out due to his controversial remarks about the Nazi employment policy, to the ÖVP. In the subsequent elections in 1994, the SPÖ lost another 8.5 per cent whereas the Freedom Party gained 4.2 per cent, thus almost achieving parity with the Social Democrats. Allowing the weakest of three parties, the People's Party to remain in the governorship meant that the FPK could set the agenda while the SPÖ was denied the benefit of reclaiming the top post in the state.

In 1999 the Social Democrats were demolished, falling to a low of 33 per cent of the vote, and the People's Party dropped to about 21 per cent in support (see Table 7.2). By contrast, the Freedom Party captured the largest share of the votes and seats in the state legislature. It was the first time in Austria's Second Republic that a so-called "third party" had achieved such success, claiming three representatives on the seven-member government council as well as the governorship. In 2004 the Freedom Party even managed to improve its performance slightly despite having lost support nearly everywhere else in Austria. Haider was again elected governor with the help of the ÖVP while the Social Democrats abstained. Subsequently, he remained governor until his death in 2008. One year later and campaigning for sympathy votes, his party topped Haider's previous electoral success, achieving an even larger share of the votes with 44.9 per cent (see Table 7.1). This was remarkable because in 2005 Haider's Carinthian branch of the Freedom Party, as already mentioned, had switched party affiliations at the national level by joining the newly formed BZÖ. Yet, to signal all but continuity at the state level, the state party continued to compete for office in Carinthia under its old label and should essentially be considered the local variant of the right-wing populist Freedom Party.[7]

Carinthia's socio-cultural cleavages and sub-state claims-making

Carinthia is known in Austria for harboring the nation's most salient and longest ethnic conflict between the regional German- and Slovene-speaking populations. In contrast to two other provinces with ethno-linguistic cleavages, Burgenland and Styria, the tensions in Carinthia have never fully subsided (Müller 2017). Dating back to an armed dispute with neighboring Yugoslavia about Carinthian territory in 1918 and 1919, the conflict shaped state politics before and after the Second World War. Even repeated interventions by national policy makers never fully defused the issue. As a result, tensions ran high between the state's German-speaking and smaller Slovenian-speaking population following the brutal oppression of the local Slavic minority especially during Nazi rule, coupled with strong assimilation pressures, forced resettlement, and the deportation of many to concentration camps.

These traumatic events had become an integral part of the collective Slovenian experience in Carinthia. After the war, the Slovenian populations continued to face political discrimination and marginalization, which sharply reduced the population that was still claiming Slovenian heritage. Armed resistance by Slovenian partisans against the German military and their local supporters and Yugoslav attempts to seize portions of the state's territory after the First and Second World Wars form other key elements in the local history. Many in the German-speaking population regarded this as treason committed by their Slovenian-speaking compatriots. Especially the local population's armed resistance against the Yugoslav military incursions in 1918 continues to be commemorated in official celebrations every year and remains a symbol of ethnic division that has been frequently exploited by political actors.

For decades after the war, the victims and perpetrators of war crimes and violent acts of revenge lived side by side in the small villages, fostering a climate of singular ethnic intolerance that the rest of Austria came to regard with a mixture of bewilderment and bemusement (Kellermann 2008). The latent conflict between the two sides served to mobilize German-nationalist and right-wing sentiments that had abated elsewhere in Austria. Thus, the Carinthians and their "German nationalism" have been a source of criticisms but also the trope of political satire in Austria, especially among intellectuals and leftwing circles in the capital Vienna. The perception of being misunderstood has added to a sense of detachment from the rest of the country and surfaces in Carinthia time and again in the public discourse (Heinisch 2002).

In the mid-1970s the conflict between German-speaking and Slovenian-speaking Carinthians escalated once again as the national SPÖ government finally decided to comply with article 7 of Austria's 1955 state treaty with the Allied Powers, obligating the country to erect bilingual signs in Carinthian towns with mixed ethnic populations. In 1972 such signs were put up in 205 communities, which prompted a massive counter reaction by the German-speaking majority population. Overnight, most of the signs were torn down, sometimes with the full complicity of the local authorities (Gstettner 1988). National media and national political leaders often expressed their dismay at the Carinthian response. In turn, this led to resentment among many German-speaking Carinthians about outside meddling, especially toward Vienna and the national government (Gstettner 2002). Both national political leaders and the local SPÖ governor were physically threatened by a mob when they tried to reason with protesters at a public gathering.

Carinthia's ethnic division provides the basis for two closely related but nonetheless distinct appeals employed by the FPK in the public political discourse in that province: (i) German-nationalist and anti-Slovenian claims coupled with overt or thinly disguised sympathies for the former Nazi regime and (ii) center-periphery arguments. The subsequent sections will explore these claims in greater detail.

Ideological affinity: the German-nationalist claims

During the conflict over the bilingual signs in the 1970s, in-state and out-of-state media coverage diverged sharply. The SPÖ-led provincial government proved unable to resolve the problem and positioned itself sharply to the right of the national party. In the wake of the political crisis, the Carinthian Social Democrats replaced their party leader and state governor Hans Sima, who had been seeking reconciliation with the Slovenes, with Leopold Wagner, formerly, a high-ranking member of the Nazi youth movement, who made no secret of his past affiliation. This was the context in which Jörg Haider, then a young out-of-state FPÖ-activist, settled, hoping to launch his political career (Heinisch 2002; Höbelt 2003). Whether motivated by genuine conviction or tactical calculus, Haider chose to play the right-wing nationalist card. He actively pursued close contacts with the exponents of the far-right German-nationalist wing of his party in Carinthia (Heinisch 2002). This opened the way for his ascendency to the post of member of the national parliament and then leader of the Freedom Party in Carinthia (Bailer-Galanda and Neugebauer 1997: 28).

As a public figure, Haider engaged in deliberate carelessness and insensitivity when making remarks about the Nazi regime, which sent signals to his far-right constituents and also provoked a maximum of attention. The following represent examples of the German-nationalist claims made in 1980s and early 1990s when the war generation and especially veterans still made up an important part of the electorate.

> One cannot simply be content with Carinthia remaining free and undivided ...
> This land [Carinthia] will only be free if it becomes a German land.[8]
>
> *(Österreich1 n.d.)*

> The FPÖ is not a successor organization to the NSDAP, for if it were, it had an absolute majority.
>
> *(Press conference held in Klagenfurt, 17 February 1985)*

> Well, this [the employment situation] did not exist in the Third Reich, because in the Third Reich, they made a proper employment policy, something which not even the government in Vienna can pull off. That needed to be said.
>
> *(Speech before the Carinthian Assembly, 13 June 1991, quoted in Czernin 2000: 31)*

This third statement cost Haider the governorship in 1991, which he held briefly following a coalition between the FP and ÖVP at the state-level. It would take him nine years to return to this office.

Even nationally, Haider's explicit overtures to pan-German activists, war veterans, traditionalists, and other far-right groups served to retain the loyalty of a key segment of the FPÖ's base, especially in Carinthia. The party's right wing had helped him take over the leadership of the Freedom Party in Carinthia and then supported him nationally. Since Haider's political strength nationally initially depended on the support in his adopted home state of Carinthia, it was there that Haider's allusions to Nazi ideology were most overt.

In 1986, Haider famously rejected the concept of an "Austrian nation" in his address to party delegates:

> Only the defeat of the Greater German Reich led to the so-called Austrian-national idea. With this, Austria confronts a choice, which will decide its development for an unforeseeable time period, and the German people [confront] the danger of losing another seven million people ... The most noble task is the defense against all attempts directed at loosening Austria's bond to its German character.
>
> *(Speech at the Innsbruck Party Congress, 14 September 1986, quoted in Czernin 2000: 17)*

In a television interview, his remarks about the nature of the Austrian nation provoked an uproar among Haider's critics and set off a national debate.

> You know as well as I, that the Austrian nation is a miscarriage, an ideological miscarriage, because belonging to a people is one thing, belonging to a state is another ... If somebody is free to consider himself a Slovene-Austrian (...) then it must be possible to consider oneself a German-Austrian. And this is what we have formulated in our program.
>
> *(Salzburger Nachrichten 2018)*

The fact that in Carinthia, politicians of all stripes had at one point or another been exploiting Carinthia's ethnic tensions to gain electoral support gave the Freedom Party some political cover. Simply put, if even the local Social Democrats were unwilling to support the demands of the ethnic minority, how would one reasonably expect a German-nationalist party to be any more sympathetic. This provided the Carinthian FP with a very powerful and at the same time seemingly legitimate issue for electoral mobilization.

When Haider returned to the governorship in 1999, he continued to engage in ethnic mobilization by playing on resentments against the local Slovene minority or by using the newly formed neighboring country of Slovenia as a proxy. By that time, he had had a history of stoking such tensions beginning with politicizing Slovenia's attempt to feature a medieval monument[9] of great symbolic value to the region's Slovenian and German heritage on Slovenia's new and short-lived currency. As the monument is located on the Austrian side of the border, Haider argued that depicting this monument, a ritual stone where the former Slovenian-speaking dukes had taken their oaths of office, threatened Austrian sovereignty. Another issue was Haider's insistence on using the German and not the Slovenian name of the Slovenian capital on traffic signs pointing to that destination despite the fact that this measure ran counter to an international convention to which Austria was a party. Governor Haider also endorsed essays in an explicitly nationalist publication, whose very title *Grenzland-Jahrbuch* (Borderland Yearbook) emphasized the notion common among far-right Carinthians that theirs was a land of the frontier and by implication a German cultural outpost confronting a Slavic menace. Incidentally, six Austrians provinces border countries in which the language and culture is not German. Yet, only Carinthia is commonly referred to, and perceived as a frontline state in need of special protection.

What sets the politics of the FPÖ in Carinthia apart from that in the rest of the country is that it continued to use German-nationalist mobilization and occasional lapses into Nazi-style rhetoric far longer than was the case elsewhere. In the rest of Austria, the FPÖ changed direction in the 1990s, opening itself to the working class and becoming more populist in the sense of emphasizing the antagonism between the good people and the elites. Outside Carinthia, the party became ideologically more flexible, embracing Austro-centric (as opposed to German-centered) patriotism and nationalism, and even seeking closer ties with the conservative wing of the Catholic Church. This was remarkable given the traditionally anti-clerical stance of the Austrian far-right and the FPÖ. Nationally, the Haider FPÖ began emulating the social and family agenda of the ÖVP. In 1997 the Freedom Party adopted even a new party program that removed the reference to Austria being part of the German nation and explicitly recognized Austria's "autochtonous minorities" (Heinisch 2002: 109–111). Haider also weakened the German-nationalist wing by replacing most of its leading figures with loyalist (Heinisch 2002: 96–97). Despite these changes,

Haider continued to play the ethnic card in Carinthia throughout his governorship and initially even opposed Slovenia's accession to the EU.

Eventually, the issue of rights for the minority population was used mainly for voter mobilization and had less to do with vestiges of pan-German nationalism in the party. As Haider himself had eliminated the German-nationalist faction from the party years earlier (Heinisch 2002); the people he subsequently recruited and promoted, dubbed by the media Haider's "boy gang" (Weinzierl 2002), were characterized by their loyalty to him rather than any ideology (Heinisch 2002: 96–97). Moreover, with the passing of the war generation, the end of Communist Yugoslavia next door, and the nearly complete disappearance of population segments in Carinthia consciously regarding themselves as ethnic Slovenes, the issue had become substantially defused already by 2000. In fact, when it was politically expedient, Haider styled himself even as an ethnic unifier, promising to reach an accommodation with the Slovene interest groups. In this context, the FP governor boasted to be learning Slovenian and frequently claimed to have treated the Slovenes better than the previous Social Democrats (*Neue Züricher Zeitung* 2001) However, whenever other problems threatened to insert themselves negatively for the FPK such as in 2004 when the national FPÖ was in turmoil and during the 2006 and 2008 campaigns when Haider fought nationally against the FPÖ on behalf of his newly founded BZÖ (Hauser and Heinisch 2016), he resurrected the ethnic issue to boost local support (Ritterband 2004).

For most of the time, the Carinthian Freedom Party resisted especially the implementation of a court-imposed compromise settlement in the issue of bilingual signs and framed the situation as "outside interference in Carinthian affairs". FP Governor Haider publicly mocked constitutional court justices and flatly refused to take the ruling seriously (News 2006). This rather straightforward arrangement had been ignored for decades, disputed, and re-negotiated until Slovenians found a way to force the issue by appealing to the Federal Constitutional Court (ORF Kärnten 2015a). In response, the Freedom Party-controlled state government vowed to resist "national interference" and even went as far as repositioning the signs to provoke a relitigation of the case and defy the court order (Zimmer n. d.).

The event led to a constitutional crisis as Governor Haider even positioned himself in opposition to the ÖVP-FPÖ government in Vienna, which was clearly embarrassed by the blatantly unconstitutional behavior by the Carinthian Freedom Party. However, Haider and his supporters within the FPÖ were too powerful to be openly called to order. Nationally, the ÖVP remained quiet for fear that the turmoil among the ranks of their coalition partner might destabilize the national government. The Carinthian FP counted on wedge issues like this for the purposes of voter mobilization (Ritterband 2004). In its discourse, the Slovene push for bilingual signs was framed as the actions of paid Slovene agitators intent on stirring up trouble in an otherwise peaceful country where everyone was content with the status quo. In fact, Haiders off-and-on again mobilization against the state's Slovene minority represents the clearest evidence of sub-national territorial claims-making (Hauser and Heinisch 2016).

Summing up, we find the Carinthian Freedom Party pursing several sub-national claims connected directly or indirectly to the state's ethnic divisions. Central to these appeals were wedge issues pitting the German- and Slovenian-speaking groups against each other and focused on German nationalism. As the war time generation faded and the issue of armed struggle in Carinthia receded, tensions lessoned. Nonetheless, claims about Carinthia as a "borderland" and "frontier state" and thus deserving of a special status remained a powerful device for framing political debates.

Regional identity: the center-periphery claims

Carinthia's ethnic and socio-cultural tensions have also served as the basis for other claims. These were directed against outside critics and served to appeal to Carinthians' strong sense of local identity to achieve political unity and silence the political opposition. The Freedom Party and especially Haider claimed that Carinthia was deserving of a greater autonomy from the federal government.

> No province has been so determined to struggle for its homeland as Carinthia ... no people has been more willing to make more sacrifices than the Carinthian people (...). The nature of the Carinthians could heal this republic. No province in our republic has done more for the unity of this country.
>
> *(Collection of quotations by Haider)*

Haider frequently framed Carinthia as "rampart in the South" (News 2007) and "the forgotten province" (ORK Kärnten 2007) that had been neglected in the past (BZÖ – Die Freiheitlichen in Kärnten 2007). The FPÖ went as far as to propose the establishment of Carinthia as a "Free State" (*Freistaat Kärnten*). Governor Haider depicted the national government as "the elite in Vienna" and thus regularly used the image of "the others" versus the Carinthian people, and argued he was "making Vienna listen" when it came to Carinthian interests and infrastructure needs (News 2007). Although the "Free State" was never implemented, the center-periphery narrative remained part of the FPK's strategy. The relationship between Carinthia and the federal government in Vienna can thus be described as especially distanced – both geographically and politically (Mölzer 1999).

Haider argued publicly that creating a Carinthian Free State was necessary to escape "Vienna's bad treatment of Carinthia" and overcome "its fate of always coming up short". He claimed that Carinthia had been the last province to get its own university (which is misleading since two Austrian states have none at all) and kept being neglected when it came to upgrading its roads and rails connections. The Carinthian Free State would "represent a commitment to our homeland and its proud history, its different character, and special situation" (BZÖ 2007).

Carinthians always took care of themselves and fought for the unity of the country (...) [but] Vienna constantly criticized Carinthian values like love of country and a sense of one's history, insisting that the province had to change its mindset.

(BZÖ 2007)

... the foreign ministry does not have the courage to put an end to the constant provocations by the Slovenes with school atlases showing half the territory as Slovenian and putting (a Carinthian monument) on their currency (...) because of our vigilance we prevent 70 years of dictatorship and Communism in Carinthia.

(Collection of quotations by Haider)

The statements by Haider are remarkable in the sense that Carinthia receives far more from the federal government and the other provinces through transfers than it actually contributes. Moreover, in terms of dictatorships, the state had lived through two fascist regimes between 1934 and 1945. Finally, in 2003 Haider announced to hold a referendum on the idea of a free state, but never followed up.

The center-periphery argument further reappeared in the context of economic policies. Despite the state's economic backsliding, Haider campaigned on turning "peripheral Carinthia" into an economic powerhouse dubbed "model Carinthia" (Lettner 2008). The center-periphery appeals played into a popular local narrative about Vienna and underscored Carinthia's relative detachment from the rest of the country. It also allowed the FPÖ leadership in Carinthia to cast blame for the economic problems onto the federal government. In order to create the impression that in fact the region was now turning around and becoming more prosperous required enormous increases in public expenditures. At the same time, Haider also raised social spending to offset cuts in popular federal programs. As a result, public debt under the FP government doubled.

Summing up, the Freedom Party was skillfully able to exploit deep seated local resentments toward outside elites especially in the media and national politics. Here, the Freedom Party was rather effective in turning the state's relative backwardness and economic malaise into an advantage for itself by suggesting that Carinthia had been forgotten and was a victim of sorts. The center-periphery discourse was subtle so as not to detract from the party's performance elsewhere in Austria but clear enough to resonate with state voters. In short, Haider and his party studiously avoided being perceived as a "Carinthian party" outside the state but locally it appeared as a "natural" political home to many voters. These claims included socio-cultural arguments against outside support for the Slovene minority and center-periphery arguments against political decisions that ran counter to the FPK agenda.

Change agents: the loss-of-legitimacy claims

Ethnic cleavages and the center-periphery condition may be considered general structural factors that were readily exploited by the FPÖ. However, there were also more specific or conditional factors that set Carinthia apart and helped the Freedom Party achieve and maintain power. Haider and his reconstituted Freedom Party also represented credible agents in the face of a manifest desire for political reform. This was due to a set of unusual political circumstances that shaped Carinthian politics, rendering them unique in the Austrian context. It was only when the old political power structure began to crumble in Austria's southernmost state in the 1980s that Haider found a path to the governorship.

Politically, the state had been dominated by the Carinthian branch of the Social Democratic Party, which had opened itself to the vast reservoir of former Nazi sympathizers. Feeding off the anti-clerical (thus anti-Conservative) sentiments of the population, the SPÖ had established a powerful political machine that ensured the party's hold on political power by delivering one absolute majority after another. As late as the 1970s, four of the top 20 members of the SPÖ-faction in the state assembly had been former NSDAP (Nazi Party) members and one had even served in the SS (Dokumentationsarchiv 2010). This unusual development was largely due to the fact that German nationalists associated the Catholic Church with protecting the ethnic Slovene minority, and resented by extension the Church's political ally, the ÖVP. As a result, the Christian Democrats remained a weak political force allowing the SPÖ to achieve a decades-long monopoly on political power. This is remarkable in light of the fact that Carinthia was not particularly industrialized.

When the local Social Democrats became caught in major scandals involving influence peddling and the abuse of power by engaging in elaborate patronage schemes in the public sector economy, their electoral fortunes declined sharply in the 1980s. The collapse of the SPÖ's political legitimacy in the state at the time is well documented as is the rampant political clientelism associated with the governing style of the then Social Democratic governor Leopold Wagner (*Die Presse* 2012). Unable to play the kind of dominant role it does elsewhere in rural Austria, the ÖVP was in no position to take advantage of this opportunity. Thus, it was Haider and the Freedom Party that effectively campaigned on exposing public corruption, eventually filling the political void and emerging as the dominate force in Carinthia.

What the FPÖ subsequently achieved was more than an ordinary election victory because it was nothing less than a complete and lasting realignment of political power in Carinthia which was only reversed in the wake of another major scandal more than a decade later. Under Haider, the Freedom Party ascended to a level of political dominance in Carinthia that was unparalleled for a "third party" in Austria. It clearly represented a reaction by the electorate not only to the political machine operated by the local Social Democrats but an indictment of the entire postwar partitocratic order not only in Carinthia but also Austrian in general. Haider presented Carinthia as a state that would be thoroughly transformed by his dynamic leadership (Heinisch 2002).

Summing up, in Carinthia, the FPÖ found conditions far more favorable than elsewhere and was thus able to dominate politically. Unlike in all the other cases, where the Freedom Party had to share the stage with an equally or even more powerful political competitor, it was electorally far more successful in Carinthia and could thus determine government formation. With Jörg Haider, it had the dominant political personality and most popular political figure in the state at the helm of the party and the state government. Whereas the ethnic cleavages and the socio-economic context provide longer-term structural conditions for sub-national claims-making, the crisis of legitimacy of state Social Democrats provided a specific set of circumstances that allowed Haider to make a play for political leadership. He could credibly present himself as an anti-politician and incorruptible change agent whose time had come and under whose leadership the state had a brighter future. Combining ethnocratic claims and center-periphery arguments with the promise to deliver the state from corruption and clientelism of the Social Democratic government, Haider and the FPÖ applied a winning formula that ensured continued political success from 1984 through 2008. Thus, we find that regionally the success of the FPÖ was based on sub-national territorial claims and conditions that pertain specifically to Carinthia.

The impact of sub-national claims in the context of populist governing

Carinthia is also a crucial case for examining the impact of a populist-led government in a sub-national territory in a country otherwise dominated by mainstream parties. When investigating the role of political claims designed to appeal to a sub-national population, we cannot only look at the FPÖ while in opposition but also need to examine how it acted in public office. Carinthia offers such an opportunity because of the extremely dominant position the party achieved there. Central to the sub-national claims Haider and his party made during that time period was the assertion that theirs was a special model designed to showcase how a state would be transformed politically and economically under FPÖ leadership.

Carinthian model: policy impact

The 14 years of the FP-led government in Carinthia constituted the longest period of a populist right-wing party in public office in Austria to date. Especially Haider, in his role as governor, was able to make a lasting impression and shape the style of politics in Carinthia. Under his leadership, the FPÖ/FPK rejected the old party tactics of campaigning as an anti-party protest movement in favor of embracing an alternative vision of governing. This was based on a new political style and the pursuit of a range of popular policy issues (including lowering rents, electric bills, the so-called baby check, administrative reforms, the privatization of state institutions such as the state bank, and the transfer of some state tasks to the private sector). The new political model was to have also an expanded plebiscitary component, which however was never implemented. Instead, it relied heavily on symbolic politics and spectacular issues to maximize support at the expense of programmatic principle and consistency. Dubbed by Haider the "Carinthian model", it combined genuine reforms with pushing several popular but financially unsustainable policies along with polarizing messages.

The Freedom Party's new form of governing became popularly known among its critics as "bread and circuses" style as it also incorporated the local fun and lifestyle culture, resulting in calculated political synergies. Taking a page from Silvio Berlusconi, Haider coaxed sponsors into creating a successful major league soccer club, over which he presided and which served as an advertising venue for his administration. Using his influence and political power to put together the financing and cut the bureaucratic red tape, the Haider government created or supported new entertainment venues along with the appropriate events ranging from pop concerts, beach volleyball tournaments, and biker meetings to soccer games and local folkloric festivities. They frequently featured the governor as the host in the requisite outfit (biker jacket, beach-surfer look, medieval costume, etc.) or some activity designed to draw a maximum of attention (i.e., the governor parachuting into the soccer stadium or bungee-jumping off the state's highest bridge). The construction of venues and the organization of numerous sports and entertainment events were arguably designed to highlight the new political departure and a popular celebrity governor (Ottomeyer and Schöffmann 1994; Ottomeyer 2000, 2009). Haider and other FP members themselves described this approach as creating a party brand[10] and as a new means of "reaching people who were otherwise not tuned into politics".[11]

In order to signal a departure from supporting high-brow art and culture that the FPÖ had dubbed elitist, Haider personally took charge of the government's cultural agency, using this position to steer state subsidies to a much larger extent than in the past toward popular festivities and local "folk culture". In due course, folkloric events and traditional regional festivals were heavily promoted whereas critical artists were attacked as out-of-touch and undeserving (Beyer 2000; Schlögl 2009). Notably, he had called Carinthia's most renowned living painter and sculptor Cornelius Kolig a "fecal artists" (Profil 2013) and withdrew funding from the state's internationally prestigious literary festival (Lutz 2000). At the same time, smaller independent organizations and projects, often politically critical of the FPÖ, were deprived of state subsidies (Beyer 2000). Symbolically, this move was designed to show how much the new government valued ordinary citizens. The FPÖ capitalized politically both on traditional festivities appealing to a sense of regional identity and events with mass popularity.

To understand how this relates to sub-national claims-making, we need to consider the three major narratives that have shaped Carinthia's postwar development and self-perception: (i) The marginalized borderland that bravely resisted a foreign incursion but was nonetheless forgotten by Vienna and the rest of the country; (ii) the state that had long suffered under an oppressive political machinery by an all-powerful and excessively clientelistic Social Democratic Party; and (iii) the Austrian South synonymous with relaxed, laissez faire attitudes, lakeside beach culture, and summer fun. The policies and related claims by the Freedom Party fed into these narratives. At the same time, the measures implemented also spoke to the widespread self-image of being a fun-loving and easy-going people whose real character was not fully appreciated by the traditional politicians (Ottomeyer and Schöffmann 1994; Ottomeyer 2000, 2009). Haider not only embraced these narratives and seemingly acted on them but was also an "international celebrity" who did not "turn his back on the province but let the people take part in his fame".[12] His luster elevated the state in the international limelight. There was the governor of tiny Carinthia on the title pages of the world's most important publications, visiting with Saddam Hussein before war in Iraq, being hosted by Libyan strongman Muammar Gaddafi, or being the center of attention in German talk shows.

Nonetheless, Haider avoided the impression of being detached from the concerns of ordinary Carinthians. He and the Freedom Party government became known for their largess and rather relaxed fiscal discipline. Various regional social benefit programs were invented to showcase that the government was giving money "back to the people". The party campaigned on the promise of providing additional social benefits such as special maternity pay ("baby checks"). Later the FPÖ government provided supplementary payments for pensioners whose federal benefits had been capped at a fixed lower rate. It should be added that this generosity stands in sharp contrast to Carinthia's comparatively meager economic and financial resources. There are numerous accounts of Governor Haider touring the state, handing out the money in person. In one such documented case from 2008 (Ritterband 2004), he handed out 100 euro notes to low income voters, claiming to compensate them for the inflation, which, according to the FP, had been caused by problems related to the newly introduced European currency (Lettner 2008).

The Freedom Party first tried to entrench itself politically by breaking open the established state administrative apparatus, which had been shaped over the decades by the Social Democrats. This combined genuine organizational reforms (flattening of hierarchies and better citizens' access) with formal and stylistic changes (partially abolishing bureaucratic titles, encouraging more casual manners, and dress code, see Kärntner Landesregierung 2003). Haider and his closest advisors involved themselves personally even in small details of political, administrative, and economic decisions, thereby reducing the traditional autonomy of civil service (Heinisch 2002). A key component was the outsourcing of state activities, ostensibly to save cost. Several departments were either reorganized or had their agenda transferred to private companies or newly created citizens' commissions (Platzer and Primosch 2011). Since the Carinthian civil service had been mostly recruited from the SPÖ, the FPÖ's campaign to "modernize Carinthia" had the added bonus of weakening their political opponents.

However, the most consequential aspect of the privatization spree was that the money generated by outsourcing ended up masking the true level of debt the state had accrued. It contributed also to an unprecedented series of corruption scandals involving individuals and groups associated with the Freedom Party and other political formations (Trend 2013; Fritzl 2016).

Furthermore, a series of prestigious but costly boondoggles of great symbolic value were initiated under the FP government the objective of which was to signal that "Carinthians too could dream big".[13] Haider not only created a major league soccer club but also a new outsized football stadium to be used in the UEFA European Championship 2008. A lakeside floating stage was just another in a series of investments that a committee of enquiry later found to be costly white elephants (Kleine Zeitung 2013). In the end, these and other projects drained much needed budgetary resources while resulting in allegations of corruption (Kordik 2010) and illegal kickbacks to finance party-political activities.[14]

The most significant and, in hindsight, financially ruinous policy decision was to provide loan guarantees for the regional Hypo Alpe Adria bank in exchange for favorable financing terms for government investment projects (Kleine Zeitung 2015). Under the FP government, Carinthia, with an annual budget of about 2 billion euro, took on liabilities of nearly 25 billion euro in support of the bank's expansion into the Balkans (*Die Presse* 2016). Its multibillion-euro investments in business ventures and real estate deals in Eastern and Southern Europe collapsed in the wake of the global financial crisis. As a result, the bank defaulted on its obligations, threatening the financial stability of Carinthia. In response, the Austrian national government decided in 2009 to nationalize the bank in an emergency move and backed Carinthia's loan obligations to stave off the regional government's bankruptcy. Assuming such an enormous financial liability represented a long-term drain on the national Austrian budget, reducing the federal government's financial room to maneuver for years to come. In addition to the banking fiasco, Carinthia had amassed a large public debt totaling 4.8 billion euro, which was twice the annual budget. In fact, under the Freedom Party governments, Carinthia's obligations doubled from 2005 to 2010 but the enormity of the state's debt was long concealed due to a lack of oversight and the outsourcing of state functions to non-state entities. In the latter case, their operations were not fully reflected in the official state budget, thus masking the true extent of Carinthia's obligations. Accounting agencies and institutions that would ordinarily exercise control had been systematically weakened. At the state level, the oversight body had been made politically pliant while at the national level, the finance ministry in charge was run by the fellow Carinthian Karl-Heinz Grasser, a political ally (and previous Haider confidant from Carinthia). Lastly, the finance expert of the main opposition party, a long-term opponent of Haider, was subject to a campaign of vicious personal attacks. Critics of the Haider government and its costly projects and those voices warning of the economic downside of his policies were labeled naysayers and enemies of Carinthia who just wanted to drag the state through the mud.

Whereas "bread and circuses" was one side of the Carinthian model, "divide and conquer" was the other. The Freedom Party strategy made use of long-standing divisions and political cleavages. In doing so, the Haider government managed to secure political majorities by playing different sub-regions off against each other or isolate Social Democratic strongholds such as the state's second largest city of Villach. As the only major source of investment in an otherwise relatively poor state, the government could use its instrument of discretionary financial allocation (*Bedarfszuweisung*) for financing local projects, initiatives, and infrastructure spending to reward political loyalty, appeal to necessary clientele groups, and punish those who appeared critical of the Haider government (Heinisch 2010). Although hardly unique to Carinthia, this policy aggravated the economic situation by spreading scarce resources needlessly thin and duplicating public projects for political support. The policy undercut necessary regional coordination and specialization in a small state while exacerbating the state's debt at an unprecedented level (for examples see Heinisch 2010). In this context, the Freedom Party routinely engaged in polarizing claims-making suggesting that critics worried about state spending wanted to deny economic opportunity to certain parts of the state.

The Freedom Party's divide-and-conquer approach extended also to coalition politics as Haider switched, when expedient, from cooperating with Christian Democrats to the Social Democrats and back again. In doing so, the Freedom Party was able to play the other two parties off against one another, enticing one or the other into backing a new project or initiative in exchange for a political concession the local SPÖ or ÖVP craved. In this way, the other parties made themselves indirectly accomplices in the financial problems and corruption scandals that increasingly overshadowed the final years of the FPK government. Overall, the much weaker ÖVP remained the preferred partner because it generally demanded a lower political price and represented less of a threat to the FPK than the SPÖ which in Carinthia was the only real political alternative to the Freedom Party. It was thus a telling indicator that one of the first persons to go to jail for public corruption once the scandals of the Haider era were eventually investigated was none other than the head of the Carinthian Christian Democrats.

When resistance threatened, Haider never hesitated to use all means at his disposal. The FPK engaged in campaigns of personal defamation of critics and political opponents far beyond of what had been the norm.[15] A special characteristic of dealing with critics was to present them either "nest defilers" besmirching Carinthia when they came from inside (BZÖ 2006; SPÖ Kärnten 2006) or as enemies of Carinthia when they were outside the state (ORF Kärnten 2015b). Particularly the courts, independent media, and national institutions tasked with oversight duties were attacked as enemies (BZÖ 2008). The dichotomous framing of "us versus them", of the good people of Carinthia versus their enemies in Vienna, in the courts, the media, among local intellectuals, the Slovenes, and the likes served to delegitimize the opposition and democratic control mechanisms.

More fundamentally, the FPK managed to create a climate in which it became politically and personally costly to oppose the governor and the FPK's policies.[16] In some cases, politicians were financially coopted such as the leader of the Carinthian ÖVP, who was one of the first state officials to be later sentenced for embezzlement and public corruption. Yet, all this does not sufficiently explain why there was so little resistance to Haider's many ill-fated policy schemes and poorly devised projects. Several of them were quite transparent as boondoggles from the start; others involved quite publically dealings with shady characters like Russian oligarchs (Hodoschek 2012) and Arab potentates, or were rife with rumors of financial improprieties. Yet, the opposition and media seemed ineffective in generating enough momentum to stop these undertakings.

Haider's unprecedented popularity, if not to say personality cult, the enormous outpouring of collective enthusiasm for him and his government throughout the state, and the political culture of what the media have dubbed the "Haider system" (Gössinger 2012) are a unique chapter in postwar Austrian political culture. The simultaneous curtailment and delegitimation of institutions of control exacerbated the problem, which in the end ruined Carinthia's economic prospects. The transfer of power from traditional state institutions and established political mechanisms to newly formed personalist networks and non-state entities clearly added to the problem. This more than anything has been the lasting legacy of RRPP in government in Carinthia.

We would argue that this political development was possible in the specific sub-national context of Carinthia. Its persistent ethnic, social, and political cleavages, the decades-long experience of political corruption and influence peddling that preceded the Freedom Party's ascend to power, the overall economic backwardness of the state, as well as Carinthia's closed political culture and fear of outside meddling all facilitated what we may call a populist mode of governing. Critics and skeptical media were dismissed as out-of-touch elites and outsiders jealous of a popular governor with big dreams in support of an underappreciated people whose dignity and historical heroism he continuously emphasized.

It took nothing less than the country's biggest financial scandal and the death of Haider to eventually break the dominance of the Freedom Party in Carinthia. Initially, his passing led locally to an unprecedented public manifestation of grief and the creation of what can only be described as a shrine to commemorate the late governor. It also engendered popular conspiracy theories about assassination plots perpetrated by the Mossad or the CIA. Many Carinthians refused to believe the forensic evidence that the governor had been intoxicated despite his history of accidents with fast cars. The amount of emotional outpouring propelled his party to yet another election victory but Haider's successor did not have the political talent to maintain either the illusion of Carinthian success or explain away the fallout from the banking scandal and public corruption. This coupled with further corruption investigations and court decisions caused the FPK to lose more than 28 per cent of their voters in 2013, which plunged from nearly 45 per cent to 16.8 per cent. The crisis also led to split in the state party in which a smaller group remained affiliated with the BZÖ whereas the large party of the FPK rejoined the FPÖ at the national level.

Conclusion

This chapter investigated the role of sub-national claims in turning Carinthia into an important stronghold for the Freedom Party, which had significant consequences for national politics. This constituted a twofold puzzle. First, Carinthia is a relatively minor state in Austria and normally does not wield much influence at the national level. Secondly, the FPÖ is not known to be a regional or sub-national party and thus one wonders how it was able to appeal especially to Carinthian voters. This chapter formulated three conditions under which one would expect a national party engaging in sub-national claims to be successful and then investigated whether they apply to the Carinthian context: (1) Sub-national territorial claims-making was more likely to be reflected in states in which political trends were most different from national and other state-level trends (general opportunity structure). (2) The FPÖ was more likely to be successful if it was able to exploit opportunity structures that are unique to a given regional context. (3) The FPÖ was more likely to be successful if it could provide a political offer that resonated especially with the voters in the region (winning formula). The evidence shows that such conditions apply to Carinthia and only to this state in Austria. The persistent ethnic and socio-cultural cleavages allowed the FPÖ to make specific nationalist appeals that resonated strongly in Carinthia due to its history and ethnic composition. This accounted also for an "us versus them" orientation that made center-periphery claims very effective and immunized the Freedom Party from the effect of outside criticism. The crisis of legitimacy that affected the locally hegemonic Social Democrats allowed the FPÖ and its leader to offer themselves as a credible alternative just when the desire for change had massively increased.

The same factors in conjunction with a closed political culture and weak institutions of democratic control also accounted for the governing model the Freedom Party created, which in the end pushed Carinthia to the brink of financial and economic collapse. The bond between Haider and the local population was so strong that it was broken only after his life had been cut short. His successors proved unable to continue the previous model in the wake of a growing economic crisis which exposed the disconnect between the claims and the political reality. When the Carinthian economy was foundering, the state had to be bailed out by the national government, local political leaders, especially from the FPÖ including Haider's successor as governor faced indictments, and national pressure eventually also settled the issue of bilingual signs.

Summing up, in Carinthia, Haider and his party found conditions uniquely favorable and were able to dominate state politics for over two decades by appealing to the local population through a winning formula of sub-national claims and policy agendas.

Notes

1 In this chapter, the term state will refer to the region or province and not the national government. Austria thus consist of nine provinces are states.
2 There have been other cases where the FPÖ was invited into government by the locally dominant party for political expediency although this was not necessary for forming a government (i.e. Vorarlberg). However, these are neither recent cases nor such in which the FPÖ had any significant power to affect public policy and we therefore exclude them from the analysis.
3 The VdU was also known as WdU, Wahlpartei der Unabhängigen (Electoral Party of Independents]
4 He had been a high-ranking member of the SS and was imprisoned from 1950 to 1953.
5 For instance, he had to accept the far-right Otto Scrinzi as deputy party leader in 1966.
6 The split with a segment of German nationalists who founded the National Democratic Party (NDP) in 1967.
7 Because the BZÖ's break with the FPÖ led by Haider at the national level was not accepted by all members of the Carinthian FP branch, a small minority remained loyal to the national FPÖ, which meant that for the time being there existed the Carinthian branch of the Freedom Party, called FPÖ, and the Carinthian branch of the BZÖ, called FPK. It is the latter however that represented the continuation of the previous Freedom Party in public office in Carinthia.
8 All excepts were translated by the author.
9 The so-called Fürstenstein [stone of dukes] was a symbol of the early medieval Slovenian-dominated precursor to modern Carinthia, which was gradually absorbed into the Holy Roman Empire and whose ethnic composition slowly changed through German migration and colonization.
10 Interview with a state tourism official and FP member (June 2004).
11 Interview with Karl Heinz Petritz, media spokesman of Jörg Haider (July 2001). Interview with Jörg Haider (July 2001).
12 Author's interview with FPK's press spokesperson, 25 June 2004.
13 Author's interview with Governor Haider, 25 June 2004.
14 Due to Haider's sudden death several of the investigations against him were terminated before it came to trials. Other cases are still pending or resulted in guilty verdicts for Haider associates and political partners (also see: Sagmeister 2012).
15 This included campaigns of personal defamation going beyond the usual: When for example the Social Democratic Party leader Gabriele Schaunig threated to block Haider's decision to guarantee the debt of the state's largest bank in exchange for the bank's willingness to finance investment projects in the state, the FPK designed a campaign depicting her as a cartoon duck "quacking against Carinthia". Some 1,500 stickers were subsequently distributed throughout the state (BZÖ 2006).
16 Interview with an ÖVP member of the Carinthian State Parliament (June 2012).

References

Alonso, S. (2012) *Challenging the State: Devolution and the Battle for Partisan Credibility: A Comparison of Belgium, Italy, Spain, and the United Kingdom*. Oxford: Oxford University Press.

Arzheimer, K. and Carter, E. (2006) "Political Opportunity Structures and Right-Wing Extremist Party Success", *European Journal of Political Research*, 45(3), pp. 419–443.

Bailer-Galanda, B. and Neugebauer, W. (1997) *Haider und die Freiheitlichen in Österreich*. Berlin: Elefanten Press.

Beyer, S. (2000) "Im Tal der Ahnungslosen", *Der Spiegel*, 14 February. www.spiegel.de/spiegel/print/d-15680712.html.

Bolleyer, N. (2008) "The Organizational Costs of Public Office". In: Deschouwer, K. (ed.) *New Parties in Government. In Power for the First Time*. London: Routledge, pp. 17–44.
BZÖ – Die Freiheitlichen in Kärnten (2006) "BZÖ präsentiert 'Gaby, die rote Quak-Ente'", *Original Text Service OTS*, 8 August. www.ots.at/presseaussendung/OTS_20060817_OTS0134/bzoe-praesentiert-gaby-die-rote-quak-ente.
BZÖ – Die Freiheitlichen in Kärnten (2007) "LH Haider: Freistaat Kärnten - ein Bekenntnis zur Heimat", *Original Text Service OTS*, 22 February. www.ots.at/presseaussendung/OTS_20070222_OTS0137/lh-haider-freistaat-kaernten-ein-bekenntnis-zur-heimat.
BZÖ – Die Freiheitlichen in Kärnten (2008) "Haider zu VfGH-Bestellung: Ein Kärnten-Feind löst den anderen ab", *Original Text Service OTS*, 30 April. www.ots.at/presseaussendung/OTS_20080430_OTS0227/haider-zu-vfgh-bestellung-ein-kaernten-feind-loest-den-anderen-ab.
Collection of Quotations by Haider: www.oesterreich1.com/meldestelle/DerKleineJoerg.html.
Czernin, H. (eds.) (2000) *Wofür ich mich meinetwegen entschuldige: Haider, beim Wort genommen*. Vienna: Czernin.
Dachs, H. (2008) "Regional Elections in Austria from 1986 to 2006". In: Bischof, G. and Plasser, F. (eds.) *The Changing Austrian Voter. Volume 16 of Contemporary Austrian Studies*. New Brunswick and London: Transaction Publishers, pp. 91–103.
Die Presse (2012) "Das rote Kärnten – es war einmal", 31 August. https://diepresse.com/home/zeitgeschichte/1285232/Das-rote-Kaernten-es-war-einmal.
Die Presse. (2016) Milliardengrab Hypo: Ein Drama in fünf Akten (16 August 2016).https://diepresse.com/home/wirtschaft/economist/1584418/Milliardengrab-Hypo_Ein-Drama-in-fuenf-Akten (accessed 19/07/2019).
Dokumentationsarchiv (2010) "Die SPÖ und ihre braunen Wurzeln", last modified 25 June 2010. www.dokumentationsarchiv.at/SPOE/Braune_Flecken_SPOE.htm.
Fritzl, M. (2016) "Kärnten. Wenn ein Land pleite geht", *Die Presse*, 6 February. https://diepresse.com/home/wirtschaft/economist/4920503/Kaernten_Wenn-ein-Land-pleitegeht.
Gössinger, A. (2012) "Das System H", *Kleine Zeitung*, 29 July. www.kleinezeitung.at/kaernten/3970058/Brisant_Das-System-H.
Gstettner, P. (1988) *Zwanghaft Deutsch? Über falschen Abwehrkampf und verkehrten Heimatdienst*. Klagenfurt: Drava.
Gstettner, P. (2002) "Kärntner Minderheitenpolitik als Mittel zum Zweck. Wie Haider seinen 'Freistaat' errichtet und damit die Republik beschädigt", *Razprave in gradivo. Treatises and Documents*, 38–39, pp. 118–129.
Hauser, C. and Heinisch, R. (2016) "The Mainstreaming of the Austrian Freedom Party: The more Things Change … ". In: Akkerman, T., de Lange, S. and Rooduijn, M. (eds.) *Radical Right-Wing Populist Parties in Western Europe. Into the Mainstream?* London: Routledge, pp. 73–93.
Heinisch, R. (2002) *Populism, Proporz, and Pariah – Austria Turns Right: Austrian Political Change, Its Causes and Repercussions*. New York: Nova Science Pub. Inc.
Heinisch, R. (2003) "Success in Opposition – Failure in Government: Explaining the Performance of Right-Wing Populist Parties in Public Office", *West European Politics*, 26, pp. 91–130.
Heinisch, R. (2010) "Von Partikularinteressen und weißen Elefanten – Ein Land auf der Suche nach einem gemeinsamen Gestaltungswillen", *Kärntner Jahrbuch für Politik*, 2010. Klagenfurt: Hermagoras, pp. 147–159.
Heinisch, R. (2016) "The Austrian Freedom Party – Organizational Development and Leadership Change". In: Heinisch, R. and Mazzoleni, O. (eds.) *Understanding Populist Party Organisation: The West European Radical Right*. Basingtoke: Palgrave Macmillan, pp. 19–47.

Heinisch, R. and Marent, V. (2018) "Sub-state Territorial Claims Making by a Nationwide Radical Right-wing Populist Party: the Case of the Austrian Freedom Party", *Comparative European Politics*, 16(6), pp. 1012–1032.

Höbelt, L. (1999) *Von der vierten Partei zur dritten Kraft. Die Geschichte des VdU*. Graz: Stocker Verlag.

Höbelt, L. (2003) *Defiant populist: Jörg Haider and the politics of Austria*. West Lafayette: Purdue University Press.

Hodoschek, A. (2012) "System Haider: Wie man in Kärnten Kassen füllt", *Kurier*, 22 September. https://kurier.at/chronik/oesterreich/system-haider-wie-man-in-kaernten-kassen-fuellt/812.376.

Kärnter Landesregierung (2003) "Verwaltungsverlagerung zu Bezirken stärkt die Regionen", *Original Text Service OTS*, 4 March. www.ots.at/presseaussendung/OTS_20030304_OTS0095/lh-haider-verwaltungsverlagerung-zu-bezirken-staerkt-die-regionen.

Katz, R. and Mair, P. (1995) "Changing Models of Party Organization and Party Democracy the Emergence of the Cartel Party", *Party Politics*, 1(1), pp. 5–28.

Kellermann, K. (2008) "Echte Tränen für hundert Euro", *Die Presse*, 17 October. https://diepresse.com/home/meinung/gastkommentar/423499/Echte-Traenen-fuer-hundert-Euro.

Kitschelt, H. (2007) "Growth and Persistence of the Radical Right in Postindustrial Democracies: Advances and Challenges in Comparative Research", *West European Politics*, 30 (5), pp. 1176–1206.

Kleine Zeitung (2013) "Die Seebühne ist zu", 23 February.

Kleine Zeitung (2015) "Protokolle: Haiders spendable Kärnten Privatstiftung", 8 August. www.kleinezeitung.at/politik/innenpolitik/4795692/960000-Euro-fuer-Seebuehne_Haiders-spendable-Kaernten-Privatstiftung.

Kordik, H. (2010) "Haider: Hypo-Beteiligung nur gegen Fußball-Sponsoring?", *Die Presse*, 10 February. https://diepresse.com/home/wirtschaft/boerse/538737/Haider_HypoBeteiligung-gegen-FussballSponsoring.

Lettner, M. (2008). "'Schöner Schein' im Land von Jörg Haider", *Profil*, 23 February. www.profil.at/home/schoener-schein-land-joerg-haider-198254.

Luther, K. R. (1995) "Zwischen unkritischer Selbstdarstellung und bedingungsloser externer Verurteilung: Nazivergangenheit, Anti-Semitismus und Holocaust im Schrifttum der Freiheitlichen Partei Österreichs". In: Bergmann, W., Erb, R. and Lichtblau, A. (eds.) *Schwieriges Erbe. Der Umgang mit Nationalsozialismus und Antisemitismus in Österreich, der DDR und der Bundesrepublik Deutschland*. Frankfurt/New York: Campus Verlag, pp. 138–167.

Lutz, B. (2000) "Ingeborg-Bachmann-Preis: Haider entzieht die Finanzierung", *Der Spiegel*, 8 February. www.spiegel.de/kultur/literatur/ingeborg-bachmann-preis-haider-entzieht-die-finanzierung-a-63401.html.

McDonnell, D. and Newell, J. (2011) "Outsider Parties in Government in Western Europe", *Party Politics*, 17(4), pp. 443–452.

Mölzer, A. (1999) "Der Landesmythos und seine Instrumentalisierung". In: Anderwald, K., Karpf, P. and Hellwig, V. (eds.) *Kärntner Jahrbuch für Politik*. Klagenfurt: KVerlag, pp. 270–275.

Mudde, C. (2007) *Populist Radical Right Parties in Europe*. Cambridge: Cambridge University Press.

Müller, W. (2017) "Kärntner Streit um 'Slowenen-Passage': 'Es tut mir weh'", *Der Standard*, 7 February. https://derstandard.at/2000052262887/Verfassungsstreit-in-Kaernten-um-Slowenen-Passage-Es-tut-mir-weh.

Neue Züricher Zeitung (2001) "Vorgeführt wie ein Tanzbär", 14 May. www.nzz.ch/arti cle7BTED-1.497585

News (2006) "Kärntens LH Haider will VfGH 'austricksen': Bleiburg-Ortstafeln um einige Meter verrückt", 8 February. www.news.at/a/kaerntens-lh-haider-vfgh-austricksen-bleiburg-ortstafeln-meter-132558.

News (2007) "'Sind das Bollwerk des Südens': Haider will Kärnten künftig 'Freistaat' nennen dürfen", 9 February. www.news.at/a/sind-bollwerk-suedens-haider-kaernten-freistaat-164089.

ORF Kärnten (2015a) "Ortstafel. Eine Chronologie", 30 September. http://kaernten.orf.at/news/stories/2734344.

ORF Kärnten (2015b) "Strutz: FPÖ hatte Kredite bei Hypo", 2 June. http://kaernten.orf.at/news/stories/2714314/.

ORK Kärnten (2007) "Aschermittwochsrede: Haider: 'Freistaat ist ernste Sache'", 21 February. http://ktnv1.orf.at/stories/173651.

Österreich1 (n.d.) "F(a)lotte(n) Sprüche vom armen, kleinen Jörgele". www.oesterreich1.com/meldestelle/DerKleineJoerg.html.

Ottomeyer, K. (2000) *Die Haider-Show: Zur Psycholpolitik der FPÖ*. Klagenfurt: Drava.

Ottomeyer, K. (2009) *Jörg Haider – Mythenbildung und Erbschaft*. Klagenfurt: Drava.

Ottomeyer, K. and Schöffmann, I. (1994) "Die Haider-Inszenierung als 'Schiefheilung' und faschistische Männerphantasie", *Journal für Psychologie*, 2(1), pp. 16–27.

Platzer, D. and Primosch, E. (2011) "Die Landesamtsdirektoren von Kärnten und die Verbindungsstelle der Bundesländer". In: Rosner, A., Fischer, H. and Bußjäger, P. (eds.) *Im Dienste der Länder – im Interesse des Gesamtstaates*. Vienna: New Academic Press, pp. 135–146.

Profil (2013) "Chaos, Kot und Katzen: Besuch bei Künstler Cornelius Kolig", 30 October. www.profil.at/gesellschaft/chaos-kot-katzen-besuch-kuenstler-cornelius-kolig-368706.

Riedlsperger, M. (1978) *The Lingering Shadow of Nazism: The Austrian Independent Party Movement Since 1945*. Stuttgart: East European Monographs.

Ritterband, C. (2004) "Kuriosenkabinett Kärnten? Zwischen 'Event' und Personenkult". In: Anderwald, K., Filzmaier, P. and Hren, K. (eds.) *Kärntner Jahrbuch für Politik*. Klagenfurt: Kärntner Druck- und Verlagsgesellschaft, pp. 53–60.

Sagmeister, S. (2012) "Sündliche Geschäfte", *Die Zeit*, 11 October. www.zeit.de/2012/42/Kaernten-Korruption-Haider-Fussball-EM.

Salzburger Nachrichten (2018) "Im 'Inlandsreport' bezeichnet FPÖ-Chef Jörg Haider die österreichische Nation als 'ideologische Missgeburt'", 18 August. www.sn.at/panorama/wissen/18-august-1988-im-inlandsreport-bezeichnet-fpoe-chef-joerg-haider-die-oesterreichische-nation-als-ideologische-missgeburt-38853997.

Schlögl, S. (2009) "Leiden an Kärnten", *Die Zeit*, 8 October. www.zeit.de/2009/42/A-Promi-Kaerntner.

Sickinger, H. (2009) *Politikfinanzierung in Österreich*. Vienna: Czernin.

SPÖ Kärnten (2006) "Kaiser: Hören Sie auf den Rechnungshof zu attackieren, Herr Haider!", *Original Text Service OTS*, 20 September. www.ots.at/presseaussendung/OTS_20060920_OTS0036/kaiser-hoeren-sie-auf-den-rechnungshof-zu-attackieren-herr-haider.

Trend (2013) "Massive RH-Kritik an Immobilien-Auslagerung in Kärnten", 28 March. www.trend.at/news/oesterreich/massive-rh-kritik-immobilien-auslagerung-kaernten-355657.

Van der Brug, W., Fennema, M. and Tillie, J. (2005) "Why Some Anti-Immigrant Parties Fail and Others Succeed: A Two-Step Model of Aggregate Electoral Support", *Comparative Political Studies*, 38(5), pp. 537–573.

Van Kessel, S. (2011) "Explaining the Electoral Performance of Populist Parties: The Netherlands as a Case Study", *Perspectives on European Politics and Society*, 12(1), pp. 68–88.

Weinzierl, U. (2002) "Wenn alle untreu werden", *Die Welt*, 23 November. www.welt.de/print-welt/article269308/Wenn-alle-untreu-werden.html.

Zimmer, L. (n.d.) "Wie Kärnten die Verfassung umgehen will". http://newsv1.orf.at/060117-95553/95539txt_story.html.

8

THE TERRITORIALIZATION OF NATIONAL-POPULIST POLITICS

A case study of the Front National in France[1]

Gilles Ivaldi and Jérôme Dutozia

Introduction

The French Front National (FN) is one of the oldest national-populist parties in Western Europe. The FN emerged as a small extreme right formation at the fringes of the party system in 1972, and it remained largely irrelevant during the 1970s (Ivaldi 2018a). The party made its first electoral breakthrough in the 1984 European elections, winning 11 per cent of the vote by politicizing and exploiting immigration and law-and-order issues. Since then, the FN has established itself as a major actor in French politics, polling an average 15 and 11 per cent of the vote in presidential and legislative elections, respectively. The FN is also competing in local, regional and European elections where it has recently achieved some of its best performances at over a quarter of the vote (see Table 8.1).

The French FN illustrates the "national-populist" party (Betz 1994; Taguieff 1995). It espouses an ideology that combines populism with nationalism and xenophobia. As Rydgren (2008: 166) suggests, the FN emphasizes ethno-nationalism which "advocates strengthening the nation by making it more ethnically homogeneous and returning to traditional values". The idealized people of the FN is primarily identified with the nation, pitted against the so-called "globalist" elite (Ivaldi 2016).

National-populist parties like the FN primarily mobilize on centralized policy prescriptions and operate on a national level. They may however engage in different strategies to exploit territorially circumscribed opportunities, and adapt to different levels of government.

This chapter focuses on the territorialization of the mobilization strategies of the FN in France. There are good reasons to consider the territorialization of FN politics. First, the ideology of the FN allows for some territorial differentiation, celebrating local community bonds and regional identities in

TABLE 8.1 FN national electoral results since 1984

Year	Election	% valid	Year	Election	% valid
1984	European	11.0	2002	Presidential[1]	17.8
1986	Legislative	9.6	2002	Legislative	11.3
1986	Regional	9.6	2004	Regional	14.7
1988	Presidential	14.4	2004	European	9.8
1988	Legislative	9.7	2007	Presidential	10.4
1989	European	11.7	2007	Legislative	4.3
1992	Regional	13.7	2009	European	6.3
1993	Legislative	12.4	2010	Regional	11.4
1994	European	10.5	2012	Presidential	17.9
1995	Presidential	15.0	2012	Legislative	13.6
1997	Legislative	14.9	2014	European	24.9
1998	Regional	15.0	2015	Departmental[2]	25.2
1999	European	5.7	2015	Regional	27.7
2002	Presidential	16.9			

1 Second-round run-off
2 Local elections with FN presence in nearly all the cantons.
Source: Ministry of Interior.

France's *terroirs* (lands and soils). Second, decentralization offers different opportunities across different levels of competition. Different political issues matter at different levels of government. The literature on multi-level party politics emphasizes the need for statewide parties to adapt their organizational and programmatic strategies to the territorialized structure of competition produced by multi-level governance (e.g. Detterbeck 2012). Finally, the FN achieves heterogeneous rates of success across different regions (Gombin 2015; Le Bras 2015). French regions have distinct socio-economic, cultural and political profiles which present specific challenges and opportunities in the pursuit of electoral support (Kestilä and Söderlund 2007).

To examine the territorialization of the FN, this chapter adopts a sub-national approach and asks to which extent the FN engages in different strategies to take advantage of specific regional and local opportunities. We argue that the current FN operates across both a cultural (identity) and socio-economic (distributional) conflict. This allows the party to adjust its supply of national-populism to different contexts and arenas where cultural and economic issues vary in salience and in the resonance they find in the political process. Additionally, we examine party organization and party competition. The FN has become institutionalized and it has recently increased its presence in sub-national politics. Different parts of the FN may diverge in the areas of elite recruitment, party programs and local campaigning, and organizational strengths may also help mobilize voters sub-nationally. Finally, different regionalized party sub-systems may produce different opportunities for the interpretation of its national-populism by the FN.

Adopting a most different systems design, this chapter draws on a comparative analysis of the 2015 regional elections across two emblematic French regions, namely Provence-Alpes-Côte-d'Azur (PACA) in the Mediterranean South, and Hauts-de-France (HDF, formerly Nord-Pas-de-Calais-Picardie) in the Northern part of the country. Both regions are electoral strongholds of the FN but show substantial variation in their socio-demographic profile, economy and political history, making them relevant cases for our analysis.

This chapter is divided into four parts. First, we present our analytical framework. Then, we describe the methods and explain the rationale for the case study, before moving onto the analysis of our two regional cases and the general discussion of our findings.

Addressing the territorialization of national-populist politics in France

The French FN illustrates the "national-populist" idiosyncrasy, combining populism with majority nationalism (Betz 1994; Taguieff 1995). The FN's nationalist ideology places primacy on the unity of the nation, which is conflated with the state and French ethnic identity (Ivaldi 2018b). The nationalism of the FN is expressed across a wide range of political, cultural and economic arguments, emphasizing an ethnically-driven definition of the nation, while strongly opposing immigration and a multicultural society. As defender of national interests, the FN also is a significant vehicle for Euroscepticism in French politics, contesting European integration and opposing the loss of national sovereignty. Finally, the nationalism of the FN finds its way into the party's economic platform. Since the mid-1990s, the FN has endorsed economic protectionism, strongly opposing free trade and "savage" globalization (Ivaldi 2018b).

Populism is another strong feature of the FN and it is linked with its nationalist ideology. In the case of the FN, the linkage between populism and nationalism is found in the identification of the nation as the "pure" people, pitted against a "corrupt" elite. The idealized people of the FN is defined as a culturally homogeneous entity which must be protected against external threats. The elite is vilified as an oligarchy and accused of betraying the nation by promoting a so-called "globalist" ideology. Ultimately, the FN claims to represent the will of the people against the elite (Ivaldi 2016).

National-populist parties like the FN emphasize national issues and primarily mobilize on centralized policy programs. Not surprisingly, most of the scholarship on national-populism has focused on the national level. As Heinisch, et al. (2018: 924) explain, "the literature on populist parties has taken the nation-state as the natural context of analysis, systematically downplaying sub-state ethno-territorial instances".

There are however important reasons to consider the territorialization of FN mobilization in France. First, while emphasizing national identity, the ideology of the FN allows for some territorial differentiation. The party celebrates traditional values of local community bonds and regional identities, evoking France's countryside and *terroirs* as the heartland of French civilization (Ivaldi and Gombin 2015). Under Jean-Marie Le Pen, the FN stressed the people's attachment to their homeland, their sense of belonging and roots in localities (*pays*) and provinces. As stated for instance in the 2002 manifesto: "our movement places man back into the natural bonds that are his own: family, local ties, profession, Nation". The FN claimed further that "France is embodied in a people and a civilization, but also in a terroir", while glorifying the "richness of France's diversity of food, landscapes, species and peoples" (FN 2002). It may therefore be the case that the FN emphasizes territorial identity and rhetoric, shifting its focus from national to regional and local.

Second, successive decentralization laws since the early 1980s have produced a complex multi-level hierarchical structure which provides different competitive opportunities across different levels of competition (Knapp and Wright 2006). Political parties in France compete at the local level across over 36,500 communes in municipal elections. Departmental elections take place across 2,054 cantons. In legislative elections, parties must achieve a local presence in 577 constituencies in metropolitan France and overseas. Regional elections take place across 18 regions.

The FN has become institutionalized, – i.e. it has achieved organizational complexity and autonomy –, and it is also increasingly embedded in sub-national politics (Ivaldi and Lanzone 2016). Different political issues matter at different levels of government. The literature on multi-level party politics emphasizes the need for statewide parties to adapt both organizationally and programmatically to territorialized structures of competition produced by multi-level governance (e.g. Deschouwer 2006; Detterbeck 2012). For national-populist parties like the FN, this means in particular translating their centralized policy prescriptions into policies relevant to the level of administration at which they compete.

Finally, as Figure 8.1 illustrates, the FN achieves heterogeneous rates of success across different regions. Typically, support for the party clusters in the North-East regions of Hauts-de-France, Grand-Est and Bourgogne-Franche-Comté, as well as in the Mediterranean South-East in PACA and Occitanie. These regions have distinct socio-demographic profiles and political traditions, which present specific challenges and opportunities for populist mobilization (Kestilä and Söderlund 2007; Gombin 2015; Le Bras 2015). Statewide parties such as the FN must refocus their strategies to address the specific needs and interests of territorialized electorates with distinct policy profiles and political attitudes (Detterbeck and Hepburn 2009). Different parts of the FN may diverge in the areas of elite recruitment, party programs and campaigning in order to "fit" the local setting.

This chapter adopts a sub-national approach to explore the territorialization of the FN in France. As Detterbeck and Hepburn (2009) suggest, the "territorialization" of political parties includes a number of dimensions. First, regional branches may adopt stronger territorial identity and rhetoric. Second, there might be a change in party discourse, emphasizing territoriality. Finally, nationwide parties may compete by identifying and prioritizing particular needs and

National-populist politics and territory 169

Regional elections 2015 (1st round)
FN share of vote by commune (% valid)

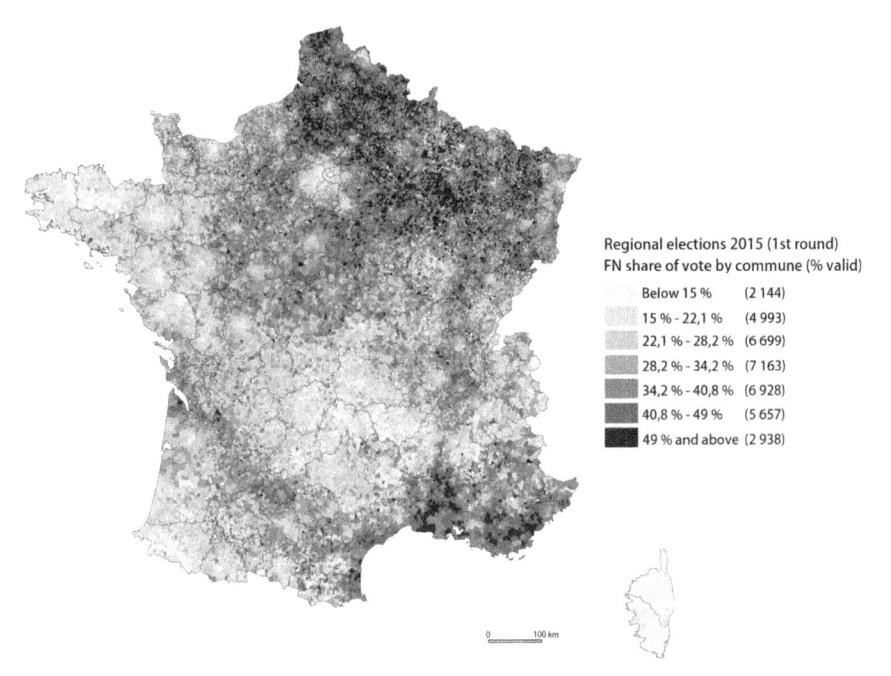

Below 15 %	(2 144)
15 % - 22,1 %	(4 993)
22,1 % - 28,2 %	(6 699)
28,2 % - 34,2 %	(7 163)
34,2 % - 40,8 %	(6 928)
40,8 % - 49 %	(5 657)
49 % and above	(2 938)

FIGURE 8.1 FN share of vote by commune (% valid) in the 2015 regional elections (1st round)

interests across different contexts and arenas, which may result in organizational and programmatic differentiation.

In this chapter we ask to which extent the FN is adapting its organizational and programmatic strategies in order to take advantage of territorialized opportunities. The concept of "political opportunities" generally refers to the external institutional or socio-economic constraints and opportunities that a particular political system sets for political parties, emphasizing both stable – e.g. the electoral system and socio-cultural cleavages – and dynamic contextual features – e.g. shifts in party competition (Arzheimer and Carter 2006; Kestilä and Söderlund 2007).

At sub-national level, a political opportunity structure can be defined as "a set of regional or local conditions that would either facilitate or hamper the attempts of the radical right to mobilize voters" (Arzheimer and Carter 2009: 337). This chapter uses the term "territorialized opportunities" to refer to the broad set of environmental conditions under which political parties operate, and which are territorially circumscribed. We take the regional level as our main reference and primarily focus on "demand-side" socio-economic contextual variables, such as economic disparities and cultural issues in the specific region. Additionally, we examine the role of "supply-side" organizational and political factors, such as regional leadership, grassroots and factions. Finally, we look at patterns of inter-party competition, variation in the support base for national parties and/or blocs across regions, and opportunities for the FN to cooperate with mainstream parties. Different regionalized party sub-systems may produce incentives for different interpretations of its national-populism by the FN.

Identity and distributional politics

Voting for PRR parties is motivated by cultural and economic factors (Golder 2016). This chapter argues that the current FN operates across both an identity and a distributional conflict in French politics, mobilizing cultural and economic grievances. This allows the party to adapt its supply of national-populism to different contexts where cultural and economic issues vary in salience and in the resonance they find in the political process.

First, the FN mobilizes a cultural (identity) conflict embedded in its nationalist ideology. FN "national-populism" focuses on the defense of national identity construed both in cultural and economic terms, which sees immigration as a threat to the fabric of French society and to its social welfare (Taguieff 1995). The FN is traditionally in favor of "national preference" – which means giving priority to the French over immigrants for welfare, housing and jobs. The party advocates a drastic reduction in immigration, as well as a range of measures to combat the so-called identitarian closure (*communautarisme*) of French Muslims (Ivaldi 2016). Electoral support for the FN is primarily driven by immigration fears (Perrineau 1995). Studies using aggregate data identify a positive correlation between immigrants and support for the FN at higher levels of aggregation (e.g. departments and regions) (e.g. Mayer 1998; Lubbers and Scheepers 2002; Della Posta 2013).

In FN discourse, immigration is linked with criminality. Immigrants are typically portrayed by the FN as the root cause of crime and public insecurity (Rydgren 2005). The party expresses an authoritarian view of society and a tough stance on law-and-order (Ivaldi 2016). High criminality rates may foster support for the FN locally. More recently the EU refugee crisis and wave of Islamic terrorism have increased the salience of immigration issues. The regional presence of refugee facilities and/or immigration hotspots may bolster local support for the FN.

Second, FN mobilization is structured by a socio-economic (distributional) conflict. During the 1990s, the FN's national-populism has attached itself to economic protectionism, associating European integration with globalization (Zaslove 2008). Anti-globalization positions and a strong criticism of international openness have become central to the contestation of "globalism" (*mondialisme*) by the FN. Predicated on the contention of France's deindustrialization, the FN has developed a policy program for the regeneration of French industry, arguing for economic nationalism and state intervention in strategic industrial sectors (Ivaldi 2015).

Recently, the FN under Marine Le Pen has also embraced economic redistribution and state regulation, opposing austerity and market liberalization. Seeking to address social decline and rural marginalization, the FN has become a strong defender of public services (Ivaldi 2015), a move which can be seen as a strategic attempt by the FN to consolidate its working class constituency (Igounet 2014). Since 2012, in particular, support for the FN has grown among lower-middle and working class voters most severely hit by the economic crisis (Gougou 2015). Locally, FN support is primarily found in peri-urban and rural municipalities which show clusters of voters with a lower socio-economic status (Fourquet et al. 2013).

Despite a marked decrease in economic liberalism over time, the FN's economic platform shows the the persistence of a small array of "residual" right-wing liberal elements which most notably include opposing decentralization and advocating tax cuts and less bureaucracy at local level (Ivaldi 2015). In 2012, Marine Le Pen's presidential platform claimed that the FN would implement "a voluntarist action plan to identify and drastically reduce unnecessary and harmful expenses for the country (...) like the cost of decentralization" (FN 2012: 3). The FN has generally been a detractor of decentralization laws on the account that decentralization has increased local bureaucracy and taxes, and fostered political corruption. As stated in the 2002 FN presidential manifesto:

> decentralization of the 1980s has been a decoy and a failure (...) Local authorities have not been de-statetised (...) Local direct taxes have increased faster than national taxes. Local authorities have pressured the taxpayer, and expenditures have exploded, often unjustifiably. This has resulted in much of the corruption of the last two decades.
>
> *(FN 2002)*

The FN's 2015 local election platforms strongly emphasized tax cuts and reducing local bureaucracy, thus showing a notable departure from Marine Le Pen's national agenda of redistribution and state intervention in the previous 2012 presidential election. The persistence of right-wing economic policies reflects the need for the party to address the diverse economic interests of its constituency. In particular, it helps the FN preserve enough room for its more traditional petty-bourgeois support (Perrineau 1995). As the analysis in this chapter suggests, the FN may also use this reservoir of right-wing policies to recalibrate its economic appeal locally in constituencies with stronger neo-liberal preferences and orientations.

Party organization and competition

The literature on the populist radical right stresses the importance of political opportunity and internal supply-side factors (Art 2011; Muis and Immerzeel 2017). Political parties are active agents capable of adapting to external constraints and opportunities through their organization. Since Marine Le Pen's accession in 2011, the FN has entered a new stage of its institutionalization in French politics. The FN is progressively developing its membership – although it remains relatively small at 51,500 (as of July 2015) –, and it is building a more complex organization (Ivaldi and Lanzone 2016). Organizational growth may help the party build up its profile and increase its presence in local constituencies, thus enhancing its potential to effectively mobilize voters.

First, the literature on populist parties highlights the predominance of leadership (Betz 1998; Lubbers et al. 2002). Recent studies of the FN confirm that personalistic features are central to Marine Le Pen's model of leadership (Ivaldi and Lanzone 2016). Regionally, the presence of candidates with national notoriety may also enhance electoral performances. Vliegenthart et al. (2012) show that media prominence and visibility may enhance electoral support for populist radical right parties like the FN.

Second, we focus on the size of grassroots membership and the presence of FN *notables* locally. Parties with strong organizations are more effective in mobilizing voters, particularly in sub-national elections where immediate and frequent contact with voters are crucial factors (Tavits 2012). Erlingsson et al. (2013) show that a local organizational presence has a substantial effect on the electoral results of anti-immigrant parties. Organizational growth on the other hand may also be seen as a consequence of previous electoral success (Ellinas 2009). Since 2011, the electoral returns of the FN in sub-national elections have substantially increased the number of elected FN representatives across the country. The FN won 11 city councils and a total of 1,544 municipal councilors in the 2014 elections. In the 2015 departmental elections, it received 25.2 per cent of the vote and won 62 local councilors nationally, as opposed to less than three on average since 1985.

In the French context, the "localness" of candidates and the presence of established *notables* are significant factors of party support (Knapp and Wright 2006: 361). New FN leaders like Sophie Montel, Julien Sanchez, David Rachline or Stéphane Ravier, for instance, have emerged locally from within the party's grassroots. While professionalization remains overall limited, the party is actively seeking to recruit a larger and better qualified pool of lower-level elites, candidates and party members, to accompany its organizational development locally. As new regional and local elites gain more autonomy and media visibility, the ideological contours of the FN's national-populist agenda may evolve and show more variation across regions, adapting to specific local issues.

Additionally, the FN mobilizes specific social groups and interests. Historically, the party has reached out to the constituency of repatriates from French Algeria (*Pieds-Noirs*) after 1962. The repatriate community has provided the FN with a network of organizations and activists, which have contributed to the electoral success of the party (Veugelers 2012).

A third aspect concerns the territorial distribution of party factions. Party factionalism has traditionally been a strong feature of the FN and it has often erupted into faction fights, party purges and organizational splits (Ivaldi and Lanzone 2016). During the 2000s, Marine Le Pen organized her modernist faction through Générations Le Pen, a think-tank that she had created in 1998. The rise of Le Pen was opposed by the party's old guard behind Bruno Gollnisch, and the conflict led to the departure of prominent national cadres like Carl Lang, Bernard Antony and Jean-Claude Martinez, as well as historical figures of the FN like Myriam Baeckeroot, Martine Lehideux and Martial Bild. This paved the way for a younger cohort of FN elites like as Marion Maréchal-Le Pen, Florian Philippot, David Rachline, Stéphane Ravier, Nicolas Bay and Julien Rochedy.

While there are no officially recognized factions within the party, current FN leaders belong to intra-party tendencies which represent different patterned sets of attitudes. Factional conflict in the FN concerns both policy and strategy, primarily revolving around economic, European integration and moral issues, and it opposes the modernist faction led by Philippot to the more traditionalist sector of the party behind Maréchal-Le Pen.[2] These factions have a strong territorial basis. They are regionally rooted and their strategies are shaped by regional opportunity structures and contexts.

Finally, we look at party competition. Electoral outcomes in France are regionalized. Statewide parties and blocs have regional strongholds. Different regionalized party sub-systems may produce different incentives for the FN to adjust its supply of national-populism. Cooperation between mainstream and populist parties may also increase the legitimacy and visibility of the populist challenger (Rydgren 2005). At national level, the French FN never shared power, but tactical alliances between the mainstream right and the FN occurred across a number of regional governments in the past, which may result in greater legitimacy for the FN.

Methods and data

This chapter adopts a qualitative case study approach. The French FN provides a good case to empirically evaluate the territorialization of national-populist parties. While embedded in the idiosyncratic features of France's political system, the findings in this chapter may be relevant to other parties in different contexts. The chapter should help improve our general understanding of how national-populist parties adapt their mobilization strategies to different contexts and opportunities.

The chapter specifically draws on a qualitative analysis of the 2015 regional elections across two French regions, namely Provence-Alpes-Côte-d'Azur (PACA) in the Mediterranean South, and Hauts-de-France (HDF) in the Northern part of the country. PACA and HDF are two of the country's largest and most densely populated regions in France, representing 5 and 6 million inhabitants respectively, and both regions are electoral strongholds of the FN. The size of the FN vote is remarkably similar across the two regions. In the 2015 elections, PACA and HDF featured two of the most prominent party leaders – Marine Le Pen herself in HDF and her niece Marion Maréchal-Le Pen in PACA –, giving the FN 40.6 per cent of the regional vote. In both cases, the

Socialist Party called for a "republican front" to defeat the FN and withdrew its candidate from the second-round race. This allowed the center-right Republicans to win the two regions, leaving however the FN as the only opposition party in both regional councils.

This chapter uses a most different systems design. PACA and HDF have in common the same dependent variable, while exhibiting significant differences in their regional socio-demographic profile, economy and political history. The salience of the socio-cultural and economic issues that drive the FN vote vary considerably across the two regions, and party competition shows significant variation.

We look specifically at the 2015 regional elections. French regional elections provide a good mix of national and local issues, which illustrates "multi-level electoral competition" (Dupoirier 2004). The 2015 elections were the first nationwide sub-national elections since Marine Le Pen's accession, thus possibly reflecting localized effects of the organizational development associated with her new leadership. These elections also took place during the EU refugee crisis, which allows to look at the impact of short-term cultural factors.

The empirical focus is on the party's regional election manifestos and discourses. We examine in particular the FN's platforms in PACA and HDF, namely *Avec Marion, une nouvelle chance pour notre région* (FN 2015a) and *Plan d'action régional. Pour une région fière et enracinée* (FN 2015b). To contextualize the FN's regional politics, we use INSEE's socio-demographic data from the 2013 census. Criminality data are available from the Ministry of Interior and we use the rate of burglaries as our main indicator. The presence of *Pieds-Noirs* is approximated by shares of repatriates in French departments from the 1968 census. We use ratios of mosques relative to the population as an indicator of the size of the Muslim community.[3]

The notoriety of lead regional candidates is measured from the Factiva Global News database. We look at data from all major national and regional news chapters during the official campaign, from 1 November to 6 December 2015. Since reliable FN membership figures are not available, we take the number of FN candidates in the 2014 municipal elections as a proxy for the party's membership base. In 2014, the FN ran more than 500 municipal lists, that is a total 19,982 individual candidates. The size of FN membership is approximated from the total number of candidates per 10,000 registered voters.

Results

The main socio-economic and political indicators for PACA and HDF show substantial variation in the contextual socio-economic and cultural conditions. These two regions have distinct socio-demographic profiles and political traditions, which may present specific opportunities for voter mobilization by the FN (see Table 8.2).

Distributional politics in Hauts-de-France

HDF has a background as a major industrial region concentrating in particular intensive coal mining, textile and metallurgic industry. Since the 1970s the region has been severely hit by deindustrialization and economic restructuration. HDF has also been strongly affected by the economic crisis since 2008 and it has the highest regional unemployment rate at 12.4 per cent. HDF has a below average median income of 18,812 euro. It has one the country's highest poverty rate with 18.3 per cent, and the share of population in social housing is well above the national average.

HDF has the country's largest working class population (27.2 per cent), and it has been a long-standing electoral bastion of the French left (Gombin 2015). According to IFOP (2013), the FN's Northern constituency shows a higher proportion of workers and voters with a low economic status, who are more supportive of economic redistribution and state intervention. HDF is highest on our measure of deindustrialization with a decrease of about 11 points in the share of industrial employment since 1989. Globalization issues have stronger resonance in the North. International trade makes up 16.9 per cent of the regional GDP as opposed to 10.3 per cent in PACA. Moreover, HDF relies heavily on European Union funds, showing the second highest rate of EU funding (240.9 euro per head).

Reflecting the economic profile of HDF, Marine Le Pen's 2015 regional manifesto strongly emphasized socio-economic themes. Regional identity issues were primarily framed as economic issues concerning territorial trademarks (FN 2015b: 9) and support to local economic actors to promote regional festivals and popular events (FN 2015b: 9). Le Pen's platform showed strong criticism of international economic integration, emphasizing "regional economic and social patriotism" (FN 2015b: 99). Le Pen pledged that she would give priority to local businesses in public tenders and that she would force companies to repay public monies in cases of relocation and offshoring. Her platform showed strong criticism of the EU and economic globalization, arguing that the region should protect against the "devastating impact" of economic globalization (FN 2015b: 3). Le Pen wrote "we no longer want to suffer the consequences of globalization and European free trade. HDF has been severely hit by globalization and its consequences: de-industrialization, unemployment, pollution" (FN 2015b: 70). The FN leader pledged that regional "subsidies to businesses would be made conditional to guarantees that jobs wouldn't be offshored and that companies would not employ posted workers" (FN 2015b: 100). Interestingly, Le Pen claimed that she would continue to accept EU monies such as the European Regional Development Fund (ERDF) and the European Maritime and Fisheries Fund (EMFF) (FN 2015b: 100 & 107).

The provision of local public services and health centers in rural areas was a key political issue of the Northern campaign by the FN (FN 2015b: 107). In HDF, no less than 27.4 per cent of the regional population live in peri-urban municipalities where highest levels of support for the FN are typically found.

TABLE 8.2 Socio-economic, cultural and election indicators compared across PACA and HDF

	Provence-Alpes-Côte d'Azur	Hauts-de-France	France[1]
Population 2015 (in million)	5.01	6.01	64.96
Density (per Sq. km)	159.5	188.9	119.41
Population in peri-urban municipalities (% of population, as per INSEE Urban Area classification)	10.6	27.4	24.4
Unemployment rate (Q4 2015, % of active pop.)	11.4	12.4	9.9
Poverty rate 2014	17.5	18.3	14.2
Social Housing 2015 (for 10 000 habs)	580	930	718
Social Health Cover 2015 (for 100 hab)	8.7	9.4	7.3
Public services (number of selected services and facilities available per 1,000 inhab. (2013))	9.0	5.1	6.5
Public jobs (as number of territorial administration staff (2014) per 1,000 inhab.)	30.9	24.1	24.8
Workers 2014 (% of active pop.)	18.8	27.2	22.2
Median available income 2014 (in euros)	19 983	18 812	20 369
Globalization (share of import and export in GDP, 2013)	10.3	16.9	15.8
Deindustrialization (change in % of industrial employment between 1989 and 2014, NA5 classification)	4.2	11.8	8.3
EU Funds (ERDF and ESF amount per head, 2007–2013)	138.5	240.9	183.1
Immigrants 2013 (% pop)[2]	10.4	5.1	9.1
Immigrants from Maghreb (% pop)[2]	4.3	2	2.7
Criminality (number of burglaries per 1,000 inhab.)	6.8	4.5	4.7
Repatriates (% of repatriates in total population, 1968 census)	6.3	0.6	1.6
FN grassroots (number of FN candidates in the 2014 municipal elections, per 10,000 registered voters)	10.4	5.8	4.3
% FN vote in 2012 presidential[3]	23.9	23.9	17.9
% FN vote in 2015 regional[3]	40.6	40.6	27.7

(1) All figures are for metropolitan France.
(2) Based on the definition of the High Council for Integration, immigrant refers to people living in France who were born foreigners abroad, irrespective of their current citizenship (www.insee.fr/en/methodes/default.asp?page=definitions/immigre.htm).
(3) As % of the valid vote cast.
Sources: Ministry of Interior, INSEE.

This compares with only 10.6 per cent in PACA. Our data also show that HDF has one of the lowest ratios of local public services of all French regions, with an average of about 5.1 services per 1,000, as opposed to 6.5 nationally, up to 9 in PACA. According to Le Pen's manifesto, "it is essential that our policies be firmly grounded in the realities of our region. Of all places, rural areas are where the sense of belonging to a community with a common destiny is the strongest" (FN 2015b: 114). Most notably, Le Pen's 4-page election brochure pledged that she would "protect the region's identity by preserving local public services across each administrative entity" (FN 2015c).

Compared with PACA, HDF shows a much smaller foreign population. Immigrants make up 5.1 per cent of the regional population, which is below the country's average and about half the percentage found in the South. The Muslim community is also substantially smaller in the North where there are about 3.6 mosques per 100,000 inhabitants, compared with 4.6 in PACA. The highest departmental average is found in the department of Nord (4.6). Muslims tend to cluster locally, however. A high Muslim population is found in particular in the urban areas of Dunkerque and Roubaix, where ratios of mosques per 100,000 are 7.8 and 13.6 respectively. Finally, criminality is just under the national average in HDF at 4.5 burglaries per 1,000 inhabitants. Criminality is higher in the larger urban areas such as Lille. A model controlling for regional socio-economic and demographic characteristics suggests that there is no specific regional effect in the case of HDF (Interstats 2015).

Traditional immigration and criminality issues were given much less attention in Le Pen's 2015 manifesto. Her regional platform had virtually no mention of immigration. Essentially, Le Pen pledged that she would defend France's Republican tradition of secularism (laïcité) against the threat of "communitarism", and this concerned primarily claims by Muslims to have separate menus in school canteens. The salience of law-and-order issues was relatively limited in Le Pen's platform which evoked criminality in public transports and schools, advocating a regional police force. However, the terrorist attacks in Paris in November 2015 provided Le Pen with the opportunity to refocus her campaign on security and immigration, thus taking it national. In her last campaign meeting, she declared: "we have no choice but to win this war. If we lose, Islamic totalitarianism will take the power in our country (...) Sharia will replace our constitution, radical Islam will replace our laws" (Le Point 2015). Immigration and identity issues were also reintroduced in the run-off campaign which featured the need to defend the "national identity", to "fight Muslim fundamentalism" and to "stop an insane and costly immigration".

In HDF, the FN was able to exploit local issues provided by the refugee crisis, seizing in particular on increasing frustration and fears about the migration transit camp of Calais. During 2015, the population of the Calais refugee camp, known as the "Jungle", increased dramatically – up to over 6,000 migrants –, which provoked growing local anger. Le Pen's election leaflet emphasized the situation around the city of Calais, which was depicted as a "total chaos". Le Pen pledged that she would use all available means to "send back all illegal immigrants and dismantle all the 'jungles' (illegal camps) in the area" (FN 2015c). During her campaign, she pledged also to "eradicate bacterial immigration" arguing that refugees were carriers of "contagious non-European diseases" (Herreros 2015). In Calais, Le Pen won 49.1 per cent of the first-round vote in 2015, and on average she polled 50 per cent across communes in the Calaisis.

Party leadership, organization and local membership are strongly associated with FN electoral success in HDF. Not surprisingly, Le Pen had the highest media profile in the 2015 campaign, totaling 2,712 news chapter articles during the official campaign, by far the highest number of all FN regional candidates – as opposed for instance to 492 for Florian Philippot and less than 150 for candidates with a much lower profile such as Philippe Loiseau, Jacques Colombier and Pascal Gannat. The vast majority of articles had a national focus, giving Le Pen a ratio of 6.2 between national and regional press releases. While Le Pen established herself in Pas-de-Calais in the late 1990s – she first ran on the FN's list in the North in the 1998 regional elections –, she has kept a national profile as party leader since 2011. The 2015 campaign featured FN *notables* well known regionally such as Philippe Eymery, Michel Guiniot and Bruno Bilde, which helped enhance Le Pen's regional profile. The campaign also emphasized the role of the party's mayors elected in 2014, Steeve Briois in Hénin-Beaumont and Franck Briffaut in Villers-Cotterêts, praising their "excellent" local government record.

The FN has developed grassroots membership in HDF. In the 2014 municipal elections, the party fielded an average 5.8 candidates per 10 000 registered voters in HDF, compared with an average of 4.3 nationally. Reflecting Le Pen's personal presence, the FN's ratio of candidates was highest in the department of Pas-de-Calais (8.4). In 2014, HDF had two FN mayors and a total of 238 FN municipal councilors, that is the second highest number after PACA. In the March 2015 departmental elections, HDF elected 26 FN local councilors, the largest number nationally.

The presence of party *notables* in HDF intersects with the territorial distribution of FN elites and factions. Northern elites such as Marine Le Pen, Steeve Briois – as well as Florian Philippot and Sophie Montel in the neighboring regions of Grand-Est and Bourgogne-Franche-Comté – notoriously embrace a social-populist agenda of economic redistribution and state intervention. The attitudes and policy preferences of the FN's Northern elites thus fit the regional context and socio-economic opportunities.

They also fit the dominant political orientation of HDF. The North has been a long-standing working class bastion of the French left providing support to both the Socialists and the Communists. While the mainstream right has recently made significant inroads in the region, NPDCP has nevertheless maintained its predominantly left-leaning profile, and the FN in the North primarily competes against the Socialist Party (PS).

Finally, leaders such as Marine Le Pen, Steeve Briois and Florian Philippot incarnate the FN's current "de-demonization" strategy which seeks to shed the extremist profile of the party (Ivaldi 2016). This was reflected in the visual language of Le Pen's 2015 manifesto which showed no explicit reference to the FN, while promoting a "peaceful France", which at the time was tipped to become her presidential campaign slogan in 2017. Le Pen's 4-page election leaflet had no reference whatsoever to the FN's name and symbols, while emphasizing the valence stature and presidential profile of Le Pen. Le Pen also sought to present a more affable personal image on social networks, regularly posting photographs of her family.

The politics of identity in Provence-Alpes-Côte d'Azur

In contrast with HDF, the 2015 FN regional campaign was characterized by its strong focus on traditional FN cultural themes and issues. Immigration and identity issues achieve higher salience in the Southern region. Compared with HDF, PACA has a much larger share of immigrants (10.4 per cent), particularly of Northern African origin (4.3 per cent). PACA is host to a large Muslim community. There are 230 mosques in the region, that is a ratio of 4.6 mosques per 100,000 inhabitants, compared with 3.6 in HDF. Locally, a strong Muslim presence is found in the department of Vaucluse as well as in the urban areas of Nice and Marseille, with ratios well above 6 mosques per 100,000.

The FN's anti-immigration rhetoric has traditionally strongly resonated in Mediterranean France (Perrineau 1995). PACA is an electoral stronghold of the FN since the mid-1980s: on average, the party has won 6.7 per cent above its national score across all presidential elections in the region since 1988. In 2015, Maréchal-Le Pen's campaign showed continuity with the old FN identity politics. Her 4-page election brochure emphasized immigration and Islam. Its title, *A Region for the French First*, was a clear reference to Jean-Marie Le Pen's book *Les Français d'abord* in the 1980s. The FN pledged that it would create a "vice-presidency for identity" in the future regional council (FN 2015a: 23). The FN objected strongly to public subsidies to immigrant associations and local organizations helping migrants. Regional political parties were accused of "breaking away from their ancestors" and of being "weak" on Muslim "communitarism", and they were strongly criticized by Maréchal-Le Pen for their "ideological blindness, electoral patronage and self-hatred" (FN 2015a: 21). She wrote "we believe we are part of an unbroken chain that we want to pass on to our children. The PS and LR have chosen renouncement, we choose identity" (FN 2015a: 21).

Unlike Marine Le Pen in the North, the campaign in PACA emphasized territorial identity and rhetoric, celebrating regional roots and local identity. It referred explicitly to four distinct sub-regional identities – i.e. Provence, Dauphiné, Comté de Nice and Alpes –, while emphasizing the link between regional and national identity. On 26 October 2015, Marion Maréchal-Le Pen launched her campaign, indicating that she would focus on family values, Christian roots and the traditional customs of Provence. In her manifesto, the FN candidate would also describe herself as a "Vauclusienne by adoption, who fell desperately in love with this land and its people", stating: "our region should be a tool to reinforce our nation and a way to unite behind a common hope" (FN 2015a: 3).

Regional identity was embedded in a broader civilizational framework of Christianity, while depicting Islam as a threat. According to the PACA manifesto: "we will assert our popular traditions and cultural heritage, notably by setting up Christmas nativity cribs in all regional council buildings" (FN 2015a: 23). During the campaign, Maréchal-Le Pen claimed that "France is no Islamic soil" and that "Muslims can only be French if they share France's customs and lifestyle which have been shaped by sixteen centuries of Christianity". She said "in our home, people don't walk around wearing jellabas, they don't wear full veils and they don't impose mosques the size of cathedrals!" (Huffington Post 2015).

During 2015, the EU refugee crisis provided further local opportunities for the FN, in particular in the areas around Menton and near Ventimiglia across the Italian border where the presence of migrants was most visible. During the campaign, Maréchal-Le Pen said the situation in Menton was comparable with Calais (Le Parisien 2015). In those areas, the FN regional score was significantly above the departmental average (37.9 per cent): Maréchal-Le Pen won for instance 44 per cent in Menton and in Castellar. The FN achieved some of its best first-round scores in the smaller border cities, polling 47.6 per cent in Fontan, 50 per cent in Castillon and 52.8 per cent in Sainte-Agnès.

Together with immigration, PACA exhibits higher rates of criminality with 6.8 burglaries per 1,000, culminating in the Bouches-du-Rhône and Var. Interstats (2015) shows that the regional effect of criminality in PACA is the strongest of all metropolitan regions, when controlling for socio-economic and demographic attributes of local areas. The region's largest cities such as Marseille, Aix, Nice, Cannes and Toulon have some of the country's highest crime rates, and criminality is a salient political issue locally. During the 2015 campaign, Maréchal-Le Pen took a strong stance on criminality and she linked it with immigration. She violently attacked "the violent scum (*racaille*) that is causing havoc and wreaking havoc in France's suburbs", while criticizing also French political elites who have "abandoned the people who live under the yoke of gangs and drug traffickers in France's suburbs" (RMC 2015).

Turning to distributional issues, PACA has a stronger economy traditionally oriented towards services, particularly tourism which represents a major component of the regional economy and a major source of employment (Gombin and Mayance 2009). Compared with both HDF and the national average, PACA shows a lower index of deindustrialization; it has a low level of embedment in international trade (10.3 per cent of its GDP) and it relies much less on EU subsidies (at 138.5 euro per head). PACA also has the highest share of local public services at 9.1 per 1,000, and a larger public sector (30.9 per 1,000). Finally, peri-urbanization is much less developed in PACA where only 10.6 per cent of the regional population live in peri-urban areas.

Reflecting the region's economic profile, the 2015 FN campaign in PACA advocated primarily right-wing economics, emphasizing in particular cuts in regional spending and bureaucracy. As explained by Maréchal-Le Pen: "Our programme is pragmatic. We will limit unnecessary expenditures and put the financial mismanagement of the region to an end. I would lie, she added, if I said that the number of public staff is not too large" (Mazerolle 2015). Her manifesto included also the promise to support small business by doubling the regional budget intended for economic development, while claiming that the FN would give priority to small entrepreneurs, craftsmen and shopkeepers. The emphasis on right-wing economics corroborates that the FN is seeking to address the specific needs and interests of its regional electorate. As IFOP (2013) suggests, FN voters in the South have a distinct socio-demographic and policy profile. Pensioners, entrepreneurs and managers are overrepresented among Southern FN voters. They are significantly more socially conservative and they favor market liberal policies.

The case of PACA confirms that organizational features are significant factors of party success at regional level. Maréchal-Le Pen had a strong media presence during the campaign, with the second highest number of newschapter articles (792). The ratio between national and regional news coverage suggests that Maréchal-Le Pen had a significant regional dimension (2.8 compared with 6.2 for Le Pen in the North). The presence of a lead candidate with both national notoriety and a regional profile may enhance electoral performances.

Unlike the FN in the North, Mediterranean elites like Marion Maréchal-Le Pen, David Rachline and Stéphane Ravier notoriously embody the hard line approach that was shaped by Jean-Marie Le Pen during his time as party leader.[4] They emphasize traditional immigration policies and ethno-culturalist discourses of the FN. During the 2014 municipal elections, Ravier ran an aggressive campaign, stigmatizing Muslims, saying for instance – "not all Muslims are extremists, yet Islam is a religion that does not blend well into the Republic" –, while using strong law-and-order themes such as "no mercy for the scum in our neighbourhood", portraying Marseille as the "reign of Kalashnikovs, corruption, Islam and uncontrolled immigration" (Beaumont 2013). In the South, FN elites cooperate with far right extremist groups such as the Bloc Identitaire (BI) and Jacques Bompard's Ligue du Sud, and they adopt ethno-racial discourses of immigration of far right intellectuals such as Aymeric Chauprade and Renaud Camus (Frigoli and Ivaldi 2019). In 2015, Maréchal-Le Pen's regional manifesto endorsed unambiguously Camus' concept of "great replacement" by warning against the imminent threat of "the substitution of population!" (FN 2015a: 21). Her regional list also accommodated two former members of the BI Philippe Vardon and Benoît Loeuillet.[5] In Fréjus, Rachline has had links with other far right groups such as Alain Soral's Egalité et Réconciliation (L'Obs 2016).

Southern FN elites also embrace social conservative views. A fervent Catholic, Maréchal-Le Pen has strong links with the traditionalist sector of the French Catholic Church such as Notre-Dame de Chrétienté and the Fraternité Saint-Pierre, and she is close to the Manif pour tous, a right-wing reactionary social movement which strongly opposed the 2013 law on same-sex marriage in France. During the 2015 campaign, Maréchal-Le Pen took an anti-abortion stand and sparked controversy by pledging that she would stop public funding to family planning centers against the official party line (L'Express 2015).

The policy preferences of the FN's Southern elites reflect regional party competition and PACA's predominantly right-wing orientation since the mid-1980s. In the 2012 presidential run-off, the socialist candidate François Hollande received only 42.4 per cent of the vote in PACA compared with 53.1 per cent in HDF. Party competition in PACA is primarily characterized by a duopolistic structure which opposes the FN to the right-wing Republicans (Ivaldi and Pina 2017).

In PACA, the FN can rely on a strong organizational base. The party has invested substantial resources in the region. On average, it was able to run 10.4 candidates per 10,000 registered voters in the 2014 municipal elections in PACA, compared with an average of 4.3 nationally. In 2014, PACA had the highest number of FN municipal councilors with a total of 338 elected representatives out of 1544, including five mayors in Marseille-7, Cogolin, Le Luc, Le Pontet and Fréjus, the largest city under FN administration (52,000 inhabitants). In 2015, PACA had also a FN deputy, Maréchal-Le Pen in Vaucluse, and two FN senators, Ravier and Rachline. In the 2015 regional elections, FN *notables* played an important role in mobilizing support for the party locally: Maréchal-Le Pen won for instance 50.4 per cent in Fréjus, 54.3 per cent in Cogolin, 52.7 per cent in Le Luc and 53.8 per cent in Le Pontet, which are FN city councils.

Finally, PACA exhibits favorable political opportunities for FN mobilization. Regional cooperation between the mainstream and the extreme right has occurred on various occasions in PACA since the mid-1980s, which may have increased the political legitimacy of the FN at the regional level. In 1986, the PACA region was won by the UDF candidate, Jean-Claude Gaudin, with the support of the FN. In 1988, the RPR/UDF coalition forged an electoral pact with the FN in the legislatives, which concerned about 25 constituencies in PACA. Prominent local right-wing politicians such as Maurice Arreckx, the mayor of Toulon between 1959 and 1985, and Jacques Médecin and Jacques Peyrat, two former mayors of Nice, have had close links with the FN. More recently, in the 2015 regional election, Maréchal-Le Pen's list featured former UMP members such as Olivier Bettati and Franck Allisio.

A second important aspect concerns the presence of a large *Pieds-Noirs* community in PACA. Our historical data show that repatriates from French Algeria represented 6.3 per cent of the regional population in 1968, up to 8.1 per cent in the Var, compared with 1.6 per cent nationally. *Pieds-Noirs* in PACA have traditionally shared a strong right-wing orientation, supporting both conservative and far right candidates. In 1965, the pro-French Algeria candidate Jean-Louis Tixier-Vignancour came in the third place in the Bouches-du-Rhône, Var and Alpes-Maritimes, winning over 15 per cent of the vote in the presidential election, as opposed to 5.2 per cent nationally.

Historically, the contribution by ex-colonials to the building of the FN's Southern constituency and party organization has been crucial in local areas such as Nice, Toulon, Carpentras, Bollène and Marignane for instance. A recent survey by IFOP (2014) suggests that the share of repatriates could be as high as 15 per cent of all registered voters in PACA, as opposed to only 2 per cent in HDF. In PACA, Maréchal-Le Pen has established links with *Pieds-Noirs* associations like the USDIFRA (Sulzer 2015). FN leaders in the South such as Rachline and Ravier, and Louis Aliot and Robert Ménard in the neighboring Occitanie region, are well known for their pro-French Algeria rhetoric and support to *Pieds-Noirs* organizations.

Conclusion

This chapter has examined the territorialization of the Front National in France. Based on a comparative analysis of the FN's regional campaigns of 2015 in Provence-Alpes-Côte d'Azur and Hauts-de-France, we found that the FN is tailoring its programmatic and organizational strategies to fit different sub-national contexts and arenas, thus aligning itself with existing cultural and economic cleavages.

Multi-level government necessitates that parties adjust how they organize and compete. The FN is successfully translating its centralized policy prescriptions into policies relevant to the regional level of administration. This is an important aspect as regional and local authorities have limited competences in France,[6] which exclude policy areas that matter most to FN supporters, such as immigration and law-and-order. However, both the PACA and HDF regional campaigns suggest that the FN is adapting its programmatic strategies to regional government, for instance by tackling immigration issues in schools and criminality in public transports.

Second, our findings suggest that statewide national-populist parties like the FN can adapt their supply of national-populism to take advantage of territorialized opportunities. The FN is seeking to achieve "goodness-of-fit" in adjusting its political message and strategies to the specific needs and interests of its targeted regional constituencies. In the richer and more culturally diverse South, the party primarily competes against the mainstream right and emphasizes immigration, identity and right-wing economics while in the more socially deprived North, where it primarily competes against the left, it focuses on redistribution, economic protectionism and the provision of public services. In PACA, the FN also embraces territorial identity and rhetoric, emphasizing regional roots and local identities, in relation to its traditional ethno-culturalist and Christian framework.

Our findings illustrate the "chameleonic" nature of the populist ideology and its potential ubiquity (Taggart 2000). Populism can attach itself to a variety of political ideologies, making it an ideologically diverse phenomenon. Our findings suggest that populism may also change face inside populist parties themselves, according to sub-national contexts and opportunities. While there are commonalities in the mobilization strategies of the FN across regions – as regards in particular the use of populist anti-establishment rhetoric –, we see different socio-economic and cultural emphases, and different regional interpretations of its populism by the FN.

Regional differences should not be overemphasized and the overall impact of the territorial dimension exaggerated, however. First, regional elections in France fit the second-order model of elections and regional campaigns are dominated by a mix of regional and national issues (Dupoirier 2004). This was illustrated by the politicization by the FN of the terrorist attacks in Paris during the regional campaign of 2015, which gave the campaign a more national tone.

Second, French regions are large units with substantial variance. This is the case of PACA which shows significant imbalances across departments in terms of income distribution. The FN's welfare chauvinist agenda may certainly find greater resonance in the region's socially deprived territories like Vaucluse where poverty is often associated with a large immigrant community, less so in the more bourgeois areas of the Riviera dominated by the mainstream right (Ivaldi and Pina 2017). Similarly, poverty in HDF is remarkably high in the Aisne, Somme and Pas-de-Calais. Differences of income are found predominantly between the region's richer urban centers such as Lille, Arras, Compiègnes and Beauvais, and the more deprived areas such as Dunkerque and Calais.

Third, we find no evidence of shifts in the party's discourse of territoriality, regional autonomy and self-government. The FN's nationalism embraces the Jacobin tradition, advocating a strong centralized state and relatively weak local autonomy. It opposes decentralization on the account that it has increased local bureaucracy and taxes, and fostered political corruption in regional and local governments. In organizational terms, the FN maintains a hierarchical structure. Power is primarily concentrated at the national level and decision-making is centralized in the hands of the national executive (Ivaldi and Lanzone 2016).

The territorial diversification of populist politics may produce greater ideological heterogeneity, possibly hampering the party's electoral prospects and organizational coherence. In the case of the FN, territorialization may lead to intra-party conflict as different parts of the party diverge in the areas of elite recruitment, policies and campaigning. The recent party split and departure of Florian Philippot illustrates the negative impact of factionalism within the party, which to some extent reflects the territorialization of the party's strategies and elites.

Additionally, the electoral geography of the FN suggests that electoral support for the party is lower in regions such as Bretagne as well as in large urban areas such as Paris and Lyon, where neither of the conflicts politicized by the FN achieve relevance, thus posing a significant challenge to the party.

We conclude by reiterating the qualitative orientation of our analysis. Rather than inferring causal relationships, our aim was to identify plausible patterns of populist territorialization. It is our hope that the findings in this chapter will inform future research on strategies of national-populist mobilization across multiple levels of competition.

Notes

1 This is an extended and revised version of our paper in *Comparative European Politics* (Ivaldi and Dutozia 2018).
2 Both recently left the FN after the 2017 elections.
3 The data were drawn from the online collaborative platform: www.trouvetamosquee.fr
4 In 2015, Maréchal-Le Pen was endorsed by Jean-Marie Le Pen after he had left the campaign over disagreement with his daughter.
5 In the departmental elections of March 2015, the FN had already run four members of Nissa Rebela, the local branch of the Identitarian movement in Nice, including its secretary general Benoît Loeuillet.
6 Regions are responsible for transport, schools, universities, research and vocational training, infrastructure and culture, including cultural heritage and monuments. The NOTRe decentralization Law of 2015 (*Loi Nouvelle organisation territoriale de la République* – NOTRe) has also given regions new albeit limited responsibilities in economic development.

References

Art, D. (2011) *Inside the Radical Right: The Development of Anti-Immigrant Parties in Europe*. Cambridge: Cambridge University Press.
Arzheimer, K. and Carter, E. (2006) "Political Opportunity Structures and Right-Wing Extremist Party Success", *European Journal of Political Research*, 45(3), pp. 419–443.
Arzheimer, K. and Carter, E. (2009) "How (Not) to Operationalise Subnational Political Opportunity Structures: A Critique of Kestilä and Söderlund's Study of Regional Elections", *European Journal of Political Research*, 48(3), pp. 335–358.
Beaumont, O. (2013) "Municipales 2014 à Marseille: Stéphane Ravier, candidat frontal", *Le Parisien*, 19 November. www.leparisien.fr/municipales-2014/en-regions/municipales-2014-a-marseille-stephane-ravier-candidat-frontal-19-11-2013-3327407.php. Accessed 15 January 2019.
Betz, H.-G. (1994) *Radical Right-wing Populism in Western Europe*. New York: St. Martin's Press.
Betz, H.-G. (1998) "Introduction". In: Betz, H. G. and Immerfall, S. (eds.) *The New Politics of the Right: Neo-Populist Parties and Movements in Established Democracies*. New York: St. Martin's Press, pp. 1–10.
Della Posta, D. J. (2013) "Competitive Threat, Intergroup Contact, or Both? Immigration and the Dynamics of Front National Voting in France", *Social Forces*, 92(1), pp. 249–273.
Deschouwer, K. (2006) "Political Parties as Multi-Level Organizations". In: Katz, R. and Crotty, W. (eds.) *Handbook of Party Politics*. London: Sage, pp. 291–300.
Detterbeck, K. (2012) *Multi-Level Party. Politics in Western Europe*. Basingstoke: Palgrave Macmillan.
Detterbeck, K. and Hepburn, E. (2009) "Party Politics in Multi-Level Systems: Party Responses to New Challenges in European Democracies". In: Swenden, W. and Erk, J. (eds.) *Exploring New Avenues of Comparative Federalism Research*. London: Routledge, pp. 165–184.
Dupoirier, E. (2004) "La régionalisation des élections régionales? Un modèle d'interprétation des élections régionales en France", *Revue française de science politique*, 54(4), pp. 571–594.
Ellinas, A. A. (2009) "Chaotic but Popular? Extreme-Right Organisation and Performance in the Age of Media Communication", *Journal of Contemporary European Studies*, 17(2), pp. 209–221.

Erlingsson, G. Ó., Loxbo, K. and Öhrvall, R. (2013) "Anti-Immigrant Parties, Local Presence and Electoral Success", *Local Government Studies*, 38(6), pp. 817–839.
FN (2002) *Pour un avenir français. Programme du Front national.*
FN (2012) *Mon Projet pour la France et les Français. Marine Le Pen, la Voix du Peuple. l'Esprit de la France.*
FN (2015a) *Avec Marion, une nouvelle chance pour notre région. Notre projet pour Provence-Alpes-Côte d'Azur.*
FN (2015b) *Plan d'action régional. Pour une région fière et enracinée.* Nord-Pas-de-Calais.
FN (2015c) *Pour notre region: Marine Présidente!,* election leaflet.
Fourquet, J., Mergier, A. and Peugny, C. (2013) *Le grand malaise. Enquête sur les classes moyennes.* Paris: Fondation Jean-Jaurès.
Frigoli, G. and Ivaldi, G. (2019) "Still a Radical Right Movement Party? Political Opportunities, Party Strategy and the Cultural Context of the Front National in France". In: Caiani, M. and Císař, O. (eds.) *Far Right "Movement-Parties" in Europe.* London: Routledge, pp. 63–80.
Golder, M. (2016) "Far Right Parties in Europe", *Annual Review of Political Science*, 19, pp. 477–497.
Gombin, J. (2015) "Le changement dans la continuité. Géographies électorales du Front national depuis 1992". In: Crépon, S. et al. (eds.) *Les faux-semblants du Front national.* Paris: Presses de Sciences Po, pp. 395–416.
Gombin, J. and Mayance, P. (eds.) (2009) *Droit(es) aux urnes en région PACA!: L'élection présidentielle de 2007 en région Provence-Alpes-Côte d'Azur.* Paris: L'Harmattan.
Gougou, F. (2015) "Les ouvriers et le vote Front National. Les logiques d'un réalignement electoral". In: Crépon, S. et al. (eds.) *Les faux-semblants du Front national.* Paris: Presses de Sciences Po, pp. 323–344.
Heinisch, R., Massetti, E. and Mazzoleni, O. (2018) "Populism and Ethno-Territorial Politics in European Multilevel Systems", *Comparative European Politics*, 16(6), pp. 923–936.
Herreros, R. (2015) "Marine Le Pen veut 'éradiquer l'immigration bactérienne'", 10 November. www.huffingtonpost.fr/2015/11/10/marine-le-pen-immigration-bacterienne_n_8519976.html. Accessed 15 January 2019.
Huffington Post (2015) "Pour Marion Maréchal-Le Pen, les musulmans ne peuvent être français que sous condition", 2 December. www.huffingtonpost.fr/2015/12/02/marion-marechal-le-pen-musulmans-elections-regionales-2015_n_8695770.html. Accessed 15 January 2019.
IFOP (2013) "Front du nord, Front du sud", *Focus n. 92*, August.
IFOP (2014) "Le vote pied-noir: mythe ou réalité?", *Focus n. 107*, March.
Igounet, V. (2014) *Le Front national de 1972 à nos jours. Le parti, les hommes, les idées.* Paris: Seuil.
Interstats (2015) "Les déterminants sociaux, démographiques et économiques de la localisation des cambriolages de logement: une modélisation statistique à l'échelle des communes françaises", *Ministère de l'Interieur, Interstats Analyse*, 2, pp. 1–8.
Ivaldi, G. (2015) "Towards the Median Economic Crisis Voter? The New Leftist Economic Agenda of the Front National in France", *French Politics*, 13(4), pp. 346–369.
Ivaldi, G. (2016) "A New Course for the French Radical-Right? The Front National and 'de-demonization'". In: Akkerman, T., de Lange, S. and Rooduijn, M. (eds.) *Radical Right-Wing Populist Parties in Western Europe. Into the Mainstream?* London: Routledge, pp. 231–253.
Ivaldi, G. (2018a) "No Longer a Pariah? The Front National and the French Party System". In: Zaslove, A. and Wolinetz, S. B. (eds.) *Absorbing the Blow. Populist Parties and Their Impact on Parties and Party Systems.* London: Rowman & Littlefield, pp. 171–196.

Ivaldi, G. (2018b) "Contesting the EU in Times of Crisis: The Front National and Politics of Euroscepticism in France", *Politics*. Online first. https://doi.org/10.1177/0263395718766787.
Ivaldi, G. and Dutozia, J. (2018) "The 'Territorialization' of the Front National's Populist Politics in France", *Comparative European Politics*, 16(6), pp. 1033–1050.
Ivaldi, G. and Gombin, J. (2015) "The Front National and the New Politics of the Rural in France". In: Strijker, D., Voerman, G. and Terluin, I. J. (eds.) *Rural Protest Groups and Populist Political Parties*. Wageningen: Wageningen Academic Publishers, pp. 243–264.
Ivaldi, G. and Lanzone, M. E. (2016) "From Jean-Marie to Marine Le Pen: Organizational Change and Adaptation in the French Front National". In: Heinisch, R. and Mazzoleni, O. (eds.) *Understanding Populist Party Organization: A Comparative Analysis*. Basingstoke: Palgrave Macmillan, pp. 131–158.
Ivaldi, G. and Pina, C. (2017) "PACA: 2017, entre permanence et bousculements des équilibres politiques", *Pôle Sud*, 47(2), pp. 179–198.
Kestilä, E. and Söderlund, P. (2007) "Subnational Political Opportunity Structures and the Success of the Radical Right: Evidence from the March 2004 Regional Elections in France", *European Journal of Political Research*, 46(6), pp. 773–796.
Knapp, A. and Wright, V. (2006) *The Government and Politics of France*. Abingdon: Routledge.
L'Express (2015) "Marion Maréchal-Le Pen part en guerre contre le planning familial", 27 November. www.lexpress.fr/actualite/politique/elections/marion-marechal-le-pen-part-en-guerre-contre-le-planning-familial_1740096.html. Accessed 15 January 2019.
L'Obs (2016) "5 choses à savoir sur David Rachline, directeur de campagne de Marine Le Pen", 17 September. www.nouvelobs.com/politique/election-presidentielle-2017/20160917.OBS8232/5-choses-a-savoir-sur-david-rachline-directeur-de-campagne-de-marine-le-pen.html. Accessed 15 January 2019.
Le Bras, H. (2015) *Le pari du FN*. Paris: Autrement.
Lubbers, M., Gijsberts, M. and Scheepers, P. (2002) "Extreme Right-Wing Voting in Western Europe", *European Journal of Political Research*, 41(3), pp. 345–378.
Lubbers, M. and Scheepers, P. (2002) "French Front National Voting: A Micro and Macro Perspective", *Ethnic and Racial Studies*, 25(1), pp. 120–149.
Mayer, N. (1998) "The Front National Vote in the Plural", *Patterns of Prejudice*, 32(1), pp. 3–24.
Mazerolle, O. (2015) "Marion Maréchal-Le Pen: 'Nous avons déjà gagné la bataille des idées'", *RTL*, 13 November. www.rtl.fr/actu/politique/marion-marechal-le-pen-nous-avons-deja-gagne-la-bataille-des-idees-7780487482. Accessed 15 January 2019.
Muis, J. and Immerzeel, T. (2017) "Causes and Consequences of the Rise of Populist Radical Right Parties and Movements in Europe", *Current Sociology Review*, 65(6), pp. 909–930.
Parisien, L. (2015) "Régionales: match à distance entre Marion Maréchal Le Pen et Christian Estrosi", 22 November. www.leparisien.fr/elections-regionales/regionales-match-a-distance-entre-marion-marechal-le-pen-et-christian-estrosi-22-11-2015-5301713.php. Accessed 15 January 2019.
Perrineau, P. (1995) "La dynamique du vote Le Pen: le poids du 'gaucho-lepénisme'". In: Perrineau, P. and Ysmal, C. (eds.) *Le vote de crise*. Paris: Presses de Sciences-Po, pp. 243–261.
Point, L. (2015) "Régionales: Marine Le Pen conclut la campagne FN en attaquant violemment Valls", 2 December. www.lepoint.fr/politique/marine-le-pen-accuse-valls-de-mener-la-guerre-totale-contre-le-fn-02-12-2015-1986736_20.php. Accessed 15 January 2019.

RMC (2015) "Marion Maréchal-Le Pen face à Apolline de Malherbe: les tweets de l'interview", 28 October. http://rmc.bfmtv.com/emission/marion-marechal-le-pen-face-a-apolline-de-malherbe-les-tweets-de-l-interview-925698.html. Accessed 15 January 2019.

Rydgren, J. (2005) "Is Extreme Right-Wing Populism Contagious? Explaining the Emergence of a New Party Family", *European Journal of Political Research*, 44(3), pp. 413–437.

Rydgren, J. (2008) "France: The Front National, Ethnonationalism and Populism". In: Albertazzi, D. and McDonnell, D. (eds.) *Twenty-First Century Populism*. New York: Palgrave Macmillan, pp. 166–180.

Sulzer, A. (2015) "Régionales 2015: en PACA, les clins d'oeil aux pieds-noirs", *L'Express*, 2 December. www.lexpress.fr/actualite/politique/elections/regionales-2015-en-paca-les-clins-d-oeil-aux-pieds-noirs_1741485.html. Accessed 15 January 2019.

Taggart, P. (2000) *Populism*. Buckingham: Open University Press.

Taguieff, P.-A. (1995) "Political Science Confronts Populism: From a Conceptual Mirage to a Real Problem", *Telos*, 1995(103), pp. 9–43.

Tavits, M. (2012) "Organizing for Success: Party Organizational Strength and Electoral Performance in Postcommunist Europe", *Journal of Politics*, 74(1), pp. 83–97.

Veugelers, J. (2012) "After Colonialism: Local Politics and Far-Right Affinities in a City of Southern France". In: Mammone, A., Godin, E. and Jenkins, B. (eds.) *Mapping the Extreme Right in Contemporary Europe: From Local to Transnational*. London: Routledge, pp. 33–47.

Vliegenthart, R., Boomgaarden, H. G. and Van Spanje, J. (2012) "Anti-Immigrant Party Support and Media Visibility: A Cross-Party, Over-Time Perspective", *Journal of Elections, Public Opinion and Parties*, 22(3), pp. 315–358.

Zaslove, A. (2008) "Exclusion, Community, and a Populist Political Economy: The Radical Right as an Anti-Globalization Movement", *Comparative European Politics*, 6(2), pp. 169–189.

9

PROGRESSIVE REGIONALIST POPULISM VS. CONSERVATIVE NATIONALIST POPULISM IN POLAND

The case of the Silesian Autonomy Movement – RAŚ

Magdalena Solska

Introduction

The national censuses conducted in Poland in 2002 and 2011 confirmed once again that Poland is one of the most ethnically homogenous countries in Europe, with 96 per cent of its citizens declaring themselves of Polish nationality in 2002 and 91 per cent in 2011.[1] To the astonishment of many observers, however, 173,200 citizens declared themselves to be of Silesian nationality in the census of 2002 (GUS 2002), rising to 809,000 in 2011 (GUS 2012).[2] Silesians thus turned out to be the largest minority in Poland, far outnumbering the country's two other main minorities, with 228,000 declaring themselves Kashubian and 109,000 declaring themselves members of the well-established German minority.

Significantly, however, the Silesians have not been recognized by the Polish state either as a national or an ethnic minority. Nor has the Silesian ethnolect, called Ślōnskŏ godka, been registered as a regional language, in spite of the fact that 529,400 respondents reported using this language at home. The Kashubian ethnolect, by contrast, with 108,000 users, has been accepted as the only regional language in Poland, while the Karaim community has been recognized as an ethnic minority despite only 45 declaring themselves Karaim.

Notwithstanding this lack of official recognition, Silesian regionalists have remained active and well organized. The Silesian Autonomy Movement (Ruch Autonomii Śląska, RAŚ) was founded in 1990, becoming the first and only ethno-regionalist party in Poland. Although RAŚ declares itself a non-partisan association, it has a collective membership and takes part in regional elections with the aim of obtaining power. From the outset the party has consistently promoted Silesia's regional and ethnic identity and the need for territorial autonomy to express and serve the ethnic and regional interests of Silesia.[3] In 2018,

RAŚ became the core of a new Silesian Regional Party (Śląska Partia Regionalna, ŚPR), bringing together other Silesian regionalist organizations, including members of the Union of Upper Silesians, the Silesians' Union, the Democratic Union of Silesian Regionalists and Ślōnskŏ Ferajna.[4] Since the launch of the Silesian Regional Party, RAŚ has pursued an adaptive strategy: while still acting only within the region, it now combines its traditional ethno-regionalist claims with positions on state-wide policy issues. On the one hand, therefore, the party continues to focus on issues related to the cultural and historical distinctiveness of the region, as well as working from within ŚPR to address various salient regional issues such as the finances of self-government and public transport. On the other hand, RAŚ has also begun to address problems relevant to the whole country, such as education and air pollution. By engaging with non-territorial matters, the party is seeking to extend its appeal beyond an ethno-territorial niche and to challenge other state-wide parties, especially since the latter clearly avoid debating the issue of state decentralization.

The activities of this ethno-regionalist force are fueled by the evident discrepancy between the Silesians' officially declared self-identification in terms of nationality and language and their lack of recognition by the state authorities. This divergence strengthens a sense of "harm done to Silesia" and the perception that Silesians are misunderstood and undervalued in cultural, economic, and political terms by a central state that has "colonized" the region. This perception has been further reinforced by hostile statements from the ruling Law and Justice party (Prawo i Sprawiedliwość, PiS), which has denounced the goals of RAŚ as "anti-Polish" and a "camouflaged German option" (PiS 2011: 34–36).

Poland's capacity to countenance regionalism and diversity has been hindered by a number of key factors, including the country's communist legacy, the unitary character of the post-communist state, and the cultivation of an ethnic and religious (Catholic) idea of national identity. In addition, there has been an overall political consensus on very limited decentralization, with the current PiS-led government even introducing some re-centralizing policies. Nonetheless, RAŚ has been consistently active for over 20 years now and has achieved a certain degree of political success and visibility. In 2010 the Silesian Autonomy Movement won three seats in the regional legislative assembly (Sejmik Województwa Śląskiego) and subsequently participated in the governing coalition together with two state-wide parties, Civic Platform (Platforma Obywatelska, PO) and the Polish People's Party (Polskie Stronnictwo Ludowe, PSL). In this regional executive (Zarząd Województwa Śląskiego) the RAŚ chairman Jerzy Gorzelik was responsible for the portfolios of culture and education. In 2014, RAŚ obtained four seats in the regional legislature. The electoral relevance of the party can thus be measured both by the mandates it has won in the regional legislature since 2010 and by the results of the 2011 census that are attributed to the party's intensive campaign. Finally, the active engagement of the party's core members has led to the establishment of the first Silesian Regional Party.

This chapter presents an analysis of the ways in which RAŚ has managed to construct its ethno-regionalist claims under the given circumstances and the mobilizing strategies it uses. The analysis focuses on the populist discourse adopted by RAŚ in response to a widespread political consensus on the futility of enhanced regional autonomy and the risks of separatism attached to regionalism (Kocyba and Riedel 2015: 271). This discourse is founded on the premise of opposition between the "regional people", constructed upon a revival of Silesian identity, and a hostile national political establishment. The case of RAŚ is relevant because it illustrates the emergence of a center-periphery cleavage within the Polish state. This phenomenon is in stark contrast with the international perspective adopted by many scholars who have applied the center-periphery analytical framework to Poland.[5] This study shows how the nascent center-periphery cleavage is also linked to a new cultural divide. The empirical research of this chapter is based on qualitative analysis of the programs and statutes of RAŚ and ŚPR, as well as statements of party leaders, national and local newspaper reports, and media interviews conducted with RAŚ members.

Ethno-regionalist demands and populist discourse

Regionalist parties can be regarded as "self-contained political organizations" that contest elections only in a particular territory of a state, since their main objective is to defend the interests and identities of "their" region (Massetti 2009: 503). Their mission is to achieve "some kind of territorial self-government" (De Winter 1998: 204), though the extent of self-government demanded can vary from cultural protectionism to outright separatism (De Winter 2001: 4). Within regionalist parties, ethno-regionalist formations can be differentiated by the characteristic claim that a party represents a distinctive ethnic group within a specific territory.

In their seminal work, Lipset and Rokkan (1967) argue that the emergence of ethno-regionalist groups is a function of the political and socio-economic development of nation states. Such groups are especially prone to appear when the center does not adjust state structures to the economic and cultural needs of the periphery (Müller-Rommel 1998: 21; see also Türsan 1998). However, the question remains as to how ethno-regionalist parties mobilize this potential within existing national political and institutional structures.

The concept of an ethno-regionalist party implies several elements that lend themselves to populist discourse. Firstly, demands for the re-organization of the power-structures of a national political system are usually associated with a critical assessment of political elites who have failed to solve the pressing problems of the region. Secondly, the demand for the recognition and empowerment of an ethno-regional collectivity implies there is a need to represent the interests of a specifically defined "regional people". This commitment to "the people" can be derived from the evocation of an idealized previous state or constructed "heartland" (Taggart 2000) to which the community is emotionally attached

(Heinisch, Holtz-Bacha and Mazzoleni 2017: 21) and which can be expressed as the historically conditioned distinctiveness of the region in which a given ethnic group is rooted. Finally, ethno-regionalist parties see themselves as "agents of change" in pursuing their goal of territorial autonomy and bringing about a new status for the community they address. In the case of RAŚ, because it has so far remained, a fringe party and is still the only ethno-regionalist political formation in Poland it is in a position to employ anti-establishment rhetoric not only against national but also regional political elites. The question then arises as to what extent this anti-establishment discourse bears populist traits in its references to the "heartland" and "the people".

Populism here refers to a discursive frame utilized to challenge the status quo, aimed at restoring power to the people and replacing the elites along with their ideas and values (Ghergina, Miscoiu, and Soare 2017: 194). Above all, populism constitutes "an appeal to a recognized authority" (Canovan 1999: 4), i.e. "the people", who are seen as the source of sovereignty. The ideational approach to populism denotes the construction of a dichotomy between an amorphous "people", typically depicted as virtuous and hardworking, and corrupted "elites" whose interests and ensuing actions pose a threat to the people (Heinisch, Holtz-Bacha, and Mazzoleni 2017: 21). In post-communist space, the "pureness" of the people is typically juxtaposed with the decadence of post-communist elites who have proved incapable of dealing with the inevitably complex problems of post-communist system transformation. Populist claims can be ambivalent and variable, however, and this malleability allows anti-establishment discourse to be applied at all levels of competition.

Given the complex strategy adopted by RAŚ, this chapter will address the following four questions. What does the party mean exactly in referring to "the people" it claims to represent? How does the party justify its demand for territorial autonomy? How does it depict the ruling elite whose dominance it intends to overcome at both regional and national levels? Where does the party position itself on the left-right spectrum in its challenge to state-wide parties?

The following section discusses the origins of the center-periphery cleavage in Upper Silesia before proceeding to a presentation of key administrative-territorial reforms in post-communist Poland. The core section of the chapter provides an analysis of the strategy of RAŚ and ŚPR followed by a summary and discussion of its findings in conclusion.

The historical roots of the center-periphery cleavage in Silesia

An understanding of a region's historical, ethno-cultural and economic characteristics should help to indicate the kinds of social grievances that might be expected to emerge within that region – grievances which ethno-regionalist parties may seek to harness in their demands for regional self-government (see Massetti 2009: 505). Silesia may be understood as a border-region where many state, national, and cultural boundaries intersect, with influences from the present-day

Czech Republic, Germany, Austria and Poland. Historically, Silesia briefly belonged to medieval Poland until the mid-14th century, when it became part of the lands of the Czech Crown within the frontiers of the Holy Roman Empire. In the 1740s, Prussia conquered almost the whole region from the Habsburgs, leaving only a portion of Upper Silesia within Austrian lands, later known as Austrian Silesia (Kamusella 2012: 48; Baranyai 2013).

Today the historical region of Silesia is absorbed within the present-day borders of the Czech Republic, Germany and Poland. Within Poland the historical region constitutes the south-west corner of the country extending north to the Czech-Polish border and eastwards to the industrial city of Katowice. Since 1998, Polish Silesia has been divided into three administrative units (voivodeships): Lower Silesia, Opole, and Silesia. The historical capital of Silesia is Wrocław, now the capital of the Lower Silesian voivodeship, populated mainly by post-war settlers from the Eastern Borderlands (Kresy) and central Poland.

Although the Silesians have inhabited German-speaking countries, they have maintained their Slavic cultural and linguistic roots as well as their Catholic faith (Buchowski and Chlewińska 2012: 11). Historically, Silesia was trilingual and dominated by the Catholic religion. German was used in public spaces such as schools, offices, and business, while Polish was the language of religion. In everyday situations and casual communication, Silesians used their own ethnolect, i.e. Slavic imbued with numerous German, Old Polish, and Czech words and structural influences from German grammar (Myśliwiec 2013b).

Whereas Lower Silesia was a part of Germany in the interwar period, the future of Upper Silesia was to be decided by plebiscite as provided in the Treaty of Versailles in 1919. That plebiscite took place on 20 March 1921 after the First (1919) and Second Silesian Uprisings (1920).[6] Every person born in Silesia was eligible to vote. While Germany offered the region broad legal and political rights, the Polish Parliament introduced the Constitutional Law of Organic Statute for the Silesian Voivodeship before the plebiscite, on 15 July 1920, to encourage the local population to vote in favor of a newly independent Poland. In the end, however, over 59 per cent voted in favor of Germany (Myśliwiec 2013a), which clearly reflected divided identities within the region. Fearing the prospect of having to introduce German law in the Silesian territory, however, the local Polish-speaking elite initiated the Third Silesian Uprising in May 1921. Finally, the region was divided between Poland and Germany, with Poland receiving the smaller (21 per cent) but more industrialized part of this disputed territory (Myśliwiec 2013a). The above-mentioned Constitutional Law of 1920 prescribed the establishment of a regional Parliament, called the Silesian Sejm, endowed with great legislative capacity, as well as a regional treasury towards which Silesians had to pay a part of their generated incomes to the state.

In May 1945 the Communist State's National Council finally revoked the Constitutional Law of the Organic Statute for the Silesian Voivodeship. The state's rapid centralization – in accordance with the main premises of a totalitarian regime – did not allow the idea of autonomy to develop any further. Polish Silesia was divided into several smaller voivodeships that became equal administrative units like all other parts of the Polish state (see Yoder 2003: 270). The whole administrative structure belonged to the central state. This so-called "democratic centralism" helped communists to control every area of social and political life, effectively suppressing local political and social activity (Myśliwiec 2013a). From an ethno-demographic perspective, it is important to note that most of Western Poland (regained from Germany after WWII), including the region of Lower Silesia, underwent a form of population exchange at the start of communist rule in Poland, whereby the native German population was expelled and Poles were settled in their place, with the latter coming mostly from the interwar Polish Eastern territories (Buchowski and Chlewińska 2012: 12). In contrast, Upper Silesia, and particularly the highly industrial and heavily populated Katowice agglomeration, has maintained a considerable proportion of the descendants of interwar inhabitants, including quite a large German minority and a smaller Czech minority (Kamusella 2012: 48). It is precisely in Upper Silesia (the western parts of the present-day voivodeships of Opole and Silesia) that RAŚ is most active and well-known.

Only after the fall of communism in 1989 was it possible for national, ethnic and territorial identities to be freely expressed and developed. EU accession in 2004 provided a further major stimulus for this process. RAŚ has since politicized the history of Upper Silesia and its people in order to advance its demand for official recognition of the Silesians as an ethnic minority and recognition of the Silesian ethnolect as a regional language. The party's quest for the territorial autonomy of the region of Upper Silesia, reviving the autonomy which the province enjoyed in the interwar period, is a natural corollary of these objectives, since self-government would help maintain Silesian identity and culture.

The Act on National and Ethnic Minorities and on the Regional Languages passed by the Polish government in January 2005 formally defined an "ethnic minority" according to the following criteria: as a group of Polish citizens less numerous than the rest of the state's inhabitants, significantly differing from other citizens in language, culture, or tradition, with an awareness of and a will to preserve its own historical national community, and with ancestors who have inhabited Polish territory for at least 100 years (Article 2).[7] While scholars agree that Silesians fulfill the criteria of an ethnic minority according to the above definition, however, Silesians have still not been recognized as such by the Polish state. It is notable, therefore, that the state authorities included the option of declaring "Silesian nationality"[8] and language in the censuses of 2002 and 2011 without having officially recognized this minority or language.

Territorial structure and territorial reform in Poland

Following a general trend (Sorens 2009), territorial reforms in Poland were heavily affected by party-political strategic interests. Electoral competition, ideological divides and territorial voting patterns all played a role in influencing the design of these reforms (Brusis 2013). In 1998 the right-wing government, composed of the Solidarity Electoral Action coalition (Akcja Wyborcza Solidarność, AWS) and the Freedom Union (Unia Wolności, UW) introduced three levels of state administration: municipalities (2,424), districts (powiaty) (308) and voivodeships (województwa) (16). This reform was framed as a step towards decommunization. Introducing district and voivodeship self-government was viewed as a strategy to "overcome the institutional and cultural legacies of centralisation and etatist thinking" (Brusis 2013: 413). The new law allocated certain powers and financial resources to the newly created self-governments. As the representative of central government in a voivodeship, the voivode (wojewoda) supervises the legality of self-government actions and controls the regionally integrated parts of the state administration (see Brusis 2013: 411). A limited level of local self-government has finally become institutionalized through directly elected councils at district and voivodeship level.

RAŚ argues that this model does not take account of the specific social and economic needs of different regions in Poland. Public finances have not been decentralized, and powers and responsibilities have not been clearly divided between state and regional administrations. Legislative competences remain in Warsaw. The national Parliament still issues laws that apply to the regions. Moreover, the regional self-government is still dominated by state-wide parties (see Czaja 2015).

In the last two decades, Polish political elites have shown a strong reluctance to countenance further decentralization. In particular, the dominant national-conservative party, Law and Justice (PiS), is committed to a centralized nation-state, portraying Polish independence as vulnerable, threatened in various ways by external powers (primarily Russia, but also the EU and Germany) and internal enemies such as former communists. The decentralized management of development policies is opposed, for instance, on the basis that it would weaken the state's authority and expose the nation state to corruption (Brusis 2013: 419; see also Zarycki 2000).

Despite this opposition to decentralization, it was under the PiS government that the first "Metropolis" was introduced in Silesia in 2017: the Metropolitan Association of Upper Silesia and Dąbrowa Basin, a group of municipalities composed of 14 neighboring cities. The purpose of forming this metropolitan union was to achieve greater efficiency in the management and development of infrastructure and to support the international competitiveness of this highly urbanized and industrially developed area. According to RAŚ, however, this solution has serious deficiencies and cannot substitute for a profound state reform – i.e. territorial autonomy – in each region. Gorzelik points out that the Polish state has still not assigned any legislative capacity to the Metropolis, nor shared with the regions its largest source of revenue, which is derived from VAT. Gorzelik also points out the lack of necessary cooperation between the Metropolis and the voivodeship, especially with regard to the modernization of public transport (Kacprzak 2018). The historically constituted status of Silesians as an ethnic minority remains unrecognized together with the party's unfulfilled quest for territorial autonomy, which has paved the way for the remarkable recent success of RAŚ.

The Silesian Autonomy Movement – from an assertive to a moderate autonomist party

RAŚ – the Silesian Autonomy Movement – was founded in 1990 in Rybnik. The movement's initial program envisaged bringing about an end to the "colonial treatment of Silesia" and establishing a stronger regional community with territorial autonomy. The organization was officially registered in 2001 and its activities have intensified since the election of Jerzy Gorzelik as leader. Over the last 15 years RAŚ has changed its image from that of an assertive autonomist party with separatist undertones to one of a moderate autonomist force (see Massetti 2009: 505). RAŚ used to issue controversial and provocative statements, such as: "Giving Silesia to Poland was like giving a monkey a watch. After 80 years it is clear that the monkey has ruined the watch (...)" (see Narbutt 2008). In an interview held on 29 November 2010 with the radio program Sygnały Dnia, Gorzelik declared: "I am a Silesian and not a Pole. I have never promised anything to Poland, so I have never betrayed it, nor do I feel obliged to loyalty towards this state".[9] Many critics denounced the party's accusation of "Warsaw colonialism" as demagogic "folklore". Today it is RAŚ that accuses the ruling party PiS of having an anti-Silesian attitude, as well as of inventing an internal foe (the "fifth German column") and of spreading fear of Silesian separatism.

RAŚ used to emphasize that its long-term objective was the establishment of a federal state. Today, however, it stresses the need for the existing Constitution to be applied more fairly, granting Silesia the official status of an ethnic minority with a regional language as well as an enhanced level of regional self-government. Besides referring back to the interwar model of autonomy, RAŚ is also highly attentive of the solutions implemented in Western European countries, especially in Spain. As noted on the party's website: "Inspired by Western European regionalism, we propose to introduce strong, autonomist, financially independent voivodeships, which would be deciding about their own affairs".[10] The movement aims at obtaining territorial autonomy as part of the country's process of "mature decentralization". In accordance with the principle of asymmetric decentralization, Poland should be a state comprised of autonomous regions with a degree of autonomy determined by the needs and capabilities of the individual regions. Furthermore, it is now clearly emphasized that "the activities of the movement on behalf of Silesian autonomy are not directed at changing state borders" (RAŚ 2011a, Article 5). The short-term goals of the organization are stated as follows:

- Fostering Silesian identity among the inhabitants of Silesia and other regions in Poland;
- Developing an active civic attitude among the Silesian population;
- Contributing to the integration of all inhabitants of Silesia, regardless of ethnicity;
- Promoting human and civil rights;

- Maintaining cultural and economic links with the Silesian diaspora and supporting their emotional attachment to the homeland;
- Promoting Silesian language and language diversity;
- Taking actions to protect the natural environment as well as the region's material and spiritual legacy;
- Serving European integration and maintaining contacts with other societies;
- Creating and promoting a positive image of Silesia.

In its key document, the Organic Statute of the Autonomous Silesian Voivodship, RAŚ describes the possible system of government of the future Autonomous Silesian Voivodeship. This system, the Statute proposes, should be based on a Silesian Parliament and Silesian Government, a Silesian Administrative Court, a Silesian Ombudsman, a Silesian Council for Mass Communication, and an independent Silesian Treasury, as had been instituted in the interwar period (RAŚ 2011c, Article 5; see Myśliwiec 2013a). The autonomous Silesian authorities will be able to formulate and collect taxes within their jurisdiction and send an agreed amount to the state. The Silesian Parliament will be given the power to adopt regional laws and thus take responsibility for its decisions. The Silesian Government should be under a President of Ministers and Ministers elected by an absolute majority of the Silesian Parliament. The Organic Statute does not, however, define the borders of the region, noting instead that "The Silesian Autonomous Voivodeship is to be created by districts connected with the region historically, culturally and economically" (RAŚ 2011c, Article 3).

In parallel with these proposals, RAŚ has also prepared a draft amendment to the existing Constitution. Countering frequent accusations of being separatist, this draft declares that "the basis of the Constitution is the indissoluble unity of the Republic of Poland (...) and it recognizes and guarantees the regions the right to autonomy and solidarity" (RAŚ 2011b, Article 3). The draft sets out the constitutional status of the districts and autonomous voivodeships. The party's proposed amendment would also grant regions much greater influence at central level. Members of the Senate would be delegated by autonomous governments in each autonomous voivodeship. What is more, the state government would be obliged to present all its legislative initiatives first to the Senate, the upper house, and only thereafter to the Sejm, the lower house of Parliament (RAŚ 2011b, Articles 100 and 117).

To realize its goals, RAŚ actively promotes Silesian culture and its own vision of the state structure it supports. For 20 years now it has published a monthly magazine, *Silesian Swallow* (*Jaskółka Śląska*), and regularly conducts activities and projects. These have included the publication of an Inventory of the Lost and Stolen Cultural Goods of Upper Silesia, the organization of Upper Silesian Days of Heritage, the digitalization of the Upper Silesian press, and an annual Mass in commemoration of deported Upper Silesians. Most crucial and conspicuous are the party's yearly commemorations of historical events not celebrated at national level. The March to Zgoda (Zgoda being a former labor camp set up by the

Soviet NKVD), for example, is devoted to the victims of Soviet repressions. "Its members follow the same distance as hundreds of Silesians did in January 1945, forced by the Soviet army ... " (Jaskółka Śląska 2009). The most prominent annual event is the Autonomy March, which, according to the event's website: "is the biggest manifestation of civil responsibility of its inhabitants for their own region. Each year it brings together hundreds of people, for whom Western European-style regional autonomy remains the best model of state decentralization".[11] RAŚ also organizes regular meetings with writers, journalists and politicians under the title "Let's talk about Silesia", devoted to the current problems of the region. A key asset for the party has been the high profile of its outspoken leader, Jerzy Gorzelik, even though different members also represent RAŚ and ŚPR at different events. Another crucial moment for the party was its accession to the European Free Alliance (EFA) of autonomist and separatist parties. RAŚ and ŚPR propagate the idea of a "Europe of regions". In March 2017, during an EFA congress in Katowice, Gorzelik stated that RAŚ did not support the radical ideological and economic ideas of, for instance, the Greens (the traditional ally of EFA in the European Parliament), nor did it share the economic ideas of other parties in the EFA. The common denominator of the Alliance is a quest for self-determination, understood in different ways according to local circumstances (Zasada 2017). Accordingly, the congress should focus above all on demonstrating that autonomy is not a dangerous solution but one that has been widely accepted and applied in Western countries.

RAŚ and ŚPR are very active in social networks and on local media. They prepare questionnaires and invite interested citizens to vote for or against certain decisions to be taken by the central state. They organize regular meetings with inhabitants to discuss the future program of the emerging Silesian Regional Party. Both direct and indirect means of communication between the party and the electorate have been skillfully used. ŚPR sees itself as a platform for promoting and facilitating civic engagement in the region, in line with its insistence that a region can become a "principle for the organization of civil society" (Keating 2003: 268).

The party's regular and consistent activities have undoubtedly contributed to raising its visibility and electoral success. Although the party usually competes only at local and regional level, in 1991 two members of the organization became deputies in the Polish Sejm – an exception due to the lack of a 5 per cent threshold at that time. Until 2010 the party managed to elect several candidates in two municipalities and it had some representatives in the city council in the town of Czerwionka-Leszczyny. It also co-governed in the Rybnik district (Zweiffel 2013: 191). The party has developed organizationally and today has around 7,000 members active in 27 units in the Silesian and Opole voivodeships (see Czaja 2015: 8). In 2010 it finally managed to win three seats in the legislative assembly of the voivodeship, increasing this number to four in 2014. Analyzing the party's electoral results at regional level, it is evident that the popularity of RAŚ is greatest in those counties that once belonged to the historic region of Upper Silesia and amongst those who declared themselves of Silesian nationality in the national censuses. In these areas the party regularly gains 10–15 per cent of the votes and appears as the third force after the most established Polish parties, Civic Platform (PO) and PiS (see Czaja 2015: 8). Within the whole Silesian voivodeship the party is placed in fourth position, after SLD in 2010, and after PSL, the oldest Polish party, in 2014 (see Table 9.1). It should further be noted that two other electoral lists were established in 2014 that managed to win some votes from RAŚ: the list for the Independent Self-Government of the Silesian Voivodeship and the list of the Minorities in Silesia (see Table 9.1). Both lists targeted similar voters while negatively assessing the activities of Poland's state-wide political parties.

At local municipality level the party is successful only in the bigger cities that historically belonged to Upper Silesia, including Katowice, Chorzów, Mysłowice and Ruda Śląska, where its support amounts to 7–11 per cent. This is due to the still weak organization of RAŚ at local level and its inability to bring forth leaders able to compete with other party candidates in elections for city presidencies (city mayors).

Additionally, RAŚ must compete with successful non-party lists, especially at local level, which are usually founded around very popular former or incumbent city presidents, rendering them typical leader-centered organizations. It is precisely these two factors, i.e. the well-entrenched position of local lists based on

TABLE 9.1 The electoral results of the regional elections to the regional legislative assembly (Sejmik) in Silesian voivodeship in 2010 and 2014

Electoral lists	Regional elections			
	2010		2014	
	Votes (%)	Seats	Votes (%)	Seats
Civic Platform RP (PO)	33.66	22	27.21	17
Law and Justice (PiS)	20.76	11	25.07	16
Democratic Left Alliance "Left Together" (SLD)	16.42	10	10.39	3
Silesian Autonomy Movement (RAŚ)	8.49	3	7.20	4
Polish People's Party (PSL)	7.11	2	13.21	5
Other lists	13.56	–	16.92	–
among others:				
Independent Self-Government of the Silesian Voivodeship	–	–	4.64	–
Minorities in Silesia	–	–	0.75	–

Source: Author's elaboration. Data comes from the State Electoral Commission (PKW). See also Czaja (2015: 5–12).

the popularity of recognizable leaders and the persisting popularity of the two state-wide parties PiS and PO that have so far hindered the party from developing more rapidly at local level.

Another aspect meriting attention in considering the electoral fortunes of RAŚ are the institutional incentives in the voting system that influence the political unity of regionalist movements (see Massetti 2009). At the level of municipalities (with up to 20,000 inhabitants) a first-past-the-post voting system is in place that favors the election of well-known candidates. In larger municipalities, districts and voivodeships, a proportional system (PR) is used that applies the d'Hondt method of allocating seats. The mandatory 5 per cent threshold of this system has also proved a challenge for RAŚ, however, together with the fact that state funding is assigned only to parties crossing a 3 per cent threshold in national elections, or to national minority parties. The party's success has thus been based primarily on programmatic and institutional development accompanied by a specific discourse.

Regionalism, populist discourse and the left-right dimension

The meaning and content of territorial autonomy for Silesia – conceived as the idealized heartland – has changed over time. The first reference point of autonomy used to be the model of the interwar period, hailed as a "revelation of the modern thinking of Polish elites in the Second Republic" (Gorzelik 2017). According to its program from 2006 (available on the website of the Opole unit: http://rasopole.org/), RAŚ intended to revive the historical borders of the two autonomous regions of Lower Silesia and Upper Silesia. The former referred to the earlier Provinz Niederschlesien and the latter to the previous Provinz Oberschlesien (before the plebiscite) and Austrian Silesia. Today, however, it refers rather to the current Silesian voivodeship, which covers only a part of historical Upper Silesia (as stated on the RAŚ official website: http://autonomia.pl/). The borders of this autonomous region are to be decided by the inhabitants themselves and the next administrative reform should include their stated preferences.

The quest for territorial autonomy is now understood and framed, moreover, as adopting a central tenet of Western democracy and European standards: "In the Western world, the autonomous regions and minority rights constitute normality. Both values are commonly respected. In Poland this postulate is presented as radical, not European (…) I believe Poland will follow countries that trust their citizens" (Gorzelik 2017). As for separation and independence, RAŚ indicates on its website[12] that autonomy is a more convenient solution for Silesia, offering the following explanation: "despite hard-working and entrepreneurial Upper Silesians, an independent five-million state would have a weaker position than a strong autonomous region within Poland. It would allow faster and efficient development". Deep decentralization is thus regarded as a way of exercising public authority. The RAŚ program for a Poland of Regions offers this solution not only for (Upper) Silesia but also for the rest of the country. Territorial autonomy is no longer presented as a privilege but as a proposal that would be good for the whole country. As further noted on the party's website:

> Autonomy will allow for deciding about our own matters: about the future of coalmines and the education of Silesian children, including the history of Silesia and not only of Poland. Decisions will be taken near us, which will enable better accountability of politicians. We will maintain our identity, because Silesian culture is not the same as Polish. It is vital for the new inhabitants to get to know these traditions. Autonomy will strengthen the prestige of Silesia. The region of Upper Silesia with five-million people deserves at least as much attention as the metropolis of Warsaw with two-million.[13]

While referring to the Silesia voivodeship as a future autonomous region within its current borders, the party also needs to take into account the fact that not all inhabitants are familiar with or affiliated with Silesian culture and traditions. This is why it has also adopted a more inclusive understanding of "regional people". RAŚ now emphasizes the diverse character of the borderland region of Silesia, with multiple languages, nationalities and traditions, and declares itself open for everyone who wants to live and work in the region, in this way seeking to combine ethnic (primarily ethno-linguistic) and civic nationalism. Silesians, in this view of RAŚ, include not only those with roots in the region who are ethnically defined as Silesian but also all persons who feel Silesian. An Upper Silesian can be a Pole, a German, or just a Silesian. Gorzelik himself has admitted that, in his view:

> Silesians have a different type of historical sensitivity. They look at their history from a bottom-up perspective. It is a history of individuals, without labelling nations, victims or perpetrators. We cannot accept the Polish version in which the color of a uniform decides whether you are on the good side or the bad side.
>
> *(Kazibut-Twórz 2010)*[14]

Given the anti-decentralization stance that characterizes all Polish state-wide parties, albeit to different degrees, the party's idea of pursuing modernization by deepening decentralization is construed in terms of an anti-establishment discourse, as per Gorzelik's statement of 2017: "We are moving against the mainstream but in accordance with the law" (Gorzelik 2017). Although RAŚ has become more moderate over time, it remains consistent in its demand for deeper self-government/territorial autonomy. The party's effort to organize and establish the Silesian Regional Party is precisely the means it has chosen to pursue this goal and distinguish itself from the state-wide mainstream parties. The predominant message generated by RAŚ is that the elites in Warsaw are indifferent to and disrespectful of the cultural, historical, and ethnic specificity of Upper Silesia, as well as being merely incompetent. As the RAŚ website declares:

> Politicians remind themselves of Silesia only during electoral campaigns or when tragedies happen in the region. In the run-up to every election we hear "we care about Silesia". The reality is different: members of the government and deputies, even if they come from Silesia, do not do much for the region.[15]

Decentralization is presented as necessary, moreover, in order to avert the usurpation of power and capture of the state by "party oligarchies".[16] From the perspective of RAŚ, the governing PiS party is pushing Poland towards the East and in many respects is perpetuating communist policies. Gorzelik points to the "totalitarian language" of the ruling party, including the phrases "total victory", "new society", "new nation" and "new political order". During an open meeting with the inhabitants of Chorzów on 16 November 2017, the RAŚ chairman claimed that PiS would lead Poland out of the EU, presumably once the current EU budget comes to an end after 2020. This prediction was made on the basis of the controversial illiberal policies introduced by the PiS government, including strengthening the executive, controlling the state media and weakening the power of judiciary and Constitutional Tribunal.[17] These legislative changes will at some point lead to questions as to Poland's future political order (Zasada 2017).

In the eyes of RAŚ, however, PiS is not the only ruling party that violates the Constitution. In fact, all previous governments have done so, for instance by assigning more competencies to the regions without granting them more funds.[18] This behavior, Gorzelik noted during the meeting, was the result of the still immature political culture of Polish political elites. RAŚ and now ŚPR are the alternative to this law-breaking government: "If we want to be an integral part of the Western world, we need to strengthen the rule of law" – an aim to be achieved through territorial autonomy.

A number of populist elements have so far been identified in RAŚ discourse. The party claims, for example, that elites merely pretend to govern for the people but only rule for themselves. RAŚ emphasizes the capacity of Silesia's inhabitants to take much more reasonable decisions favoring their region than those taken by the Polish elites. The "civic values and engagement" of Silesians are held up in contrast with the hypocrisy of the elites. A utopian element can also be detected, with the "populist heartland" epitomized by references to the Organic Statute of the interwar period, modified by the RAŚ Organic Statute.

However, other elements of typical populist discourse are clearly missing. RAŚ does not appeal to the morality or pureness of the "people". It does not perceive itself as the only "authentic representative of the will of the people" but recognizes other ethno-regionalist organizations such as those representing the German minority. Despite its harsh criticism of the establishment and its placing them in the "communist past", no other "simplifying means" are applied to the complicated Silesian reality. (The example of the possibility of "Polexit" is rather related to the fact that in 2016 the EU indeed initiated a "rule of law probe" into the country.) Although RAŚ regards territorial autonomy as a remedy for regional problems and state capture by elites, it also points to the very complex issue of historical truth in Poland and the diversity of questions facing the region.

The party's construction of a "heartland" and a "regional people", together with its employment of severe anti-establishment rhetoric, have been the means by which RAŚ has promoted a distinct ethnic and regional identity and historical narrative as the basis for its demand for territorial autonomy. This has constituted the core of the party's activity. The movement has not produced any clear political program that would address economic, health, social policy or other issues. RAŚ does not identify with any state-wide party on the left or the right. As stated on the website of the RAŚ Opole unit: "Our regionalist character better expresses the identity of RAŚ than the left-right scheme. However, our attachment to traditional values, individual and economic freedom, and rejection of ubiquitous bureaucratic structures place RAŚ among the 'groups of freedom'".[19] ŚPR, however, has developed more concrete responses to the pressing problems of the region.

Moving the party beyond a narrow focus on the center-periphery axis has entailed seeking ways to escape its previous niche position by challenging state-wide parties on traditional left-right issues. The newly created Silesian Regional Party intends to address such hitherto unaddressed problems while bringing together other regionalist organizations. On its official website, the party stresses the following:

> We create the program for Silesia and want to decide about the future of this region because we know its weaknesses and strengths. We are from here; we do not act upon instructions from Warsaw. We want to decide together. This is why every voice is so important. Everyone is welcome.[20]

The ŚPR program rests on the four premises of self-government, dialogue, innovation and identity, thus combining the postulates of RAŚ with a number of targeted policies. ŚPR seeks to realize its aims in accordance with the existing Constitution, although territorial autonomy remains one of its long-term goals. Given the currently low level of state decentralization in Poland, some of the steps postulated by ŚPR, such as its demand for profound reform of education, are necessarily of a state-wide character. According to ŚPR, the creation of an innovative economy, the key to overcoming the semi-peripheral status of Poland, is possible only on the basis of modern education. The latter should constitute a policy priority for the government, and spending on education should rise to 6 per cent of GDP.

(ŚPR 2018).

With its 12.4 per cent contribution to Poland's GDP, the Silesian voivodeship is the second richest region in the country and the second biggest contributor to the state's revenue (after the Mazowieckie voivodeship, which includes Warsaw) and is regarded as an attractive place for investments. It is also the second most populated region in the country (Tygodnik Powszechny 2017). The concentration of industry in this one region (including coal mining, iron and steel, transport, energy and chemicals) gives Silesia great economic potential and lends it some distinctive regional characteristics. However, rising emigration and high levels of air pollution remain crucial challenges. To ensure a real improvement in quality of life, ŚPR argues, any reform agenda must go beyond the state's hitherto applied understanding of the region as the "state's store for raw material resources" (Portal Samorządowy 2017).

The Polish government's Program for Silesia (Czoik 2017) has been treated by the Silesian Regional Party as an opportunity to enter into discussions over the future of the Silesian voivodeship. As noted by ŚPR, the scale of the region's problems is reflected in the 2016 EU Regional Social Progress Index, according to which the Voivodeship of Silesia ranks 250th in terms of quality of life out of 272 regions in Europe. The government's plan to construct two more coalmines has been subject to especially vehement criticism from ŚPR (Portal Samorządowy 2017):

> The Minister of Energy, who accused the Silesian self-government of blocking the development of coalmines, has demonstrated that the government perceives our region as the state's raw material resource, an "internal colony" predestined to be completely exploited (...) We have been experiencing the costs of such policies for a long time, while revenues have been transferred to the center. The predatory economic policies conducted by the central government in Upper Silesia, which has clearly been sacrificed for the modernization of other regions, have left lasting wounds.

It is on the basis of these claims that ŚPR declares, in the same statement, that it is ready to overtake responsibility and develop better policies for the region.

The ŚPR further emphasizes that the pressing problems of the region are not adequately tackled in the government's program and that the proposed expenditures do not address the real needs of the region. For example, while the government proposes a program entitled "Flat +", promising to build new flats in the suburbs of Silesian cities, the party objects that the exploitation of heavy industry in Silesia has left a legacy of degraded inner-cities and quarters that could be renovated and made habitable. It is precisely this devastated infrastructure, as well as a lack of attractive public spaces, that has led to the increasing depopulation of the region. Furthermore, reviving the economies of areas affected by Poland's post-communist transformation will not be possible without significant financial incentives for entities willing to invest in brownfield land (i.e. degraded post-industrial terrains). Without such innovative policies and mechanisms, ŚPR maintains, many municipalities will stagnate. A major additional issue is that the cities of Silesia are notorious for having the worst air quality in the EU. ŚPR stresses that connecting thousands of households to the heating network is an urgent need but one that cannot be financed by the self-government. What can be done, according to ŚPR, is to bring about a "decolonization of the regions" (an expression used by Jerzy Gorzelik at the inauguration of ŚPR). Self-governments – as the main pillars of modernization – should therefore participate in the revenues derived from VAT. Specifically, the party suggests a percentage from VAT should go to every level of self-government, allocated in proportion to the number of inhabitants (ŚPR 2018).

Discussion

The ethno-regionalist claims advanced by RAŚ and ŚPR are centered around a demand for territorial autonomy that is presented not only as a solution for at least some of the problems of the Silesian region but also as a remedy for the weaknesses of Polish democracy. Territorial autonomy is no longer regarded as a privilege but as a "normal state" and an ordinary form of self-government in Western Europe. Autonomy is presented as a means of ensuring "development", since it would enable investment in the strong and essential sectors of the region rather than in those sectors determined by the central government. Autonomy would secure better management of the region, it is argued, as well as greater transparency in expenditure. The construction of an ideal "heartland" enables RAŚ and ŚPR to adopt an inclusive conception of "the people" that encompasses all targeted voters. Accordingly, "ideological pluralism" is also a noticeable feature of the party. Given that various interest groups exist among the community it seeks to represent, and given that the very aim of ŚPR is to bring together members of different organizations, RAŚ and ŚPR are compelled to refrain from defining their ideological leaning. Their program is rather a result of consensus, and the overall well-being of the community is presented as more important than particular interests. This approach can be termed a form of "civic regionalism".

However, several general distinctions can still be made. On the value axis, RAŚ and ŚPR have adopted a more pro-European and cosmopolitan approach, although this does not involve abandoning their promotion of the traditional values of the region. In terms of the economic proposals of ŚPR, the type of discourse it uses could be interpreted as a form of "bourgeois regionalism discourse" (see Massetti and Schakel 2015: 867) based on grievances about exploitative state policies that transfer resources from a wealthy region to poorer regions. In this sense, RAŚ and ŚPR can be positioned on the left of the value axis but on the right in terms of their economic program, especially in the case of ŚPR. Both of these positions contrast clearly with the political program of the ruling PiS. On these issues RAŚ and ŚPR are closer to the Civic Platform party, with which RAŚ was in coalition, since this state-wide party declares itself pro-European and center-right.

The case of RAŚ and ŚPR seems to confirm the following tendencies observed in Western democracies (Massetti and Schakel 2015: 867–868):

- Regionalist parties in relatively well-off regions are more attracted to right-wing neoliberal discourses that highlight long-term grievances about the exploitation of their resources for the benefit of poorer regions;
- Such rightist positions are typically linked to moderate autonomist claims;
- Regionalist parties tend to adopt positions on the left-right axis (the secondary dimension) similar to those of the dominant state-wide party in the region, in this case the Civic Platform (PO) party, although PiS has also recently become more popular on account of its social program.

It must be noted that RAŚ and ŚPR strive to distance themselves from all "Warsaw parties" in their endeavor to identify and represent the key priorities and problems of "their" voivodeship. Indeed, RAŚ sees a "window of opportunity" for its autonomist agenda in the centralizing policies of the PiS-led government, since the more such divisive policies and rhetoric are pursued, the more the idea of territorial autonomy may become attractive. At some point, political parties such as RAŚ, especially now as part of ŚPR with a different vision of the state (and facing a currently helpless opposition), may become a feasible alternative.

The liberal values promoted by RAŚ and ŚPR, including multiculturalism and support for the idea of a "Europe of regions", stem from the particular history of the region and are quite new on the Polish political scene, since the post-communist "liberal consensus"[21] of the elites was very much restricted to economic policy. The strategy of RAŚ and ŚPR in promoting a more liberal, Europeanized, and secularized vision of politics, based above all on civic engagement, is clearly in conflict with the currently enforced state politics of national sovereignty, supported by a social policy of redistribution and the privileged position of the Catholic Church. It is too early to tell, however, whether the new center-periphery cleavage will subsume the left-right dimension.

Conclusion

The persistent initiatives that have contributed to the electoral success of RAŚ have been concerned first and foremost with demands for the recognition of the Silesian ethnic minority and regional language, together with many other activities aimed at protecting and promoting Silesian ethnic and regional identity. As long as these issues remain unresolved, the new center-periphery cleavage will persist;[22] and because the state authorities are unwilling to respond to these demands, the party's discourse will inevitably employ populist anti-establishment features in denouncing current and previous ruling elites. These populist tones are moderated and subdued, however, by "civic regionalism". Neither RAŚ nor ŚPR can be characterized as "anti-pluralist" or "illiberal" (see Müller 2016), since they encourage wider political engagement and greater civic responsibility. As Jerzy Gorzelik stated in a radio program (Rozmowa Dnia) on 11 January 2018, Silesianness is a "community of memory" and a "political program"; only by engaging in politics can this community and its cultural traditions be protected and its development ensured. In this sense the country's political elite only serves to strengthen the center-periphery cleavage in Silesia in its unwillingness to countenance the regionalist demands of RAŚ.

At the same time there has been an evolution in the meaning of "territorial autonomy" that also affects the party's construction of the "people" and the features of its anti-establishment discourse, which now includes a "democracy dimension". Through ŚPR, RAŚ now addresses not only salient regional problems but also issues relevant to the whole country. The party's strong anti-establishment discourse and its criticism of incompetent and undemocratic elites may encourage more engagement on the part of other regions. The economic proposals of the party remain eclectic, affording only a very general conclusion as to the position of the party on the left-right dimension. The territorial dimension remains the issue that RAŚ and ŚPR strive to make most salient in inter-party competition.

The case of RAŚ and the emergence of the first regional party in post-communist Poland is relevant, as it relates to present European developments and values. The EU membership inevitably weakens nation states and activates ethno-regionalist movements. In case of Poland, this leads to a tension between the Polish core nation and the centralizing state politics on the one hand, and the actually changing Polish society on the other. To date, Poland has viewed the EU more through the prism of economic advantages than in terms of European values. This is why the development of RAŚ and ŚPR merits particular academic attention, especially against the background of Poland's current conflict with the EU over the rule of law in the country and the rising question of a more suitable system of government.

Notes

1 In the interwar period, the ethnic and national minorities constituted one third of the population. The current homogeneity is predominantly the result of the Second World War and the Holocaust. See Hermanowski and Kosmala (2001).
2 The possibility of declaring two nationalities was introduced for the first time in the 2011 census. Among 809,000 declared Silesians 362,000 declared Silesian nationality as their only one and 415,000 added another nationality, in most cases the Polish one (GUS 2012).
3 The historical Upper Silesia constitutes only a western part of Silesian voivodship and almost whole Opole voivodship of today. The eastern part of the Silesian voivodship used to belong to the region of Lesser Poland. This is also why the RAŚ criticizes

the administrative reform of 1998 as it has not taken into account the historical legacies of the respective regions and thus weakens the potential appeal of the RAŚ ethno-regionalist claims. To emphasize its inclusive approach, the RAŚ usually refers to "Silesia" and "Silesian people" in general, or to Upper Silesia in historical terms.
4   The Silesian Regional Party was finally registered in May 2018. Because it also represents the claim for territorial autonomy and most RAŚ members – e.g. Henryk Mercik is the leader of the ŚPR and the vice-chairman of the RAŚ – are engaged in this party, it is treated here as a continuation of the RAŚ, notwithstanding the shift of focus on salient issues, addressed later in this chapter. Other members stem from regionalist organizations traditionally committed to foster the history and culture of Silesia (Portal Samorządowy 2018).
5   According to Zarycki (2000), Poland has had a constant status of a periphery, and the configuration of power between the foreign centers has changed considerably over time. Polish national culture, viewed as peripheral one, resisted the Russian, Prussian, Austrian occupation, Soviet and German invasion, and finally, the influence of the West (EU). Another constant feature has been the alliance of the Catholic Church with the national opposition (resistance) in their struggle against foreign centers. This is why the religious, national, culturally traditional, anti-communist, but also EU critical stance characterizes the right specter of the political landscape in Poland, today represented by PiS.
6   Whereas the Polish authorities regard the Silesian Uprisings as a pro-Polish move and the will of Silesians to join Poland, many Silesians argue that in those Uprisings, their ancestors were fighting for autonomy, some for autonomy within Polish state, and some within the German state. This is why Silesians often refer to those events as a "civil war" (Zweiffel 2013: 181).
7   The national minority, in turn, has to fulfill all these criteria and additionally it must identify with a nation organized in a state. This is why the Silesians cannot be regarded as a national minority in Poland. The act recognizes nine national minorities: Czech, Lithuanian, Belarusian, German, Armenian, Russian, Slovak, Ukrainian and Jewish; and four ethnic minorities: Karaim, Lemko, Roma and Tatars. The act has also recognized Kashubian as a regional language.
8   "Nationality" was understood as belonging to an ethnic or national community (GUS 2012).
9   https://www.polskieradio.pl/7/158/Artykul/278382,Nie-straszcie-secesja-i-separatyzmem
10 https://autonomia.pl/
11 http://marszautonomii.pl/
12 https://autonomia.pl/faq-najczestsze-pytania/
13 https://autonomia.pl/faq-najczestsze-pytania/
14 Gorzelik refers here to the fact that during the war many Silesians were conscripted into the *Wehrmacht*, often against their will. Up until today the "Silesian grandfather from *Wehrmacht*" has a very pejorative meaning in Poland.
15 https://autonomia.pl/faq-najczestsze-pytania/. A pilot research "The political consciousness of Polish citizens in the Silesia Voivodship" conducted in 2009 and then repeated in 2010 demonstrated that most respondents believed, politicians at the central level did not understand the needs of the Silesia region – 66 per cent (44.9 per cent definitely agree and 21.15 agree), whereas only 7.3 per cent respondents answered otherwise. See Muś (2017: 164–168).
16 Jerzy Gorzelik (2017) maintains that the power monopoly of the central government leads to the state capture by the "party oligarchies". The lack of the constitutionally guaranteed territorial separation of powers is a threat for the society, similar to the one resulting from the lack of separation between executive, legislative, and judicative branches on national level.

17 Liberal democracy has been thoroughly defined by Giovanni Sartori (1995) as consisting of two dimensions – constitutional dimension, i.e. political liberalism (rule of law) and the electoral dimension.
18 http://rasopole.org/
19 http://partiaslaska.pl/
20 The Polish Constitution stipulates in art. 167 that "Units of local government shall be assured public funds adequate for the performance of the duties assigned to them."
21 On the weakness of liberalism in Poland, see Szacki (1995). On the recent "illiberal tendencies" see Hanley and Dawson (2016).
22 See Rohrschneider and Whitefield (2009) for the longevity of political cleavages.

References

Baranyai, N. (2013) "Regionalism in Upper Silesia: The Concept of Autonomous Regions in Poland". In: Pálné Kovács, I. and Kákai, L. (eds.) *Ten Public Policy Studies*. Pécs: University of Pécs, Department of Political Studies, pp. 9–28.

Brusis, M. (2013) "Party Strategies and Administrative-Territorial Reforms in Poland", *West European Politics*, 36(2), pp. 405–425.

Buchowski, M. and Chlewińska, K. (2012) *Tolerance of Cultural Diversity in Poland and Its Limitations*, report written within "Accept Pluralism" 7th Framework Programme Project. San Domenico di Fiesole: European University Institute, Robert Schuman Centre for Advanced Studies.

Canovan, M. (1999) "Trust the People! Populism and the Two Faces of Democracy", *Political Studies*, 47(1), pp. 2–16.

Czaja, M. (2015) "Pozycja Ruchu Autonomii Śląska w systemie partyjnym województwa Sląskiego po wyborach samorządowych". In: Czaja, M. and Gutowski, S. (eds.) *Wybory samorządowe 2014 w województwie Śląskim*. Katowice: Towarzystwo Inicjatyw Naukowych, pp. 6–26.

Czoik, T. (2017) "Premier Morawiecki zaprezentował Program dla Śląska. To 70 inwestycji o wartości 40 mld zł", *Gazeta Wyborcza Katowice*, 21 December. http://katowice.wyborcza.pl/katowice/7,97222,22818797,premier-morawiecki-zaprezentowal-program-dla-slaska-to-70-inwestycji.html. Accessed 12 July 2018.

De Winter, L. (1998) "Conclusion. A Comparative Analysis of Electoral, Office and Policy Success of Ethno-Regionalist Parties". In: De Winter, L. and Türsan, H. (eds.) *Regionalist Parties in Western Europe*. London: Routledge, pp. 204–247.

De Winter, L. (2001) *The Impact of European Integration on Ethno-Regionalist Parties*. Barcelona: Institut de Ciències Polítiques i Socials.

Ghergina, S., Miscoiu, S. and Soare, S. (2017) "How Far does Nationalism Go? An Overview of Populist Parties in Central and Eastern Europe". In: Heinisch, R., Holtz-Bacha, C. and Mazzoleni, O. (eds.) *Political Populism. A Handbook*. Baden-Baden: Nomos, pp. 193–207.

Gorzelik, J. (2017) "Mieliśmy rację. Rzeczpospolita Polska nie jest państwem prawa", *Silesion*, 15 July. https://silesion.pl/gorzelik-to-jest-marsz-pod-prad-15-07-2017. Accessed 12 July 2018.

GUS (2002) *Narodowy Spis Powszechny*. Warszawa: Główny Urząd Statystyczny.

GUS (2012) *Wyniki Narodowego Spisu Powszechnego Ludności i Mieszkań 2011*. Warszawa: Główny Urząd Statystyczny.

Hanley, S. and Dawson, J. (2016) "East Central Europe: The Fading Mirage of the 'Liberal Consensus'", *Journal of Democracy*, 7(1), pp. 20–34.

Heinisch, R., Holtz-Bacha, C. and Mazzoleni, O. (2017) "Introduction". In: Heinisch, R., Holtz-Bacha, C. and Mazzoleni, O. (eds.) *Political Populism. A Handbook*. Baden-Baden: Nomos, pp. 19–37.

Hermanowski, M. and Kosmala, G. (2001) "Contemporary Regionalism in Poland", *Geographica Slovenica*, 34(1), pp. 149–162.

Jaskółka Śląska (2009) "Marsz pamięci ofiar obozu 'Zgoda'", 22 November. www.jaskolka slaska.eu/2009/02/05/marsz-pamieci-ofiar-obozu-zgoda/. Accessed 12 July 2018.

Kacprzak, I. (2018) "Śląsk musi wymyślićsię na nowo", *Rzeczpospolita*, 9 January. www .rp.pl/Zycie-Slaska/301099858-Slask-musi-wymyslic-sie-na-nowo.html. Accessed 12 July 2018.

Kamusella, T. (2012) "Poland and the Silesians: Minority Rights à la carte?", *Journal of Ethnopolitics and Minority Issues in Europe*, 11(2), pp. 42–74.

Kazibut-Twórz, E. (2010) "Gorzelik: Odłączyć Śląsk od Polski? Nie mam takich zamiarów", *Dziennik Zachodni*, 10 December. www.dziennikzachodni.pl/artykul/ 343827,gorzelik-odlaczyc-slask-od-polski-nie-mam-takich-zamiarow,id,t.html. Accessed 12 July 2018.

Keating, M. (2003) "The Invention of Regions: Political Restructuring and Territorial Government in Western Europe". In: Brenner, N., Jessop, B., Jones, M. and MacLeod, G. (eds.) *State/Space: A Reader*. Oxford: Wiley-Blackwell, pp. 257–277.

Kocyba, P. and Riedel, R. (2015) "Polskie partie polityczne wobec kwestii Śląskiej na przykładzie stosunku do Ruchu Autonomii Śląska", *Myśl Ekonomiczna i Polityczna*, 2 (49), pp. 263–277.

Lipset, S. M. and Rokkan, S. (1967) *Cleavage Structures, Party Systems and Voter Alignments*. Chicago, IL: The Free Press.

Massetti, E. (2009) "Explaining Regionalist Party Positioning in a Multi-Dimensional Ideological Space: A Framework for Analysis", *Regional and Federal Studies*, 19(4–5), pp. 501–531.

Massetti, E. and Schakel, A. H. (2015) "From Class to Region: How Regionalist Parties Link (and Subsume) Left-Right Into Centre-Periphery Politics", *Party Politics*, 21(6), pp. 866–886.

Müller, J.-W. (2016) *Was ist Populismus? Ein Essay*. Berlin: Suhrkamp Verlag.

Müller-Rommel, F. (1998) "Ehno-Regionalist Parties in Western Europe. Theoretical Considerations and Framework of Analysis". In: De Winter, L. and Türsan, H. (eds.) *Regionalist Parties in Western Europe*. London and New York: Routledge, pp. 17–27.

Muś, A. (2017) "'Zjednoczeni dla Śląska' – Support of Upper Silesians for Regional Initiative", *Political Preferences*, 14, pp. 157–174.

Myśliwiec, M. (2013a) "The Spanish Autonomous Model in Poland? The Political Concept of the Silesian Autonomy Movement". In: López Basaguren, A. and Escajedo San-Epifanio, L. (eds.) *The Ways of Federalism in Western Countries and the Horizons of Territorial Autonomy in Spain*. Berlin: Springer, pp. 179–190.

Myśliwiec, M. (2013b) "Ślōnskŏ godka - praśny folklor, czy język regionalny?", *Przegląd Prawa Konstytucyjnego*, 3(15), pp. 99–120.

Narbutt, M. (2008) "Zegarek z napędem autonomicznym", Rzeczpospolita, 25 May.

PiS (2011) *Raport o stanie Rzeczypospolitej*. www.rodaknet.com/raport_o_stanie_rzeczypos politej.pdf. Accessed 12 July 2018.

Portal Samorządowy (2017) "Śląska Partia Regionalna odpowiada ministrowi: Nie jesteśmy surowcowym zapleczem dla państwa", 4 December. www.portalsamorzadowy.pl/wydar

zenia-lokalne/slaska-partia-regionalna-odpowiada-ministrowi-nie-jestesmy-surowco wym-zapleczem-dla-panstwa,101165.html. Accessed 12 July 2018.

Portal Samorządowy (2018) "Śląska Partia Regionalna zaprasza do współpracy regionalne środowiska", 21 February 2018. www.portalsamorzadowy.pl/polityka-i-spolec zenstwo/slaska-partia-regionalna-zaprasza-do-wspolpracy-regionalne-srodowiska, 104390.html. Accessed 12 July 2018.

RAŚ (2011a) *Statut Ruchu Autonomii Śląska*. http://autonomia.pl/statut-ruchu-autonomii-slaska/. Accessed 12 July 2018.

RAŚ (2011b) *Projekt Konstytucji RP*. http://autonomia.pl/projekt-konstytucji-rp/. Accessed 12 July 2018.

RAŚ (2011c) *Statut Organiczny Śląskiego Województwa Autonomicznego*. http://autonomia.pl/statut-organiczny/. Accessed 12 July 2018.

Rohrschneider, R. and Whitefield, S. (2009) "Understanding Cleavages in Party Systems. Issue Position and Issue Salience in 13 Post-Communist Democracies", *Comparative Political Studies*, 42(2), pp. 280–313.

Sartori, G. (1995) "How Far Can Free Government Travel?", *Journal of Democracy*, 6(3), pp. 101–111.

Sorens, J. (2009) "The Partisan Logic of Decentralization in Europe", *Regional and Federal Studies*, 19(2), pp. 255–272.

ŚPR (2018) *Program dla Śląska*. http://partiaslaska.pl/program-dla-slaska/. Accessed 12 July 2018.

Szacki, J. (1995) *Liberalism after Communism*. Budapest: Central European University.

Taggart, P. (2000) *Populism*. Buckingham: Open University Press.

Türsan, H. (1998) "Introduction. Ethno-Regionalist Parties as Ethnic Entrepreneurs". In: De Winter, L. and Türsan, H. (eds.) *Regionalist Parties in Western Europe*. London: Routledge, pp. 1–16.

Tygodnik Powszechny (2017) "Siła Regionu", 31 October. www.tygodnikpowszechny.pl/sila-regionu-150677. Accessed 3 November 2017.

Yoder, J. A. (2003) "Decentralisation and Regionalisation after Communism: Administrative and Territorial Reform in Poland and the Czech Republic", *Europe-Asia Studies*, 55(2), pp. 263–286.

Zarycki, T. (2000) "Politics in the Periphery: Political Cleavages in Poland Interpreted in Their Historical and International Context", *Europe-Asia Studies*, 52(5), pp. 851–873.

Zasada, M. (2017) "Jerzy Gorzelik: W świecie zachodnim autonomia regionów to normalność", *Dziennik Zachodni*, 31 March. www.dziennikzachodni.pl/opinie/wywiady/a/jerzy-gorzelik-w-swiecie-zachodnim-autonomia-regionow-to-normalnosc,11940211/. Accessed 12 July 2018.

Zweiffel, L. (2013) "Ruch Autonomii Śląska", *Studia Politologica*, XI, pp. 178–199.

10

REGIONALIST POPULISM IN CROATIA

The case of the Croatian Democratic Alliance of Slavonia and Baranja – HDSSB

Marko Kukec

Introduction

A crucial component in the strategies of regionalist parties in their promotion of regional self-government is a clear differentiation of the region from the central state at both societal and elite levels. At the societal level, however, regionalist parties cannot always rely on pre-existing regionally-based social cleavages rooted in specificities such as language/dialect, history, geography or ethnicity (Brancati 2007: 135–36). In such circumstances, regionalist parties must typically act in the manner of "regional entrepreneurs" (Türsan 1998: 5–6), identifying various latent grievances held by the regional population and molding these into coherent and electorally appealing mobilization strategies. The success of such efforts depends largely on the ability of regionalist parties to increase the salience of these grievances above national-level issues. At elite level, "regionalist entrepreneurs" are ideally politicians who originate from the region and are independent from national politics (De Winter 1998: 222). However, many regionalist politicians are veterans of national parties and thus face strong credibility constraints in presenting themselves as the champions of regional interests. By studying the case of the Croatian Democratic Alliance of Slavonia and Baranja (HDSSB), this chapter aims to advance the theoretical and empirical understanding of how populism is employed to surmount these constraints by sharpening regional differentiation at both societal and elite levels.

In the years after its establishment in 2005, HDSSB shook the duopoly of the two strongest parties in Croatian politics, the Croatian Democratic Union (HDZ) and the Social Democratic Party (SDP). It did so by opening up a different conflict line from the value cleavage that has traditionally structured the Croatian party system, focusing instead on regionalist claims. Organizationally and programmatically, the party is rooted and restricted to the region of

Slavonia and Baranja, but this strategy elevated the party to national relevance: during the 2011–2015 term, the party held seven seats in the 151-member Croatian parliament, equaling one-fourth of the MPs returned by the two Slavonian constituencies. Another organizational feature of HDSSB is that it originated as a splinter party of HDZ and was established by Branimir Glavaš, who had earned the rank of a general during the Croatian war of independence and had been the most prominent HDZ figure in the region until 2005.

The strategy applied by HDSSB in striving for regional differentiation is often labeled "populist", not only by domestic politicians and media but also in the international scholarly literature (Inglehart and Norris 2016: 44). Within the Croatian political debate, the populist label is mostly used pejoratively as a strategy by its competitors to portray HDSSB as a non-credible and uncooperative party rather than on the basis of any rigorous empirical assessment. As this chapter will show, however, this assertion does have some empirical and theoretical merit. Populism, most commonly defined as pitting "the good people" against "the bad elite" (Mudde 2004), may indeed serve as an instrument of regionalist parties with which to consolidate regional identity through the construction of a regional "heartland" and to fuel resentment among the regional population towards national elites. Regionalist party elites entangled in the web of national politics may attempt to shift the boundaries of the "elite" category in order to distance and exclude themselves from the category of national elites (Albertazzi and McDonnell 2005: 958–59). This is possible because the entities of "the people" and "the elite" are not fixed in the populist narrative but highly prone to redefinition and adaptation to concrete circumstances (Mudde and Kaltwasser 2013: 168; Kriesi 2014: 369). In addition, insistence on the adversarial relationship between "the regional people" and "the national elite" can transcend issue-based political competition (Hawkins 2009: 1044), which benefits regionalist parties that find it difficult to organize their appeal around a set of policy issues.

The present analysis attempts to uncover which dimensions of populism are present in the regionalist platform of HDSSB. In doing so, the analysis goes beyond the pejorative use of the term "populism" in considering HDSSB, while also adding another case to the comparative literature on populism and, of particular relevance for this volume, ascertaining a link between regionalism and populism. If the "minimal" definition of populism as a "thin-centered ideology" is adopted, then the precise application of populist rhetoric needs to be studied in conjunction with another ideology. While always applying the people-elite dichotomy, populism also draws on grievances that characterize a particular context or the particular ideological orientation of a populist actor. In other words, populism often serves as an amplification of the grievances peculiar to a certain ideology by homogenizing two opposing sides and assigning a moral dimension to a conflict. While HDSSB may be positioned on the classic left-right and new politics ideological spectrum, the defining feature of its political platform is regionalism. In accordance with the themes of this edited volume, therefore, the chapter examines how HDSSB combines populism with regionalism in promoting regional self-government. In addition to presenting an in-depth analysis of how "the regional people" and "the elite" are constructed by HDSSB, the chapter also explores the solutions offered by the party in response to the subordinate position of the region in relation to the central state.

The empirical analysis component of the chapter rests on a qualitative content analysis of newspaper articles from the Slavonian daily newspaper *Glas Slavonije* and content produced by HDSSB itself during the formative and peak periods of the party (2005–2013). The analysis of this data systematically applies the concept of populism defined by the ideational approach (Hawkins and Kaltwasser 2017), highlighting those elements of party communications that indicate populism, i.e. discourse employing the two components that form the central dichotomy of populism: "the people" and "the elite". The results of this analysis show that HDSSB has sought to portray Slavonia and Baranja as the "heartland" of Croatia that has been forgotten by the national "elite" while striving to blur any internal differences amongst the Slavonian "people". The elite is carefully constructed in this discourse as a combination of the current leadership of HDZ, other mainstream parties, the media, and "regional traitors", while the leadership of HDSSB are portrayed as mavericks who are nevertheless loyal to the founding principles of HDZ and to the first Croatian president, Franjo Tuđman.

The following section introduces the concept of populism derived from the ideational approach to the phenomenon, relating its components to the basic tenets of regionalism. Before the thematic analysis of HDSSB populism on the two components (people and elite), data sources are introduced. The concluding section reflects on the interrelationship between populism and regionalism in light of the case of HDSSB.

The intersection of populism and regionalism

The phenomenon of populism has appeared across many different world regions and time periods, though most prominently in the United States, Latin America and Western Europe. As a consequence, it is the populist actors in these three regions that have received the greatest amount of theoretical and empirical scholarly attention, leading to vast but often regionally segregated literatures on populism. In shifting from one region and time period to another, the concept of populism has been adapted to the peculiarities of specific contexts such as socio-economic characteristics or particular constellations of power among societal groups (Akkerman, Mudde and Zaslove 2014: 1326). According to the specific opportunity structures in which they operate, and depending on their right- or left-wing orientation, populist actors may mobilize opposition to globalization, the media, big businesses and state bureaucracy, and have adopted a variety of modes in expressing their discontent.

The concept of populism has accordingly been assigned various, often context-specific components in the literature. Rooduijn (2014), for example, lists no fewer than 12 such components. Intuitively, such intension of the concept hampers its extension, or its ability to cross regional boundaries and its application to (somehow) similar phenomena in other contexts. This is of particular relevance to the study of populism emerging in new contexts such as Central and Eastern Europe, with populist political actors mobilizing grievances that have so far received less treatment in the literature. For this reason, applying a stringent concept of populism would disregard its chameleonic nature, i.e. the ability of populism to adapt to contextual specificities (Meny and Surel 2002a: 6; Arter 2010: 490–91).

Recent literature has settled on a number of key components of populism, however, encompassed by the "ideational" approach to populism (Pauwels 2011: 99; Bornschier 2017: 301). Stripping the concept of the contextual and organizational features of populist actors, the ideational approach focuses on a minimal definition of populism as a set of ideas about how the political world operates (Hawkins 2009: 1043; Mudde and Kaltwasser 2013: 150; Hawkins and Kaltwasser 2017), and this approach has been supported in recent studies of commonalities among populists from different regions (Rooduijn 2014). Proponents of this approach refer to populism as a "thin-centered ideology", since it separates ideas from structures and actions while still lacking the comprehensiveness of the problem statements and solutions offered by more established "thick" ideologies such as socialism and conservatism (Canovan 2002: 32; Mudde 2004: 544; Pauwels 2011: 99). The relatively restricted scope of populism allows for and even necessitates that populism be combined with another ideology, typically by recasting the grievances of a specific social group within a populist framework.

Adopting the minimal definition of populism has advantages for this chapter, particularly in theorizing the ways in which populism interacts with regionalism. In the remainder of the theoretical section, I attempt to analytically relate regionalism and populism by highlighting the compatibility of their central tenets. Specifically, I discuss how the first underlying component of regionalism, i.e. identity politics, fits into the populist people-elite framework, while the second component of regionalism, i.e. the demand for self-government, is just another way to include the voice of the people in politics.

The people

The two basic components of populism as conceived by the ideational approach are "the people" and "the elite", both of which are depicted as homogeneous entities (Mudde and Kaltwasser 2013: 151). Populists regard the collective entity of "the people" as the essence of society, often referred to as the "silent majority", who are held to be the bearers of sovereignty (Akkerman, Mudde and Zaslove 2014: 1327). While the exact meaning of "the people" is dependent on context, the entity is romanticized as pure, virtuous and hard-working. They (the "ordinary" or "common" people) are believed to share interests and characteristics that can be aggregated to form a "general will" which populists claim to represent (Jagers and Walgrave 2007: 324; Mudde and Kaltwasser 2013: 151). Any socio-structural or political divisions within a society are downplayed by populists in the attempt to homogenize their audience and present a unified front against the elite. Emphasizing the undivided character of "the people", populists often refer to them in the singular, e.g. as *el pueblo*, *das Volk*, or *narod*. The self-assigned responsibility of populists is nothing more nor less than to ensure that the outcomes of decision-making processes reflect the will of the people (Jagers and Walgrave 2007: 323).

In the real world it would be difficult to find empirical references to any societal groups embodying all of the characteristics assigned to "the people". The imagined character of "the people" is emphasized by Taggart's (2002) concept of "the heartland" that is home to "the people" and constitutes the ideal community that populists claim to represent. To ascertain the real meaning that populist actors attribute to "the people" and how populism relates to regionalism, it is thus necessary to understand the meaning of "heartland" as that term is employed by a populist actor (Taggart 2002: 67; Kriesi 2014: 362).

In the same vein, while regions and regional identities may be based on certain observable characteristics such as language, religion or residency, regions are often constructed or imagined (Anderson 1983; Paasi 2009: 132; Fitjar 2013). Both the physical and the symbolic boundaries of a region are contested, and as such are malleable to the needs of actors involved in the process. Regionalist political entrepreneurs are often the most outspoken actors in defining the essential characteristics of a region and in defining the criteria for membership of the regional community. Rather than operating in a vacuum, however, regionalist entrepreneurs often rely on well-established discourses pertaining to the qualities of the regional population and the overall socio-economic position of the region within a polity. These qualities are then adapted to the specific interests of regionalist actors. The constructivist perspective on regions and regional identity thus closely resembles the concept of the "heartland", where an ideal and pure community of people with common interests is (re)created for the purposes of political mobilization. Led by these theoretical considerations, this analysis systematically traces the efforts of HDSSB to construct "the regional people".

The elite

The pure and virtuous people are contrasted with a corrupt and self-serving elite who have betrayed the will of the people (Barr 2009: 31; Pauwels 2011: 100). To the detriment of the popular will, members of the elite pursue their own selfish interests or sell themselves out to a foreign agent such as international business or political oligarchy. Drawing mostly from Latin American experience, many authors describe populist discourse as a Manichaean struggle between "good" and "evil" that achieves cosmic proportions and goes beyond any current political circumstances (Hawkins 2009: 1043). More generally, the elite is constructed as an exact opposite to the definition of the people, and thus the two opposite poles mutually reinforce each other and present a clear division. As the notion of the people is "blurred around the edges" (Taggart 2002: 67), populists aim to solidify its definition by clearly specifying who does not belong to the people.

Like the concept of "the people", the concept of "the elite" is hollow and malleable according to specific contexts (Mudde and Kaltwasser 2013: 151; Rooduijn 2014: 575). For example, Latin American left-wing populists often contrast poor people with a wealthy land-owning elite that is attuned to the imperialist aspirations of United States. In Europe, meanwhile, right-wing populists contrast ethnic majority populations with an establishment that is responsible for high levels of immigration. Whether the elite is a political, economic, cultural, intellectual or media elite, it is always external to the people, often only symbolically but sometimes also physically, as in the case of the global business elite or central governments. Elites are also regarded as interconnected and homogeneous, working in unison to undermine the general will and perpetuate their domination over the people.

Power to the (regional) people

A defining programmatic feature of regionalism is the pursuit of some form of regional self-government (De Winter 1998: 204; Türsan 1998; Dandoy and Sandri 2007: 6) that will empower the regional community which regionalists claim to represent. These proposals may take the form of demands to protect the already established rights of a certain regional community, to decentralize existing regions, to establish new regions or introduce federalization, with secessionism as the most extreme demand (Dandoy 2010). Regionalist parties often promote regional self-government on the pragmatic basis that the benefits will include more efficient and responsive regional government than central government can provide. In addition to these functional grounds, regionalists often invoke symbolic grounds in calling for self-government as the way for a regional population to take power into its own hands. The latter appeal may be further emphasized by resorting to populism.

Although not a defining feature of the minimal concept of populism, populist actors often accuse elites of capturing the institutions of the state and depriving the virtuous people of their voice within these institutions. Rooted in their belief that democracy entails an expression of the popular will in its pure form, unmediated by the institutions of representative democracy, populists demand more direct involvement of the people in politics (Meny and Surel 2002b: 8; Kriesi 2014: 363). In other words, they seek to circumvent any obstacles impeding the popular will from accessing the decision-making process.

In combining regionalism with populism, regionalist parties might advocate bringing the institutions of representative democracy closer to the people as a means of removing obstacles to the realization of the popular will. When the "heartland" is territorially delineated, bringing government closer to the people entails political, administrative, and fiscal decentralization (Schneider 2003: 33), allowing a territorially bounded community to take political matters into its own hands. Previous literature on populism has scarcely acknowledged the territorial dimension of populist reform proposals. However, McDonnell's (2006) study of the Italian Northern League has provided a blueprint example of a party combining populism with regionalism in describing how the Northern League defended its drive for further autonomy for northern Italian regions on the basis of a populist appeal against the Italian elites in Rome. In this chapter, the communication of HDSSB is analyzed to ascertain the extent to which the party's demand for the territorial restructuring of the state is likewise grounded in populist appeals.

Regional characteristics and the rise of HDSSB

The martyrdom, victimhood and poverty of Slavonia and Baranja

The region that HDSSB aims to represent encompasses three sub-regions: Slavonia, the largest sub-region, and Baranja and Western Sirmium. Administratively, the territory of the region is divided into five counties that were created in the early 1990s as units of the central state but were later granted self-government (Koprić 2010: 373). Geographically, the region is situated in eastern Croatia, sharing a border with Bosnia and Herzegovina to the south, Hungary to the north and Serbia to the east. This geographic position has played a major role in shaping the history and contemporary narratives of the region. Once situated at the periphery of the Austro-Hungarian Monarchy on its southeastern border, the region long served as a frontier with the Ottoman Empire. Being on the front line of defense against the Ottomans, the region played a vital role in the security of the Monarchy and of Christian Europe, earning it the epithet of *antemurale christianitatis* (Grgin 2003: 88; Holjevac 2006: 104–05). More recently, the narrative of Slavonian martyrdom was further reinforced during the Croatian war for independence, as the Slavonian population again showed their readiness to defend Croatia. This narrative continues to dominate contemporary characterizations of the region.

The violence sustained by the region throughout this war resulted in significant human casualties and major damage to its infrastructure and economy. This destruction is deeply embedded in the collective memory of the people; and victimhood is thus another important narrative of the region alongside martyrdom. In addition to combat casualties, the war in Slavonia was marked by a number of appalling war crimes against civilians, the most severe of which was the Ovčara Massacre, now commemorated by a "memory walk" in Vukovar every year. Besides these tragic incidents, Slavonia and Baranja also suffered enormous economically during the war, with industrial capacity falling by 90 per cent, leading to a dramatic rise in unemployment (Smoljan 2010: 29–30). The region's economy still lags behind that of other regions and the national average today, especially when compared to the capital, Zagreb, and the wealthy north and west of the country. The protraction of this poor economic situation is often blamed on the negligence of the central government, which is accused of having failed to honor the sacrifices made by the region during the war and of continuing to exploit the hard-working Slavonian farmers without making further investments in the development of the region. In spite of the national identity shared between Croatia and Slavonia, therefore, Slavonia's particularly turbulent history has given rise to a number of regional characteristics which HDSSB has been able to exploit in order to mobilize the Slavonian population.

The regionalism of HDSSB

Osijek, the largest city in eastern Croatia, is one of the region's cities celebrated for their sacrifices in the war for independence. The commander of the city's defense was Branimir Glavaš, who was awarded the rank of major general for his role in the war. In parallel with his military career, Glavaš pursued a highly successful political career during the early 1990s, becoming one of the founders of HDZ. As a strong supporter of Franjo Tuđman, the first Croatian president, he enjoyed considerable influence within Tuđman's regime and was rewarded for his support with a significant degree of control over Slavonian political and economic affairs. With the establishment of local and regional self-government in 1993, Glavaš became the governor of Osijek-Baranja County, a position he held until 2000, relying on a combination of the strong support base of HDZ in the region and his personal charisma as a war hero. At national level, meanwhile, he served as an MP throughout the 1990s and early 2000s. In the elections for the presidency of HDZ held after the death of Tuđman in 1999, Glavaš – as he has since admitted – rigged the voting process in favor of Ivo Sanader, who won and eventually became prime minister in 2003. In spite of this backing, Sanader had no tolerance for the new regionalist platform that Glavaš was developing, and which he announced just before the local elections in 2005. The central party leadership of HDZ regarded this as an act of serious disobedience, leading to a purge of Glavaš and his close associates from HDZ and the public offices they held. The new platform nevertheless achieved its first electoral breakthrough in the 2005 local elections, transforming itself into the Croatian Democratic Assembly of Slavonia and Baranja, a parent organization of multiple local associations established in the five Slavonian counties. At national level, three Slavonian MPs splintered away from the parliamentary party group of HDZ and established a separate parliamentary party group, ensuring the visibility and legislative influence of HDSSB in parliament.

Soon after this electoral breakthrough for HDSSB, however, testimonies began to emerge about wrongdoings committed by Glavaš during the defense of Osijek. One of his subordinates accused him of war crimes against Serbian civilians, and this was corroborated by several other witnesses, leading the state chief prosecutor to initiate a formal investigation and order his arrest, eventually leading to his imprisonment. Glavaš rejected these accusations as a politically motivated "witch hunt" staged by Prime Minister Ivo Sanader and launched a campaign for his liberation, presenting himself as the victim of Sanader's government. Glavaš was jailed and released multiple times over the course of the trial before he was eventually sentenced to ten years in prison by a county court in 2008. He initially eluded imprisonment by escaping to Bosnia and Herzegovina (to his birthplace of Drinovci) shortly before the verdict, where he was able to hide as a dual citizen of Croatia and Bosnia and Herzegovina (BH). Following the Supreme Court's confirmation of the verdict in 2010, however, Glavaš was arrested by the BH authorities and, at his own request, began serving his sentence there instead of in Croatia.

The accusations and the trial against Glavaš did not damage HDSSB either organizationally or electorally. In May 2006 the Croatian Democratic Alliance of Slavonia and Baranja was founded, carrying the same acronym (HDSSB) as the previously established platform. Organizationally, the Alliance party headed by Vladimir Šišljagić coexisted with the Assembly headed by Glavaš, who retained control over the party through joint monthly meetings of the Alliance and Assembly in Drinovci, and later on inside the prisons where he was serving his sentence. Under the leadership of Šišljagić, the party attracted members and followers and established a firm presence on the ground, thus demarcating the territory that it claimed to represent and that would be included in the new region as foreseen by the party leaders (Figure 10.1). The parliamentary wing of the party, despite consisting of only three members, was highly visible in parliament, often surpassing the activity rankings of other MPs. Organizational density and regionally-focused parliamentary activity, together with the strategy of exploiting the victimization of Glavaš, led to the party doubling its number of legislative seats at the 2011 national elections, which together with the defection of one Social Democrat MP, resulted in seven mandates for HDSSB in the 2011–2015 legislative term.

The main programmatic feature of HDSSB is its demand for the redrawing of Croatia's territorial units and the transfer of more extensive powers of self-government to the regions. Specifically, the party advocates the replacement of the current 21 counties with five regions, including the region of Slavonia and Baranja, which would span the territory of the five counties indicated in Figure 10.1. The five regions would be assigned more competencies than the counties currently enjoy and would be headed by a directly elected governor and regional legislature. The regions would also need to be represented at national level through the Chamber of Regions as the second chamber of the national parliament. The party bases these demands on the historical continuity of the Slavonia-Baranja region throughout Croatian history (Glas Slavonije 2011a; HDSSB 2012). In its efforts to deepen regional Slavonian identity, the party often invokes narratives of

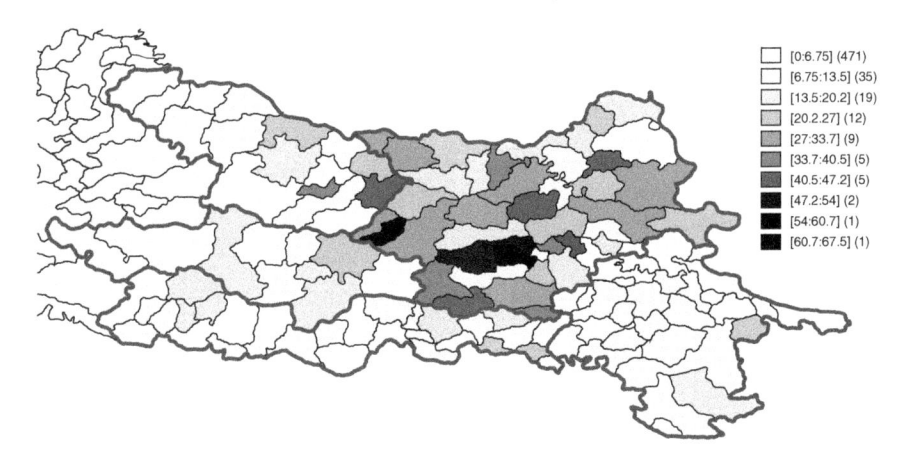

FIGURE 10.1 Party results (per cent) at 2013 local elections (the red lines are the borders of the five Slavonian counties)

martyrdom and victimhood, while being careful to present the Slavonian identity not as separate from the national Croatian identity but as the very essence of Croatian identity.

In reinforcing its demand for self-government HDSSB also adopts "economic regionalism", drawing on the relative poverty of Slavonia and particularly on the poor condition of agriculture, the region's main economic sector. By employing the argument of "internal colonialism" (Hechter 1973; Fitjar 2010: 528) and portraying Slavonia as a region that has been exploited, if not completely forgotten, by the central government, HDSSB has skillfully tapped into a widespread sense of negligence harbored by the local population. The central government is accused of having taking advantage of the hard work of Slavonian farmers and of having distributed once prosperous Slavonian agricultural firms among politically favorable entrepreneurs. In response, the party demands a fairer distribution of funds from the state budget sufficient to enable the development of a fiscally sustainable Slavonian region. These demands place the party on the left of the socio-economic ideological spectrum (Inglehart and Norris 2016: 44), confirming the general tendency of regionalist parties in relatively poor regions to adopt this position (Massetti and Schakel 2015: 871).

Following this outline of the regionalist appeal of HDSSB, the empirical analysis in the next section demonstrates how the party has combined these regionalist messages with populism, applying the theoretical arguments presented above on the linkages between these two ideologies. The combination of these two ideologies is found at all three levels envisaged in the theory, since the party employs populism to strengthen Slavonian identity, to aggravate the resentment of regional people towards national elites, and to frame the goal of self-government as a means of bringing the government closer to the people.

Empirical analysis

Case study design

In recent years the literature on populism has seen an increase in quantitative and comparative research designs that pay particular attention to the measurement of populism (Hawkins 2009; Rooduijn and Pauwels 2011; Schultz, et al. 2018). While this approach has been effective in showing how the concept of populism traverses different time periods and regions, particularly if defined minimally as a set of ideas, the approach is less mindful of the contexts in which specific populist actors operate. In studying how populism is combined with other ideologies such as regionalism, moreover, contextual characteristics are highly informative in ascertaining the choices that populist actors make in combining ideologies. For this reason, a case study design is undertaken in this chapter, affording us in-depth insights into the strategy of HDSSB and the party's efforts to develop a regionalist populist platform.

The data are based on a qualitative content analysis of newspaper articles covering the activities of HDSSB as well as contents produced by the party such as manifestos, press releases, and party speeches. The newspaper articles are from *Glas Slavonije* (Voice of Slavonia), a regional newspaper, which has covered the work of HDSSB extensively and even supported the party's initiative in its early days. Applying a purposeful sampling strategy (White and Marsh 2006: 36–37; Forman and Damschroder 2008: 43), only articles published one month prior to elections were collected; more specifically, articles published one month prior to the local elections of 2005 and one month before the national elections of 2007 and 2011. This is because the party-political messages of most interest for the purposes of this analysis are likely to be concentrated in the pre-election period. The press articles were collected from the archives of the National and University Library in Zagreb, while the party-produced content was downloaded from the website of HDSSB and the personal website of Glavaš. The analysis is deductive in that it traces the two components of populism (the people and the elite) in the communications of HDSSB, but also inductive in that the concrete entities defined as the people and the elite needed to be inferred from the analyzed content.

Who are the people?

If populism is defined minimally as referring to the "people", in accordance with the narrow conceptualization proposed by Jagers and Walgrave (2007), then the frequent references made to "the people" in HDSSB discourse confirm that the party is populist. In line with the party's regionalist agenda, the leaders of HDSSB often present the residents of Slavonia and Baranja as their "heartland", asserting that "between mechanically raising our hands up with tape across our mouths and struggling for the better life of Slavonians and our region, we have chosen the harder way" (*Glas Slavonije* 2005b). Interestingly, the residents of Western Sirmium (Srijem) are only specifically mentioned in a few instances and are left out of the title of the party. One reason might be that this sub-region is also omitted in everyday and general references to the whole region (as in this chapter), as well as the fact that Western Sirmium comprises only a small part of Sirmium while Eastern Sirmium is larger and is located in Serbia.

The residents of the heartland are idealized as virtuous and hard-working, as is common in portrayals of "the people" in populist narratives. As a traditionally rural region with agriculture as its main economic activity, Slavonia is presented as having been a self-sustainable region of "the Slavonian people who have always lived from their own work" (*Glas Slavonije* 2005a) and could continue to do so if the government changed its approach and stopped "underestimating Slavonian wisdom and common sense" (*Glas Slavonije* 2005f). Emphasizing the common sense of the regional population is another strategy aimed at promoting the case of the potential capacity of the "people" for self-government and advancing the claim that they should have greater control over decisions pertaining to the region. Back in the mythical "golden ages", Slavonians could provide for themselves through their own hard work and thrift. Today, by contrast, they suffer the impoverishment that characterizes the region as a result of central government neglect. In spite of this setback, the party maintains, the Slavonian people have resisted in the past and will continue to resist now. The leaders of HDSSB declare that they "feel the Slavonian defiance, awakening and acceptance of HDSSB's program as their own" (*Glas Slavonije* 2011b). This idea of "defiance" permeates the narrative of HDSSB, drawing on the martyrdom and resilience of the Slavonian people so salient throughout the region's history.

In its efforts to build regional identity, however, HDSSB does not seek to set exclusive boundaries between the regional population and other Croats. Rather, Slavonia is understood as the essence of Croatia and Slavonians are considered an integral element of the Croatian people. In its political communications HDSSB has needed to maintain a fine balance between these regional and national identities to avoid seeming overly biased towards either of them. This strategy evolved in response to a context in which the party was not in a position to build a completely new regional identity but instead had to mold existing identities and link them to the implementation of its political platform. On the one hand, the success of regionalist mobilization does require a certain identification with the region, which HDSSB appeals to with its populist references to the Slavonian people. On the other hand, HDSSB has had to refrain from defining Croats as "other", since Slavonians also have a strong attachment to the national Croatian identity, especially since their region bore a disproportionate burden of the suffering and costs of the Croatian war for independence. Insisting on an exclusive Slavonian identity would certainly have alienated the majority of the Croatian regional population, and more importantly would have undermined the efforts of Glavaš to present himself as a Croatian war hero as part of his liberation campaign. The complexity of HDSSB regionalism and populism is captured in the following party statement: "In Slavonia, where Croatia was created, we have to bring pride to Croatian people ... " (*Glas Slavonije* 2011c). Slavonia is thus portrayed as the heartland of Croatia, sharing the nation's exposure and resistance to external control and embodying all the virtues attributed to the Croatian people at large, such as diligence and honesty.

Another common theme in populist narratives is that the people form a homogeneous entity whose "general will" populist parties claim to represent. Internal social and political differences are deliberately blurred in an attempt to mobilize a unified front against the external enemy/elite, to the detriment of the heterogeneous interests that inevitably exist in any community and which deserve electoral expression. HDSSB has both a narrow (Slavonian) and a wider (Croatian) conception of the people, though the empirical material suggests that the Slavonian people are deemed a more homogeneous entity than the Croatian people. Particularly in its early days, HDSSB aimed at establishing a broad and inclusive coalition of Slavonians, with the call to "forget disputes, political differences and personal bigotry – let us gather around one program, a program for a happy and rich Slavonia within the framework of the Croatian state" (*Glas Slavonije* 2005d). With this approach the party sought to foreground the center-periphery grievance and emphasize the ultimate goal of increasing the prosperity of Slavonia, thus pushing internal regional grievances to one side.

To maintain the center-periphery grievance, however, the party has been compelled to adopt a polemical approach vis-à-vis the central state and other Croatian regions. HDSSB often decries the centralization of the Croatian state, complaining that "from 90 billion kuna [12.1 billion euro] of budget funds, only 10 billion goes to local self-government, of which nearly half goes to Zagreb" (*Glas Slavonije* 2005e). In several instances, the regions of Dalmatia and Istria are also deemed to benefit disproportionately from the national budget. Arguably, regionalism very often depicts a zero-sum game among the regions, which is well understood by HDSSB. Thus, if there is any negative differentiation present between the Slavonian people and other Croats, it is mostly of an economic rather than cultural nature, employed for the purpose of highlighting the economic inequalities between regions and to criticize the "internal colonialism" to which the Slavonia-Baranja region has been subjected. For this reason Inglehart and Norris (2016), based on data from the Chapel Hill Expert Survey, classify HDSSB as a populist-left party, with the "leftist" label referring to an emphasis on economic injustice and the need for redistribution.

Who are the elites?

To whom, then, does HDSSB attribute the blame for the economic hardships to which the Slavonians are still exposed? While the city of Zagreb receives a disproportionate amount of public funds, it is "Zagreb", and more precisely the central government, which is presented as standing behind this unfair distribution. As the "center of political and economic power", Zagreb is an ideal target in the populist narrative of HDSSB, pitting a powerful and remote central elite against the simple and hard-working people of the region of Slavonia and Baranja. The central elite is not only accused of neglecting the region, moreover, but also of willfully conspiring against regional interests:

> HDZ and the Sanader government not only did not care about the equal development of all Croatian regions, but have intentionally directed the funds from the state treasury towards Dalmatia, Istria and Zagreb, the result of which is that Slavonia and Baranja is the poorest Croatian region.
>
> *(Glas Slavonije 2007c).*

In another instance, on 22 February 2011, the party issued the following statement in response to an incident of wheat stolen from the state reserves:

> HDSSB considers as hypocritical and shameless the attempt of the current government to present payments to the robbed peasants as caring for the problems of the Slavonian peasants. The Croatian government is not giving anything to the peasants but is only returning what was stolen in the robbery for which the government is most responsible.

Politicians who are native to the region of Slavonia but who remain loyal to the central government are portrayed as "domestic traitors". Employing similar claims to those of the Lega dei Ticinesi party (Albertazzi and McDonnell 2005: 135), HDSSB claims that "Slavonians with a Zagreb address" have forgotten and abandoned their own people to show their loyalty to the leaderships of their parties. This is particularly the case in references to the national parliament, where Slavonian politicians are accused of having failed to lobby for Slavonian interests or of having broken the party unity necessary for the benefit of Slavonia, preferring instead to sell themselves out in return for the perks of national office. In the months preceding the establishment of HDSSB (Assembly) in 2005, Glavaš and two other MPs bypassed the HDZ leadership by submitting several legislative amendments that would enable the allocation of greater funds to Slavonia. Recalling this episode in an interview in 2007, Šišljagić criticized Vladimir Šeks, an Osijek-born speaker in the parliament, for failing to support their legislative efforts:

> He compromised himself in his relation to Slavonia and Baranja, especially in the vote on the amendments by which Glavaš, Drmić and myself sought money for Slavonia, and Šeks, as the speaker of the parliament, was against investments into this region.
>
> *(Glas Slavonije 2007c).*

On account of their negligence of Slavonia, HDSSB pits regional elites who have remained subordinate to national elites on the opposing side of the Slavonian people, claiming that these domestic elites have betrayed the trust of Slavonians and even worked against the interests of their own region.

Glavaš himself, as well as his associates, were by no means newcomers to the national political scene. Glavaš had long served as the governor of Osijek-Baranja County and as a senior MP of HDZ, and therefore had direct access to the "center of political and economic power". The literature on populism and the literature on regionalism both often emphasize the importance of a charismatic leader who is an outsider to the political establishment (De Winter 1998; Hawkins and Kaltwasser 2017: 523). Barr (2009: 38), for example, excludes "insiders" from his definition of populism, as insiders cannot credibly claim to be outside of the establishment. Conceived minimally as a set of ideas about the relationship between the people and the elite, however, populism may well be adopted by former insiders, as demonstrated in the case of HDSSB. The arguments employed by Glavaš and his associates to distance themselves from the elites complement their efforts at societal level, where they promote a Slavonian regional identity in parallel with acknowledging the well-rooted Croatian identity in the region.

Glavaš and other defectors from HDZ to HDSSB had the particularly delicate task of convincing Slavonians that HDZ was a corrupt and alienated party, while avoiding criticizing the legacy of Tuđman, the first president of HDZ, who is considered the founder of modern Croatia. In doing so, the defectors had to present themselves as mavericks and to confine their criticisms to the actions of HDZ after 2000, in contrast with the romanticized period of Tuđman's reign. In expressing allegiance to the legacy of the first Croatian president, they went so far as to make the following statement:

> All candidates from the non-partisan local list of Dinko Burić gave unconditional support to the manifesto of Branimir Glavaš, and even though the list of HDZ no longer exists in Belišće, these candidates are most sincerely committed to the original principles of HDZ.
>
> (Glas Slavonije *2005c*).

Glavaš himself has claimed on multiple occasions that he never left HDZ but was expelled against his will. The position taken by HDSSB is that HDZ is no longer the noble movement that brought about Croatian independence but has been hijacked by crooked and unresponsive elites. In this account, the group only decided to leave HDZ and form a separate regionalist political platform because all the intra-party avenues for expressing the popular concerns of Slavonians had been blocked. HDZ has long been a dominant political party in the region, particularly on account of its role in the war for independence, and thus Glavaš and his associates are constrained in criticizing the early HDZ, as this would not be well-received by the Slavonian electorate.

The criticisms leveled by HDSSB against national elites extend beyond the leadership of HDZ to other parties, most notably to the opposition Social Democratic Party (SDP), as well as encompassing the media and big business. In addition to its criticism of these separate actors, the leadership of HDSSB warns about their interconnectedness, signaling a certain level of elite homogeneity. Together with the homogeneity of "the people", this perceived homogeneity of the elite is an important indicator of populism as conceived by the ideational approach, reinforcing the "us" versus "them" narrative with no gray areas in between (Pauwels 2011: 100; Poblete 2015: 205). While HDZ and SDP might have policy differences, "the reign of HDZ and SDP was marked by numerous scandals, corruption has risen to intolerable level, and now they squabble, led by desire for power and a new fraud of voters" (*Glas Slavonije* 2007a). The leaders of the opposition are also portrayed as incompetent and pleasure-loving, and any possibility of a coalition with either of these two parties was strongly rejected, leaving the party in permanent opposition throughout most of its existence. The media, meanwhile, are portrayed as agents of the political elite. In an interview given on 25 May 2009, Glavaš stated that "the Croatian public does not know, thanks to the politically directed media, the kind of mafia that rules Croatia". The exact profile of the media criticized by HDSSB varies according to which party is in power, ranging from "the regime media under the control of HDZ and Ivo Sanader" (*Glas Slavonije* 2007b) to a more general qualification of the "fascistic leftist media", as Glavaš characterized some of them in a letter to HDSSB dated 29 August 2010. These statements serve as a further illustration of the chameleonic nature of populism (Taggart 2002: 70; Arter 2010: 490).

In addition to political and media elites, populists often denounce "big businesses" as elitist, both in respect of their levels of wealth and the networks they maintain with top politicians (McDonnell 2006: 128; Mudde and Kaltwasser 2013: 159). Such economic elites have served as major targets of populists in economic contexts as varied as Latin America and Western Europe. In Eastern Europe, new elites emerged in the 1990s as societies underwent traumatic periods of transition in adapting to neoliberal economic policies implemented across the region (Mudde 2000), a period characterized by the rise of the so-called "winners of transition" (Marks et al. 2006), amongst whom the privatization tycoons were the most prominent. Slavonia was mostly on the losing side of the shady Croatian privatization process, in which many of its large agricultural conglomerates went bankrupt. In a press release of 21 February 2010, HDSSB expressed a regional grudge against the "agromafia, which enjoys the protection of the Croatian government and state institutions". An MP of HDSSB, Boro Grubišić, also pointed out that corporations with links to "high" politicians were not allowing the citizens of Slavonski Brod to breathe clean air (*Glas Slavonije* 2011b), referring to the pollution from the oil refinery in the nearby Bosnian town of Bosanski Brod.

Criticism of "big business" typically extends to the European Union in populist narratives (Ivaldi, Lanzone, and Woods 2017: 360) on the basis of the claim that EU integration has led to deregulated markets, stripped people of their control over domestic politics and handed it over to capitalists. In contrast, HDSSB is surprisingly supportive of the EU and accepts globalization as given. More concretely, the party expressed support for Croatia's EU membership as well as for the idea of a "Europe of the Regions" (Hepburn 2007; Paasi 2009). There are at least two possible explanations for this position. First, the pro-EU stance of HDSSB might stem from its regionalist character, despite the party also being populist. According to research by Jolly (2007: 112), regionalist parties are typically more supportive of European integration than other parties, since integration entails a weakening of the central state and a more supportive environment for the expression of regional interests. This is an unlikely explanation for HDSSB's stance, however, given the party strong orientation in favor of Croatia's national sovereignty, even though Krešimir Bubalo pointed out in a speech of 6 April 2013 that "projects from Slavonia and Baranja meet with greater understanding and acceptance in Brussels than in Zagreb".

A more plausible explanation is that this pro-EU stance developed out of the "permissive consensus" (Hooghe and Marks 2009) that emerged among all parties in Croatia in the period prior to joining the EU (Kocijan and Kukec 2016; Raos 2016). All parties favored EU accession as a strategic goal for Croatia and a "return to Europe" to which the country had always belonged (Lindstrom 2003), as well as an opportunity for Croatia to attract financial resources from EU funds. Inter-party competition over the issue of Europe in the years before accession thus revolved around the question of who was most competent to "absorb" EU money, a capacity HDSSB claimed to possess on multiple occasions during the 2011 campaign. In its support for the EU, therefore, HDSSB stands out from the majority of other European populist parties who see Brussels as even more distant from the people than national elites.

Bringing government closer to the people

As the analysis so far has revealed, HDSSB adopts populism to amplify its grounds for demanding more extensive self-government for the region of Slavonia and Baranja. Populism is used in promoting Slavonian identity and denouncing national elites for the poverty of the region. Extending this analysis, the data was studied to ascertain whether HDSSB has other populist features.

In terms of the organizational features of the regionalist movement in Slavonia and Baranja, no additional populist features are discerned. Populist movements are often characterized by having a strong charismatic leader with a direct connection to the people that in practice overrides conventional party organization (Weyland 2001: 13; Albertazzi 2006: 136). From the outset, HDSSB was controlled by its "founder and preacher" Branimir Glavaš, even while he was serving a prison sentence in Bosnia and Herzegovina, where senior party members would visit him on a regular basis. As a splinter party of HDZ, however, HDSSB inherited a strong party organization which it has only ever further developed rather than dismantled. In addition, again contrast to some populist movements, the party has never explicitly advocated the introduction of direct democracy measures. The party's MPs, while critical of the idle and dependent colleagues of larger parties, have often stressed the homogeneity and activism of their parliamentary group.

Nonetheless, some traces of populist rhetoric can be found in the party's demands for reforms of the regional government and public finances. In addition to calling for a higher degree of self-government for Slavonia and Baranja as one of the five regions within Croatia, HDSSB advocates direct elections for regional governors and regional legislatures. The party formulates these demands as aimed at bringing the institutions of government closer to the Slavonian people, who will then finally be able to take political affairs into their own hands. In the words of the former president of HDSSB, Šišljagić:

> The high level of centralization, where one person or one party decides on the distribution of the state funds, is the cause of crime and corruption, and creates privileges for the governing party (...) This part of Croatia has the natural resources and people necessary to respond to the greatest challenges and crises and to bring economic growth with its own labor.
>
> *(Glas Slavonije 2011a).*

In particular, the party advocates transferring the Ministry of Agriculture to Osijek, the would-be capital of the envisaged region. As the economic activity in the region is strongly attached to agriculture, this would allow Slavonian farmers direct access to the Ministry and place the fate of the region's most important economic sector into the hands of its people.

In addition to demanding the territorial restructuring of the second tier of government, HDSSB calls for a fairer distribution of funds from the national budget. These economic demands are a common feature of regionalist actors, especially since complaints of imbalances in budgetary transfers among regions are raised by both richer and poorer regions. In this sense there is nothing inherently populist in the demands put forward by HDSSB. However, as suggested by Hawkins and Kaltwasser (2017: 524), populists are known for their arbitrary and unscientific economic thinking, which reflects "popular know-how and common sense" rather than rigorous economic analysis. The math employed by HDSSB in stating its long-standing demand for higher budget allocations, for example, is simplistic: "If 20 per cent of citizens live in Slavonia and Baranja, then we have the right to expect 20 per cent of the state budget" (*Glas Slavonije* 2007a). While intuitive and seemingly fair, this proposition, like the list of priorities presented to the Slavonian voters, is not grounded in any rational analysis. The "economic regionalism" of HDSSB is thus supplemented by a populist solution in addressing the problem of what would constitute a fair distribution of funds among Croatia's regions.

Conclusion

The credibility of a regionalist party's drive for more extensive self-government crucially depends on a clear differentiation between the region and the central state at societal and elite levels. However, many new regionalist parties do not emerge in pre-existing conditions favorable for establishing such a clear differentiation. In these circumstances they need to increase the salience of various separate regional narratives and grievances held by the regional population against the center and combine these into a viable electoral strategy. This chapter has described the strategy applied by a regionalist party in such circumstances to sharpen these differences by combining regionalism with elements of populism.

The Croatian region of Slavonia and Baranja is hardly the most obvious candidate for regionalist mobilization. However, the Croatian Democratic Alliance of Slavonia and Baranja (HDSSB) have skillfully exploited the raw material available to them in developing a regionalist mobilization strategy. As regionalism entails a certain degree of group consciousness, the region's identity needed to be reinvented. While Slavonians are understood to be an integral part of the Croatian people, the party has exploited narratives of the martyrdom and victimhood of Slavonian people to appeal to a common Slavonian identity, while the "economic regionalism" of HDSSB is grounded in the relative poverty of Slavonia and Baranja. At the elite level, although party leader Branimir Glavaš and his lieutenants enjoyed long careers within the governing HDZ, the largest Croatian party, they have had to portray themselves as outsiders of the political establishment in the center.

Applying the minimal concept of populism, this chapter has undertaken a qualitative content analysis of newspaper articles and party-produced literature to study the concrete application of populist rhetoric by a party seeking to amplify regionalist claims. This analysis has found that two defining dimensions of populism are present in the messages of HDSSB. First, the party refers to the Slavonian people, whom they attempt to homogenize by blurring any internal divisions among the regional population while at the same time avoiding any denial of the people's national Croatian identity in order to avoid alienating potential supporters. Rather than a separate community, Slavonia is therefore presented as the "heartland" of Croatia and the region which defended the whole nation in Croatia's war of independence. This legacy of conflict in the region has been further exploited by HDSSB in building the region's identity by holding up the Slavonian people as especially defiant and resilient. Slavonians are typically represented by the party as simple hard-working farmers who make their living from their own labor, an image that not only reflects the importance of agriculture in Slavonia but is also a commonly applied populist narrative.

The elite is presented as a combination of the political establishment, the media and "domestic traitors", all of whom are deemed corrupt and negligent of the Slavonian people. To distance themselves from HDZ, the leadership of HDSSB pits Slavonians against the central political establishment, symbolized by the former PM Ivo Sanader, who was accused of conducting a "witch hunt" against Glavaš. The party holds a particular grudge against "domestic traitors", i.e. Slavonian politicians who have sided with the Zagreb establishment for the sake of retaining their lucrative posts. Nevertheless, the party and its leadership remain loyal to the founding principles of HDZ and the first Croatian president, Franjo Tuđman, whose legacy still resonates strongly in the region of Slavonia.

The analysis once again confirms that regionalism is an ideology well adept at combining with populism, especially when a regionalist party needs to respond to a certain set of constraints. From a programmatic perspective, the synthesis between regionalism and populism is evident in the plan of bringing government closer to the people. Indeed, the key objective of HDSSB is the creation of a separate Slavonian region as one of five future Croatian regions. The separate region would have a wide array of competences, a directly elected leadership, and should be allocated at least 20 per cent of the national budget. This objective clearly resonates with the populist rhetoric of bringing the voice of the people into government. At the same time, some of the party's features do not fit with certain trends commonly found amongst populist parties and movements. For instance, HDSSB does not level criticism at the institutions of representative democracy, nor takes an anti-EU or anti-globalization stance. On the contrary, the party's parliamentary group has often emphasized that its legislative activities are aimed at the redistribution of public funds towards the region.

References

Akkerman, A., Mudde, C. and Zaslove, A. (2014) "How Populist Are the People? Measuring Populist Attitudes in Voters", *Comparative Political Studies*, 47(9), pp. 1324–53.

Albertazzi, D. (2006) "The Lega Dei Ticinesi: The Embodiment of Populism", *Politics*, 26 (2), pp. 133–39.

Albertazzi, D. and McDonnell, D. (2005) "The Lega Nord in the Second Berlusconi Government: In a League of Its Own", *West European Politics*, 28(5), pp. 952–72.

Anderson, B. (1983) *Imagined Communities. Reflections on the Origin and Spread of Nationalism.* London: Verso.

Arter, D. (2010) "The Breakthrough of Another West European Populist Radical Right Party? The Case of the True Finns", *Government and Opposition*, 45(4), pp. 484–504.

Barr, R. R. (2009) "Populists, Outsiders and Anti-Establishment Politics", *Party Politics*, 15 (1), pp. 29–48.

Bornschier, S. (2017) "Populist Mobilization Across Time and Space: An Introduction", *Swiss Political Science Review*, 23(4), pp. 301–12.

Brancati, D. (2007) "The Origins and Strengths of Regional Parties", *British Journal of Political Science*, 38(1), pp. 135–59.

Canovan, M. (2002) "Taking Politics to the People: Populism as the Ideology Of Democracy". In: Meny, Y. and Surel, Y. (eds.) *Democracies and the Populist Challenge*. New York: Palgrave Macmillan, pp. 25–44.

Dandoy, R. (2010) "Ethno-Regionalist Parties in Europe: A Typology", *Perspectives on Federalism*, 2(2), pp. 194–220.

Dandoy, R. and Sandri, G. (2007) "Regionalism and Party Programs: Comparative Analysis of the Content of the Manifestos of Regionalist Parties in Europe". Paper presented at the *Società Italiana di Scienza Politica Conference*, Catania.
De Winter, L. (1998) "Conclusion: A Comparative Analysis of the Electoral, Office and Policy Success of Ethno-regionalist Parties". In: De Winter, L. and Tursan, H. (eds.) *Regionalist Parties in Western Europe*. London: Routledge, pp. 204–47.
Fitjar, R. D. (2010) "Explaining Variation in Sub-State Regional Identities in Western Europe", *European Journal of Political Research*, 49(4), pp. 522–44.
Fitjar, R. D. (2013) "Region-Building in the Arctic Periphery: The Discursive Construction of a Petroleum Region", *Geografiska Annaler*, Series B, pp.71–88.
Forman, J. and Damschroder, L. (2008) "Qualitative Content Analysis". In: Jacoby, L. and Siminoff, L. A. (eds.) *Empirical Methods For Bioethics: A Primer*. Oxford: Elsevier, pp. 39–62.
Glas Slavonije (2005a) "Ugledni građani zajedno za jaku i razvijenu Slavoniju i Baranju", 21 April.
Glas Slavonije (2005b) "Glavaš na izbore kao nezavisni, HDZ sinoć sastavio nove liste", 22 April.
Glas Slavonije (2005c) "Burićevi 'nezavisni' za Glavaša", 29 April.
Glas Slavonije (2005d) "Glavaš pozvao na zaboravljanje razmirica u interesu Slavonije", 29 April.
Glas Slavonije (2005e) "Ivan Drmić: Regionalizacija nije autonomaštvo", 6 May.
Glas Slavonije (2005f) "Vrijeme je za promjene", 13 May.
Glas Slavonije (2007a) "Bubalo: HDZ-u i SDP-u ne odgovara regionalna opcija", 6 November.
Glas Slavonije (2007b) "Nevenka Mesić laže", 9 November.
Glas Slavonije (2007c) "Između Sabora i Osijeka biram Osijek", 17 November.
Glas Slavonije (2011a) "Vladimir Šišljagić: Jake regije pokrenut će razvoj cijele Hrvatske", 26 November.
Glas Slavonije (2011b) "Misli hrvatski, djeluj slavonski", 28 November.
Glas Slavonije (2011c) "U Slavoniji gdje se stvarala Hrvatska moramo vratiti ponos hrvatskom narodu", 28 November.
Grgin, B. (2003) "The Ottoman Influences on Croatia in the Second Half of the Fifteenth Century", *Historical Contributions*, 23(23), pp. 87–102.
Hawkins, K. A. (2009) "Is Chavez Populist?: Measuring Populist Discourse in Comparative Perspective", *Comparative Political Studies*, 42(8), pp. 1040–67.
Hawkins, K. A. and Kaltwasser, C. R. (2017) "The Ideational Approach to Populism", *Latin American Research Review*, 52(4), pp. 513–28.
HDSSB (2012) *Program Hrvatskog Demokratskog Saveza Slavonije i Baranje*. www.hdssb.hr/index.php/component/content/article/83-o-nama/97-program-rada-hdssb-a.
Hechter, M. (1973) "The Persistence of Regionalism in the British Isles, 1885–1966", *American Journal of Sociology*, 79(2), pp. 319–42.
Hepburn, E. (2007) "The Rise and Fall of a 'Europe of the Regions': The Territorial Strategies of Substate Political Parties 1979–2006". Paper presented at the *European Union Studies Association (EUSA) Annual Conference*, Montreal.
Holjevac, Ž. (2006) "Vojna Krajina u Hrvatskom Identitetu". In: Marinović, M. (ed.) *Povijesno Nasljeđe i Nacionalni Identiteti*. Zagreb: Zavod za školstvo Republike Hrvatske, pp. 101–11.
Hooghe, L. and Marks, G. (2009) "A Postfunctionalist Theory of European Integration: From Permissive Consensus to Constraining Dissensus", *British Journal of Political Science*, 39(1), pp. 1–23.

Inglehart, R. and Norris, P. (2016). "Trump, Brexit, and the Rise of Populism: Economic Have-Nots and Cultural Backlash". In: *Faculty Research Working Paper No. RWP16-026*, John F. Kennedy School of Government. Cambridge, MA: Harvard University, pp. 1–52.

Ivaldi, G., Lanzone, M. E. and Woods, D. (2017) "Varieties of Populism Across a Left-Right Spectrum: The Case of the Front National, the Northern League, Podemos and Five Star Movement", *Swiss Political Science Review*, 23(4), pp. 354–376.

Jagers, J. and Walgrave, S. (2007) "Populism as Political Communication Style: An Empirical Study of Political Parties' Discourse in Belgium", *European Journal of Political Research*, 46(3), pp. 319–345.

Jolly, S. K. (2007) "The Europhile Fringe?: Regionalist Party Support for European Integration", *European Union Politics*, 8(1), pp. 109–130.

Kocijan, B. and Kukec, M. (2016) "From Hard Consensus to Soft Euroscepticism: Attitudes of Croatian MPs on EU Integration", *Historical Social Research*, 41(4), pp. 38–60.

Kopric, I. (2010) "Karakteristike Sustava Lokalne Samouprave u Hrvatskoj", *Hrvatska javna uprava*, 10(2), pp. 371–386.

Kriesi, H. (2014) "The Populist Challenge", *West European Politics*, 37(2), pp. 361–378.

Lindstrom, N. (2003) "Between Europe and the Balkans: Mapping Slovenia and Croatia's 'Return to Europe' in the 1990s", *Dialectical Anthropology*, 27(3–4), pp. 313–329.

Marks, G., Hooghe, L., Nelson, M. and Edwards, E. (2006) "Party Competition in the East and West: Different Structure, Same Causality", *Comparative Political Studies*, 39(2), pp. 155–175.

Massetti, E. and Schakel, A. H. (2015) "From Class to Region: How Regionalist Parties Link (and Subsume) Left-Right into Centre-Periphery Politics", *Party Politics*, 21(6), pp. 866–886.

McDonnell, D. (2006) "A Weekend in Padania: Regionalist Populism and the Lega Nord", *Politics*, 26(2), pp. 126–132.

Meny, Y. and Surel, Y. (eds.) (2002a) *Democracies and the Populist Challenge*. New York: Palgrave Macmillan.

Meny, Y. and Surel, Y. (2002b) "The Constitutive Ambiguity of Populism". In: Meny, Y. and Surel, Y. (eds.) *Democracies and the Populist Challenge*. New York: Palgrave Macmillan, pp. 1–21.

Mudde, C. (2000) "In the Name of the Peasantry, the Proletariat, and the People: Populisms in Eastern Europe", *East European Politics and Societies*, 14(2), pp. 33–53.

Mudde, C. (2004) "The Populist Zeitgeist", *Government and Opposition*, 39(4), pp. 541–63.

Mudde, C. and Kaltwasser, C. R. (2013) "Exclusionary vs. Inclusionary Populism: Comparing Contemporary Europe and Latin America", *Government and Opposition*, 48(2), pp. 147–74.

Paasi, A. (2009) "The Resurgence of the 'Region' and 'Regional Identity': Theoretical Perspectives and Empirical Observations on Regional Dynamics in Europe", *Review of International Studies*, 35(S1), pp. 121–46.

Pauwels, T. (2011) "Measuring Populism: A Quantitative Text Analysis of Party Literature in Belgium", *Journal of Elections, Public Opinion and Parties*, 21(1), pp. 97–119.

Poblete, M. E. (2015) "How to Assess Populist Discourse through Three Current Approaches", *Journal of Political Ideologies*, 20(2), pp. 201–18.

Raos, V. (2016) "Transformation of the Croatian Party System in the Process of EU Accession". In: Maldini, P. and Pauković, D. (eds.) *Croatia and the European Union: Changes and Development*. London: Routledge, pp. 159–75.

Rooduijn, M. (2014) "The Nucleus of Populism: In Search of the Lowest Common Denominator", *Government and Opposition*, 49(4), pp. 572–98.

Rooduijn, M. and Pauwels, T. (2011) "Measuring Populism: Comparing Two Methods of Content Analysis", *West European Politics*, 34(6), pp. 1272–83.

Schneider, A. (2003) "Decentralization: Conceptualization and Measurement", *Studies in Comparative International Development*, 38(3), pp. 32–56.

Schultz, A. et al. (2018) "Measuring Populist Attitudes on Three Dimensions", *International Journal of Public Opinion Research*, 30(2), pp. 316–326.

Smoljan, J. (2010) "Socio-Economic Aspects of Peacebuilding: Untaes and the Organisation of Employment in Eastern Slavonia", *International Peacekeeping*, 10(2), pp. 27–50.

Taggart, P. (2002) "Populism and the Pathology of Representative Politics". In: Mény, Y. and Surel, Y. (eds.) *Democracies and the Populist Challenge*. New York: Palgrave Macmillan, pp. 62–80.

Türsan, H. (1998) "Introduction: Ethno-regionalist Parties as Ethnic Entrepreneurs". In: De Winter, L. and Türsan, H. (eds.) *Regionalist Parties in Western Europe*. London: Routledge, pp. 1–16.

Weyland, K. (2001) "Clarifying a Contested Concept: Populism in the Study of Latin American Politics", *Comparative Politics*, 34(1), pp. 1–22.

White, M. D. and Marsh, E. E. (2006) "Content Analysis: A Flexible Methodology", *Library Trends*, 55(1), pp. 22–45.

11
ETHNIC POLITICS AND COMPETITION BETWEEN RIGHT-WING POPULIST PARTIES IN HUNGARY

Edina Szöcsik

Introduction

The success of radical right-wing populist parties can only be understood with reference to issues and policies surrounding ethnic minorities. Nativism is the central ideological feature of such parties, according to which the nation-state should ideally be inhabited exclusively by members of the native group, since non-native persons and ideas are perceived as a threat to that state (Mudde 2007: 22). Immigrants, as well as autochthonous minorities, are undesirable and must not be allowed to challenge the prerogatives of natives. The policies on immigration and the rights of minorities generated by this nativist ideology have proven key to the successful mobilization and electoral entry of radical right populist parties (e.g. Rydgren 2005; Bustikova 2014). The literature has explored the consequences of the success of these parties on Hungary's immigration and integration policies, including the programs of other parties. Scholarly debate focuses both on the *direct* influence of radical right populist parties on immigration and integration policies through the inclusion of such parties in government (e.g. Akkerman 2012), as well as their *indirect* influence as a consequence of their impact on the behavior of their mainstream competitors.[1] Some scholars argue that mainstream parties have significantly adjusted their behavior when radical right populist parties have become an electoral threat (Bale et al. 2010; van Spanje 2010; Han 2015; Abou-Chadi 2016), while others argue that the impact of radical right populist parties has been overstated (Mudde 2013; Akkerman 2015; Meyer and Rosenberger 2015).

This chapter explores competition in the field of ethnic minority politics between two Hungarian right-wing parties, Jobbik ("The Movement for a Better Hungary") and Fidesz ("Fidesz – Hungarian Civic Alliance"), in the period 2010–2014. In Hungary, two ethnic minority groups stand out in terms of their political importance: the Roma minority and the various minority populations of Hungarians in states outside Hungary. The Roma constitute the largest ethnic minority group in Hungary, comprising approximately 7.5 per cent of the total population. As well as suffering widespread social discrimination and a lack of social integration, Roma are poorly represented politically. While other national and ethnic minority groups within Hungary comprise only 1 per cent or less of the Hungarian population, there are large Hungarian minorities present in Slovakia and Romania, as well as smaller but substantial minorities in Serbia, Ukraine and Croatia. These external Hungarian minorities have a historical home base and have formulated territorial and cultural demands addressed to the central governments of their respective countries. The number of immigrants and asylum seekers in Hungary has historically been very low except during the wars in the Balkans of the early 1990s. In the summer of 2014, however, a large number of refugees arrived at the southern borders of Hungary, and immigration and asylum have become increasingly politicized in Hungarian politics since early 2015. This study focuses on the period 2010–2014 and does not cover the most recent political developments.

Jobbik entered the Hungarian Parliament for the first time in the national elections of 2010 with a vote share of 16.7 per cent. The anti-Roma and populist appeal of Jobbik played a central role in this electoral breakthrough (Karácsony and Róna 2011). The winner of the 2010 elections was Fidesz, which won a landslide victory in an electoral coalition with KDNP (the Christian Democratic People's Party), receiving 52.7 per cent of the votes. In Hungary's highly disproportional mixed-electoral system, this vote share translated into more than two-thirds of all parliamentary seats. With such a majority, Fidesz and its junior partner KDNP had the power to amend the constitution without the support of the opposition. In the struggle for power between left and right, these results signified a strong shift to the right. This shift was the outcome not only of the increased electoral share of right-wing populist parties and the advent of a strong new right-wing populist government with a new radical right populist party in opposition, however, but also of the ideological radicalization of Fidesz.

While researchers have noted that the mainstream right party Fidesz became an increasingly populist and strongly nationalist party after 2002,[2] the electoral entry of Jobbik raises the question of whether it was Jobbik's success that fueled the radicalization of Fidesz. Political pundits and scholars have argued that Jobbik managed to influence policy formulation and supported the radicalization of Fidesz (Pytlas and Kossack 2015: 113–115; Minkenberg 2017: 130–142). According to these scholars, Fidesz was compelled to accommodate Jobbik's policy demands because Jobbik presented an electoral threat for Fidesz from the right. Indeed, 37 per cent of Jobbik voters in the 2010 elections had previously voted for Fidesz (Karácsony and Róna 2011).[3] Fidesz, it is argued, therefore implemented a number of Jobbik's most important policy goals, either directly or in a slightly watered-down version. As evidence of this influence, scholars cite the similarities between the policy proposals in Jobbik electoral program of

2010 and the policies implemented by Fidesz between 2010 and 2014 (Bíró-Nagy et al. 2013; Róna 2014: 151–183; Krekó and Mayer 2015: 192; Political Capital 2015; Bíró-Nagy and Boros 2016; Böcskei and Molnár 2016; Enyedi 2016: 12; Minkenberg 2017: 138). There has been no comprehensive and exhaustive study of this influence to date, but there are numerous relevant examples in a variety of policy fields.

This chapter explores Jobbik's impact on Fidesz with regard to the issues of the external Hungarian minorities and the internal Roma minority. In doing so it draws a distinction between the parties' discourses and their actual policies, on the basis that discourses and policies are two independent dimensions of parties' electoral strategies. The aim is to identify and evaluate the similarities and differences between the discourses and policies of the two parties and whether these converged or diverged from each other in the period under analysis. This comparative analysis draws on party manifestos, party press releases and parliamentary debates, as well as the speeches of the two charismatic party leaders, Gábor Vona of Jobbik and Viktor Orbán of Fidesz, since these leaders dominated the directions and public image of their respective parties in this period. In the case of Jobbik it is also necessary to include other members of the party leadership, since Vona became increasingly associated with a moderation process in the party that was not unequivocally supported by the party leadership.

On the one hand, analysis shows that the longstanding commitment of Fidesz to improving the situation of external Hungarian minorities, including the introduction of dual citizenship with voting rights, proved electorally rewarding in the 2014 elections, in which many members of external Hungarian minorities participated in the Hungarian elections for the first time and overwhelmingly supported Fidesz. While Jobbik pursued a similar discourse and proposed similar policies, it was unable to challenge the loyalty of external Hungarian communities to Fidesz. On the other hand, Jobbik's mobilization of anti-Roma sentiment was one of the main reasons for its electoral breakthrough in 2010, gaining its greatest support in counties in north-eastern Hungary with large Roma minorities. Although Fidesz denounced Jobbik's anti-Roma prejudices, it nevertheless implemented several policies first proposed by Jobbik. Fidesz's strategy proved unsuccessful, however, in challenging Jobbik's electoral strongholds in north-eastern Hungary in the 2014 elections. Accordingly, this chapter argues that it was the competition dynamics between these two state-wide right-wing populist parties in the field of minority politics that resulted in their regionally different patterns of electoral success.

The chapter is structured as follows. The first section discusses the debate on the impact of the success of populist radical right parties on the behavior of mainstream parties, differentiating between two stances in the literature as to the nature and extent of this impact, i.e. one group of scholars argue that mainstream parties have adjusted their behavior in response to their radical right populist challengers, while another group claim that the impact of radical right populist parties has been overstated. The second section of the paper outlines the role of minority groups in the discourses and policies of radical right populist parties. The third section presents an overview of Fidesz and Jobbik and discusses the driving forces behind their electoral successes in the elections of 2010. The fourth section presents the findings of the analysis of the discourse and policies of the two parties with regard to external Hungarian minorities, while the fifth section presents the findings related to the Roma minority, leading to the overall conclusion of the chapter.

The impact of radical right populist challenger parties on their mainstream competitors

One of the most pressing questions related to the consequences of the success of radical right populist parties is whether and in which ways they have an impact on the behavior of their mainstream competitors. Do radical right populist parties have a "contagious" impact, compelling their mainstream competitors to shift their positions on core issues closer to the positions of radical right populist parties? Do such parties increase the salience of their core issues in the programs of mainstream parties? And finally, do mainstream parties more broadly adapt their own discourses on these core issues to the discourses of radical right parties?

In the context of Western European political parties, different answers to these questions have emerged. One group of scholars has argued that radical right populist success has caused mainstream parties to adjust their behavior. One reason for this, it is argued, is that by emphasizing issues such as immigration and nationalism, which are related to the cultural values dimension in the two-dimensional post-industrial political space, radical right populist parties present a fundamental challenge to their mainstream competitors, who mainly emphasize issues related to an economic left-right dimension (Abou-Chadi and Krause 2018). In the literature on niche parties, it has been shown that when radical right populist parties present an electoral threat, mainstream parties have an incentive to shift their position towards the position of radical right populist parties (Meguid 2005). By adapting in this way, mainstream parties seek to seize ownership of the issues that radical right parties emphasize. By challenging radical right populist parties' ownership of these issues, mainstream parties hope to win back votes – and even win new voters – from their radical right populist challengers. In her work on niche political parties, Bonnie Meguid (2005) calls this an "accommodative strategy", and her research shows that when mainstream parties have moved closer to the position of radical right parties on their core issues, the outcome has resulted in reduced electoral success for radical right parties. Several cross-country studies have found that mainstream parties do adjust their positions, specifically with regard to immigration, integration and multiculturalism (Bale et al. 2010; van Spanje 2010; Han 2015; Abou-Chadi 2016; Abou-Chadi and Krause 2018), as well as more broadly on cultural aspects (Minkenberg 2001; Wagner and Meyer 2017). These studies show that the mainstream right and left are both affected by the success of the radical right, although the effects are (slightly) more pronounced for parties of the mainstream right.

A second group of scholars have questioned the impact of radical right populist parties on the behavior of their competitors (Akkerman 2015; Meyer and Rosenberger 2015). For example, Mudde (2013: 8–9) has argued that assessments of the impact of radical right populist parties on the behavior of mainstream parties have overstated this impact. Radical right populist parties, according to this view, have no impact on their left-wing competitors and only a limited impact on their right-wing competitors, mostly in relation to the issue of immigration control but not to the issue of integration. Furthermore, although radical right populist parties may increase the salience of immigration issues, they have not forced their competitors to change their actual policy positions, even if these competitors increasingly borrow elements from the discourse of radical right populist parties. Similarly, Akkerman (2015) has argued that while immigration has become a salient political issue in most European democracies, this development cannot be attributed to the success of the radical right. For example, van Heerden et al. (2014) have argued that mainstream parties competed over this issue even before there was a successful radical right party in the Netherlands.

A similar debate has emerged about the consequences of the success of radical right populist parties in Eastern Europe, although the context of this success in that region differs to some extent. An important difference between party competition in Eastern Europe and Western Europe is that inter-party competition in many Eastern European countries is dominated by socio-cultural issues. A second difference is that the issue of immigration was not politicized in Eastern Europe until the recent refugee crisis; rather, it is the issue of national minorities that has played the central role in the mobilization of radical right populist parties in Eastern Europe (Bustikova 2014). Despite these contextual differences, Minkenberg (2017: 130–142) has argued that the mechanisms underlying the contagious impact of radical right populist parties are the same in Eastern Europe and that the "radical right's effect occurred primarily in shifting the overall political agenda to the right in the dimension of identity politics" (Minkenberg 2017: 134). In a comparative study of the impact of radical right populist parties in Eastern Europe, Pytlas and Kossack (2015) have argued that mainstream parties on the right not only shift their positions concerning identity-related issues but also co-opt the narrative frames of radical right populist parties.

In this study I focus on the question of whether a formerly mainstream right-wing party adjusted its discourse and policies on ethnic minorities when challenged by an electorally successful radical right populist party. I concentrate on the issues of ethnic minorities, since these played a central role in the mobilization strategies of radical right populist parties in Hungary and other Eastern Europe states. Accordingly, I postulate that mainstream parties are most likely to adjust their behavior to that of radical right populist parties regarding issues related to ethnic minorities. In the following section, I outline the important role of national and ethnic minorities in the ideology of right-wing populist parties.

Minorities in the discourse of right-wing populist parties

The discourse of radical right-wing populist parties combines populism, nationalism, and nativism. The thin ideology of populism separates society into two homogeneous and mutually antagonistic groups: "the pure people" versus "the corrupt elite" (Mudde 2004). Each group has shared feelings and interests, and the distinction between them is drawn on a moral basis, with populist actors claiming to express the will of the people in their discourse and accusing elites of betraying the people. Nationalism as a political doctrine "strives for the congruence of the political and the cultural unit, i.e. the nation and the state" (Mudde 2007: 16). Every nationalist discourse revolves around the question of who is and who is not a member of the nation (i.e. who is *in* or *out*) and the opposition between the nation and its out-groups (De Cleen 2017). Populist and nationalist discourses partially overlap in conceiving of "the people" as the nation, i.e. as a "culturally and ethnically bounded collectivity with a shared and distinctive way of life" (Brubaker 2017: 362). A central feature of right-wing populist discourse is thus the exclusion of "others", i.e. of groups who do not belong to the nation (Kriesi and Pappas 2015: 5). As a result, the discourse of right-wing populist parties combines a vertical opposition between the people and the elite and a horizontal opposition between "the people" and outside groups, i.e. those who do not belong to the nation, including those forces that threaten the nation. Right-wing populist parties link these two oppositions in their discourses by blaming domestic or national elites for prioritizing or privileging those who do not belong to the nation while ignoring the problems of the people or nation (Brubaker 2017: 363–364). A core belief and concern of nativism is the idea that elites and the state should serve on behalf of the nation, and that those who belong to the nation should enjoy prerogatives over those who are not part of the people and the nation. According to nativist ideology, the state would ideally be inhabited exclusively by members of the native group, since non-native persons and ideas are perceived as a threat to the nation-state (Mudde 2007: 22). As Mudde argues (2007: 22), nativism is an aggressive form of nationalism that constitutes the key ideology of radical right populist parties. Given this core nativist ideology, such parties conceive of immigrants and ethnic and national minorities as out-groups in their discourses and promote measures to restrict the rights of these minorities in their policies.

The context of the electoral success of Fidesz and Jobbik in 2010

Fidesz emerged in 1988 as a youth party with a radical liberal and strongly anti-communist profile. The party has been represented in the Hungarian Parliament ever since the country's first free elections were held in 1990 and has since been in power three times (1998–2002, 2010–2014, 2014–present). Over time, the ideological orientation of Fidesz has changed profoundly. In the early 1990s it re-established itself as a center-right party (Enyedi 2005; Waterbury 2006: 490–494). This shift to the ideological center paid off when Fidesz won the elections in 1998. After Fidesz went into opposition in 2002, however, Viktor Orbán strengthened his position in the party as the ideological course of Fidesz became radicalized. Orbán set about transforming Fidesz into a mass movement beyond the parliamentary arena, organizing so-called "Citizens' Circles" (polgári körök) for the mobilization of his followers (Krekó and Mayer 2015: 188).

Jobbik is a much younger party than Fidesz, both as an organization and in terms of the age of its party base. It was formed by students as a youth association in Budapest in 1999. Some prominent members of Jobbik had been members of the far-right Hungarian Justice and Life Party (MIÉP), while others had ties to Fidesz. When Orbán initiated the establishment of civic circles in 2002, he personally invited the participation of Gábor Vona, who later became the Jobbik party president. Vona was also the head of Fidesz's student section at that time (Krekó and Juhász 2017: 95–96). Fidesz's electoral loss and the failure of MIÉP to gain seats in parliament in 2002 motivated Jobbik's leadership to form their own party a year later. The goal was to build a modern party to represent a radical right-wing position in Hungarian politics. Jobbik justified its abstention from the European parliamentary elections in 2004 as a means of showing its opposition to the conditions Hungary was obliged to fulfill in order to access the EU. In the national elections of 2006, Jobbik participated in an electoral coalition with MIÉP. Cooperation between the two parties ended, however, when they won only 2.2 per cent of the votes and failed to gain parliamentary representation. In 2009, Jobbik managed to enter the European Parliament on its own with a vote share of 14.8 per cent, and in 2010 it gained representation in the Hungarian Parliament with 16.7 per cent of the votes.

Jobbik's supporter base is made up mainly of young male voters. Jobbik does not mobilize the very lowest socio-economic class, but rather those who still have something to lose.[4] Voters who sympathize with Jobbik tend to be more nationalistic and more strongly opposed to immigrants, the Roma minority, the elite, and the project of European integration, while also seeking to revise the borders of Hungary (Bíró-Nagy and Róna 2011: 270). Jobbik's voters predominantly live in towns and villages. While Jobbik is a state-wide party, it has regional strongholds in the counties of north-eastern Hungary where living standards are lower and the proportion of the Roma population is highest compared with other counties (Bartlett et al. 2012: 24). In contrast to these counties where Jobbik received more than 20 per cent, in Budapest the party received its lowest vote share, with 10.1 per cent of the votes in the elections of 2010 (Bíró-Nagy and Róna 2011: 267).

The landslide victory of Fidesz and the electoral entry of Jobbik were both driven by the political and economic crises that occurred in the period 2006–2010 (Enyedi 2015: 249). Just a few months after the elections in 2006, a speech of the re-elected socialist prime minister, Ferenc Gyurcsány, was leaked, revealing that he had claimed his government had lied about the state of the economy in the election campaign. Riots broke out in the capital, and the space in front of the Parliament was occupied for two weeks with the symbolic support of Fidesz politicians. The upheaval peaked on October 23, the anniversary of the 1956 anti-communist revolution, when Orbán called for a large demonstration of his followers. The demonstration escalated as extremist rioters clashed with the police and succeeded in drawing violent police into the peaceful crowd of Orbán's demonstration, with the result that peaceful Orbán followers were beaten up by the police. The 2006 riots were crucial for Jobbik too, enabling radical right extremist rioters to present themselves as victims of Gyurcsány's "dictatorial police state" (Krekó and Mayer 2015: 190). The brutality of the police against the protestors further eroded the political authority of the socialist-liberal government coalition. Two years later, the financial crisis of 2008 hit Hungary particularly severely. Hungary became the first country to require help from the IMF, signing a stability package in October 2008. Austerity measures fueled public discontent and further undermined support for the government. The combination of these political and economic crises led to alienation and strong anti-elite sentiments.

These sentiments in society were addressed by Fidesz and Jobbik through a common set of populist narratives and a similar construction of the crisis of the socialist-liberal government (Krekó and Mayer 2015). Both parties argued that the crisis of the post-communist government was a symptom of "insufficient" transition, which ended the communist regime in 1989 but failed to bring about a fundamental change in the political game.[5] Fidesz claimed that the transition had been stolen by the former communist elite still represented by MSZP, the post-communist successor party, as well as by international capital (Krekó and Mayer 2015: 186). Both parties criticized the international establishment and its domestic supporters for upholding cosmopolitan and liberal attitudes that did not serve Hungarian interests. The foreign-minded actors that comprised this elite include, among others, "Brussels", "Washington", foreign-owned multinational companies and international civil society actors. Both parties equate the left with liberalism, which they claim is conspiring against the Hungarian nation (Krekó and Mayer 2015). They criticize the West for not acknowledging that multiculturalism erodes the Christian roots of Europe and Hungary and leads to the decline of nation-states (Enyedi 2016). While both parties share these elements of populist discourse, Jobbik has sought to portray Fidesz as a party of the establishment, accusing Fidesz and MSZP of exploiting the transition for their own corrupt interests.

External Hungarian minorities as an integral part of the Hungarian nation

Hungary is one of the most ethnically homogenous countries in Eastern Europe. At the same time, there remain large Hungarian communities in Romania and Slovakia, as well as smaller communities in Croatia, Serbia and the Ukraine. These Hungarian minorities lived in the territory of the Hungarian Crown before the First World War. With the defeat and dissolution of the Dual Monarchy of Austria-Hungary, Hungary lost two-thirds of its territories, and one-third of ethnic Hungarians suddenly found themselves outside of the borders of Hungary after the Treaty of Trianon of 1920.

The Hungarian right consider "Trianon"[6] a national tragedy, and the fate of the Hungarian external minorities had become a central concern for the national-conservative wing of the emerging democratic opposition already by the end of the 1980s. Prime Minister Antall, who headed the first freely elected national-conservative government in 1990, declared himself the prime minister of 15 million Hungarians "in spirit" (Waterbury 2006: 488). He thus understood himself not only as the prime minister of the 10.5 million Hungarians living in Hungary, but also of the external Hungarian minority communities in neighboring countries and of the Hungarian diaspora scattered throughout the world.

When Fidesz came to government in 1998, it pursued a more active and even aggressive diaspora policy than either the previous left-wing government or the first national-conservative government. In its governing program it stated that it intended to create an "organic relationship of Hungarian communities to the motherland even after EU accession" and made clear that its goal was "unification without border revisions" (Waterbury 2006: 497). The Fidesz government extended financial assistance to a number of cultural and political organizations of external Hungarian minorities to support the survival and reproduction of Hungarian communities in their home countries, providing considerably more assistance than the previous Hungarian government.

The Fidesz government also became closely involved in the political affairs of Hungarian minority parties and organizations. The development of the Status Law in 2001 was the culmination of Fidesz's extensive client-building and co-opting of ethnic Hungarian organizations. This piece of legislation granted special benefits and subsidies, mainly in the realm of culture but also including temporary labor permits to members of external Hungarian communities. To receive these benefits, individuals had to apply for an ethnic identity card (officially called a "Certificate of Hungarian Nationality") so that they could be recognized as members of the Hungarian "nation". The adoption of the Status Law created considerable tensions both between Hungary and its neighboring countries and between Hungary and the EU. Neighboring countries argued that the privileged access of ethnic Hungarians to Hungary's labor market and education system was discriminatory against non-ethnic Hungarian citizens. Criticism also came from within Hungary and from external Hungarian communities, pointing out that the Status Law created dependencies and encouraged paternalism, thereby undermining the self-governing projects undertaken by Hungarian minority communities (Waterbury 2006: 504). During the years in which Fidesz was out of power and in opposition, between 2002 and 2008, it continued to mobilize around the issue of external Hungarian minorities and supported a popular initiative for introducing dual citizenship for members of external Hungarian minorities.

A vote on this initiative was held in 2004 and received a slight majority of 51.6 per cent. The initiative failed, however, since turnout did not reach the threshold of 25 per cent of all votes.

Even before the emergence of Jobbik, then, the issue of the external Hungarian minorities had played a central role in Fidesz's nationalist ideology, discourse and nation-building policies. When Fidesz regained executive power in 2010 it almost immediately submitted a law (after only three days of taking office) offering dual citizenship in combination with voting rights without residence requirements for Hungarians living in neighboring countries. By autumn 2013, more than 525,000 people had applied for Hungarian citizenship (Hungarian Ministry of Public Administration and Justice 2013). Fidesz also passed a law declaring June 4 to be an annual "Day of National Unity" to commemorate the Treaty of Trianon. The new constitution adopted in 2011 neatly illustrates Fidesz's conceptualization of the Hungarian nation and the duties the Hungarian state should perform, as shown in the following excerpt from Article D of the new constitution:

> Bearing in mind that there is one single Hungarian nation that belongs together, Hungary shall bear responsibility for the fate of Hungarians living beyond its borders, shall facilitate the survival and development of their communities, shall support their efforts to preserve their Hungarian identity, the effective use of their individual and collective rights, the establishment of their community self-governments, and their prosperity in their native lands, and shall promote their cooperation with each other and with Hungary.[7]
>
> *(Hungarian Government 2011)*

The issue of the external Hungarian minorities was also essential for Jobbik. In its foundational document, Jobbik describes its self-conception as follows:

> The Jobbik Movement for Better Hungary is a national party; its political foundation relies on the protection of national values and interests. This is why we stand up against the increasingly open intention to eliminate the nation as the primal community of human life. In the age of globalization and consumerism, it is increasingly pressing that we build one nation of Hungarians living in the torn-away territories so that we strengthen our national feeling of belonging – in and outside the borders – and that we familiarize the coming generation with the vital energy of our national identity.
>
> *(Jobbik 2003)*

As this excerpt shows, a central goal of the party is to strengthen the Hungarian nation, which it argues can only be achieved by strengthening ties with Hungarians beyond the borders. Jobbik's policy proposals on the issue of the external

Hungarian minorities resembled the policies of Fidesz (Jobbik 2010: 55–58). As in the case of Fidesz, it promoted the adoption of dual citizenship without residence requirements for ethnic Hungarians beyond the borders. It also supported the cultural and economic reunion of the Hungarian nation and the establishment of self-governing institutions for Hungarian communities abroad. Perhaps the most aggressive policy idea that Jobbik presented in its electoral program was the demand that Hungary should become the protector state of Hungarian minorities abroad, following the example of Austria and the German minorities in South Tyrol (Jobbik 2010: 57). However, it did not expand on this idea in its electoral program.

To summarize these findings, both Fidesz and Jobbik consider the external Hungarian minorities to be part of the Hungarian nation, and therefore the goals of strengthening the linkages between the Hungarian state and unifying the external Hungarian minorities have been important for both parties. However, neither the discourse nor the policies of Fidesz have changed since the electoral entry of Jobbik. As a right-wing challenger party, Jobbik could not easily question Fidesz's credibility on this issue, nor could it easily outbid Fidesz with more extreme demands, since Fidesz has had a long track record of internationally controversial policies regarding external Hungarian minorities. As a result, Jobbik was not able to successfully challenge Fidesz's ownership of the issue of external Hungarian minorities, as is shown by the overwhelming political support for Fidesz among members of these communities. Following the introduction in 2011 of dual citizenship with voting rights, 128,000 members of Hungarian external minorities participated in the elections of 2014, and 95 per cent of them voted for Fidesz (Republikon Intézet 2014: 19).

The Roma minority: a threat, a burden, or a hidden asset?

According to the results of the Hungarian census held in 2011, Roma comprise 3.2 per cent of the Hungarian population, with approximately 315,000 people self-reporting themselves as Roma (Hungarian Central Statistical Office 2013). These numbers may underestimate the size of the Roma minority, however, since many Roma choose not to identify as such on account of the stigma associated with that identity. The Council of Europe has estimated the actual size of the Roma population to be between 500,000–1,000,000, amounting to 7.5 per cent of the Hungarian population as of 2012 (Council of Europe 2012). The overwhelming majority of Roma speak only Hungarian, and only a small number are bilingual. The Roma minority differs from other ethnic minorities in Hungary in multiple ways (see Schafft and Kulcsár 2015: 554–555). First, the Roma comprise by far the largest of the thirteen officially recognized minorities in Hungary, outnumbering all other groups combined. Second, the Roma minority is characterized by a high level of internal diversity, comprising at least three main groups: the Vlach Roma, who speak a dialect of Romani; the Boyash Roma, who speak a dialect of Romanian; and Hungarian-speaking

Roma who refer to themselves as Romungro. Third, the Roma are not of European origin, having arrived in Hungary between the fourteenth and fifteenth centuries from northern India, which they had left in the sixth century. As a consequence, the Roma are a stateless minority and do not have a historic homeland; nor do they have a kin state that could protect their interests. Finally, the Roma have suffered a history of political and socio-economic exclusion in Hungary and throughout Europe.

In the period of socialism in Hungary, the Roma were not recognized as an ethnic minority (Kállai 2005: 15). The Hungarian Socialist Working People's Party tackled the "Gypsy question" as a poverty issue and sought to ameliorate the socio-economic grievances of the Roma through paternalistic policies of assimilation (Schafft and Kulcsár 2015: 560). Industrialization in the 1960s and early 1970s provided job opportunities and steady incomes for many Roma. The housing situation of the Roma minority improved, and the integration of Roma children in the educational system was supported. While these efforts enhanced the socio-economic well-being of many Roma, they also reinforced the cultural assimilation of Roma and reproduced severe inequalities between Roma and non-Roma in Hungarian society. According to Schafft and Kulcsár (2015: 560), a widely shared perception has emerged in non-Roma society that while the state provides significant resources to help the Roma, the Roma themselves have personal traits that are not amendable to succeeding in society. For example, the stereotype of "lazy and unemployed Gypsies" continues to be widespread in public discourse.

The impacts of Hungary's post-socialist transformation were especially severe for the Roma. While the Roma population became to some extent more urbanized between the 1970s and 1980s, the majority still live in villages and regions where the impacts of economic transition, including the collapse of agriculture and industry, have been particularly harsh (Schafft and Kulcsár 2015: 562–563). The gap between the socio-economic status of Roma and non-Roma widened significantly in the early 1990s.

Hungary's first national-conservative government addressed the problems of the Roma minority as an ethnic group with a culture distinct from the Hungarian majority society and in need of protection. The Roma were recognized as an ethnic minority among twelve other national and ethnic minorities officially in the 1993 Act on the Rights of National and Ethnic Minorities. This act guaranteed cultural autonomy for national and ethnic minorities in the realms of culture, education and the media, and was motivated among other reasons by the hope that neighboring countries would reciprocate by providing cultural autonomy for Hungarian minorities (Majtényi 2004: 136). As minority self-government organizations had a real say only in cultural matters, however, they did not have the capacity to address the socio-economic grievances of the Roma (Molnár and Schafft 2003). Throughout the 1990s it became increasingly clear that the socio-economic misery of the Roma needed to be addressed by means of public policies. The first Action Plan for Improving the Living

Standards of the Roma was adopted by a socialist-liberal government in 1997 and covered the areas of education, employment, housing and discrimination. Subsequent governments adopted new action plans, which mainly varied in priorities but essentially pursued the same goals (Vizi 2013: 135–138). The European Commission exerted pressure on Eastern European member candidates to adopt policies supporting the societal integration of Roma, while also providing financial means to carry out ambitious action plans. The Commission feared that, given the socio-economic misery of the Roma, a large number of them would migrate to Western European countries when Eastern European countries became members of the EU (Vizi 2013: 129). At this time, however, the Roma issue was of relatively low priority and was not a matter of ideological contestation between Fidesz and the various socialist governments (Vizi 2013: 127). The impact of all these different action plans was negligible: statistics show that socio-economic disparities between Roma and non-Roma remained large in terms of education, occupational categories, and employment (UNDP/World Bank/EC 2011). In 2011, for example, 22 per cent of Roma in Hungary had completed only primary education, compared to 6 per cent of the non-Roma population, while 56 per cent of Roma had completed only lower secondary education compared to 35 per cent of non-Roma. Almost two-thirds of the Roma working population were unskilled workers in 2011, compared to only a quarter of the non-Roma population in this occupational category. Half of the Roma declared themselves unemployed, compared to 24 per cent of non-Roma.

The anti-Roma appeal of Jobbik played a central role in its electoral breakthrough in the European Parliament elections of 2009, and then again in the Hungarian parliamentary elections of 2010 (Karácsony and Róna 2011). In early 2006, a series of violent conflicts between Roma and non-Roma occurred. Jobbik, an insignificant party at that time, formed a paramilitary organization called the Hungarian Guard in order to "strengthen the nation's ability to defend itself on both the physical and spiritual level" (Feischmidt and Szombati 2017: 324). Karácsony and Róna (2011) have shown that the marches of the Hungarian Guard in response to "gipsy crimes" and the ensuing media attention helped Jobbik to appropriate the Roma issue. It is therefore no surprise that the issue of the Roma minority played a central role in the nationalist discourse found in Jobbik's programmatic party documents, wherein the Roma minority were presented as an existential threat to the Hungarian nation. In the words of Gábor Vona in his New Year's speech of 2011:

> There is no political cure that would lead to the growth of the Hungarian population under the current domestic and international circumstances that would be competitive with the explosive growth of the Roma population (…) it is only a matter of time [until] the Gypsies become the majority (…). This is not to say that the problem is that there are going to be more brown than white people, because this fact, by itself, would not

constitute a problem. The trouble lies in the inferiority of the socio-cultural level of the Gypsies and their inability to integrate, which is almost certain to lead to an anarchic state of civil war.

(Vona 2011)

Vona thus sought to convince his audience he was not racist by arguing that the problem was not one of different skin color but of cultural differences between the Hungarians and the Roma minority, including the claim that, despite enormous material efforts made by non-Roma to support their integration, the Roma "lack the motivation to break out from poverty" (Jobbik 2010: 40). Jobbik blamed the left for inciting the political mobilization of the Roma and turning them against Hungarians. Jobbik further claimed that aggressive actions by Roma were frequently motivated by racism.

Jobbik's declared goal was the "ending of Gypsy-criminality", and the party formulated a number of law-and-order policies to achieve this aim, including strengthening the police and establishing a gendarmerie (Jobbik 2010). In its first party program, issued in 2007, Jobbik even demanded the establishment of a special extra organizational unit within the police for the prevention and investigation of Roma crimes in areas of most tension (Jobbik 2007: 10). Jobbik also aimed to end the dependency of the Roma on social welfare provision, promising to provide a job for anyone willing to work in public workplaces. In addition, the party declared its intention to reform public education, endorsing the controversial proposal of segregated schools, arguing that the allegedly special needs of Roma pupils could be better addressed in such schools.

The issue of the Roma had certainly been of low priority for Fidesz before the electoral rise of Jobbik. In none of its previous electoral campaigns had Fidesz prominently addressed the situation of the Roma, even when it had entered on various occasions into electoral coalitions with Roma parties (see Fidesz 2010). Once Jobbik had won seats in parliament, however, Fidesz and Viktor Orbán were compelled to take a position on this issue. In one instance, a Jobbik MP attacked Orbán during a parliamentary debate for stating at a meeting with Roma political representatives that the Roma do not represent a problem but a hidden asset for Hungarian society. The Jobbik MP argued that the Roma had received an enormous amount of financial support over the years without any visible results. Indirectly, the Jobbik MP was blaming the Roma and their political leadership for this lack of success. He pointed out that almost half a million well-educated Hungarians had left the country during the same period in search of a better future, raising the question of who would represent this hidden asset of Hungarian society.[8] Orbán countered this claim in the following words:

> If we raise the question, if I understand you correctly, that according to your opinion the Hungarian Roma are not resources of Hungary, not a hidden asset of Hungary, then I do not agree with you. Everybody

represents a hidden asset of Hungary who wants to work and is able to do so but does not have a job (...) whether we are speaking about pregnant women, men and women approaching the age of retirement, or the Roma. Our conception is that the task of the Hungarian government is to provide opportunities so that all people who have the will and the capability can work.

(Orbán 2013)

In his response, Orbán accused Jobbik of prejudices against the Roma and distanced himself and Fidesz from Jobbik by emphasizing that his government valued everyone who wanted to work, regardless of gender, age or ethnicity.

At a policy level, it is less clear to what extent Fidesz has sought to distinguish itself from Jobbik. In the first half of 2011, when Hungary held the Presidency of the Council of the European Union, the European Commission adopted the "European Framework on National Roma Integration Strategies Up to 2020". The goals of this EU Roma Framework were to close the gaps between Roma and non-Roma in education, employment, healthcare, and housing, obliging member states to submit national strategies or sets of policy measures for Roma integration by 2012. These strategies and measures would further be subject to an annual report by the Commission on their implementation. The adoption of the EU Roma Framework was celebrated by the Fidesz government as one of the most important achievements of its presidency (Euractiv 2011). The Open Society European Policy Institute praised the establishment of the Framework as a success that represented the "most comprehensive, robust and best-equipped institutionalized Roma-specific policy to-date" (Mirga 2017: 7). However, the EU Framework had been a long time in the making and thus the involvement of the Fidesz government should not be exaggerated. Another factor that should be taken into account is that the Fidesz government was receiving a great deal of international attention and criticism for its plan to adopt a new constitution at the time it adopted the Framework. Nevertheless, it is difficult to imagine that Jobbik would have praised the adoption of the EU Framework in the same way as Fidesz if it had been in government.

At the same time, a number of policies originally proposed by Jobbik were implemented by the Fidesz government (Róna 2014: 175–177). For example, the Fidesz government adopted several laws aimed at improving public security through increases in the severity of penalties, which was an approach very much in line with Jobbik's commitment to combating "Roma crime" by increasing penalties. The government was also receptive to Jobbik's demand for the imposition of stricter conditions on eligibility for social assistance payments. Such payments were now made dependent upon the applicant performing public work and upon their children attending school. Applicants for social assistance payments were even threatened with inspections to assess the orderliness of their homes. In the realm of education, too, the government introduced a number of reforms in line with ideas set out by Jobbik in its electoral manifesto. For example, the government lowered the compulsory school age from 18 to 16, making easier for pupils to drop out without completing secondary level of education (Roma Educational Fund 2015). New and controversial legislation allowing for school segregation caught the attention of the European Commission, which launched an infringement procedure in June 2016 to investigate whether Hungarian legislation and administrative practices enabled school segregation (European Roma Rights Center 2016).

To sum up, Jobbik was the first party to politicize the Roma issue in the Hungarian party competition and managed to mobilize a considerable part of the electorate with its anti-Roma appeal. Fidesz accommodated many of Jobbik's policy proposals on this issue while at the same time striving to distance itself from Jobbik's radical discourse. Fidesz's strategy was to attempt to accommodate Jobbik's demands while simultaneously presenting itself as a moderate right-wing party in the European political mode, seeking thereby to avoid alienating moderate right-wing voters.

Conclusion

Issues of national identity are central to the discourse of radical right populist parties. Successful radical right populist parties own these issues and present themselves as the defenders of the nation. In such nativist discourse, minorities are presented as a threat to the nation. This chapter has explored how issues related to external Hungarian minorities and the Roma minority impacted on the competition between two right-wing populist parties, Jobbik and Fidesz in the period 2010–2014. The rhetoric surrounding these two ethnic minorities was central to the mobilization of right-wing populist parties in Hungary. This chapter has argued that the issue of the external Hungarian minorities has been a core issue for the right in Hungary since the breakdown of the socialist regime and a cause that has been successfully championed by Fidesz. The electoral rise of Jobbik has not threatened Fidesz's ownership of this issue, particularly since Fidesz made a number of major policy concessions to these minority groups, even introducing dual citizenship with voting rights for members of external Hungarian minorities. This chapter has also highlighted how the politicization of the issue of the Roma minority played a central role in Jobbik's successful mobilization. Jobbik presented the Roma minority as a socio-economic and security threat for non-Roma Hungarian society. Fidesz responded by accommodating several of Jobbik's policies related to the Roma minority. At the same time, however, Fidesz strived to present itself as a moderate party, denouncing Jobbik as a racist party.

While focused on the case of Hungary, this chapter also contributes to the wider debate on the impact of radical right populist parties on their mainstream competitors. The transformation of Fidesz into a radical right populist party, for example, raises the question of whether this transformation was triggered or supported by the electoral rise of Jobbik. Analysis has found that Fidesz accommodated a number of policy demands related to the issue of the Roma minority that were originally formulated by Jobbik in its electoral campaign. These findings support the claim that radical right populist challenger parties do indeed have an impact on mainstream right parties. The analysis also indicates that mainstream right parties are most likely to respond only to the issues at the heart of radical right populist parties' mobilization strategies and ones that have not formerly been politicized along the main divisions of party competition. For example, Jobbik was unable to challenge Fidesz's ownership of the issue of external Hungarian minorities, in large part because Fidesz had championed this issue long before the emergence of Jobbik. This finding highlights that identity politics include a range of issues, and it is not necessarily the case that all of these issues are championed by the radical right. Furthermore, the findings point toward the stickiness of issue ownership. Thus, when Jobbik tried to outbid Fidesz by proposing a more aggressive role for Hungary in the promotion of the rights of external Hungarian minorities, the external Hungarian minorities who now possessed (dual) Hungarian citizenship and voting rights did not turn their support to Jobbik in the national elections of 2014.

Notes

1 For a recent overview of the consequences of the electoral success of radical right populist parties, see Muis and Immerzeel (2017).
2 There is an ongoing debate as to how best to characterize the ideology of Fidesz (see Mudde 2016; Minkenberg 2017: 136–139).
3 Further, 21 per cent of Jobbik voters had previously voted for MSZP, while 20 per cent declared they could not remember their previous vote choice (Karácsony and Róna 2011).
4 Scholars have argued that levels of education and income do not influence sympathy with Jobbik (Bíró-Nagy and Róna 2011: 270; Krekó and Juhász 2017: 80–82). With regard to the impact of education, Pytlas (2015) has argued that the most educated segment of society support Jobbik, Bíró-Nagy and Róna (2011: 270) have argued that the least educated individuals are underrepresented in Jobbik's voter base compared to groups with higher levels of education. Along similar lines, Pirro (2015) has argued that the middle class is an important voter base for Jobbik.
5 The centrality of the narrative of the "failed regime transition" in Jobbik's discourse can be illustrated by the opening statement of Jobbik's founding document, which began: "Today, in 2003, a real regime transition has not yet occurred" (Jobbik 2003).
6 The Treaty of Trianon of 1920 was a peace agreement whereby the Allies of World War I and the Kingdom of Hungary defined the new borders of Hungary.
7 All excerpts from Hungarian documents have been translated by the author.
8 The debate between Ádám Mirkóczki (Jobbik MP) and Viktor Orbán on 7 October 2013 can be retrieved from the homepage of the Hungarian parliament: www.parlament.hu.ed.

References

Abou-Chadi, T. (2016) "Niche Party Success and Mainstream Party Policy Shifts: How Green and Radical Right Parties Differ in Their Impact". *British Journal of Political Science*, 46(2), pp. 417–436.
Abou-Chadi, T. and Krause, W. (2018) "The Causal Effect of Radical Right Success on Mainstream Parties' Policy Positions: A Regression Discontinuity Approach". *British Journal of Political Science*. Online first. Doi:10.1017/S0007123418000029.

Akkerman, T. (2012) "Comparing Radical Right Parties in Government: Immigration and Integration Policies in Nine Countries (1996–2010)". *West European Politics*, 35(3), pp. 511–529.

Akkerman, T. (2015) "Immigration Policy and Electoral Competition in Western Europe: A Fine-Grained Analysis of Party Positions over the Past Two Decades". *Party Politics*, 21(1), pp. 54–67.

Bale, T., Green-Pedersen, C., Krouwel, A., Luther, K. R. and Sitter, N. (2010) "If You Can't Beat Them, Join Them? Explaining Social Democratic Responses to the Challenge from the Populist Radical Right in Western Europe". *Political Studies*, 58(3), pp. 410–426.

Bartlett, J., Birdwell, J., Krekó, P., Benfield, J. and Gyori, G. (2012) *Populism in Europe: Hungary*. London: Demos.

Bíró-Nagy, A. and Boros, T. (2016) "Jobbik Going Mainstream: Strategy Shift of the Far-Right in Hungary". In: Jamin, J. (ed.) *L'extrême droite en Europe*. Brussels: Bruylant, pp. 243–264.

Bíró-Nagy, A., Boros, T. and Vasali, Z. (2013) "More Radical than the Radicals: The Jobbik Party in International Comparison". In: Melzer, R. and Serafin, S. (eds.) *Right-Wing in Europe*. Berlin: Friedrich Ebert Stiftung, pp. 229–253.

Bíró-Nagy, A. and Róna, D. (2011) "Tudatos Radikalizmus. A Jobbik Útja a Parlamentbe (2003–2010)". In: Lánczi, A. (ed.) *Nemzet és Radikalizmus. Egy Új Pártcsalád Felemelkedése*. Budapest: Századvég Kiadó, pp. 242–283.

Böcskei, B. and Molnár, M. (2016) "Kormányon a Radikális Jobboldal? A Jobbik Ígéretei a Magyarországi Törvényalkotásban (2010–2014)". *Politikatudományi Szemle*, 16(1), pp. 55–76.

Brubaker, R. (2017) "Why Populism?". *Theory and Society*, 46(5), pp. 357–385.

Bustikova, L. (2014) "Revenge of the Radical Right". *Comparative Political Studies*, 47(12), pp. 1738–1765.

Council of Europe. (2012) "Estimates on Roma Population in European Countries". www.coe.int/en/web/portal/roma. Accessed 26 December 2018.

De Cleen, B. (2017) "Populism and Nationalism". In: Rovira Kaltwasser, C., Taggart, P. A., Espejo, P. O. and Ostiguy, P. (eds.) *The Oxford Handbook of Populism*. Oxford: Oxford University Press, pp. 342–362.

Enyedi, Z. (2005) "The Role of Agency in Cleavage Formation". *European Journal of Political Research*, 44(5), pp. 697–720.

Enyedi, Z. (2015) "Plebeians, Citoyens and Aristocrats or Where is the Bottom of Bottom-Up? The Case of Hungary". In: Kriesi, H. and Pappas, T. S. (eds.) *European Populism in the Shadow of the Great Recession*. Colchester: ECPR Press, pp. 235–250.

Enyedi, Z. (2016) "Paternalist Populism and Illiberal Elitism in Central Europe". *Journal of Political Ideologies*, 21(1), pp. 9–25.

Euractiv. (2011) "At Presidency Midterm, Orbán Denounces EU 'Absurdities'". 15 April. www.euractiv.com/section/central-europe/news/at-presidency-midterm-orban-denounces-eu-absurdities/. Accessed 3 March 2018.

European Roma Rights Center. (2016) "EU: Commission Probe Must Spell the End of Romani Segregation in Hungarian schools". www.errc.org/article/eu-commission-probe-must-spell-the-end-of-romani-segregation-in-hungarianschools/4485. Accessed 17 January 2018.

Feischmidt, M., & Szombati, K. (2017). Understanding the rise of the far right from a local perspective: Structural and cultural conditions of ethno-traditionalist inclusion and racial exclusion in rural Hungary. *Identities*, 24(3), pp. 313–331.

Fidesz. (2010) "Nemzeti ügyek politikája". http://nezopontintezet.hu/files/2012/03/Nem zeti-Ügyek-Politikája-2010.pdf. Accessed 17 January 2018.
Han, K. J. (2015) "The Impact of Radical Right-Wing Parties on the Positions of Mainstream Parties Regarding Multiculturalism". *West European Politics*, 38(3), pp. 557–576.
Hungarian Central Statistical Office. (2013) "A Népesség a Nemzetiségi Hovatartozást Befolyásoló Tényezők Szerint". www.ksh.hu/nepszamlalas/tablak_nemzetiseg. Accessed 25 June 2018.
Hungarian Government 2011. The fundamental law of Hungary. Adopted on April 25, 2011. Available at: https://www.kormany.hu/download/e/02/00000/The%20New%20Fundamental%20Law%20of%20Hungary.pdf. (accessed July 25, 2019)
Hungarian Ministry of Public Administration and Justice. (2013) "Policy for Hungarian Communities Abroad. Strategic Framework for Hungarian Communities Abroad". http://bgazrt.hu/_files/NPKI/Jogszabály/policy_2013.pdf. Accessed 17 January 2018.
Jobbik. (2003) "Alapító Nyilatkozat". www.jobbik.hu/jobbikrol/alapito-nyilatkozat. Accessed 3 March 2018.
Jobbik (2007): Bethlen Gábor program.
Jobbik. (2010) "Radikális Változás". A Jobbik Országgyűlési Választási Programja a Nemzeti Önrendelkezésért és a Társadalmi Igazságosságért. www.jobbik.hu/sites/default/files/jobbik-program2010gy.pdf. Accessed 3 March 2018.
Kállai, E. (2005) *Helyi Cigány Kisebbségi Önkormányzatok Magyarországon*. Budapest: MTA Etnikai-nemzetiségi Kisebbségkutató Intézet – Gondolat Kiadói Kör.
Karácsony, G. and Róna, D. (2011) "The Secret of Jobbik. Reasons Behind the Rise of the Hungarian Radical Right". *Journal of East European & Asian Studies*, 2(1), pp. 61–108.
Krekó, P. and Juhász, A. (2017) *The Hungarian Far Right. Social Demand, Political Supply and International Context*. Stuttgart: Ibidem Verlag.
Krekó, P. and Mayer, G. (2015) "Transforming Hungary – Together?". In: Minkenberg, M. (ed.) *Transforming the Transformation?: The East European Radical Right in the Political Process*. London: Routledge, pp. 183–205.
Kriesi, H. and Pappas, T. S. (2015) "European Populism in the Shadow of the Great Recession". In: Kriesi, H. and Pappas, T. S. (eds.) *European Populism in the Shadow of the Great Recession*. Colchester: ECPR Press, pp. 1–22.
Majtényi, B. (2004) "Minority Rights in Hungary and the Situation of the Roma". *Acta Juridica Hungaria*, 45(1–2), pp. 131–148.
Meguid, B. M. (2005) "Competition between Unequals: The Role of Mainstream Party Strategy in Niche Party Success". *American Political Science Review*, 99(3), pp. 347–359.
Meyer, S. and Rosenberger, S. (2015) "Just a Shadow? The Role of Radical Right Parties in The Politicization of Immigration, 1995–2009". *Politics and Governance*, 3 (2), pp. 1–17.
Minkenberg, M. (2001) "The Radical Right in Public Office: Agenda-Setting and Policy Effects". *West European Politics*, 24(4), pp. 1–21.
Minkenberg, M. (2017) *The Radical Right in Eastern Europe: Democracy under Siege?* New York: Palgrave Macmillan.
Mirga, A. (2017) "Revisiting the EU Roma Framework Assessing the European Dimension for the Post-2020 Future". www.opensocietyfoundations.org/reports/revisiting-eu-roma-framework-assessing-european-dimension-post-2020-future. Accessed 20 March 2018.
Molnár, E. and Schafft, K. A. (2003) "Social Exclusion, Ethnic Political Mobilization, and Roma Minority Self-Governance in Hungary". *East Central Europe*, 30(1), pp. 53–73.
Mudde, C. (2004) "The Populist Zeitgeist". *Government and Opposition*, 39(4), pp. 541–563.

Mudde, C. (2007) *Populist Radical Right Parties in Europe*. Cambridge: Cambridge University Press.
Mudde, C. (2013) "Three Decades of Populist Radical Right Parties in Western Europe: So What?". *European Journal of Political Research*, 52(1), pp. 1–19.
Mudde, C. (2016) "Viktor Orbán and the Difference between Radical Right Politics and Parties". In: Mudde, C. (ed.) *On Extremism and Democracy in Europe*. London: Routledge, pp. 43–50.
Muis, J. and Immerzeel, T. (2017) "Causes and Consequences of the Rise of Populist Radical Right Parties and Movements in Europe". *Current Sociology*, 65(6), pp. 909–930.
Orbán, V. 2013. 136. Felszólalás. Available at: https://www.parlament.hu/web/guest/a-partok-kepviselocsoportjai-es-a-fuggetlen-kepviselok-aktualis-?p_p_id=hu_parlament_cms_pair_portlet_PairProxy_INSTANCE_9xd2Wc9jP4z8&p_p_lifecycle=1&p_p_state=normal&p_p_mode=view&p_auth=znEa1RXv&_hu_parlament_cms_pair_portlet_PairProxy_INSTANCE_9xd2Wc9jP4z8_pairAction=%2Finternet%2Fcplsql%2Fogy_naplo.naplo_fadat%3Fp_ckl%3D39%26p_uln%3D308%26p_felsz%3D136%26p_szoveg%3D%26p_felszig%3D136. Accessed at July 25, 2019.
Pirro, A. L. P. (2015) *The Populist Radical Right in Central and Eastern Europe: Ideology, Impact, and Electoral Performance*. London: Routledge.
Political Capital. (2015) "Jobbik's Policy Proposals Realized by Fidesz: A Summary in 10 Points". *Political Capital*, 15 May. www.riskandforecast.com/post/flash-report/jobbik-s-policy-proposals-realized-by-fidesz-a-summaryin-10-points_818.html. Accessed 8 March 2018.
Pytlas, B. (2015) *Radical Right Parties in Central and Eastern Europe: Mainstream Party Competition and Electoral Fortune*. London: Routledge.
Pytlas, B. and Kossack, O. (2015) "Lighting the Fuse. The Impact of Radical Right Parties on Party Competition in Central and Eastern Europe". In: Minkenberg, M. (ed.) *Transforming the Transformation?: The East European Radical Right in the Political Process*. London: Routledge, pp. 105–136.
Republikon Intézet. (2014) "Republikon Intézet Választási Elemzése". http://republikon.hu/media/9504/valasztasok_2014_ri.pdf. Accessed 25 June 2018.
Roma Educational Fund. (2015) "Changes in Hungary's Public Education Act Hurt Disadvantaged Roma Children and Youth". www.romaeducationfund.hu/sites/default/files/documents/changes_in_hungarys_public_education_act_hurt_disadvantaged_roma_children_and_youth_web_final.pdf. Accessed 17 January 2018.
Róna, D. (2014) "Jobbik-jelenség. A Jobbik Magyarországért Mozgalom Népszerűségének Okai". PhD Diss, Corvinus University of Budapest.
Rydgren, J. (2005) "Is Extreme Right-Wing Populism Contagious? Explaining the Emergence of a New Party Family". *European Journal of Political Research*, 44(3), pp. 413–437.
Schafft, K. A. and Kulcsár, L. J. (2015) "The Demography of Race and Ethnicity in Hungary". In: Sáenz, R., Embrick, D. G. and Rodríguez, N. P. (eds.) *The International Handbook of The Demography of Race and Ethnicity*. Dordrecht: Springer, pp. 553–573.
UNDP/World Bank/EC. (2011) "UNDP/World Bank/EC Regional Roma Survey 2011". www.eurasia.undp.org/content/rbec/en/home/ourwork/sustainable-development/development-planning-and-inclusive-sustainable-growth/roma-in-central-and-southeast-europe/roma-data.html. Accessed 26 December 2018.
van Heerden, S., de Lange, S. L., van der Brug, W. and Fennema, M. (2014) "The Immigration and Integration Debate in the Netherlands: Discursive and Programmatic Reactions to the Rise of Anti-Immigration Parties". *Journal of Ethnic and Migration Studies*, 40 (1), pp. 119–136.

van Spanje, J. (2010) "Contagious Parties: Anti-Immigration Parties and Their Impact on Other Parties' Immigration Stances in Contemporary Western Europe". *Party Politics*, 16(5), pp. 563–586.

Vizi, B. (2013) *Európai Kaleidoszkóp. Az Európai Unió és a Kisebbségek*. Budapest: L'Harmattan.

Vona, G. 2011. Félnünk pedig semmitől sem szabad, mert az igazság szabaddá tesz. Available at: https://www.jobbik.hu/rovatok/orszagos_hirek/vona_gabor_felnunk_pedig_semmitol_sem_szabad_mert_az_igazsag_szabadda_tesz. Accessed at July 25, 2019.

Wagner, M. and Meyer, T. M. (2017) "The Radical Right as Niche Parties? The Ideological Landscape of Party Systems in Western Europe, 1980–2014". *Political Studies*, 65 (1), pp. 84–107.

Waterbury, M. A. (2006) "Internal Exclusion, External Inclusion: Diaspora Politics and Party-Building Strategies in Post-Communist Hungary". *East European Politics and Societies*, 20(3), pp. 483–515.

12
A CLASH OF MYTHS

Populism and ethno-nationalism in Serbia

Bojan Vranić

Introduction

Serbia has undergone major territorial and political changes since the early 20th century. In the Balkan Wars it expanded its territory by annexing the regions of Kosovo and Macedonia, later forming a new federal state with other Slavic nations in the Balkans. More recently, Serbia has struggled to prevent some of its regions from declaring independence. Kosovo's[*][1] declaration of independence in 2008 was certainly the most serious manifestation of regional grievance, unsettling political and national identity and expanding the already fertile ground for both nationalism and populism in the Serbian party landscape. Given the complexity of Serbian inter-party dynamics, however, the relationship between party politics, populism and nationalism are, as Bieber (2005: 167) points out, "notoriously hard to classify". To regard populism and nationalism in Serbia as examples of radical right-wing ideology would thus be to oversimplify matters.

The territorial cleavage related to Kosovo has raised a serious challenge to Serbian sovereignty and is the main factor that makes Serbian party populism explicitly peculiar. In terms of political ideologies, Serbian party populism fits well with Mudde's (2007: 24) concept of nativism, occupying a space somewhere between authoritarianism and xenophobia. In this respect it does not diverge greatly from other (Western) European cases. Rather, the peculiarity of Serbian party populism lies in the cultural meanings that agents invest in strategies of populist mobilization. Serbia belongs to what Brubaker (2009: 57) defines as a nationalizing state, i.e. one that is "conceived" as a nation state despite being "ethnically heterogeneous". Serbian populist parties that base their strategies on territorial disputes and regional grievances are mainstream, national and often catch-all parties that frame disputes as questions of national identity pertaining to the survival of the Serbian nation. In accordance with Brubaker's triadic configuration of nationalisms, Serbian populist parties make use of ideas typically associated with minority nationalism, such as the idea of a homeland or heartland, to buttress their mobilization strategies. Within Serbia, Kosovo is politically constructed as the heartland that has been occupied by national minorities.

This chapter shows that populism is the baseline for the main parties in Serbia, which have a strong tendency towards instrumentalizing territorially-based ethno-nationalism as a situational reaction to the political agendas of Serbia's ethnic minorities. The situationally defined notion of ethno-nationalism (Eriksen 2010: 56) implies that populist parties in Serbia exploit different spatial and temporal upheavals in identity (caused by real or imaginary threats from minorities) to buttress their mobilization strategies and legitimize their policies.

The first part of this chapter presents an analytical framework for interpreting the logic of Serbian party populism and its relation to territorial disputes. The second part uses this framework to compare three selected cases of Serbian parties that include territorial claims in their official party programs and manifestos: the Serbian Socialist Party (known by its Serbian initials, SPS), the Serbian Radical Party (SRS) and the Serbian Progressive Party (SNS). These are not the only populist parties in Serbia, but I have chosen them because each has at some point been either a governing party or in a coalition with one of the others, thus gaining uncontested political power to shape institutional policy on the territorial issue of Kosovo. In the final part of the chapter I show that none of these parties have demonstrated political consistency in the evolution of their programs in relation to the Kosovo issue, meaning that ethno-nationalist mobilization strategies have been peripheral and situational within an overarching populist strategy. The key reason for these parties having moderated their stances in recent years, moving away from the radical positions they took in the 1990s, can be found, I argue, in the actions and influences of external supranational actors, including the European accession process, which has become a principal legitimizing formula for (governing) populist parties since 2008.

The people, the territory and the riddles of national identity

In conceptual terms, the question of territorial cleavages in Serbia may be translated into questions of national identity. However, when related to populism, questions of national identity tend to be conceived as symptoms of structural challenges, such as growing economic competition in a global market or the problem of adequate political representation (Spruyt, Keppens and Van Droogenbroeck 2016: 337). These accounts often ignore cultural aspects of national identities, leading to a lack of understanding of the political consequences of disturbances to identity caused by territorial cleavages in post-communist, semi-consolidated democracies. Recent research shows that populist regimes in European post-communist societies emerge and draw their legitimacy from ethnically based cleavages (Minkenberg 2017), leading to a significant overlap between populism and ethno-nationalism, though there is no link between them. This chapter argues that a link can be established from fundamental elements of the concept of *cultural identity*, since questions of national identity in Eastern Europe are deeply embedded in historical meanings and legacies. This particularly applies to the Western Balkan region, where national identities resulted from the actions of what Bieber (2005: 168) refers to as an "emancipatory national movement directed against big empires governing most of the Balkans until the late nineteenth and early 20th centuries".

In recent literature on populism (Mudde and Kaltwasser 2017), the concept of cultural identity is always related to the issue of the cleavage between the "true" people and the "elite". In post-communist Europe, the role of elites as enemies of the "true" people is often assigned instead to ethnic minorities (Mungiu-Pippidi 2004; Mudde 2007; Krause 2015) who have political or territorial aspirations that contest the national sovereignty of the "people" (i.e. the majority). In this respect, populism in Eastern Europe ideologically resembles nationalism. As Canovan (2002: 34) argues, populist parties tend to define people territorially, turning ethnically drawn borders into "boundaries of polity". Serbia is no exception to this rule but is nevertheless a special case. As I will show in the case of Kosovo★, populism in Serbia has three layers of mobilization strategy depending on whether they are used in regional (Kosovo), sub-regional (North Kosovo) or supranational contexts (directly connected to the European Union integration process).

J. W. Müller's recent attempt to define populism is very helpful in explicating the Serbian case. Müller (2015: 83) defines populism as "a particular *moralistic imagination of politics*, a way of perceiving the political world which places in opposition a morally pure and fully unified people against small minorities, elites in particular, who are placed outside the authentic people". The explanatory potential of Müller's definition lies in its emphasis on *the moralistic imagination* as a fundamental element in the cleavage between the "true people" and minorities. With regard to populist mobilization strategies, this implies that populist parties and their leaders draw legitimacy from reinventing national myths of territorial rights, for example by constructing the notion that the heartland of the true people has been occupied by (ethnic) minorities.

A populist mobilization strategy based on moralistic imagination can only be successful if it is congruent with a particular political culture of nationalism that imagines the community as a social construct sustained by cultural myths. In his seminal book *Imagined Communities*, Benedict Anderson offers a definition of the relationship between populism and nationalism that may serve as a good starting point for this chapter. As he argues, the nation is imagined as a community "because, regardless of the actual inequality and exploitation that may prevail in each, the nation is always conceived as a deep, horizontal comradeship" (Anderson 2006: 7). An implicit consequence of the nation's embeddedness in imagined cultural myths of fraternity is an insensitivity to the divergent cultural identities of other members of the community, such as national minorities, leading to their political under-representation. Thus conceived, nationalism is fertile ground for populism and its tendency to simplify the relations between the "people" (i.e. the nation) and minorities as an "us versus them" type of social cleavage.

The relationship between nationalism and populism becomes explicit in the context of territorial cleavages. The moralistic imagination of "the people" serves as an endogenous legitimacy principle. However, by itself this cannot offer a straightforward explanation of how populist parties turn national identity questions into tools for their political mobilization. Rather it must be theoretically supplemented by a concept of populism that incorporates external actors with the power to lend institutional legitimacy to the political goals of populist parties and thereby make their mobilization strategies sustainable.

Recent literature on multi-level populism (Mazzoleni 2005) and the influence of supranational institutions on populist rhetoric (Elias 2009) can help to reconcile these two elements, at least in the case of Serbia. As Mazzoleni (2005: 211) argues:

> The more institutional opportunities there are, the more the actions and the claims [of populist parties] become not only regional, but also national and supranational. This question becomes central where the relationship between the institutional levels (sub-national, national, supranational) is changing, for example in the context of supranational integration.

The concept of multi-level populism contributes in at least two major respects to our explication of the relationship between populism and nationalism in the context of territorial grievances. First, it emphasizes regional grievances, providing analytical tools for understanding the dynamics of populist mobilization strategies based on campaigning against minorities. Second, it introduces the role of supranational actors, which in this case refers especially to the European Union. The EU provides minority parties with an "external support structure that makes arguments about the feasibility and sustainability of self-determination much easier" (Elias 2009: 5). The EU has thus been the game changer, leading populist parties to revise their strategies by adopting different kinds of rhetoric when addressing different levels of politics. As Mazzoleni (2005: 211) argues: "the political actor combines the use of the regional, national and transnational institutions and connects it with other parties within or outside the national context".

The next part of this chapter will apply this conceptual framework to the Serbian context and analyze the evolution of the party programs of the Serbian Socialist Party (SPS), the Serbian Radical Party (SRS) and the Serbian Progressive Party (SNS), demonstrating the shift from authoritarian to multi-level populism in Serbia.

People beyond territory: party politics in Serbian semi-competitive pluralism

The Serbian populist potato: the Kosovo Myth

Party pluralism was institutionalized by the Serbian constitution in 1989 and Serbia has had a dynamic party landscape ever since, offering nuanced alternatives to established political positions. This is a paradoxical situation, since, despite appearing to offer many options over the past three decades, the Serbian political landscape has always comprised either a single dominant party and a circle of loyal midsized parties or a state of polarized pluralism. The former applied in the period of Slobodan Milošević's rule, while the latter is characteristic of the governments and party coalitions that have emerged since the democratic changes of 5 October 2000.

Under Milošević's autocratic regime (1989–2000), Serbia became an inward-looking and closed society marked by xenophobia, intolerance towards minorities, and ethnic clashes. In 1998 a civil war broke out in Kosovo that led to a mass exodus of both Albanians and Serbs from the region and NATO bombings in 1999. The 1990s provided fertile ground for both populism and ethno-nationalism. In this period the party landscape was dominated by SPS, often supported by SRS (known as the "red-black" coalition), which formed a strong nationalist bloc that was consistently quite repressive of the highly fragmented opposition (Bieber 2005: 177).

After 5 October 2000 a power shift occurred and a democratic (civic) opposition gained political power in Serbia. Democratization ushered in power-sharing processes that enabled minorities to pursue their political agendas more openly and, in the case of Kosovo, in the form of separatism. The key changes that occurred in Serbian politics from this time include a shift towards a predominantly pro-European course, market liberalization, constitutional revision (formally completed and enacted in 2006) and overall modernization. The pace of political reforms in Serbia was slow, however, due largely to the country's devastated economy, combined with the EU's carrot-and-stick policy on the war crimes of the 1990s and the issue of Kosovo in particular (Börzel and Grimm 2018: 123). These societal and political issues led to the polarized pluralism that characterized the Serbian party landscape after 2000, which broadly consisted of "a civic, pro-EU bloc (...) that was campaigning against a nationalist, anti-EU bloc" (Zuber and Džankić 2017: 225). This polarization came to an end after the 2012 elections when the centrist SNS became the dominant party, turning the polarized system into "a system with a predominant party" (Lončar 2017: 49).

There have thus been three main periods in the evolution of the contemporary Serbian party system: the dominant party system under SPS (1990–2000); polarized pluralism under DS and SRS (2001–2012); and the dominant party system again, now under SNS (2012–present). With the exceptions of the 2000 and 2008 elections in which the center-left (civic) Democratic Party (DS) became a core party, nationalist parties enjoyed the greatest success in Serbia over this time. A prima facie conclusion would therefore be that Serbian voters prefer radical right-wing and ethno-nationalist parties. However, the situation is less straightforward if we compare the cultural dimensions of the party's ideological standpoints with their positions on ethno-nationalism. Figure 12.1 shows the positioning of political parties after the elections to the National Assembly of 2016. (Note that only those parties that passed the 5 per cent threshold have been considered).

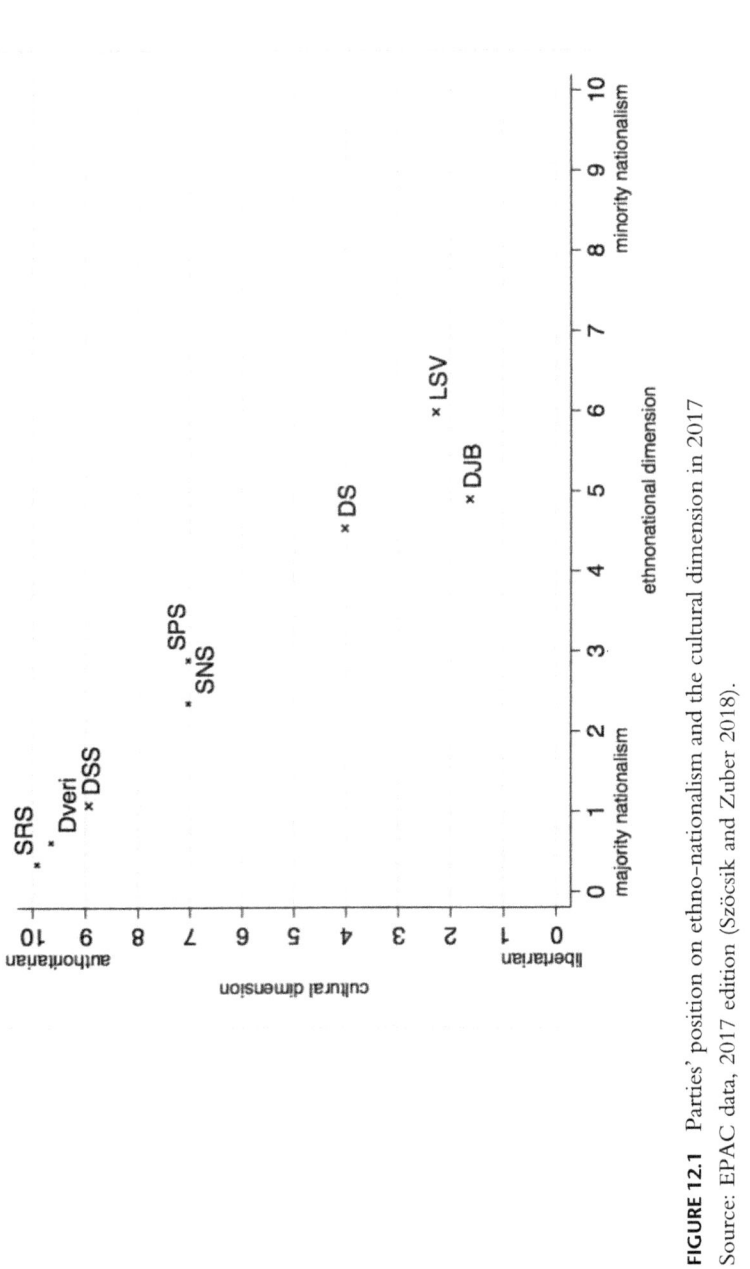

FIGURE 12.1 Parties' position on ethno-nationalism and the cultural dimension in 2017

Source: EPAC data, 2017 edition (Szöcsik and Zuber 2018).

As shown in Figure 12.1, SPS and SNS, the core parties from 1990 to the present, have positioned themselves as center-right parties on the ideological spectrum. Meanwhile, SRS has remained consistent in its authoritarian nationalism and has now become an almost irrelevant political option (see Figure 12.2). This implies that the key formula for electoral success in Serbia is not the consistent application of majority nationalism, although such nationalism has played an important role in mobilization strategies. Rather, as will be shown in the following analysis, the dominant mobilization strategy of Serbian national parties is a populist one that instrumentalizes ethno-nationalism situationally by using territorial grievances to legitimize their policies and political campaigns.

The strongest link between populism, territorial grievances and party mobilization strategies in Serbia over the past twenty-five years has been the case of Kosovo. Four days after Kosovo★ declared independence on 17 February 2008, Serbia's governing and opposition parties organized a mass rally under the slogan "Kosovo is Serbia" (21 February). The nationalist Prime Minister Vojislav Koštunica (of the Democratic Party of Serbia, or DSS) frantically asked the protesting masses: "What is Kosovo? Whose is Kosovo? Is there anyone among us who is not from Kosovo?" (Politika 2008). These rhetorical questions sublimated the symbolic meaning represented by Kosovo for (populist) parties in Serbia, since Kosovo was constructed by political elites as the heartland of the true people. In relation to nationalism, Kosovo is what Ernest Gellner terms "the potato principle", referring to the territorial rootedness of nationalist ideology (cited in Eriksen 2002: 66).

From a historical perspective it was the Battle of Kosovo on 28 June 1389 between the medieval Serbian state and the Ottoman Empire that served as the foundation of this myth. This battle ended in the defeat of the medieval Serbian kingdom, which then became a vassal state of the Ottoman Empire. Two symbolic meanings, albeit not always compatible, have been derived from this loss of territory. The first is the myth of Prince Lazar (captured in the battle and beheaded by the Ottomans) and his devotion to Orthodox Christianity, which transcends territories in its bearing on the cultural and spiritual life and experiences of all Orthodox peoples. This part of the Kosovo myth has served as the foundation of *populism* in Serbia, and I will refer to it here as "the wise people myth". The second part of the Kosovo myth is what Russell-Omaljev (2017: 88) judiciously terms a Serbian "historical victimization" discourse. The descriptive part of this narrative consists of glorifying the sacrifices made by Serbian warriors to protect Europe from "the Ottoman horde", while the moral narrative tells a tale of an unjust Europe that never truly recognized the Serbs' achievements of that time. The symbolic meanings of this victimization discourse became a core element of ethno-nationalist politics in the aftermath of the breakdown of socialist Yugoslavia.

Both parts of the Kosovo myth rest on a discourse of lost territory and a promised return to the true peoples' heartland as a "favorite theme of Serbian ethno-nationalism" (Kecmanović 2002: 168). This discourse entered the

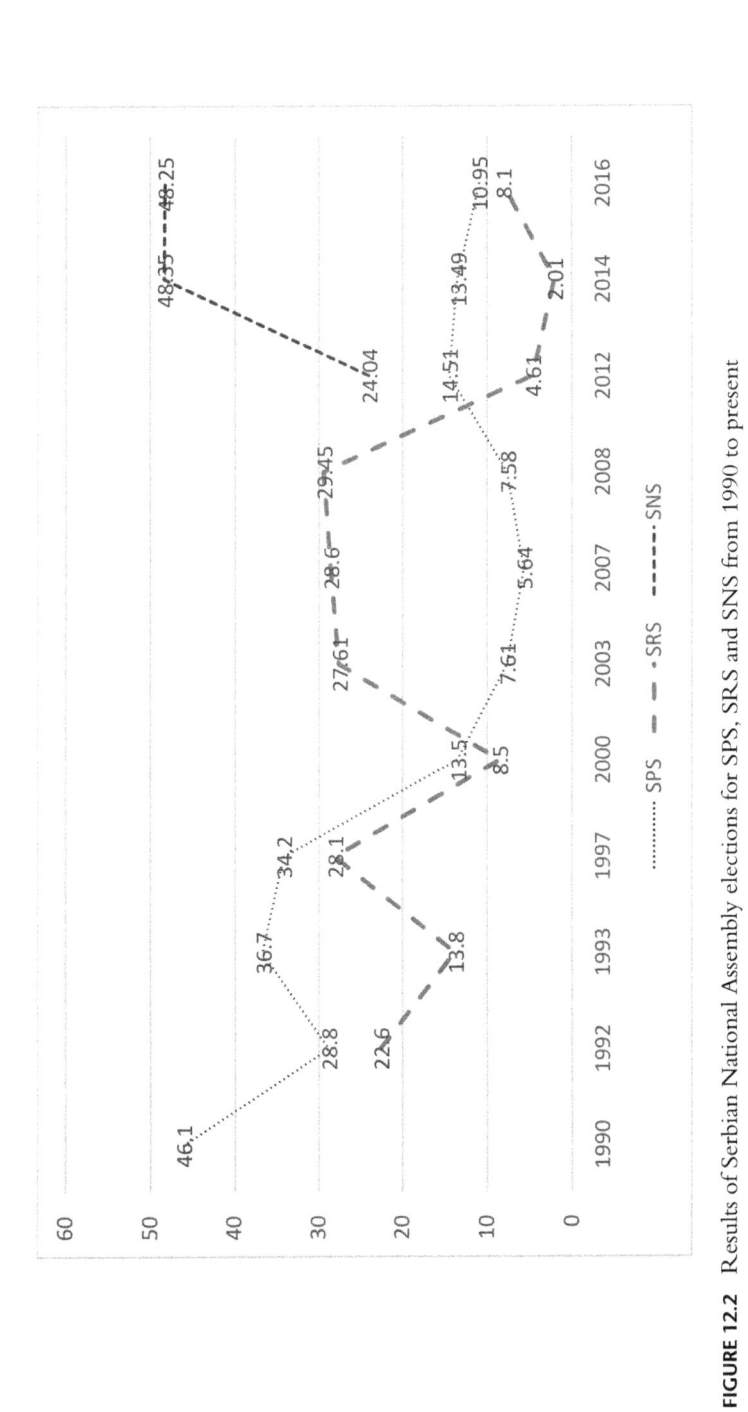

FIGURE 12.2 Results of Serbian National Assembly elections for SPS, SRS and SNS from 1990 to present

Source: Republic Electoral Commission (www.rik.parlament.gov.rs/latinica/arhiva.php).

competitive space between political parties in Serbia after the 1989 constitutional reforms which legalized party pluralism. The pluralization of the party landscape coincided closely with the six-hundredth anniversary of the Battle of Kosovo in 1989, which generated nationalistic euphoria among Serbian national parties. This euphoria was buttressed by the notorious Memorandum of the Serbian Academy of Arts and Sciences (SANU) drafted by nationalist members of the intelligentsia in 1986. Those intellectuals who accepted the ideas of the Memorandum "became the chief media propagandists disseminating the images and language of hatred and fear for the national cause" (Malešević 2006: 196). The authors of the Memorandum presented Kosovar Albanians as the arch-enemy of Serbian national interests. As such, the Memorandum shaped a victimization pattern that has continued to define Serbian ethno-nationalism up to the present day:

> The question [of provinces] concerns the Serbian nation and its state. A nation that regained its own state after a long and bloody struggle, that fought for and achieved a civil democracy and that lost 2.5 million of its members in the last two wars, has lived to see the day when the Party committee of apparatchiks decrees that after four decades in the new Yugoslavia it alone is not allowed to have its own state. A worse historical defeat in peacetime cannot be imagined.
> *(Mihajlović and Krestić 1995: 127)*

This excerpt from the SANU Memorandum help us to specify Serbian ethno-nationalism as a conservative form of nationalism in which questions of identity are connected to the "continuity and destiny of a culturally unique community" (Vincent 2015: 465). The relationship with populism can be seen in the way the Memorandum treats the notion of democracy as ideologically linked to nativism (Mudde 2007; Betz and Johnson 2017), reflecting the will of the true people unlike forms of representative democracy. Nationalist sentiments and the ascendance of nationalist parties in Serbia led to a series of demonstrations and political violence in protest over Kosovo in 1989, which then continued sporadically over the next decade, ultimately leading to the civil war of 1998 and the NATO bombardment of 1999. The 1989 riots were not the first to occur on a large scale but were a turning point for separatism as a regional grievance that became a true threat to Serbian sovereignty. The success of Albanian separatism (resulting in the proclamation of the independence of Kosovo★ in 2008) occurred in positive correlation with the introduction of party pluralism and the breakdown of socialist Yugoslavia. As Gourevitch (1979: 319) argues, as long as there is a strongly centralized state (political core), regional grievances and territorial cleavages represent only a minor threat at most in ethnically divided societies. After 1989, however, and following democratic changes in 2000, Serbia lost its authoritarian and centralized system of governance, which led to Kosovo★ declaring independence.

Nationalistic euphoria about Kosovo and anti-Albanian sentiment led to the rise of nationalism in the early 1990s. The question thus arises as to how populist parties exploited the ascendance of ethno-nationalism over Kosovo as a tool for political mobilization in Serbia. This exploitation was achieved primarily through a process of ideological and rhetorical simplification, reducing the problem of territorial grievance to the problem of political elites. An example of this simplification can be found in Slobodan Milošević's infamous speech in 1989 on Gazimestan (near the location of the Battle of Kosovo). In this speech, Milošević (Vreme 2009) blamed corrupt Albanian and Serbian communist elites as the source of territorial disputes over Kosovo. In doing so, Milošević framed the political discourse on Kosovo to fit a populist mobilization strategy by exploiting existing anti-Albanian sentiment generated by Serbian intellectuals in the 1980s.

The success of this mobilization strategy in the 1990s depended on the charisma of the political leader and his ability to inflame the moralistic imagination and sentiments of the people. After the democratic reforms of 2000, the mobilization strategies of populist parties changed significantly. Kosovo remained the main source of fuel for mobilization strategies, but the form of these strategies changed to multi-level populism. Below I will show that at least three levels of populist strategies have been adopted in relation to the contested territory of Kosovo since the democratic changes in Serbia.

On the first level, the independence of Kosovo* and the violent events that ensued in 2009 caused the formation of the sub-region of North Kosovo. The political symbol of this sub-region is the town of Kosovska Mitrovica, which is divided between an ethnic Serbian section in the north and an ethnic Albanian section in the south. From 2009 onwards, Kosovska Mitrovica and North Kosovo became the prime objects of territorial contestation, with Serbia aiming to make this territory an autonomous region, while Kosovar Albanians claimed the territory was within Kosovo's* sovereignty. When trying to legitimize their political agendas in this sub-region, Serbian populist parties employed rhetoric focused on nourishing the myth of national preservation, designating Kosovar Serbs in terms of the "wise people myth", as guardians of a territory that belongs to Serbia by historical and cultural right.

The second level of populist rhetoric is national. When populist parties and their leaders have sent political messages to the nation at large they usually emphasize the military supremacy of Serbia over Kosovar Albanians, buttressed by Serbia's strong relationship with Russia, and convey images of reliving the Battle of Kosovo.

Finally, on the third, supranational level, populist parties tend to represent themselves as pro-European peacekeeping actors dedicated to regional stability. At this contextual level, the populist pattern focuses on the "victimization discourse", designating the negotiations mediated by the EU as unjust to the Serbian people while at the same time justifying the talks as a necessary institutional arrangement for preserving peace in the region.

Analysis of the party programs of SPS, SRS, SNS

The context of the 1990s and the aftermath of Kosovo's* independence from Serbia in 2008 determined the positions adopted by national political parties towards Kosovo and Kosovar Albanians. The specific circumstances that led to the employment of ethno-nationalism by populist parties are clearly discernible in the parties' programs. In the following discursive analysis I will examine the official party programs of SPS (1990, 1992, 2010), SRS (1990, 1991) and SNS (2011) and their stances towards the following ideas: majority, minority, elites, diaspora and Kosovo. These programs were selected on the basis that it was these manifestos that preceded the greatest electoral successes in the National Assembly ever achieved by SPS, SRS and SNS (Figure 12.2). From a discourse analysis of the selected programs I deduce seven important points that shaped party mobilization strategies after the introduction of party pluralism in Serbia. An overview of the analysis is given in Table 12.1.

The 1990s: plebiscitary Caesarism and the self-government of the people

Although party pluralism and free and fair elections were constitutionally affirmed in 1989, the political outcome of these constitutional reforms was the dominance of a single party, the ex-communist Socialist Party of Serbia (SPS), whose only true competitor – though also its greatest ally – was the far-right Serbian Radical Party (SRS). Overarching authority and power belonged to Slobodan Milošević, the President of Serbia and Yugoslavia from 1990 to 2000 and the charismatic leader of SPS. For this reason it is often argued (Goati 1995; Podunavac 1995; Golubović 2004) that the Serbian political system was a type of plebiscitary Caesarism during the 1990s, characterized by the charismatic rule of the "father" of the nation.

In the early 1990s, SPS and SRS were ideological counterparts of the same ethno-nationalist and populist ideology. While both parties had "the people" and territory at their ideological core, SPS was initially positioned on the left of the ideological spectrum while SRS was on the right. The context of the war in the 1990s indubitably led both SPS and SRS to increase their use of ethno-nationalist ideas in their party programs, resulting in policies of "latent imperialism" (Kellas 2004: 159) legitimized by ideas and myths about the historical right of the Serbian people to specific territories.

Both SPS and SRS found justification for such latent imperialism in the "myth of the wise people". In the case of SPS, the party's program of 1990 set the foundation of this myth by promoting the nineteenth-century idea of the "self-government of the Serbian people" (*narodna samouprava*) (SPS 1990: 3). The program postulated that only Serbs as the majority held the political, historical and cultural rights of self-government, derived from "a sense for freedom and justice in the centuries-long suffering of our people" (SPS 1990: 3). The

TABLE 12.1 Populism and ethno-nationalism in party programmes (SPS, SRS, SNS) in Serbia: 1990–2017

Party	Programme	Definition of majority	Relation to minorities	Definition of the elites	Relations to Serbian diaspora in the region	Relation to Kosovo	Overall ideological core
SPS	1990	The people	No specified rights; assimilationist tendencies	Communist bureaucracy	Traces of expansionist nationalism	Territorial dimension; political oppression as a solution	Authoritarian populism
	1992	The people	Cultural rights; minorities seen as instability factor; Albanians as dangerous others	Anti-national bureaucracy and parties	Cultural relations	Symbolic and territorial dimension; ethnic cleansing discourse; political oppression as a solution	Ethno-nationalism
	2010	Citizens	Cultural rights	Neoliberal elites	Cultural relations	Territorial dimension; opting for a balanced solution; no proposed solution	Multi-level populism
SRS	1990	The people	Minorities treated as Serbs with different cultural backgrounds; Albanians as dangerous others	Communists as the anti-national bureaucracy	Open expansionist nationalism; Great Serbia project	Heartland of Serbia; ethnic cleansing discourse; war as a solution	Ethno-nationalism
	1991	The people	Minorities have political rights only if loyal to Serbian way of life; Albanians as dangerous others	Communist as the anti-national bureaucracy	Open expansionist nationalism; Great Serbia project	Heartland of Serbia; ethnic cleansing discourse; immigration of Serbian population; war as a solution	Ethno-nationalism
SNS	2011	Citizens	Cultural right, catch-all party solutions to representation	Tycoons and corrupt political elites (after 2000)	Cultural relations	Equal rights of Serbs and Albanians to territory but not to state; referendum as a political solution	Multi-level populism

same notion was preserved in the party's 1992 program, despite the minor change of introducing the term "citizens" instead of "the people", and SPS rhetoric would retain a strong majoritarian nationalist tone throughout the 1990s.

The establishment of the populist pattern in the SPS program is also evident in references to "elites". Although SPS had inherited members, leaders and assets from the old communist party (Goati 1995: 201), it made a decisive break with communist politics in its 1990 program by declaring communist bureaucrats to be enemies of the people who were impeding the *national interests* of Serbia (SPS 1990: 4–5). The 1992 program toned down this "elite versus the people" discourse, shifting to what was more of a revisionist than a populist stance, no longer placing all the blame for the people's suffering on the elites, though insisting that the obligation of the elite was to govern not as "a master but a servant to the people" (SPS 1992: 16). The program declared the party's aim to remove all obstacles between the people and the moral political elite, in this case meaning Slobodan Milošević, thereby deepening the bond between the charismatic leader and the nation.

The program of the radical right-wing SRS was founded upon the same principles. The origins of the Serbian Radical Party date from 1990 when its future leader, Vojislav Šešelj, founded the Serbian Chetnik Movement (*Srpski četnički pokret*) as a movement with a clearly "neo-fascist" tone (Gagnon 2004: 105). In 1991 this movement merged with the Peoples' Radical Party led by Tomislav Nikolić (later to become the President of Serbia, 2012–2017) to form the Serbian Radical Party (SRS). After Vojislav Šešelj had surrendered himself to the International Criminal Tribunal for the Former Yugoslavia (ICTY) in the Hague in 2003, Tomislav Nikolić acted as party leader until 2008 when he formed the Serbian Progressive Party. Prior to the 2008 split, the ideological impact of SRS on the Serbian political landscape was notorious for promoting ethno-nationalist political agendas, with grave consequences. SRS is still promoting the same ideas today, albeit with negligible electoral success.

Ethno-nationalism as a leading ideological concept of SRS was established in its first program in 1990 (SRS 1990: 2), which stated the party's primary political aim as follows:

> The renewal of a free, independent and democratic Serbian state in the Balkans that joins together all Serbians, meaning a state that will include the presently imposed federal unit along with Serbian Macedonia, Serbian Montenegro, Serbian Bosnia, Serbian Herzegovina, Serbian Dubrovnik, Serbian Dalmatia, Serbian Lika, Serbian Kordun, Serbian Banija, Serbian Slavonia and Serbian Baranja.

The key idea contained in this excerpt from the party's manifesto has remained the same in every SRS program ever since (Table 12.1). It promotes the idea of Greater Serbia, advancing the cultural and historical territorial claims of the Serbian people over regions in Bosnia, Croatia and Macedonia. The justifying principle of the 1990 program was drawn from the idea of the democratic interests of the Serbian people. This created an explicit relationship between ethnonationalism and populism, since territorial expansion was justified on the basis of *the will of the people* to live under one government. During the wars in Bosnia and Croatia, Šešelj's guerrilla groups attempted to enforce this general "will" through extreme violence, "terrorizing both the Serbian and non-Serbian population" (Gagnon 2004: 105). In all SRS programs "the people" are perceived in what Canovan (2002: 34) defines as "a corporate body with a continuous existence over time". This is seen most clearly in the position taken by the 1990 program towards religious "minorities" living in the listed territories, which claimed that Muslims, Catholics and Protestants were all of Serbian origin and thus included in this imaginary general will (SRS 1990: 2).

After Šešelj and Nikolić formed SRS in 1991, the party enacted a program that became the template for all populist parties in Serbia. The new program gave the populist policies of SRS a clear territorial dimension, positioning Greater Serbia as both a political goal and a principle of legitimacy. Greater Serbia was now defined by borders, not by provisional ethnic boundaries. To the west, for example, the borders of Serbia were to be established in east Croatia "on the line of Karlobag-Ogulin-Karlovac-Virotitica" (SRS 1991a: 6).

The populist logic behind the ethno-nationalism of SPS and SRS in the early 1990s can best be seen in the positions they adopted towards ethnic minorities. In its programs of 1990 and 1992, SPS chose to recognize "specific national, historical and cultural features of the areas" (SPS 1990: 34–35) inhabited by minorities. However, SPS never offered to guarantee cultural or political rights to these minorities; it merely recognized the cultural specificity of these *areas*. The geographical dimension of this program implied that SPS was willing to recognize minority cultures as variations of Serbian culture in territories such as Kosovo, but not willing to grant specific minority cultural and political rights. The 1992 program went even further in rejecting and diminishing the political rights of minorities and their rights of representation. This program defined a "national minority" as one that already possesses its own state outside of Serbia (SPS 1992: 20). The program denounced the right of such national minorities to self-determination, claiming that it was illegitimate for a national minority to seek an independent state when it already had a "home country".

Positioning itself on the right of the party spectrum, SRS opted for a sharp "us versus them" distinction in referring to the political rights of minorities (SRS 1991a). The SRS manifesto of 1991 created a discourse that distinguished "loyal" minorities from "disloyal" minorities. Only "loyal" minorities should be guaranteed the same rights as Serbian citizens (SRS 1991a), and even these excluded any representational rights that might have made such cultural rights of any import.

The positions adopted by these two major political parties of the 1990s towards minorities were tailored in a number of special ways to address the issue of Kosovo and the Kosovar Albanians. The scale of grievance over the Kosovo issue can be seen in the intense efforts made by both SPS and SRS to elaborate and adapt their stances on this issue in their party programs. Thus, SPS dedicated a separate section to Kosovo in every one of its programs in the 1990s, with the following paragraph unchanged in each:

> The Socialist Party of Serbia asserts that Kosovo and Metohija is a national, ethical, historical and state question of the Serbian people [that is] of the greatest importance and an inseparable part of Serbia. The basis of our politics is the national equality (...) of Albanians, Serbs, Montenegrins, Muslims, Croats, Turks, Roma and all other nationalities. The Socialist Party will decisively act in order to prevent emigration and to ensure the return of exiled Serbs and Montenegrins. (...) We are committed to doing everything to ensure that the world knows the whole truth about Kosovo and Metohija, about the causes and the grave effects of Albanian chauvinism and separatism.
>
> *(SPS 1990: 38–39)*

At least four conclusions can be drawn from these lines about the ethno-nationalist dimension of SPS populism in the 1990s. Firstly, Kosovo was presented as the paramount Serbian national question and one that could be solved by letting "the people" decide, probably in the form of a referendum – thus calling on a Serbian trope of "self-government". This constituted a political agenda that all other nationalist parties came to accept, derived from the "wise people myth" that the Kosovo issue could only be solved through a nationwide referendum in which the Serbian people were to decide the fate of their heartland. Second, although Albanians and other minorities were to be included in this process, they were not to enjoy any special political rights of representation, and since Serbs comprised two-thirds of the population it was clear that minorities would remain under-represented by this solution. Third, the fairness of this political end was derived from a discourse of victimization: a conspiracy that "chauvinist" Albanian elites from Kosovo were working to bring about the systematic emigration of the non-Albanian population. Finally, the program set out a clearly populist position in calling for "evil" and "corrupt" Albanian "elites" inclined to separatism to be combated and discriminated against in favor of the "true" Albanian people, while the latter should be given the same constitutional rights as citizens of Serbia.

The SPS program of 1992 further emphasized this ethno-nationalist dimension, pulling SPS farther to the radical right. An addition was made to the previously cited paragraph from the 1990 program, stating that Kosovo holds "significant symbolic meaning for Serbian people" (SPS 1992: 55). The program claimed that Albanians had long been set on occupying Kosovo and that Serbs needed to liberate and retain the territory. The term "ethnic cleansing" was also invoked, with a call to reverse the effects of Albanian migration (SPS 1992: 56). In conceptual terms the 1992 program is a prime example of a populist radical right-wing version of democracy, molded in a "nativist ideology" which holds that state policies "should comprise 'natives' and that 'non-natives' are to be treated with hostility" (Mudde 2007: 138). The more SPS shifted to the right in its program, the more it matched the description of a right-wing populist party seeking to "radicalize its core base while antagonizing (...) other parties" (Heinisch and Mazzoleni 2016: 9). The fact that this policy was pursued by the dominant party in Serbia was one of the main reasons why Albanian parties boycotted all of the elections held in the 1990s. As Orlović (2015: 108) argues, Albanian boycotting of elections reflected the failure of the central government to integrate the country's largest national minority in institutional settings, causing a center-periphery cleavage between dominant and minority cultures in Serbia that would eventually lead to civil war in Kosovo.

SRS took a strongly negative political stance towards Kosovar Albanians from the very beginning, calling for the suppression of Albanian separatism "by all means necessary" in its program of 1990 (SRS 1990: 3). The measures that SRS proposed to achieve this aim included the "deportation of 360,000 Albanian emigrants and their descendants", the "suspension of state funding for the Albanian national minority", the "declaration of a state of war on Kosovo", the "creation of a 20–50-kilometer-wide military zone between Albania and Serbia" and a return to the ethnic make-up of Kosovo "from before 6 April 1941" (SRS 1990: 3). The 1990 program thus contained a blatant call for ethnic cleansing, and this would be a core element in SRS's 1991 manifesto.

The ethno-nationalist solutions that SPS and SRS proposed to the Kosovo territorial problem had devastating effects on the political values of Serbian voters. A series of studies on values and attitudes in Serbia in the period 1993–1996 showed that levels of xenophobia soared in these years. In 1993, a staggering 77 per cent of Serbian citizens demonstrated xenophobic attitudes, regardless of their ideological political orientations (Pantić 1995). By 1996, however, this had fallen to 36 per cent, and the situation was dampened still further following the democratic reforms of 2000. This pacification was largely brought about by the EU through its role as a mediator in institutionally-based negotiations between the Serbs and the Kosovar Albanians. The institutionalization of the process gained added legitimacy in the context of a pro-European climate in Serbia that culminated in the breakdown of SRS in 2008 and the formation of the Serbian Progressive Party (SNS), which became a populist center-right party. This change in the dynamics of the Serbian party-political scene, together with the introduction of supranational actors, changed the strategies of the populist parties, which shifted to become more in line with a form of multi-level populism targeting different actors (regional, national, supranational) with different types of rhetoric.

After the 2000s: levels of populism in Serbia

In the September and December elections of 2000, the Caeseristic regime of Slobodan Milošević was replaced by a coalition of ideologically diverse democratic parties led by the Democratic Party (DS). For the next twelve years DS held political power more or less successfully, beginning processes of political and economic modernization. One of the key elements of legitimization during this period was a clear and uncontested devotion to European integration.

This new legitimizing political formula caused significant changes in party and inter-party dynamics. There was a new ideological cleavage in Serbia, with democratic and left-wing parties taking a pro-EU stance and right-wing parties (led by SRS and their leader Tomislav Nikolić)[2] taking an anti-EU stance. Anti-EU sentiment continued on a downward trend, reducing the capacity of SRS to form a coalition and rendering it incapable of forming a government. Pro-EU sentiment remained above 60 per cent (Serbian European Integration Office 2008) even after Kosovo★ declared independence in February 2008. In the parliamentary election that followed Kosovo's★ declaration of independence, SRS managed to gain second place in the polls with an impressive 29.4 per cent of the votes (see Figure 12.2), but failed to form a government with the other anti-EU parties who gained seats in parliament. This was due to the decision of SPS to position itself as a pro-EU party and form a coalition with DS (who came in first place with 39.4 per cent of the votes). This caused a split in SRS, with Tomislav Nikolić and Aleksandar Vučić forming SNS, a pro-European center-right party. The radical right never subsequently recovered its political strength in Serbia.

There were at least two reasons for this change. The first was clearly connected to changed circumstances in intraparty dynamics. The pro-EU formula of legitimization was an important change in this regard after the 2008 election, reaching a peak after the 2014 elections in which every parliamentary party was pro-EU (Zuber and Džankić 2017: 226). The second radical change was in the nature of the territorial disputes. After Kosovo★ declared independence, territorial issues became focused on the sub-region of North Kosovo, where Serbs were presented as a minority struggling for rights of political representation rather than a majority exercising their general will over Kosovar Albanians. By spatially limiting questions of ethno-nationalism to North Kosovo, the territorial dispute over Kosovo lost its potency and ability to mobilize. The general pro-EU stance and altered territorial status of Kosovo thus had a significant impact on the populist mobilization strategies of parties in Serbia, bringing about a shift from radical and authoritarian strategies to more stable, multi-level populist strategies. This shift was reflected in the party programs of the two major populist parties in Serbia, SPS and SNS, after 2008.

In the aftermath of the civil war in Kosovo and the breakdown of the Milošević regime in 2000, SPS lost its influence on the Serbian political scene. In 2004 the party embarked upon a long process of consolidation under the leadership of Ivica Dačić, resulting in it becoming part of the governing coalition in 2008 (with DS) and remaining in power since then (in coalition with SNS after 2012). This consolidation was fully realized in 2010 with the adoption of a new party program which was social democratic in its ideological core and stripped of its ethno-nationalist dimension, albeit with the preservation of some populist elements.

The key change to the new SPS program was its abandonment of the narrative about the "people". Instead, the program now affirmed the idea that all "citizens" should be treated equally. However, this new orientation of the program still failed to provide an adequate answer to the question of the political rights of minorities. It adopted the position that cultural rights should be granted to minorities and that the state should not remain neutral when enacting laws to guarantee these rights in everyday life, while still expounding the view that minorities posed a potential threat to "stability, territorial integrity and sovereignty" (SPS 2010: 13). This was a milder version of ethno-nationalism, though retaining vestiges of the position taken by the party in its programs of the 1990s.

Significant revisions were made to the text of the old program in relation to Kosovo; indeed the issue was hardly mentioned in the new manifesto. Kosovo was presented as an integral element of Serbian national identity and a constitutive part of its statehood. A reference to Kosovo★ was also included in the part of the program that blamed Kosovar Albanian elites for the NATO bombings in the 1999 war. The parts about "ethnic cleansing" were removed, and instead the Kosovo★ authorities were accused of ghettoizing Serbs and other non-Albanian population groups.

After the 2008 election, ethno-nationalism became a secondary strategy of mobilization for the SPS. Instead the party now turned to criticizing privatization processes and tycoons from the 2000s, adopting new tactics more in line with a Western European version of populism that connects mobilization strategies with societal issues neglected by former elites (Canovan 2002: 27). After the 2012 election, however, SPS changed its partnership in the governing coalition, joining forces with SNS. This coalition gave Ivica Dačić the position of Prime Minister for a year. In this period the government led by SPS and SNS signed a Brussels agreement with Kosovo★ mediated by the EU High Representative for Foreign Affairs and Security Policy (Catherine Ashton). This agreement established a new era of relations between Serbia and Kosovo★, no longer as relations between a centralized state and a region but between two political entities (although Serbia has not recognized Kosovo★ as an independent state). The first paragraph of the agreement declared the establishment of an Association of Serb-Majority Municipalities in North Kosovo (*Zajednica srpskih opština*), thereby de facto creating a new sub-region and fully legitimizing a new multi-level populist formula for mobilization.

Such revisions of populist formulas for mobilization were evident in the 2011 program of the Serbian Progressive Party (*Srpska napredna stranka*), officially founded on 21 October 2008 after Tomislav Nikolić created a faction within SRS in September of the same year. From 2008 to 2011, SNS underwent a phase of consolidation in which it positioned itself as a center-right party and distanced itself from the radical right-wing SRS. The political actions of SNS and its leader Aleksandar Vučić after the 2012 elections were also a turning point in the mobilization strategies of nationalistic parties.[3] SNS made populism the ideational core of its party ideology, skillfully adapting various peripheral concepts to correspond more closely to situational changes and levels of political action, from ethno-nationalism to liberal pluralism. Thus SNS has both supported the election of the first female and openly LGBT prime minister in Serbian history (Ana Brnabić, Prime Minister from 2017 onwards) and yet has a leader in Aleksandar Vučić who has stated that the ICTY's verdict against Ratko Mladić was "unjust" (Al Jazeera Balkans 2017).

The SNS's official program (*The White Book of Reforms*) was enacted in 2011, one year before SNS took over power from DS. The program represented a radical turn away from the previously extreme right-wing position of SRS, while adopting anti-elitist attitudes and declaring "war on corruption". The main body of the program was anti-elitist, targeting the "democratic political elites" who held power from 2000 to 2005 ("the gravest affairs" period; SNS 2011: 80). The legitimacy pattern for this type of politics is typical of all European populist regimes and includes accusations of what Mudde and Kaltwasser (2017: 2) term "economic mismanagement", corrupt privatization and the creation of a new class of clientelist bourgeoisie that is parasitic in its relation to the suffering people. In the opening section of its program, SNS affirmed the "wise people myth" as its political standpoint:

> The Serbian Progressive Party trusts in its people and their historical experience, trusts in the still sleeping strength of Serbia and her human and material potential. We believe that only united can we prevent the further decay of Serbia and pull our country out of crisis and allow every citizen in Serbia to live a better and happier life.
>
> *(SNS 2011: 2)*

The pivotal point of SNS's program is the party's relation with the "true" people, making it a decidedly populist the program. The second layer to the program's rhetoric is its reference to the citizens of Serbia, denoting all the other people with whom the "true" people share their daily lives. While these other citizens are declared to be as deserving of happiness as "the people", it is nevertheless the task of the "people" to ensure this overarching societal happiness.

In relation to minorities the SNS program went one step further than SPS's new program. It not only recognized the cultural rights of minorities but also supported political rights such as the establishment of minority councils as political bodies (SNS 2011: 45). However, the program only guaranteed equal political treatment for minorities if they become voters for SNS.

Regarding Kosovo, the SNS of 2011 program set out various new political solutions and revived some old ones. Firstly, the program indirectly recognized the political status of Kosovo★ as an entity. Although the program decisively asserted that SNS would never recognize the independence of Kosovo★, it did demonstrate an awareness that the political reality was such that negotiations with Kosovar★ authorities were necessary (SNS 2011: 37). Secondly, the territorial dimension of the dispute over Kosovo was still upheld, although the discourse about Serbia's monopoly of the symbolic significance of Kosovo was removed. The program addressed issues relevant to Kosovar Serbs but treated them as people who needed to coexist with Kosovar Albanians. Thirdly, the political solution that SNS offered in this manifesto was a referendum in Serbia that would put the fate of the agreement into the hands of the "wise people". The program reminded its audience, however, that before a referendum could be held the consequences of "ethnic cleansing" in Kosovo first needed to be redressed and removed by letting the Serbian population return to their properties (SNS 2011: 38). These three solutions demonstrate SNS's maneuvers in negotiating peripheral ideas of populism, moving the party away from a politics of reconciliation towards ethno-politics.

Kosovo's role in the SNS program is a clear example of multi-level populism derived from a territorial dispute. The first layer, the one that establishes a relation with Kosovo*, adopts rhetoric in alignment with supranational interests. The second layer is connected to rhetoric that directs SNS's focus towards the sub-region of North Kosovo, while the final layer is directed towards the national level (the idea of a national referendum). These three layers are not complementary but in conflict with one another. The first and third layers could not be achieved together because supranational and regional actors would never agree to a referendum in Serbia as a means of reaching a decision on the status of Kosovo*, since if they did so it would result in the return of a centralized state that would deprive ethnic minorities of the rights of representation. A national referendum conflicts with the second layer, moreover, because it would never result in a zero-sum game for Kosovar Serbs and Albanians. However, when taken together, all three layers allowed SNS to present itself as a pro-EU party dedicated to peace and regional stability, making it an acceptable partner for national, regional and supranational actors.

Concluding remarks on the territorial layers of Serbian populism

This chapter has analyzed the relationship between territorial cleavages and the ascendance of populism in recent and contemporary Serbian political contexts. The case of Kosovo was selected for this analysis because it represents the most serious grievance in relation to Serbian sovereignty and one that has shaped populist discourse in Serbia over the past century. The analysis showed that the genesis of Serbian populism cannot be perceived as having developed in a continuous line uninterrupted by external influences from regional, national and supranational actors. From the disintegration of communist Yugoslavia to the fall of Slobodan Milošević's regime and up to the present day, populist parties in Serbia have shifted positions significantly in terms of the dispute over Kosovo, from an authoritarian and Caesarist political style to a more moderate approach. The actions and mobilization strategies of contemporary populism in Serbia are more decentralized and more sensitive in reflecting the context of territorial cleavage, i.e. in responding to sub-regional, national and supranational actors.

The case of Serbia challenges the prevailing understanding of populism in post-communist societies and the tendency of the literature on populism to restrict analysis of political mobilization to a "people versus elite" cleavage in what is typically framed as a far-right political discourse. As this chapter has shown in the example of Kosovo, territorial cleavages lead to redefinitions of both "the people" and "the elites" and blur the usual ideological and behavioral differences between left-wing and right-wing parties. When confronting territorial disputes, the ability to redefine the "people versus elite" cleavage is not merely a mobilization strategy of populist parties – regardless of ideological standpoint – but an essential capacity that allows parties to adapt skillfully to changing political circumstances over time.

This chapter has also demonstrated the partial paradox that processes of democratization allowed populism to thrive in Serbia through their strategies of redefining the concepts of "the people" and "the elites". Extrapolating from this it could be said, more broadly, that the more authoritarian a system is in nature, the fewer options populist parties have for selectively defining these concepts. As Canovan (2002: 28) has insightfully shown, the cluster of different definitions of political life that democracy generates allows populists to make their policies opaque by simplifying political solutions as either for or against the people – a generalization that leads to essentially undemocratic institutional outcomes. In analyzing the case of Serbia, this chapter has made this feature of the concept of populism explicit through comparative analysis of the political party programs of SPS, SRS and SNS from the 1990s and 2000s and the positions these manifestos adopted towards the territorial dispute over Kosovo. During the authoritarian regime of the 1990s, populist parties leaned heavily on nationalist and culturally determined notions of the people and the elites, relating and dividing them along territorial cleavages, as either patriots or betrayers of Serbian national interests. This ethno-nationalist discourse was constructed by combining the myth of Kosovo with the actual threat of regional riots and wars. Slobodan Milošević adopted this discourse as an overarching national ideology, thereby determining the strategies of political mobilization during the 1990s. After democratic reforms in 2000, the political arena was opened up to different political actors and influences, including not only national but regional and supranational actors. Over the past two decades, populism has thus evolved from a crude strategy for nationalist mobilization to more flexible strategies of addressing the people and targeting different elites in different political contexts.

Finally, these evolutionary steps are quite explicit when placed in the context of the territorial cleavage generated by the status of Kosovo★. After Kosovo★ declared independence and gained political support from the EU, populist parties in Serbia adapted to these newly changed political circumstances by taking a multi-level approach to mobilization strategies. Populist parties, and SNS in particular, have skillfully adapted their rhetoric, redefining the "people versus elite" cleavages when addressing different levels of actors in sub-regional, national and supranational contexts.

The findings of this chapter remain open-ended and need to be further explored and substantiated by empirical data on the actual extent to which populist parties influence mobilization outcomes and their voters. In the case of Serbia, recent research on populism (Lutovac 2017) has shown that the connection between populism and the territorial issue of Kosovo is still a strong formula for legitimization. In terms of territorial cleavages, today's Serbia is a divided society, though not so much along ethnic lines as along ideological ones. Serbian populist parties have sought to generate an ideological discourse that takes the fact of ethnic heterogeneity and transforms it into a claim that Serbia is an ethnically divided society in order to lend legitimacy to nationalist mobilization strategies. A broader comparative study is needed to determine whether Serbia is an isolated case or whether the findings of this chapter may be applied to other post-communist European societies with ethnic divides and territorial disputes.

Notes

1 I use the terms Kosovo and Kosovo* to refer to a territorial entity and a political entity respectively. When used territorially, I refer to the province of Kosovo and Metohija (hereafter: Kosovo) as defined by UN Security Council Resolution 1244. When referring to it as political entity as defined by the Brussels Agreement of 2013, I use the term Kosovo* with an asterisk.
2 Vojislav Šešelj was prosecuted for war crimes committed during the 1990s at the International Criminal Tribunal for the Former Yugoslavia at The Hague from 2002 and was not present in Serbia.
3 Tomislav Nikolić resigned from the seat of party president after he was elected President of Serbia in May 2012.

References

Anderson, B. (2006) *Imagined Communities*. London/New York: Verso.
Balkans, Al Jazeera (2017) "New York Times: Srbija tone u nacionalizam". 27 November. http://balkans.aljazeera.net/vijesti/new-york-times-srbija-tone-u-nacionalizam. Accessed 21 January 2018.
Betz, H. -G. and Johnson, C. (2017) "Against the Current – Stemming the Tide: The Nostalgic Ideology of the Contemporary Radical Populist Right". In: Mudde, C. (ed.) *The Populist Radical Right: A Reader*. London: Routledge, pp. 67–82.
Bieber, F. (2005) "Serbia in the 1990s: The Case of Ethnic Semi-Democracy". In: Smooha, S. and Järve, P. (eds.) *The Fate of Ethnic Democracy in Post-Communist Europe*. Budapest: Local Government and Public Service Reform Initiative and European Centre for Minority Issues, pp. 167–189.
Börzel, T. and Grimm, S. (2018) "Building Good (Enough) Governance in Postconflict Societies & Areas of Limited Statehood: The European Union & the Western Balkans", *Daedalus*, 147(1), pp. 116–127.
Brubaker, R. (2009) *Nationalism Reframed*. Cambridge: Cambridge University Press.
Canovan, M. (2002) "Taking Politics to the People: Populism as the Ideology of Democracy". In Mény, Y. and Surel, Y. (eds.) *Democracies and the Populist Challenge*. London: Palgrave Macmillan, pp. 25–44.
Elias, A. (2009) *Minority Nationalist Parties and European Integration*. London: Routledge.

Eriksen, T. H. (2010). *Ethnicity and Nationalism. Anthropological Perspectives*. New York: Pluto Press (2 ed.).
Gagnon, V. P. Jr. (2004) *The Myth of Ethnic War*. Ithaca, NY: Cornell University Press.
Goati, V. (1995) "Socijalna osnova političkih partija u Srbiji". In Pavlović, V. (ed.) *Potisnuto civilno društvo*. Beograd: Eko Centar, pp. 199–200.
Golubović, Z. (2004) "Autoritarno nasleđe i prepreke za razvoj civilnog društva i demokratske političke culture". In: Vujadinović, D. et al. (ed.) *Između Autoritarizma i demokratije*. Beograd: Centar za demokratiju, pp. 233–256.
Gourevitch, P. A. (1979) "The Reemergence of 'Peripheral Nationalisms': Some Comparative Speculations on the Spatial Distribution of Political Leadership and Economic Growth", *Comparative Studies in Society and History*, 21(3), pp. 303–322.
Heinisch, R. and Mazzoleni, O. (2016) "Introduction". In: Heinisch, R. and Mazzoleni, O. (eds.) *Understanding Populists Party Organization: The Radical Right in Western Europe*. London: Palgrave Macmillan, pp. 1–18.
Kecmanović, D. (2002) *Ethnic Times: Exploring Ethno-Nationalism in the Former Yugoslavia*. London: Praeger.
Kellas, J. G. (2004) *Nationalist Politics in Europe: The Constitutional and Electoral Dimension*. London: Palgrave Macmillan.
Krause, K. D. (2015) "Potpuni i parcijalni rascepi u post-komunističkim društvima", *Srpska politička misao*, posebno izdanje, pp. 35–56.
Lončar, J. (2017) "Stanje demokratije u Srbiji kroz prizmu izborne kampanje 2016. Godine". In: Pilipović, G. and Stojiljković, Z. (eds.) *Stranke i javne politike: Izbori u Srbiji 2016. godine*. Beograd: Konrad-Adenauer-Sriftung, pp. 49–68.
Lutovac, Z. (2017) "Odnos građana prema političkoj eliti i reprezentativnoj demokratiji". In: Lutovac, Z. (ed.) *Građani Srbije i Populizam: Javno mnjenje Srbije 2017*. Beograd: Institut društvenih nauka i Centar za politikološka istraživanja i javno mnjenje, pp. 13–40.
Malešević, S. (2006) *Identity as Ideology*. London: Palgrave Macmillan.
Mazzoleni, O. (2005) "Multi-level Populism and Centre-Periphery Cleavage in Switzerland: The Case of the Lega dei Ticinesi". In Mény, Y. and Caramani, D. (eds.) *Challenges to Consensual Politics: Democracy, Identity, and Populist Protest in the Alpine Region*. Brussels: Peter Lang, pp. 209–227.
Mihajlović, K. and Krestić, V. (1995) *Memorandum of the Serbian Academy of Sciences and Arts*. Belgrade: Serbian Academy of Sciences and Arts.
Minkenberg, M. (2017) "The Radical Right in Postcolonial Central and Eastern Europe: Comparative Observations and Interpretations". In: Mudde, C. (ed.) *The Populist Radical Right: A Reader*. London: Routledge, pp. 386–403.
Mudde, C. (2007) *Populist Radical Right Parties in Europe*. Cambridge: Cambridge University Press.
Mudde, C. and Kaltwasser, C. R. (2017) *Populism: A Very Short Introduction*. Oxford: Oxford University Press.
Müller, J-W. (2015) "Parsing Populism", *Juncture*, 22(2), pp. 80–89.
Mungiu-Pippidi, A. (2004) "Miloševićevi birači – objašnjenje za nacionalizam u postkomunističkoj Evropi koji je potekao iz masa". In: Mungiu-Pippidi, A. and Krastev, I. (eds.) *Nacionalizam posle komunizma*. Beograd: BFPI, pp. 47–91.
Orlović, S. (2015) "Društveni rascepi i njihov uticaj na partijski sistem Srbije", *Srpska politička misao, posebno izdanje* [special issue], pp. 103–124.
Pantić, D. (1995) "Dominantne vrednosne orijentacije u Srbiji i mogućnost nastanka civilnog društva". In: Pavlović, V. (ed.) *Potisnuto civilno društvo*. Beograd: Eko Centar, pp. 71–105.

Podunavac, M. (1995) "Princip građanstva i priroda političkog režima u post-komunizmu: slučaj Srbija". In: Pavlović, V. (ed.) *Potisnuto civilno društvo*. Beograd: Eko Centar, pp. 221–238.

Politika (2008) "Data je reč, dok živimo – Kosovo je Srbija". 21 February. www.politika.rs/sr/clanak/33766/Politika/Rec-je-data-dok-zivimo-Kosovo-je-Srbija. Accessed 21 January 2018.

Russell-Omaljev, A. (2017) *Divided We Stand: Discourses on Identity in "First" and "Other" Serbia*. Stuttgart: Ibidem Press.

Serbian European Integration Office. (2008) *The EU Perspective of the Serbian Citizens Trends: Results of Public Opinion Poll*, www.mei.gov.rs/upload/documents/prezentacije/european_perspective_serbia_dec_2008.ppt, Accessed 27 December 2018.

SNS. (2011) *Bela knjiga "Programom do promena"*. www.sns.org.rs/sites/default/files/bela-knjiga_0.pdf. Accessed 21 January 2018.

Spruyt B., Keppens G. and Van Droogenbroeck, F. (2016) "Who Supports Populism and What Attracts People to it?" *Political Research Quarterly*, 69(2), pp. 335–346.

SPS. (1990) *Programske osnove i Statut Socijalističke partije Srbije*. Beograd: SPS.

SPS. (1992) *Osnove programa: predlog*. Beograd: SPS.

SPS. (2010) *Program Socijalističke partije Srbije*. www.sps.org.rs/documents/PROGRAMME%20SPS.pdf. Accessed 21 January 2018.

SRS. (1990) *Politički program srpskog četničkog pokreta*. www.srpskaradikalnastranka.org.rs/files/izdavastvo/velika_srbija/VS0001.pdf. Accessed 21 January 2018.

SRS. (1991a) *Program Srpske radikalne stranke*. www.srpskaradikalnastranka.org.rs/files/izdavastvo/velika_srbija/VS0009.pdf. Accessed 21 January 2018.

Szöcsik, E. and Zuber, C. I. (2018) "The Second Edition of the EPAC Expert Survey on Ethno-nationalism in Party Competition: Testing for Validity and Reliability", *Regional and Federal Studies*. Online first. Doi:10.1080/13597566.2018.1512975.

Vincent, A. (2015) "Nationalism". In: Freeden, M, Sargent, L. T. and Stears, M. (eds.) *The Oxford Handbook of Political Ideologies*. Oxford: Oxford University Press, pp. 452–473.

Vreme. (2009) "O Srbima, bitkama i Jugoslaviji". 25 June. www.vreme.com/cms/view.php?id=872091. Accessed 22 May 2018.

Zuber, C. I. and Džankić, J. (2017) "Serbia and Montenegro. From Centralization to Secession and Multi-Ethnic Regionalism". In Schakel, A. H. (ed.) *Regional and National Elections in Eastern Europe*. London: Palgrave Macmillan, pp. 207–238.

13
POPULISM AND ETHNO-TERRITORIAL POLITICS – CONCLUSIONS

Bridging legacies in understanding party mobilization

Reinhard Heinisch, Emanuele Massetti and Oscar Mazzoleni

This book has aimed to conceptualize the relationship between populism and territory-related dimensions in order to develop a new perspective for understanding current trends in party mobilization across Europe. What role does the territorial dimension play in state-wide populist party mobilization? How do regionalist and state-nationalist claims interact with populist discourses? A common denominator is found in their equation of "the people" with certain ideas of ethnos and territory and their antagonistic relationship with elites, including both internal elites and those external to the territory in question. However, the analysis reveals that the relationship between populism and territorial dimension is varied and complex. In line with the main objective set out in the introductory chapter, this conclusion will first highlight the importance of populism in regionalist mobilization before going on to show the crucial influence of the territorial dimension in shaping populist strategy. Finally, it will summarize the contributions made in this book to the scholarship on links between nationalism, regionalism and populism.

The relevance of populist claims

The chapters dedicated to the analysis of regionalist and minority nationalist parties have shown how deeply populism can be intertwined with political mobilizations based on the center-periphery cleavage. Through regionalism or minority nationalism, actors politicize the distinctive features of the population of a specific sub-state region vis-à-vis the population of the state as a whole (Fitjar 2010). Given that the extent of self-government demanded by regionalist parties can vary considerably, populists can select their own approach from within a wide range of possible claims-making. At the same time, regionalist parties themselves can develop populist strategies in an effort to avail themselves of new opportunity structures (e.g. by exploiting the impact of economic deprivation on a region, to give an example from this book) or to distinguish themselves from competitors. From these studies of regionalist parties, it emerges that the relations of such political actors with populism vary considerably.

Three qualitatively distinct levels of regionalist engagement with populist discourses emerge. First of all, some regionalist or minority nationalist parties develop strong populist claims. Indeed, it is difficult for some parties to disentangle populist and territorial claims. This is the case, for example, with Lega Nord in Italy, Lega dei Ticinesi in Switzerland and the Belgian Vlaams Belang, since these parties' anti-immigrant nationalist stances intersect so closely with regionalist claims. In other regionalist parties, however, populist discourse is barely in evidence. This is the case with the Silesian Regional Party in Poland and the liberal regionalist DeFI party in Belgium, for example, in which populism is almost completely absent. Finally, there is an intermediate level of adoption of populist discourse, whereby regionalist parties appropriate populist themes and rhetoric only in response to certain circumstances. This evolution in the positions adopted by some regionalists within political systems thus reveals a complex relationship to populist stances. For instance, regionalist parties in Catalonia and in the Celtic peripheries of Britain have adopted only partial populist discourses or adopted a populist stance only temporarily. Specifically, Catalan regionalist parties have employed populism in their recent shift to a secessionist stance that emphasizes the right to self-determination of the Catalan people vis-à-vis Spanish elites (see chapter by Barrio et al.). The Scottish National Party (SNP) and Plaid Cymru in the UK, by contrast, have engaged with populism in two distinct ways at different stages in their history: adopting a form of centrist populism in their formative phases (1920s–1960s); and, since 2010, a type of left-wing populism (see the chapter by Massetti).

Where populism is a predominant element, the "enemies" in its discourse tend to be derived primarily from national and ethnic "others", often seen as allied with national elites of one sort or another. In this case populists may develop a national in-group-out-group discourse that seeks to immunize a certain electorate against outside criticism while tagging political opponents as compromised on account of their connections with "alien" influences. In a second case, populist discourse makes a generic reference to an unspecified "heartland" or hinterland that finds itself in an antagonistic relationship with metropolitan elites. In a third case, populist discourse includes claims about specific people in a specific region. Here, populist actors may depend on that region as their principal powerbase, either because their focus is primarily regionalist or because the area serves as a stronghold and springboard for competing at national level. Alternatively, the region may embody a certain symbolic significance for the national narrative, so that strength of support in that region confers some special legitimacy to a national political actor, and thus populists employ this discourse for the purpose of national competition.

Populist themes are incorporated differently into the ideological repertoires and discourses of regionalist or minority nationalist parties. In some cases, these different combinations occur with the same party across time. As mentioned above, the chapter by Massetti shows how such a populist discourse has been employed in very different ways by the SNP and Plaid Cymru in two distinct periods: in their formative phase and then later during the recent economic crisis. In the first period, populism was used as a back-up to regionalism so as to avoid adopting a clear position in left-right politics. After having developed a left-leaning ideological outlook in the period from the 1970s to the 2000s, however, the two "Celtic" parties operated a new programmatic synthesis in the context of the Great Recession by mixing regionalist, populist and leftist ideological elements. In particular, they embraced an anti-austerity left-wing populist discourse reminiscent of some state-wide populist parties in Southern Europe such as Podemos, Syriza, and to some extent also the Movimento 5 Stelle. The chapter on Spain by Barrio, Barberà and Rodríguez-Teruel presents us with mainstream regionalist parties and civil society organizations that have drifted towards employing populist discourse and strategies as a result of a mix of disillusionment with Spanish institutional processes and economic dissatisfaction. Compared to the cases in the UK, the strategic repositioning among these Spanish parties has even resulted in their pushing the boundaries of institutional politics in liberal democracies to the limits. Claims about the right of the Catalan "people" have led to open defiance of the Spanish constitutional order and public calls for unilateral secession. These parties thus represent the most radical cases (in terms of center-periphery politics) in our analysis.

The importance of the territory

This book has also explored how nation-state populist parties consider territorial opportunities and constraints when shaping their national messages. The focus on nation-state populist parties has shown how these parties have tried to reconcile state-nationalist ideology with region-specific or even regionalist demands. For instance, the state-nationalist French Front National (today the Rassemblement National) has clearly adapted its discourse to different regions (see the chapter by Ivaldi and Dutozia), while in Germany the AfD has developed regional nativism in seeking to represent the grievances of people in Eastern Germany (chapter by Betz and Habersack). The Freedom Party of Austria (FPÖ), meanwhile, has openly engaged in unionist regionalism since its Carinthian regional branch adopted a confrontational stance vis-à-vis Vienna, while at the same time targeting the Slovene ethnic minority in that region (see the chapter by Heinisch).

What the above mentioned chapters demonstrate is that even the staunchest state-nationalist party needs to calibrate its populist discourse to regional specificities across the state. Borderlands may be more affected by immigration, for example, whereas industrial decline due to globalization will resonate in some parts of a country more than in others. The concurrence of regional development and populist discourse is thus an important factor in the affinity between national populists and regions. For instance, the chapter on the Front National shows very clearly that in Southern France the party primarily competes against the mainstream right and therefore emphasizes immigration and identity, whereas in the economically depressed North it essentially competes against the left and therefore focuses on economic redistribution and protectionism. Another example is provided in the chapter on Germany where, as already mentioned, the AfD has found a special opportunity in Eastern Germany largely because of grievances against the political dominance of West Germans, economic deprivation, and the westward drift of the leftist populist Die Linke party, which originated in (and once sought to represent) Eastern Germany.

Multi-level electoral competition pushes even ultra-nationalist populist parties to politicize regional peculiarities (see the chapter by Vranić). Some chapters show very clearly this interplay between party orientation and the territorial dimension, as well as how potentially conflicting ethno-territorial ideologies such as state nationalism and regionalism are taken up. Populist claims serve to mitigate or obfuscate such conflicts and allow parties to reduce risks while increasing their political opportunities. For political actors to succeed, they need to master political communications across different levels of government and thus demonstrate sophistication and a profound understanding of the interactive effects between regional and national settings. Competing in multi-level arenas also necessitates that nation-state populist parties adjust the way in which they organize and develop their claims. For instance, centralized as it is, the FN has still needed to translate its policy prescriptions into policies relevant to the regional level of administration. Among the challenges that populists may face are that such implementation can often be rather technical and that regional authorities have only limited competence in matters that are very important to the supporters of populist parties. At regional and local level, therefore, national-level mobilization strategies or discourses about blocking immigration or hiring more police, for example, may not be effective. This means populist parties have to adapt their programmatic strategies. Of course, mainstream parties have to do this as well and routinely translate national policy initiatives into regional contexts by pointing to specific applications and consequences. The problem for populist parties, as shown in the chapters on the FN and the FPÖ, is that they can ill afford to come across as ordinary parties in the eyes of their supporters but rather need to draw a distinction between themselves and the mainstream. Some chapters here also emphasize the "chameleonic" traits of populist claims (Taggart 2000), entailing a high degree of adaptability to context. As a result, these formations have often responded effectively to situational circumstances, including different regional contexts and territorial settings.

The ambivalence inherent in all these populist stances, which include and exclude people often on the basis of only the vaguest criteria and thus raise the question of where the "heartland" begins and ends, also shapes political demands and programmatic positions. As a result, demands often do not involve bargaining over specific policy issues in contention between the national and the regional levels but are rather about more diffuse calls for a radical change in the relationship between the national and regional levels.

Employing multi-level frames leads to extensive ambivalence on the part of populist actors when they engage in claims-making. This also applies to claims as to who precisely the "true people" are in whose name populist parties purport to act (see the chapters by Mazzoleni and Ruzza and by Heinisch and Marent). Are they the "native" born people of the entire nation-state threatened by immigrants and minorities? Do they live in an imagined "heartland" marginalized by metropolitan elites? Or are they the people of a particular region who merit special consideration because of some special circumstances? All three cases involve populist conceptions of "the people" as homogenous and amorphous entities in need of special protection and elevation. Nonetheless, there are clear variations in the claims and discourses employed.

In most cases of regionalist populism (or populist regionalism), "the people" are equated with the regional population (or the minority nation) while "the elites" are equated with the central institutions of the nation-state. Conversely, in most cases of state-nationalist populism (or populist state-nationalism), "the people" are identified as the (majority) nation while "the elites" are synonymous with the supra-national (EU) and/or international institutions in liaison with allegedly anti-patriotic internal political and economic forces. In between these two clear-cut patterns we find a considerable number of possible combinations. For instance, there are regionalist populist parties that target EU elites as much as they target national elites (e.g. the Vlaams Belang party in Belgium), or that target the latter even more than the former (e.g. the Ticino League in Switzerland). We also find regionalist parties which began their secessionist struggle from a marked Europhile perspective but then became disillusioned by the EU's position on their cause (e.g. the Catalan European Democratic party and the Republican Left of Catalonia party). In addition, we find state-nationalist parties that target national elites not only from a national-populist perspective but also from a regionalist populist perspective (e.g. the Carinthian regional branch of the FPÖ in Austria and the Eastern German branches of the AfD in Germany). Finally, we also encounter populist regionalist parties that are turning into state-nationalist-oriented parties (e.g. the Lega in Italy). What we do not find, however, are any cases of populist state-nationalist parties that do not target EU elites. Indeed, to the same extent as criticism of nation-state elites is a key characteristic of regionalist populism, Euroscepticism seems to be a clear fixture of state-nationalist populism. In this respect, state-nationalism can be seen as a form of regionalism in relation to the emerging EU super-state.

Central and Eastern Europe

Another feature intended to set this book apart is the inclusion of cases from Central and Eastern Europe. Despite the extensive literature on the widespread appeal of nationalism throughout this broader European region, such analysis is often still not well-integrated into the wider literature, as if to suggest special theories would be required to understand political developments in Central and Eastern Europe. Undoubtedly, the region does present certain important historical, socio-economic and socio-cultural differences vis-à-vis Western Europe. As the studies here have shown, however, the patterns of interaction between nationalism, regionalism, and populism can be understood very much along the same lines as they exist in Western Europe. Notwithstanding these similarities, this book has also drawn attention to three important differences whose impact has been significant in the analyses here. Firstly, in parts of Eastern Europe there are historical grievances and competing narratives in the formation of majority nationalist and regionalist accounts that have only been allowed to surface openly since the collapse of Communism. Secondly, the diaspora of majority and minority kinship groups throughout the region, coupled with religious cleavages, can be a factor in mobilizing popular support and informing populist strategies. Moreover, the process of accession to the EU under economically difficult circumstances and, in most cases, as junior partners to the most powerful Western member states, has created a regional identity in which the latter are seen as culturally foreign and economically exploitative (see the chapter by Betz and Habersack, alluding to the case of Eastern Germany). European integration has also affected regions differently, creating winners and losers and divisions that can easily be exploited by political actors and integrated in their populist claims-making.

The case of the Silesian Autonomy Movement (RAŚ) in Poland, and its offshoot, the recently created Silesian Regional Party (ŚPR), is analyzed by Magdalena Solska. Within this Polish center-periphery cleavage it is the regionalists that present themselves as a "civic" political force vis-à-vis state authorities unwilling to respond to their regionalist demands and a government currently subject to international criticism for its nationalist, illiberal and anti-pluralist tendencies. At the same time, the discourse of RAŚ includes anti-establishment and populist features when making claims against current and previous ruling elites. These claims are tempered, however, by the party's emphasis on civic engagement and responsibility. In this case we see a clash of territorial conceptions that pits a nation-state which has often been partitioned and has only recently attained full sovereignty against a regional population whose recognition would pose a challenge to the national majority narrative. Populist claims on both sides, and the anti-establishment discourse of the regionalists, are part of the pattern of interaction. Solska's analysis also reminds us that Poles have thus far seen the EU primarily through the prism of economic advantages, though this may change due to the territorial dimension in domestic politics as this conflict becomes increasingly intertwined with the issue of European values and the question of which party is more apt to represent these values, the nationalist Law and Justice party (PiS) or the regionalist RAŚ/ŚPR.

Edina Szöcsik's analysis of the Hungarian case finds that national identity represents the core issue in the discourse of successful radical right populist parties. These parties style themselves as defenders of the nation and present internal minorities as a threat. In the Hungarian case this means that the Roma minority has been a special target and even a source of competition in the rivalry between the two main national-level right-wing populist parties, Jobbik and Fidesz, especially in the period from 2010 to 2014. In addition, the matter of external Hungarian minorities and their protection is another source of legitimacy for Hungary's nationalist parties and has served as a constitutive issue of the Hungarian right since the collapse of Communism. The role of territory is particularly interesting in this political contest. Whereas external Hungarian minorities are seen as closely connected to clearly circumscribed territories whose loss is regarded as a stain on the Hungarian nation, the Roma present a de-territorialized threat. Indeed, it is precisely on account of their lack of a clear territorial connection that the Roma are presented as alien to the nation and a threat to law and order, though not as a threat to the territorial integrity of the state. It is especially this policy toward the Roma that has been a constant source of conflict between Brussels and Budapest. Since the accession process the European Commission has exerted pressure on Eastern European EU member states like Hungary to adopt policies supporting the societal integration of the Roma. The Euroscepticism promoted by Fidesz and similar parties thus draws on both nationalism and populism and is centered on discourse about the treatment of sub-state groups and minorities.

In the chapter by Bojan Vranić, the relationship between ethno-territorial cleavages and the ascendance of populism in contemporary Serbia is analyzed. This chapter focuses on the issue of Kosovo, since this region represents not only the most profound challenge to Serbia's sovereignty but is also, as a territory, a core constitutive element in Serbia's national majority narrative. The analysis shows an evolution in parties' nationalist mobilization strategies, shifting from a more authoritarian stance in the past to a more decentralized populist mode. This shift reflects the changing context of territorial cleavages, especially in the relationships between sub-regional (North Kosovo), regional (Kosovo), and supra-national actors (the EU and the international community). The case of Serbia again confirms the capacity of populism to interact extremely well with nationalist parties of all ideological orientations. In this case, the issue of Kosovo exemplifies territorial cleavages but blurs the usual political differences in terms of ideological and behavioral conventions between left-wing and right-wing parties. The chapter suggests that this territorial discourse has remained the central constant among these parties, which have otherwise adapted to changing political circumstances over time. While the myth of Kosovo and the underlying ethno-nationalist discourse persists, its use has become more subtle in the form of varying the "people versus elite" discourse in order to target different elites in different political contexts. Kosovo's independence and its political support by the EU have forced populist parties in Serbia to adapt again to a multi-level arena and recalibrate their mobilization strategies when addressing actors in regional, national, and supra-national contexts.

The chapter by Marko Kukec investigates the strategy of a Croatian regionalist party that combines elements of regionalism and populism to sharpen the center-periphery conflict lines. The Alliance of Slavonia and Baranja (HDSSB) party is clearly a case of unionist regionalism (Massetti 2009), whereby Slavonians advance claims of regional specificity but also identify themselves strongly with the whole nation and thus with Croat majority nationalism. HDSSB thus sees Slavonia as the "heartland" of Croatia, and Slavonians as the quintessential Croats, exemplifying the people's fighting spirit (and their extreme sacrifice for the nation), strong work ethic and modest lifestyles. These characteristics are presented as virtues related to the region's farming economy and traditionalist socio-cultural fabric, which the party cultivates in its overall discourse. The populism of HDSSB becomes evident in the way the party pits the qualities and needs of the Slavonian people against the alleged corruption and indifference of the Croat elites in Zagreb. In turn, this premise also represents the main justification for regionalist demands for autonomy and more power and resources, i.e. the demands the party has been pushing since its establishment. This is the clearest example among our European cases of a regionalist party sharing a state-nationalist narrative but employing populist claims to pursue regionalist goals.

Rethinking nationalism, regionalism, Euroscepticism and populism

As a general aim, this book has sought to make a genuine contribution to scholarship by drawing together concepts such as populism, regionalism, and nationalism. Most academic analysis has tended to focus either on the populist or the regionalist/nationalist nature of parties analyzed but has devoted little or no attention to the linkages and interactions between them. This tendency in the scholarship on party politics implies a false dichotomy of sorts, presenting populism and territorially-rooted ideologies, especially regionalism and nationalism, as somehow juxtaposed, unrelated or even incompatible. By contrast, this work highlights the heuristic relevance of disentangling nationalism and regionalism as territorial ideologies. This is not to say that the relationship between populism and nationalism has gone unnoticed, of course; the identification between "the people" and "the nation" has long been subject to debate (e.g. Mény and Surel 2000: 204–214). However, works that systematically focus on this relationship from a dual perspective are rather rare (see De Cleen 2017) and generally do not distinguish conceptually between majority nationalism and regionalism/minority nationalism.

Majority nationalism and to a lesser extent minority nationalism share a common demand for protecting the nation from outsiders and external threats. As such, nationalism can be directed against both internal targets such as immigrants and external targets such as supra-national powers. Indeed, as European democracies found themselves increasingly constrained by the strengthening of the EU, so Euroscepticism has become a notion uniting different populist parties across the continent. Eurosceptic claims are not exclusively manifestations of state-nationalism; such claims are also sometimes expressed by regionalist forces criticizing the impact of European integration on their particular region rather than on the member-state as a whole. Given the centrality of the national sovereignty question, i.e. the issue of perceived interference in national decision-making by supra-national institutions, however, Euroscepticism does tend to converge with state nationalism. Indeed, national-level actors concerned about "sovereignism" and the influence of transnational institutions and global markets also tend to view the EU as a conduit for such trends rather than as a form of protection from them.

This study also contributes to analyzing populism not in its isolation but in conjunction with other and already longer established political concepts. Independently of whether populism is considered as a ("thin-centered") ideology or as a discourse, the chapters in this book show the capacity of populism to be attached to, or combined with the territorial dimension. Indeed, one of the lessons learned from this study is that a large and growing number of relevant parties in contemporary democracies do not fall fully or neatly within any single one of the three full-fledged ideologies (conservatism, liberalism and socialism) but rather profess a mix of elements taken from the three big ideologies as well as from thin-centered ideologies and looser political discourses.

This study also contributes directly to the literature on populism, above all in identifying the crucial implications for the contemporary (populist) politics along territorial and multi-level dimensions. Populist discourse appears to be fueled by (or is used to politicize) perceived inequalities in the distribution of powers and resources, whether horizontally or vertically or both, which raise issues of legitimacy. Grievances channeled through populist discourse are particularly effective when there are perceived disparities between the allocation of powers/resources and territorially-based identities (e.g. national identities vs. EU powers, or regional identities vs. nation-state powers), since such disparities allow populist actors to point to an alleged detachment between "their" people and the elites. In other words, ethno-territorial and multi-level politics serve to magnify the populist predicament in two ways. Firstly, ethno-territorial politics allows populist actors to denounce the gulf between people and elites not only in terms of daily policy preferences but also in terms of values and identity. Secondly, multi-level politics provides populist actors with the institutional means to challenge elites at different (usually higher) levels. An important contribution made here to the study of populism is the confirmation that, even within Europe and when combined with different ethno-territorial ideologies, populism can take on different ideological orientations along the left-right axis.

This book also speaks to the development of scholarship on ethno-territorial ideologies, and in particular to the literature on regionalist parties. It does so in two ways. First, it extends the literature on regionalist parties by presenting an analysis of two regionalist parties that have emerged in former Communist Europe: RAŚ in the Silesian region of Poland and HDSSB in the Slavonian region of Croatia. The investigation of these regionalist parties in this part of Europe by itself constitutes an important broadening of empirical research on political regionalism, since the literature on regionalist parties to date has focused predominantly on Western Europe (De Winter 1998; Massetti 2009; Mazzoleni and Mueller 2016), while the literature on Central-Eastern Europe has traditionally been more concerned with ethnic minority parties (Bugajski 2015). Secondly, this book highlights the many possible levels of synergy between regionalism and populism. The lightest form of synergy is represented by the regionalist populist dichotomy (regional people vs. nation-state elites), which can be reached starting both from the regionalist-only dichotomy (region vs. nation-state) or from the populist-only dichotomy (people vs. elites).

The strength with which this regionalist populist dichotomy is used may depend on various factors: from the compatibility/incompatibility between the regional and nation-state identity to the intensity of a regionalist struggle against the nation-state. For instance, a high-intensity struggle such as that pursued in Catalonia is supported by a strong regionalist populist dichotomy that aims to delegitimize the Spanish elites and institutional processes while legitimizing the unilateral decisions taken by the Catalan people and their regional representatives. Regionalist populism (or populist regionalism) becomes more evident, however, when populist discourse serves not only in a regionalist struggle but also in other important policy areas in which there appear to be crucial disparities between the preferences of the regional people and the policies imposed on them from the nation-state's central institutions, especially if all state-wide parties appear to converge on these policies. Clear examples of this type of broader synergy can be found in the right-wing anti-immigrant populism practiced by the Belgian VB since the 1980s or the Italian Lega Nord and the Swiss Lega dei Ticinesi since the 1990s, and the left-wing anti-austerity populism of the SNP and Plaid Cymru in recent years in the UK. Overall, the most important contribution of this work to the literature on regionalism is its widening of the empirical investigation into how regionalist parties, which were once considered to be single-issue parties, have extended their ideological outlooks and discourse beyond their core concerns. Adding populism to traditional left-right and new left-right issues in this way serves as a response to the call made more than a decade ago by De Winter et al. (2006: 252) to widen the comparative study of regionalist parties' ideologies.

References

Bugajski, J. (2015) *Ethnic Politics in Eastern Europe: A Guide to Nationality Policies, Organizations and Parties*. Abingdon: Routledge.

De Cleen, B. (2017) "Populism and Nationalism". In: Kaltwasser, C. R., Taggart, P., Ostiguy P. and Ochoa Espejo, P. (eds.) *The Oxford Handbook of Populism*. Oxford: Oxford University Press, pp. 342–362.

De Winter, L. (1998) "Conclusion: A Comparative Analysis of the Electoral, Office and Policy Success of Ethnoregionalist Parties". In: De Winter, L. and Türsan, H. (eds.) *Regionalist Parties in Western Europe*. London: Routledge, pp. 190–235.

De Winter, L., Gomez-Reino, M. and Lynch, P. (2006) "Conclusion: The Future Study of Autonomist and Regionalist Parties". In: De Winter, L., Gomez-Reino, M. and Lynch, P. (eds.) *Autonomist Parties in Europe: Identity Politics and the Revival of the Centre-Periphery Cleavage*. Barcelona: ICPS. Vol. II, pp. 247–270.

Fitjar, R.D. (2010) *The Rise of Regionalism: Causes of Regional Mobilization in Western Europe*. Oxon: Routledge.

Massetti, E. (2009) "Explaining Regionalist Party Positioning in a Multi-dimensional Ideological Space: A Framework for Analysis", *Regional and Federal Studies* 19(4/5), pp. 501–531.

Mazzoleni, O. and Mueller, S. (eds.) (2016) *Regionalist Parties in Western Europe: Dimensions of Success*. London: Routledge.

Mény, Y. and Surel, Y. (2000) *Par le Peuple, Pour Le Peuple. Le Populisme et la Démocratie*. Paris: Fayard.

Taggart, P. (2000) *Populism*. Buckingham: Philadelphia Open University Press.

INDEX

Advisory Council for the National Transition, ACNT (Catalonia) 101
Alternative für Deutschland, AfD 13, 113–129, 282–284
Akkermann, T. 1, 4, 214–215, 235, 239
Alleanza Nazionale (Italy) 74
Alliance Future Austria 142
Albertazzi, D. 1–2, 5, 20, 44, 70, 75, 213, 225, 228
Allisio, F. 182
Anderson, B. 216, 258
Annemans, G. 46–47
Anselmi, M. 5
Antony, B. 173
Arreckx, M. 182
Art, D. 171
Arter, D. 215, 227
Arzheimer, K. 67, 110, 112, 122, 137, 169
Aslanidis, P. 4
Assemblea Nacional Catalana 91
Association of Towns for the Independence (Catalonia) 101–102
autonomist 6, 71–72, 80, 196, 198, 206

Baeckeroot, M. 173
Bale, T. 4, 235, 238
Barberà, O. 12, 88, 91, 282
Barr, R. 216, 226
Barrio, A. 12, 88, 91, 100, 281, 266
Bartlett, J. 241
Bay, N. 173
Beaumont O. 181
Berlet, C. 4

Berlusconi, S. 70, 79, 154
Bettati, O. 182
Betz, H.-G. 1, 4–5, 13, 20, 89, 110, 112–113, 124, 165, 167, 172, 264, 282, 285
Bieber, F. 256, 258, 260
Bignasca, G. 78
Bild, M. 173
Bilde, B. 178
Biorcio, R. 1, 71, 90
Biró-Nagy, A. 237, 241, 251
Blair, T. 28
Bloco de Esquerda (Portugal) 21
Bloc Québécois 43
Böcskei, B. 237
Bolleyer, N. 138
Bompard, J. 181
Bonikowski, B. 27
Borghezio, M. 74
Bossi, U. 72–73
Breuilly, J. 42, 65
Brexit 31, 33
Briffaut, F. 178
Briois, S. 178
British Conservative Party 7
Brown, G. 27
Brubaker, R. 42, 114, 240, 256
Bündnis Zukunft Österreich, BZÖ 141–142, 144, 149–150, 157, 159–160

Caiani, M. 66, 74–75
Camus, R. 181

Canovan, M. 4, 95, 192, 215, 258, 269, 273, 276
Candidatura d'Unitat Popular, CUP (Catalonia) 93–94, 102
Carter, E. 67, 137, 169
Casa Pound (Italy) 74
Catalan European Democratic Party, PDeCAT 93–94, 100, 284
catalan secessionism 88–89, 92
Catalonia's Democrats 93
Catalunya Sí Que Es Pot 100
cleavages: center-periphery cleavages 3, 43, 45, 191, 192, 206, 207, 271, 280, 285; ethnic cleavages 2, 152–153; diversity 1–2; divisions 1, 150
Christian Democratic Austrian People's Party 139
Christen-Democratisch en Vlaams, CD&V (Belgium) 46, 47, 49, 57
Ciudadanos (Spain) 94, 98
Civic Platform (Poland) 190, 199, 206
Claes, L. 47
Clerfayt, G. 46
Colombier, J. 178
Convergence and Union, CiU (Catalonia) 92
Convergencia Democratica de Catalunya/ Partit Demòcrata Català 12–13, 76
Conversi, D. 42, 91
Corbyn, J. 32–33, 34
Croatian Democratic Alliance of Slavonia and Baranja *see* HDSSB
Croatian Democratic Union, HDZ 212–214, 216, 218–231, 286–288

Dandoy, R. 6, 49, 217
Danish Folkspartei, DF 66, 112
Declaration of Independence (Catalonia) 94–96, 100, 104–106
Declaration of Independence (Kosovo) 256, 272
De Cleen, B. 81, 240, 287
Démocrate fédéraliste indépendant, DéFI (Belgium) 12–13, 41, 44–46, 48–54, 56–59
De la Torre, C. 4–5, 68
democracy 5, 8, 24, 66, 74, 76, 89–91, 95–97, 102, 104, 106, 112–114, 118, 200, 205, 207–208, 217, 229, 231, 264, 270, 276; liberal democracies 8, 110, 282
Democratic Convergence of Catalonia, CDC 13, 92, 93–95, 98, 100, 102–103, 105

Democratic Union of Catalogna, UDC 108–109, 118
Democratic Party, DS (Serbia) 260, 262, 271–272, 274
Deschouwer, C. 45, 48, 148
Detterbeck, K. 2, 68, 166, 168
De Winter, L. 6, 9, 47, 66, 90, 191, 212, 217, 226, 289
Die Linke 21, 35, 125, 127, 283
Di Rupo, E. 57
Di Tella, T. 4
Dupoirier, E. 174, 184
Dutozia, J. 12, 165, 185, 282
Džankić, J. 260, 272

economic protectionism 11, 167, 170, 183
Electoral mobilization 98, 100, 148
Elias, A. 6, 9, 20, 27, 36, 76, 259
Esquerra Republicana de Catalunya, ERC 13, 93–96, 100, 102–103, 105
ethnic cleavages *see* cleavages
ethnicity 1, 196, 212, 249
ethno-nationalism *see* nationalism
ethno-territorial ideologies 3, 5, 9–10, 12, 283, 288
European Free Alliance (EFA) 198
european integration 2, 9, 11, 65–66, 69–70, 76, 167, 170, 173, 197, 228, 241, 272, 285, 287
european political systems 2–3, 12
European Union 5, 9, 47, 70, 175, 227, 249, 258–259
euroscepticism 2–3, 5, 9,11, 13, 14, 65–67, 69, 73, 75, 77, 79–80, 82, 105, 110, 136, 167, 284, 287–288
Evans, G. 24–25
Eymery, P. 178

Fabbrini, S. 10
Fella, S. 69
Fidesz 13, 235–238, 240–245, 247–251, 286
Finchelstein, F. 5
Findeisen, S. 116
Fitjar, R. D. 5, 216, 221, 280
Five Star Movement, 5SM (Italy) 21, 34, 71–72
Flemish Christian Democrats 46
flemish independence 47, 55, 58
Flemish Nationalist Party 47
Flemish People's Party 47
Front démocratique des francophones, FDF (Belgium) 48–49

Front national, Rassemblement national, FN (France) 13, 165–185, 283
Forza Italia 74
Freeden, M. 4, 7, 14, 43
Freiheitliche Partei Österreichs, FPÖ 13, 65, 110, 136–144, 146–160, 282–284
fringe party 7, 192

Gagnon, G. A. 65, 268–269
Gellner, E. 42, 65, 262
general will 4, 42, 89, 100, 215, 217, 224, 269, 272
German Free Democrats 140
Glavaš, B. 213, 219, 226, 228, 230
German Longitudinal Election Study, GLES 121–122, 128, 130
globalization 2, 9, 79, 80, 115–116, 124, 125, 129, 167, 170, 175–176, 214, 228, 231, 244, 282
Gibb, D. A. 23, 35
Gidron, N. 43, 115–116, 124
Giugni, M. 77–78
Goati, V. 266, 268
Gobbi, N. 61–62
Goebel, J. 117
Gollnisch, B. 173
Gombin, J. 166, 168, 175, 180
Gomez-Reino Cachafeiro, M. 9, 66, 90
Gorzelik, J. 190, 196, 198, 205, 207–208
Grimm, S. 110, 260
Grubišić, B. 227
Guiniot, M. 178
Gyurcsàny, F. 241

Habersack, F. 13, 110, 282, 285
Hagen, K. 125–127
Haider, J. 136, 142–143, 146, 153, 160
Hawkins, K. A. 213–216, 222, 226, 229
Harmsen, R. 2, 10–11, 66
Hrvatski demokratski savez Slavonije i Baranje, HDSSB (Slavonia) 13, 212–214, 216, 218–231, 286–288
Hechter, M. 106, 221
Heinisch, R. 17, 69, 81–82, 89–90, 136, 140, 142–143, 145–146, 148–150, 152, 155, 157, 167, 192, 271, 280, 282, 284
Hellmann, O. 67
Henderson, K. 10–11
Hepburn, E. 2, 6, 168, 228
Hermet, G. 42
Hix, S. 9
Höbelt, L. 139, 146
Hobsbawm, E. 42
Holtz-Bacha, C. 192

Hooghe, L. 9, 11, 66, 228
Hussein, S. 155

identity politics 2, 179, 215, 239, 251
Iglesias, D. 43, 50
Ignazi, P. 65
Immerfall, S. 20
immigrants *see* migration
independence referendum 28–29, 93, 101–102
independentist 6, 72, 93
Inglehart, R. 79, 213, 221, 224
Ishiyama 10–11
islamization 113, 115
Ivaldi, G. 13, 21, 88, 165, 167–168, 170–171, 178, 181–182, 184–185, 227, 282

Jagers, J. 20, 42–43, 216, 222
Jansen, R. 4, 117
Jeffery, C. 1, 9, 41, 43
Jobbik 13, 235–238, 240–242, 244–245, 247–251, 286
Johnson, C. 264
Jolly, K. S. 9, 66, 228
Jones, R. P. 114
Juhász, A. 241, 251
Junqueras, O. 96, 105
Junt pel Sì, JxSì (Catalunya) 13, 93, 100
Junts per Catalunya, JxCAT (Catalunya) 94, 100

Kacprzak, I. 195
Kállai, E. 246
Kamusella, T. 193–194
Karácsony, G. 236, 247, 251
Katsambekis, G. 1, 21
Katz, R. 137
Kazibut-Twór, E. 201
Kazin, M. 4
Keating, M. 9, 24, 28, 35, 65–66, 68, 76, 198
Kecmanović, D. 262
Kellas, J. 266
Kellermann, K. 145
Kenny, M. 119
Kestilä, E. 166, 168–169
Kioupkioli, A. 21
Kitschelt, H. 11, 67, 90, 137
Greek communist party, KKE 43
Kollig, C. 154
Koopmans, R. 67
Kopecky, P. 9
Kopetsch, C. 116, 124

Kossack 236, 239
Koštunica, V. 262
Krause, D. 258
Krause, W. 238
Krekó, P. 237, 241–242, 251
Kriesi, H. 5, 72, 89, 95–96, 213, 216–217
Krouwel, A. 2
Kubiak, D. 118–119
Kukec, M. 13, 212, 228, 286
Kulcsár L. J. 245–246

Laclau, E. 4–5, 7, 22, 97
La France insoumise 21, 34
Lagasse, A. 46
Lang, C. 173
Lanzone, M. E. 88, 168, 172, 184, 227
Law and Justice (Poland) 190, 195, 199, 285
Lega dei Ticinesi (LT) 12–14, 64, 67, 69, 75–80, 82–83, 90, 225, 281, 284, 289
Lega (Nord), Italian Northern League 1, 12–14, 43, 64, 66–67, 69, 70–75, 79–80, 82–83, 89–90, 136, 218, 281, 284, 305
Lehideux, M. 173
Leonard, R. 33
Le Bras, H. 166, 168
Le Pen, J.-M. 168, 179, 181, 185
Le Pen, M. 75, 170–175, 178–179
Lettner, M. 151, 155
Lewis, S. 22, 24, 35
Liberals, PLR (Belgium) 49
Loeuillet, B. 181, 185
Loiseau, P. 178
Lubbers 170, 172
Lutte Ouvrière 43
Lynch, P. 20, 25–27, 36, 90
Lyons, N.M. 4

MacEwen, A. 35
Machowecz, M. 125–127
Madron, A. 70, 72
Maggi, A. 74
Maingain, O. 46, 49
majority nationalism *see* nationalism
March, L. 1, 5, 21, 29, 35
Majtényi, B. 246
Malešević, S. 264
Maréchal-Le Pen, M. 173, 179–183, 185
Marent, V. 13, 143, 284
Marks, G. 227–228
Maroni, R. 73
Martinez, J.-C. 173
Mas, A. 93, 97, 105–106
Maspoli, F. 76, 78

Massetti, E. 17, 20, 24, 26–27, 35–36, 41, 68, 90, 191–192, 196, 200, 205–206, 221, 280–282, 287, 289
Mazzoleni, O. 17, 20, 41, 43, 64, 69, 74, 76–78, 81, 89–90, 94, 192, 259, 271, 280, 284, 289
McDonnell, D. 1–2, 5, 20, 44, 89, 138, 213, 218, 225, 227
McGann, A.J. 90
McIntyre, R. 35
McKee, I. 32
McSmith, A. 29
Meguid, B. 238
Ménard, R. 183
Mény, Y. 94, 215, 217, 287
Mercik, H. 208
Meyer, D. 67
Meyer, S. 235, 239
Meyer, T. 238
migration (immigrants) 2, 42, 57, 66, 68, 73–74, 77, 79, 82, 121, 123–125, 160, 170, 176–177, 179, 235–236, 240–241, 270, 284, 287
Mihajlović, K. 264
Miliband Ed 28, 31
Milošević, S. 260, 265–266, 268, 271–272, 275–276
Minkenberg, M. 4, 10–12, 236–239, 251, 257
Mladić, R. 274
majority nationalism *see* nationalism
minority nationalism *see* nationalism
Mirkóczki, A. 251
Moffitt, B. 90, 95, 101
Molnár, M. 237
Molnár, E. 246
Montel, S. 172, 178
Morel, M.-R. 48
Moreno, L. 43
Mudde, C. 1, 4, 8–9, 20–22, 29, 35, 41–43, 65, 88–90, 97, 137, 213–217, 227, 235, 239–240, 251, 256, 258, 264, 271, 274
Mueller, S. 6, 41, 43, 76, 289
Müller, J.-W. 4, 8, 145, 207, 258
Müller-Rommel, F. 191
Muslim Community 113, 174, 177, 179
Mysliwiec, M. 193–194, 197

nationalism: ethno-nationalism 256–257, 260–261, 264–269, 272–274; majority nationalism 3, 7–8, 14, 65, 69, 167, 262, 287; methodological nationalism 1, 41; minority nationalism 3, 6, 34, 65, 83, 257, 280, 287; minority nationalist 1, 3,

6, 20, 22, 33–35, 68, 82, 280–282; national identity 8, 22, 23, 65, 114, 167, 170, 177, 179, 190, 219, 244, 250, 256–259, 273, 285; national integrity 8, 11; national-populist politics 165, 167; national sovereignty; *see also* sovereignism 9–11, 65, 76, 78, 167, 206, 228, 258, 288
National Democratic Party (Austria) 139, 160
National Pact for the Referendum 102
National Pact for the Right to Decide 101–102
nativism 8, 10, 89–90, 110–112, 126, 136, 235, 240, 256, 264, 282
Nazi Party, NSDAP 139, 147, 152
Neumayer, L. 11
Newell, J. 138
Nikolić, T. 268–269, 272–273, 277
NL *see* Northern League 64
Norris, P. 79, 213, 221, 224
New-Flemish Alliance, N-VA 41, 44–59

Olzak, S. 67
Omnium Cultural 91, 97–98, 100, 102
Open VLD (Flemish) 57
Orbán, V. 237, 241–242, 248–249, 251
Orlović, S. 271
Ordemann, J. 116
Otjes, S. 5
Ottomeyer, K. 154–155
Österreichische Volkspartei, ÖVP 139, 141, 144, 147–149, 152, 157–158, 160

Paasi, A. 216, 228
Panizza, F. 4
Pappas, T.S. 5, 88–89, 95, 240
Partit Demòcrata Català 12
political party: competition 2, 5, 10–12, 67–69, 79, 97, 166, 169, 173–174, 182, 207, 228, 239, 250–251; mobilization 2–3, 69, 262, 266, 280; party-populist mobilization 1, 3; *see also* regionalist parties
Passarelli, G. 69, 71
Pauwels, T. 1, 4, 44, 47–48, 50–54, 56, 58, 83, 215–216, 222, 227
Party of Democratic Socialism (Germany), PDS 35, 119–120, 127
Peeters, A. 46
Pegida 115, 117–118
Perrineau, P. 170–171, 179
Petritz, K. H. 160
Peyrat, J. 182

Philippot, F. 173, 178, 184
Pilet, J.B. 45–46, 48–49
Pina, C. 182, 184
Pirro, A. L. P. 4, 251
Prawo i Sprawiedliwość (Poland), PiS 190, 195–196, 199–200, 202, 206, 208, 285
Plaid Cymru 12–13, 20–31, 33–36, 43, 281–282, 289
Platforma Obywatelska (Poland), PO 190, 199–200, 206
Poblete, M.E. 227
Podemos 21, 34, 282
Polish People's Party 190, 199
Polskie Stronnictwo Ludowe (Poland), PSL 190, 199
Pontida 71, 73–75
Popular Party (Spain), PP 98, 106
populism: multi-level populism 10, 69, 78, 259, 265, 267, 271, 275; party-based populism 1–2, 4; populist attitudes 123–130; populist discourse 3, 5–7, 9–10, 12, 20–23, 25, 28–29, 33–34, 64, 68, 74–75, 79, 88–89, 94, 112, 114, 191, 200, 203, 216, 240, 242, 275, 280–283, 288–289; populist drift 88, 104; populist radical right 8, 14, 43, 47, 80, 82, 113, 124, 136, 171–172, 237, 270; populist rhetoric 4, 90, 104, 112–113, 213, 229–231, 259, 265; populist themes 22, 33, 281–282; radical right populist parties, RRPP 138, 141, 158; right-wing populism 1, 8, 110–111, 114, 118; pure people 2, 4, 42, 89, 137, 167, 240
PRL *see* Liberals
Puigdemont, C. 93–94, 96–97, 103, 105–106
Pujol, J. 93
Pytlas, B. 236, 239, 251

Quadri, L. 78–79

Rachline, D. 172–173, 181–183
radical-left 5–7, 9
radical-right 5–9, 13–14, 79–82
Rajoy, M. 105
Raos, V. 228
Rassemblement National *see* Front national 13, 65, 282
Ravier, S. 172–173, 181–183
regionalism: Catalan regionalist parties 88, 97, 281; regionalist parties 1, 3, 5–9, 12–13, 21, 33, 43, 64–66, 68–69, 80–81, 88–91, 97–100, 104, 191–192, 206,

212–213, 217, 221, 228, 230, 280–282, 284, 288–289; regional nativism 110, 282
Reinbold, F. 115
Reinthaller, A. 139
Rensmann, L. 114
Rico, G. 117
Riedel, R. 191
Riedlsperger, M. 138–139
Riishøj, S. 11
Ritterband, C. 149, 155
Rochedy, J. 173
Rodríguez-Teruel, J. 12, 88, 91, 100, 282
Rohrschneider, R. 208
Roma (minority) 13, 208, 236–238, 241, 245–250, 270, 285–286
Rooduijn, M. 4, 50, 116, 124, 214–215, 217, 222
Rosenberger, S. 235, 239
Rovira Kaltwasser, C. 4, 41, 68, 90
Rovny, J. 12
Rudolph, N. 119
Russell-Omaljev, A. 262
Rydgren, J. 1, 5, 20, 165, 170, 173, 235
Ruzza, C. 2, 12–13, 64, 69–70, 284

Sagmeister, S. 160
Salheiser, A. 118
Sallés, Q. 106
Salmond, A. 36
Salvini, M. 70–73, 75, 82–83
Sanader, I. 219–220, 225, 227, 231
Sandri, G. 217
Sarrazin, T. 114–115
Sartori, G. 208
Schafft, K.A. 245–246
Schakel, A.H. 6, 41, 205–206, 221
Schaunig, G. 160
Scheepers, P. 170
Schmidt, C. 118
Schmidt, M. 113
Schmidt, V.A. 67
Schiltz, H. 46
Schmitt-Beck, R. 110, 122, 124
Schneider, A. 218
Schöffmann, I. 154–155
Schweizerische Volkspartei *see* Swiss People's Party
Scottish Greens 27, 33
Scottish National Party, SNP 12–13, 20–36, 281–282, 289
Scottish Socialist Party, SSP 27, 29, 35
Scrinzi, O. 139, 160
secessionist 6–8, 12–13, 70, 72, 81, 88, 90–91, 93–105, 281, 284

self-government 6–7, 21, 24, 35–36, 52, 55–56, 91, 184, 190–192, 194–196, 199, 201, 203–205, 212, 214–215, 217–221, 223–224, 228–230, 244, 246, 266, 270, 280
Serbian Progressive Party, SNS 257, 259–260, 262–263, 266–267, 271–276
Serbian Radical Party 13, 257, 259, 266, 268
Serbian Socialist Party 13, 257, 259
Silesian Autonomy Movement, RAŚ 13–14, 189–192, 194–203, 205–208, 285, 288
Silesian Regional Party 190, 198, 201, 203–204, 208, 281, 285
Sima, H. 146
Sinardet, D. 43–44, 51–54, 56
Śląska Partia Regionalna (Silesia), ŚPR 190–192, 198, 202–208, 285
Social Democratic Party (Austria) 139, 152, 155, 160
Socialist Democratic Party (Croatia), SDP 212, 227
Socijalistička Partija Srbije (Serbia), SPS 13, 257, 259–260, 262–263, 266–274, 276
Söderlund, P. 166, 168–169
Solska, M. 13, 189, 285
Soral, A. 181
Sorens, J. 194
Soros, G. 5
sovereignty 9–11, 65, 76–78, 83, 89–90, 102, 148, 167, 192, 206, 215, 228, 256, 258, 264–265, 273, 275, 285–286, 288
Spaak, A. 46
Spanish People's Party 7
Socialist Democratic Party, SPD (Germany) 119, 127
Spiering, M. 11
Sozialdemokratische Partei Österreichs, SPÖ 139, 141, 144–146, 152, 155, 157
Spruyt, Keppens and Van Droogenbroeck 257
Srpska napredna stranka, SNS 13, 257, 259–260, 262–263, 266–267, 271–276
Srpska radikalna stranka, SRS 13, 257, 259–260, 262–263, 266–269, 271–274, 276
Stanley, B. 4, 89–90
Steffen, T. 110
Steger, N. 140
Strache, H.-C. 142
Stravakakis, Y. 1
Sturgeon, N. 30–31
Südekum, J. 116

Sulzer, A. 183
Surel, Y. 94, 215, 217, 287
Swinney, J. 26, 36
Swiss Democrats 77
Swiss People's Party, SVP 81, 76–79, 80, 110, 136
Syriza 21, 34, 282
Szczerbiak, A. 9, 65
Szöcsik, E. 13–14, 235, 261, 285
Šeks, V. 225
Šešelj, V. 268–269, 277
Šišljagić, V. 220, 225, 229

Taggart, P. 2, 4–6, 9–10, 22, 65, 68–69, 89–90, 183, 191, 216–217, 227, 283
Taguieff, P.-A. 4, 165, 167, 170
territorialization 165–168, 173, 183–184
territory 1–3, 42, 48, 52, 56, 111, 145, 151, 153, 191, 193–194, 218, 220, 242, 256–257, 259, 262, 265–267, 270, 280, 282, 286
Thatcher, M. 26
thin ideology 4–5, 7, 240
Thomas, D.E. 36
Thompson, L. 32
Tillie, J. 137
Topaloff, L.K. 65
Torra, J. 94
Tournier-Sol, K. 2
Treaty of Trianon 243–244, 251
Tuđman, F. 214, 219, 226, 231
Tuorto, D. 69, 71
Türsan, H. 191, 212, 217

UKIP (United Kingdom Indipendent Party) 29–30, 66
Ulster Unionist Party (UK) 7
Unió Democràtica de Catalunya 92
Union of Navarrese People (Spain) 7

Valentine, L. 35
Valkeniers, B. 46, 48
Vampa, D. 20
Van der Brug, W. 1, 137
Van der Elst, F. 46
Van Grieken, T. 46, 48
Van Haute, E. 12–13, 41, 44–48, 51–54, 56, 58
Vanhecke, F. 46–48
Van Kessel, S. 89, 137
Vankrukelsven, P. 46
Van Spanje, J. 235, 238
Vardon, P. 181
Vasilopoulou, S. 9

Venturi, F. 23
Verband der Unabhängigen, VdU (Austria) 138, 160
Verney, S. 66, 89
Verstrepen, J. 48
Veugelers, J. 172
Vignancour, J.-L. 182
Vilaregut, R. 99
Vlaams Belang (Belgium), VB 1, 12–14, 41, 43–59, 66, 83, 136, 281, 284, 289
Vlaams Blok (Belgium) 47, 90
Vlaams-Nationale Partji, VPN 47
Vlaamse Volkspartij, VVP 47
Vliegenthart, R. 172
Vogel, L. 118
Volksunie (Belgium), VU 45–47
Vona, G. 237, 241, 247–248
Vorländer, H. 115, 117–118
Vranić, B. 13, 256, 283, 286
Vučić, A. 272–274

Wagemans, H. 46
Wagner, L. 146, 152
Wagner, M. 238
Walgrave, S. 20, 42–43, 216, 222
Waterbury, M.A. 241, 243
Watson, B. 35
Watts, M. 35
Webb, P. 36
welfare (state) 11, 28–29, 66, 76, 112, 170, 184, 248
Welsh Labour 27, 36
Welsh language 21–22, 24, 35
Welsh Wales 22–24, 35
Weyland, K. 4, 228
White, M.D. 222
Whitefield, S. 208
Wincott, D. 1
Wodak, R. 42
Wood, L. 30
Woods, D. 88, 90, 227
Wyn, J. R. 27

xenophobia 43, 120, 165, 256, 260, 271

Yoder, J.A. 194
Young, D. 22–23

Zakaria, F. 89
Zasada, M. 198, 202
Zarycki, T. 195, 208
Zaslove, A. 170, 214–215
Zuber, C.I. 14, 260–261, 272
Zweiffel, L. 198, 208